Max Planck Institute for Innovation and Competition

More information about this series at
http://www.springer.com/series/7760

MAX-PLANCK-GESELLSCHAFT

MPI Studies on Intellectual Property and Competition Law

Volume 27

Edited by

Josef Drexl
Reto M. Hilty
Joseph Straus

Kung-Chung Liu • Reto M. Hilty
Editors

Remuneration of Copyright Owners

Regulatory Challenges of New Business Models

Springer

Editors
Kung-Chung Liu
Singapore Management University
Singapore, Singapore

Reto M. Hilty
Max Planck Institute for Innovation and Competition
Munich, Germany

ISSN 2191-5822 ISSN 2191-5830 (electronic)
MPI Studies on Intellectual Property and Competition Law
ISBN 978-3-662-53808-1 ISBN 978-3-662-53809-8 (eBook)
DOI 10.1007/978-3-662-53809-8

Library of Congress Control Number: 2017936055

Printed on acid-free paper

This Springer imprint is published by Springer Nature
The registered company is Springer-Verlag GmbH Germany
The registered company address is: Heidelberger Platz 3, 14197 Berlin, Germany

Introduction

One of the core purposes of copyright law is to remunerate right holders for use of their works. This was not a particular challenge during the early years of copyright law. Remuneration was a contractual issue between right holders and exploiters (primarily publishers, phonogram producers, theaters, or concert houses) in the first place. From the middle of the nineteenth century on, collecting societies were established to ensure remuneration. These self-help organizations of right holders searched for public cultural activities, requested compensation from the organizers, and distributed the revenues to their members.

Technological development made the control of unauthorized uses increasingly difficult. In particular the emergence of sound recordings allowed performances of music without the consent of right holders, for instance, in a coffee house. The first fundamental change occurred with the emergence of copying devices, such as audiotapes, and later on photocopying machines, which allowed private reproduction of works on a large scale. Right holders faced substantial losses as more and more legitimate copies were substituted by private reproduction. One vinyl record could be reproduced on many tape cassettes; students no longer needed to buy overpriced books, but contented themselves with copying the relevant parts.

Legislators all over the world reacted differently. Some simply prohibited such forms of private use (e.g., USA, UK), while others (Germany or France as front runners), realizing that they could never effectively control private behavior, legalized it and established at the same time a compensation (levy) system, under which copying devices and blank media were charged with fees, respectively, and collecting societies were involved to distribute the revenues among the right holders.

Critics of both approaches never died down. Whereas it was obvious that prohibition could not be effectively enforced—private copying took place anyway without compensating right holders—it was also undeniable that remuneration through collecting societies hardly compensated actual losses of right holders. Nevertheless, the compensation system had one strong argument on its side: creators (the original right holders) could be compensated. Even after assigning their rights to commercial exploiters, statutory provisions could oblige collecting societies to split revenues among different groups of right holders. For some creators, such compensation systems were the only source of compensation.

The rising digital technology combined with the possibility of disseminating works via the Internet changed the copyright economy dramatically. Not all right holders, however, took these developments as opportunities and transformed their previous business models into new ones. In particular the entertainment industries and above all the music industry delayed the breakthrough for roughly one decade by insisting on trade only with offline carriers, most importantly compact discs. They perceived the new technologies as threats and tried to criminalize independent providers of online business models, which used copyright-protected material without authorization. Right holders only slowly understood that technical protection measures could be implemented to gain back their control over the use of works.

In view of that possibility, optimists—or pessimists, depending on the perspective—proclaimed the incipient end of collecting societies. We know by now that this prediction was more than wrong. Although the copyright economy is about moving away from physical copies toward business models that rely on access to decentralized and hosted content, from downloading to cloud storage and streaming, collective rights management is not dead.

Now new forms of use have evolved and various business models coexist. However, the core questions remain the same as at the very beginning of copyright law: How can adequate remuneration to right holders for uses of their works be ensured? Has it become easier—or more difficult? Has compensation become fairer? Does copyright law also serve the economic interests of creators? Do consumers accept onerous payment systems—or are high prices fostering illegal behavior? Has the "burden" of complying with copyright law simply become unacceptable for the general public?

Many concerns in fact might be rooted in deficiencies and uncertainties connected with copyright law. One first—although not new—issue is that the whole remuneration system is hardly comprehensible. This is not least due to the complexity of substantive copyright law. In fact, payment mechanisms are strongly related to the structure of copyright law, which is largely unclear per se. One simple act of use can involve a whole bundle of overlapping economic rights (including neighboring rights) and various groups of right holders. Therefore, improving the transparency of payment systems is necessarily linked with a more streamlined copyright protection—but again how can such streamlining be achieved?

Secondly, collective rights management systems as such lack transparency. Certainly, collecting societies have mostly adapted their activities to new technological reality, and new administration structures have emerged. However, this is still an ongoing process, and alternative approaches might be necessary for simplifying the management of copyrights and legalizing usage activities in ways that are more efficient and legally watertight. The Scandinavian model of the "extended collective licenses" might be one approach, which legalizes uses of works from unknown right holders or right holders who are not members of collecting societies.

At the same time, collecting societies, to a large degree as monopolists in more or less shielded national markets, are organized as private entities and yet perform activities in public interests. Appropriate governance structure is a copyright as well as competition law issue. What role should states play in regulating that very specific branch of the copyright economy?

Large parts of the copyright industries, however, no longer rely on collective rights management systems. Equally important payment mechanisms based on individual licensing are on the rise. Thanks to business models enabled by technical measures, right holders are about to gain back control over the use of their works that they lost decades ago. Additional impetus is given by new actors who come into play, above all Internet service or mobile providers (ISPs/MP). ISPs/MPs are in fact in the best position not only to monitor usage activities but also to collect fees. From an economic point of view, it might even make sense to require ISP/MPs to pay copyright owners on behalf of their subscribers and charge the latter individually either a lump sum or per-use payment. The potential of ISP/MPs in lowering transaction costs is obvious.

As desirable as all these advancements may seem to be at first glance, they give rise to a third group of multifaceted concerns. Above all—and beyond the questions addressed here—copyright may be used (and abused) as a lever to control user activities beyond the scope covered and justified by copyright law. In particular, ISP/MPs are collecting not only fees from users but also data. Even from the mere remuneration perspective, business models that allow copyright industries and ISP/MP exclusive technological control, respectively, are a double-edged sword. Fair consumer prices are by no means ensured, since no independent price control applies (in contrast to legally disputable tariffs of collecting societies). At the same time nothing guarantees the participation of creators, especially after they have entered into sell-out agreements. If one core issue of copyright law is the adequate remuneration of creators, the field cannot be left entirely to such players. Special regulation may be required to protect the interests of other parties involved—but what should it look like?

Finally, since we increasingly live in a collaborative economy, right holders and disseminators of content are no longer necessarily identical. Independent market players, such as startups, quite often are more innovative in anticipating future consumer preferences. Even the most sophisticated and sought-after platforms need content to become meaningful. Voluntary licensing, however, is very often refused since new business models are seen as a threat to traditional ones. If right holders are not interested in using online technologies themselves, they most likely will also not grant licenses to independent platforms, including e-book producers, perceiving the latter as rivals in technology competition. A prominent example was the Google book scanning project. What Google wanted to accomplish was precisely what the modern information society is in need of—providing the world online access to the existing knowledge in printed form, some of which is quite often out of stock.

Book publishers, however, remonstrated all over the world. This is not without irony if we think back to one of the core purposes of copyright law, namely, to remunerate right holders for the use of their works. In fact, instead of prohibiting

Google's activities, publishers could have requested adequate compensation—also and not the least for the benefit of the authors of the books. Such cases suggest a fourth regulatory challenge for modern copyright economy: If voluntary licensing of independent suppliers of innovative business models does not happen, are we then in need of legal intervention, e.g., based on compulsory or statutory licenses? To what extent can competition law be a remedy?

Overall, the copyright economy is increasingly moving away from the world of physical copies (such as books, DVDs, or other storage media). New business models rely on access to decentralized hosted content instead. This evolution currently is speeding up with the rise of wireless and mobile Internet access (in China, for instance, mobile Internet access has surpassed that of PCs), and cloud computing, in particular, is replacing downloads with streaming activities. All this makes ubiquitous uses of copyright-protected works more widespread and instantaneous than ever before.

The question about how to make sure that copyright owners are reasonably remunerated for the use of their works has become far more complex and pressing. This insight prompted the editors of this book to devote the 6th "Conference on European and Asian Intellectual Property," a joint effort between the Institutum Iurisprudentiae of the Academia Sinica, Taiwan, and the Max Planck Institute for Innovation and Competition in Munich, Germany, that started in 1999, to the topic "Exploring Sensible Ways for Paying Copyright Owners." The conference took place from 11 to 12 June 2015 in Taipei, with the Applied Research Center for Intellectual Assets and the Law in Asia (ARCIALA), Singapore Management University, as the third co-host. More than 20 speakers, mainly from Asian and European countries, gathered together and reflected on the related questions. Different from many anthologies, the present book follows a structured approach similar to that of the conference. Experts in this specific field of copyright law were invited to study and explore predetermined issues in order to assemble a consistent whole.

The major concern of the present book is to evaluate existing mechanisms and find new ones for the adequate payment of copyright owners for the consumption of their works. The underlying assumption is that adequate rewards to creators and subsequent right holders will continue to be one goal of copyright law (particularly to incentivize further creation and investment). Searching for sensible ways in the first place focuses on the reduction of transaction costs. New technologies are promising in that respect, but further development and broader application of new mechanisms might be necessary to enhance adequacy and efficiency of payment systems. The more onerous payment systems are, the more irrelevant copyright risks become due to lack of acceptance, and the less they might fulfill their functions.

Finally, we would like to thank all the contributors for their support and cooperation. In addition, we'd like to thank the following institutions in Taiwan for sponsoring the conference: Institutum Iurisprudentiae Academia Sinica; the Judicial Yuan; the Ministry of Science and Technology; the Fair Trade Commission; College of Law, National Taiwan University; Research Center for Humanities and Social Sciences and Institute of Law for Science and Technology, National Tsing Hua University; the Science and Technology Law Institute under the Institute for Information Industry; and Formosa Transnational Attorneys at Law. Last but not least, we are grateful to the English editor Kent M. Suarez and to Ms. Ingrid Bolland for their excellent work.

Contents

Overlapping Rights in Different Business Models

Jyh-An Lee

Contents

Abstract This chapter provides an overview of the problems stemming from the fragmented copyright system. The multitude of rights and right holders has led to huge transactions costs for the exploitation, license, dissemination, and enforcement of copyright. Copyright divisibility and fragmentation also result in legal issues surrounding overlapping exclusive rights in a single subject. This problem may not only bring about controversies over copyright license, but also generate uncertainties for startup companies that build their business models on digital content. This chapter then evaluates current policy proposals addressing the issues of fragmented copyright and overlapping exclusive rights. Those proposals include consolidating current bundles of exclusive rights, and adopting an implied license

---

Jyh-An Lee is Assistant Professor at the Faculty of Law at the Chinese University of Hong Kong.

J.-A. Lee (✉)
Faculty of Law, The Chinese University of Hong Kong, Hong Kong, People's Republic of China
e-mail: jalee@cuhk.edu.hk

K.-C. Liu, R.M. Hilty (eds.), *Remuneration of Copyright Owners*, MPI Studies on Intellectual Property and Competition Law 27, DOI 10.1007/978-3-662-53809-8_1

doctrine to the incidental use of copyrighted work based on one single exclusive right. Finally, this chapter assesses whether a more streamlined collective copyright management mechanism can solve the issue of overlapping rights.

1 Introduction

When we talk about copyright, there is not only one right involved. Copyright actually consists of a bundle of different exclusive rights. For example, in the United States, copyright includes rights of reproduction, adaptation, distribution, performance, display, and digital sound recording transmission rights.[1] In the United Kingdom, copyright consists of rights of reproduction, adaption, communication to the public, performance, and broadcasting.[2] Each of these rights can be owned, transacted, and enforced separately.[3] This is called copyright divisibility.[4] The exclusive rights sometimes overlap; therefore, the same act may infringe different exclusive rights simultaneously.[5] Copyright divisibility and overlapping exclusive rights have created enormous transaction costs for copyright clearance. Digital technologies and the Internet, however, have not ameliorated the problem, but made it more perplexing.[6] Compared to activities in the physical world, those in cyberspace are more often associated with different overlapping exclusive rights.[7]

This chapter provides an overview of the problems stemming from the fragmented copyright system. The multitude of rights and right holders has led to huge transactions costs for the exploitation, license, dissemination, and enforcement of copyright. Copyright divisibility and fragmentation have also resulted in legal issues surrounding overlapping exclusive rights in a single subject. This problem may not only bring about controversies over copyright license but also generate uncertainties for startup companies that build their business models on digital content.

This chapter then evaluates current policy proposals addressing the issues of fragmented copyright and overlapping exclusive rights. Those proposals include consolidating current bundles of exclusive rights and adopting an implied license

---

[1]17 U.S.C. §106.

[2]CDPA 1988 ss. 16-23.

[3]17 U.S.C. §201(d)(2); CDPA 1988 ss.90(2)(b).

[4]A. Kohn / B. Kohn (2000), 362; M.A. Lemley (1997), 570; J. Litman (2010), 20; J.W. Natke (2007), 486, 495.

[5]M.A. Leaffer (2010), 294.

[6]M.A. Lemley (1997), 574; J.W. Natke (2007), 486.

[7]J.W. Natke (2007), 486.

doctrine for the incidental use of copyrighted work based on one single exclusive right. Finally, this chapter assesses whether a more streamlined collective copyright management mechanism can solve the issue of overlapping rights.

2 Fragmented Copyright

2.1 The Multitude of Rights and Right Holders

Copyright involves a collection of exclusive rights in relation to creative works.[8] Different exclusive rights have been designed to cover new technological use.[9] Each sub-right underlying a copyrighted work can be transferred or licensed to different parties.[10] The benefit of copyright divisibility is that authors can exploit their works in different ways by different entities.[11] Divisibility was also recognized by the US Supreme Court.[12] When sub-rights of the same work are owned by different parties, users are required to obtain multiple authorizations from those rights holders.[13] Rights holders may have incentives to license different rights to different copyright management organizations (CMOs) whose businesses are designed to manage specific rights.[14] In practice, it is quite possible that unrelated parties own different exclusive rights to the same copyrighted work.[15]

Sometimes there are multiple copyrighted works on one single subject.[16] For example, a film contains a bundle of screenplay, characters, music, and other copyright works.[17] Producers, directors, and actors in some jurisdictions can claim their rights independently in the same film.[18] A pop song may include different copyrighted works owned by respective copyright holders, such as

[8]Text accompanying note 1-2.

[9]P. Goldstein (2003), 189.

[10]Text accompanying note 3; W. Cornish / D. Llwelyn / T.F. Aplin (2013), 525; D. Gervais (2010), 10.

[11]J. Litman (2004), 18.

[12]N.Y. Times Co. v. Tasini, 533 U.S. 483, 495-96 (2001).

[13]D. Gervais (2010), p. 10.

[14]*See, e.g.,* P. Mysoor (2013), 183-84; J.W. Natke (2007), 497.

[15]*See, e.g.*, M.A. Lemley (1997), 570.

[16]D. Gervais / A. Maurushat (2003), 15, 20.

[17]D. Gervais (2010), 13.

[18]*See, e.g.,* D. Gervais (2000), 81; D. Gervais / A. Maurushat (2003), 21. Some commentators argue that by allowing each contracting country to decide upon the relationship between audiovisual performers and film producers, Article 12 of the Beijing Treaty on Audiovisual Performances actually weakens the protection for performers, who are principally in an inferior bargaining position. G. Pessach (2014), 86-89. Similar criticisms are made on the "statutory presumptions," a proposal that copyrights are systematically transferred to corporate entities. T. Lüder (2007), 26-27.

producers, composers, lyricists, performers, and publishers.[19] Therefore, a single use of a song requires separate licenses from different right holders and CMOs, such as an author's society, a producer's society, and a performer's society.[20] Copyright clearance on occasion becomes challenging when rights holders, such as producers/performers[21] and composers/publishers[22] may have different views regarding how the subject work should be exploited. Even when there is only one author holding copyright over a work, he may still be represented by different copyright collecting societies for different types of rights.[23] Moreover, all these subdivisions may be co-owned by co-authors or their successors.[24] Digital technologies, however, have made copyright fragmentation more common and legally confusing.[25] One example is the Internet transmission of music in the US, which involves, at least, both license for public performance and license for distribution. However, the former is administered by the American Society of Composers, Authors, and Publishers (ASCAP) and BMI, whereas the latter is licensed by the Harry Fox Agency, a subsidiary of the National Music Publishers Association.[26]

From a user's perspective, if overlapping rights are administered by different CMOs, the costs of right clearance may increase significantly. Users need to identify who are the right holders and negotiate with them separately.[27] The transaction costs stemming from searching and negotiation are significant.[28] Whether multiple rights on a single work are administered by one single CMO may differ from jurisdiction to jurisdiction. For example, in some jurisdictions, the author's right of reproduction and right of communication to the public are managed by different CMOs, whereas in other jurisdictions, these rights are administered by one single CMO.[29]

2.2 The Tragedy of the Anticommons

The theory of the tragedy of the anticommons was first conceptualized by Michael Heller's 1998 Harvard Law Review article, in which he used the post-Soviet property system as an example to illustrate the market failure resulted from

[19] *See, e.g.*, D. Gervais (2010), 10, 12; T. Lüder (2007), 23-24, 41; W.W. Fisher III (2004), 59-67.

[20] *See, e.g.*, T. Lüder (2007), 23-24; W.W. Fisher III (2004), 46-59.

[21] *See, e.g.*, E. Vanheusden (2007), 47; S. Dusollier / C. Colin (2011), 834.

[22] Information Infrastructure Task Force (1995), 213-225.

[23] D. Gervais / A. Maurushat (2003), 22.

[24] *See, e.g.*, D. Gervais (2010), 2.

[25] *See, e.g.*, J. Litman (2007), 1917; J.W. Natke (2007), 495-498.

[26] Information Infrastructure Task Force (1995), 213-225.

[27] M.A. Lemley (1997), 570; J. Litman (2004), 21.

[28] R.P. Merges (1996), 1317; J.W. Natke (2007), 500.

[29] T. Lüder (2007), 24-25.

fragmented property rights and coordination breakdown.[30] Heller discovered that in the post-socialist economy, property rights of real estate were fragmented and distributed to multiple stakeholders in Russia.[31] As it was quite difficult to obtain permission from all the rights holders,[32] new entrepreneurs preferred to start up their businesses in kiosks, rather than stores.[33] Therefore, the significant amount of empty and underused stores in the market was viewed as an example of the tragedy of the anticommons by Heller.[34] He defined anticommons as[35]:

> [m]ultiple owners are each endowed with the right to exclude others from a scarce resource, and no one has an effective privilege of use. When there are too many owners holding rights of exclusion, the resource is prone to under use—a tragedy of the anticommons.

When proposing the theory of anticommons in 1998, Heller was aware that this theory may have wide implications in the study of intellectual property (IP).[36] He and Rebecca Eisenberg further applied this theory to biomedical research and argued that patenting upstream biomedical research produced anticommons property where "too many owners hold rights in previous discoveries that constitute obstacles to future research."[37] Anticommons becomes a tragedy when it is too costly for users to obtain all essential licenses.[38]

The tragedy of the anticommons takes place in the context of divided copyrights as well. As Heller points out, "[g]overnments can create too many property rights and too many decision-makers who can block use."[39] When specific rights subsist in the same work are administered by different copyright collecting societies, the costs of copyright clearance will increase significantly.[40] Transaction costs, strategic behaviors, and cognitive biases may all hinder efficient negotiation.[41] However, it does not mean that CMOs or entities who obtain any of the subdivision right should be blamed for the tragedy. It is natural that "[a]fter initial entitlements are set, institutions and interests coalesce around them, with the result that the path to private property may be blocked and scarce resources may be wasted."[42]

---

[30] M.A. Heller (1998), 621.

[31] *Id.*, 637-639.

[32] *Id.*, 39.

[33] *Id.*, 633-635.

[34] *Id.*, 633-635, 659.

[35] *Id.*, 624.

[36] M.A. Heller (1998), 626.

[37] M.A. Heller / R.S. Eisenberg (1998), 698, 700.

[38] *Id.*, 699.

[39] M.A. Heller (1998), 625.

[40] N. Elkin-Koren (2005), 381.

[41] M.A. Heller (1998), 625-626; M.A. Heller / R.S. Eisenberg (1998), 698.

[42] M.A. Heller (1998), 659.

The perverse result will be that every right holder has the exclusive right to prevent others from using the underlying work,[43] and eventually no single party can legally exploit the subject copyrighted work.[44] To put differently, gridlock in relevant industries and holdup behaviors would become a serious problem because of copyright divisibility.[45] Consequently, a single piece of exclusive right may become less valuable,[46] and the consumption of copyrighted works may come below the socially optimal level.[47] Copyright divisibility results in the tragedy of the anticommons.[48] In the end, the multitude of rights and right holders on the same copyrighted work leads to a classic example of market failure.[49] What is worse is that "[o]nce anticommons property is created, markets or governments may have difficulty in assembling rights into usable bundle."[50]

3 The Problem of Overlapping Rights

Traditionally every type of copyright use mostly fits nicely with individual subdivision of copyright.[51] If I make a copy of a book without a copyright owner's permission, I may infringe his right of reproduction. If I broadcast a song via radio, this involves the right of communication to the public. Nevertheless, a single act may also fall into the overlapping zones of different rights and violate all those rights at once.[52] The distinction between different economic rights is sometimes unclear, which create uncertainties for copyright enforcement or CRM. If a user gets license to make certain use of a work, it doesn't mean that his exploitation of the work is entirely legal. If other overlapping rights involved are incidental to or necessary to a certain use, the user may still need to get additional licenses associated with those overlapping rights.[53]

As the Internet and digital technologies have increasingly transformed the clear distinction between different uses and accompanying rights, issues concerning overlapping rights are increasingly common.[54] Professor Jessica Litman once asked: "When someone views a website or listens to a song over the Internet, is

---

[43] D. Gervais (2010), 13; J.W. Natke (2007), 500.
[44] M.A. Lemley (1997), 57-72.
[45] L.P. Loren (2003), 698.
[46] M.A. Lemley (1997), 571.
[47] L.P. Loren (2003), 700; L. Lessig (2004), 223.
[48] M. Heller (2008), 37-43.
[49] L.P. Loren (2003), 677.
[50] M.A. Heller (1998), 659.
[51] J.W. Natke (2007), 496.
[52] H.R. Rep. No. 94-1476 (1976), 61-62.
[53] J. Litman (2007), 1916-1917; M.A. Lemley (1997), 571.
[54] D. Gervais (2010), 10-11; M.A. Lemley (1997), 568; J.W. Natke (2007), 486.

she committing a reproduction, a distribution, a performance or display, or all of them at once?"[55] She indicated that every Internet related use of copyrighted works involves rights of reproduction, distribution, public performance, and public display in the United States.[56] Take the media-on-demand service for example; such a business model may be built upon all those rights, plus the right of communication to the public and right of making available in some other jurisdictions. It is, therefore, very easy for unwary users to infringe copyright even if they have already obtained a license for any of the single exclusive rights.[57] Some scholars have rightfully pointed out that the problem of overlapping rights in the digital space stems from the fact that the divisibility doctrine does not take Internet transmission into consideration.[58] Just like the anticommons in biomedical research, the spiral of overlapping rights in the hands of different owners may constitute obstacles to new product development and innovation.[59] In this section, we will discuss some cases and issues concerning overlapping rights in the physical world, and then turn to those in the digital arena.

3.1 Rights of Communication to the Public and Public Performance

The problem of overlapping rights may exist in traditional use of copyrighted work. For instance, the difference between the right of communication to the public and the right of public performance once troubled the British courts. In *Football Association Premier* League *v QC Leisure*, a number of publicans used a foreign decoder to show on television screens the broadcast of Premier League games in their pubs.[60] Kitchin J. gave a provisional view that the publicans had not communicated the broadcasts to the public, as there had been no further re-transmission by wire or otherwise.[61] However, the Court of Justice of the European Union (CJEU) had a different viewpoint, stating that transmitting the football matches on television screens did constitute a communication to the public.[62] Commentators suggested that the opinion held by the CJEU has substantially expanded the scope of the right of communication to the public and blurred the line between it and the right of public performance.[63] Kitchin, who later became Lord Justice, believed that

[55]J. Litman (2010), 42; D. Gervais (2010), 10.

[56]J. Litman (2004), 19-20; M.A. Lemley (1997), 567-68; J.W. Natke (2007), 486.

[57]M.A. Lemley (1997), 571; *see also* J.W. Natke (2007), 498, 501.

[58]M.A. Lemley (1997), 568; L.P. Loren (2003), 716; J.W. Natke (2007), 495-496.

[59]M.A. Heller / R.S. Eisenberg (1998), 698-699.

[60]FAPL EWHC 1411 (2008) (Ch); 3 C.M.L.R. 12 (2008).

[61]FAPL EWHC 1411 (2008) (Ch); 3 C.M.L.R. 12, 262 (2008).

[62]FAPL (C-403/08)(2011) E.C.D.R. 8, 202-203.

[63]P. Mysoor (2013), 173.

the CEJU's opinion suggested that there is an overlap between the right of communication to the public and the right of public performance.[64]

3.2 *Right of Making Available to the Public*

Copyright in the digital environment occasionally involves three types of exclusive economic right:[65] right of reproduction,[66] right of communication to the public,[67] and the right of making available online.[68] New business models enabled by digital technologies, such as IPTV, music streaming, and other web-based content delivery services, have led to copyright controversies, mostly over which type of copyright is involved in a certain transaction. This issue is important for copyright practice, especially when different rights are owned by different right holders or administered by different CMOs. For example, whether digital transmission falls in the scope of right of distribution was once an issue.[69] Another instance is the creation of the "right of making available to the public," which originates from the inability of the Berne Convention for the Protection of Literary and Artistic Works to cover interactive or on-demand transmission of copyrighted works, enabled by the Internet.[70] As those interactive services may not fall into traditional public performance and recitation, broadcasting, and cable transmission[71] which cover only traditional "push" technology,[72] copyright holders had problems claiming rights over interactive and individualized use of their works.

In order to solve this difficulty, the WIPO Copyright Treaty (WCT) and the European Union Copyright Directive (the Directive 2001/29/EC of the European Parliament and of the Council of 22 May 2001 on the harmonisation of certain aspects of copyright and related rights in the information society), classify the right of "making available to the public" as a type of more general right of communication to the public.[73] This right covers various interactive uses of copyright works, including offer for download, streaming music works, pay-per-view TV channels,

---

[64]FAPL EWHC 108 (2012) (Ch); 2 C.M.L.R. 16, 63 (2012).

[65]T. Lüder (2007), 14.

[66]WCT Art. 9(4); WPPT Art. 7, 11, and 16; E.C. Copyright in the Information Society Directive Art. 2.

[67]WCT Art. 8; E.C. Copyright in the Information Society Directive Art. 3.

[68]WCT Art. 8; WPPT Art. 10, 14, and 16; E.C. Copyright in the Information Society Directive Art. 3.

[69]D. Gervais (2000), 81.

[70]K.E. Beyer (2014), pp. 6-7; P. Goldstein / P.B. Hugenholtz (2010), 328.

[71]Berne Convention, 1971 Paris Text Art. 11, 11*bis*, and 11*ter*.

[72]P. Mysoor (2013), 168.

[73]WCT Art. 8; EU Copyright Directive Art. 3(1).

and file sharing over peer-to-peer networks.[74] Articles 10 and 14 of the WIPO Performers and Phonograms Treaty (WPPT) similarly provide performers and producers of phonograms with the right of "making available to the public." As this right of making available to the public is different from but sometimes overlapping with the right of reproduction, a legitimate interactive online service involving both rights may require two different clearance transactions.[75] In countries like the US that have not legislated the right of making available to the public, one common argument against such legislation is its potential overlap with the rights of performance and display.[76]

3.3 *Rights of Reproduction and Public Performance*

Rights of reproduction and public performance are two rights that tangle in a number of new business models,[77] especially when users have already obtained a license for pubic performance, but not for reproduction. Courts in different jurisdictions may have different approaches to the overlapping of these two rights. Here we provide examples from the US and Germany to illustrate the judicial heterogeneity.

3.3.1 The MP3.com Case in the US

In the early days of the digital music revolution, MP3.com purchased CDs and reproduced the music to facilitate its streaming business model. Although the company acquired public performance licenses from ASCAP and BMI,[78] it was held liable for willful infringement of the reproduction right.[79] MP3.com argued that the acquisition of CDs includes a performing right license, accompanied by an implied license for reproduction insofar as necessary to perform the music.[80] The US District Court for the Sothern District of New York disagreed and held that[81]:

[74]P. Goldstein / P.B. Hugenholtz (2010), 329; T. Lüder (2007), 33-36.

[75]D. Gervais (2000), 82; T. Lüder (2007), 26. There is one distinction between the right of making available to the public and the traditional right of communication to the public: the former is granted to authors, performers, and producers; whereas the latter is only accorded to authors. EU Copyright Directive Art. 3.

[76]K.E. Beyer (2014), 11.

[77]M.A. Lemley (1997), 574; W.W. Fisher III (2004), 160; D. Gervais (2010), 10.

[78]J. Litman (2004), 19.

[79]Country Road Music, Inc. v. MP3.com, Inc., 279 F. Supp. 2d 325, 333 (S.D.N.Y. 2003).

[80]*Id.*, 327.

[81]*Id.*, 327-328.

> "Performance" and "reproduction" are clearly and unambiguously separate rights under the Copyright Act of 1976. Here, the performing rights licenses themselves, as their name implies, explicitly authorize public performance only, do not purport to grant a reproduction right in music compositions...Moreover, the performing rights societies themselves do not, and do not purport to have, the authority to grant such a right.

In other words, even though MP3.com had secured performance rights licenses from the performing rights societies, the court held that the company still infringed copyright because such licenses did not include right of reproduction.

3.3.2 The MyVideo Case in Germany

In Germany, although an online service provider MyVideo already acquired a pan-European license from GEMA for public performance, it was still sued for the infringement of mechanical right (right of reproduction) by a CMO named CELAS, a joint venture of GEMA and PRS for Music. MyVideo then sought declaratory judgment against CELAS. Both the Munich District Court and Munich Court of Appeals ruled against CELAS because the courts opined that requesting a license purely for mechanical right does not make economic sense.[82] This decision was based on the German copyright rule that prevents rightholders from over-fragmenting exclusive rights.[83] Therefore, the courts ruled that rightholders can only license rights that are economically feasible.[84] This case illustrates a different approach than the US one coping with the overlapping reproduction right and public performance right.

3.3.3 Comparison

The similarity between the above two cases is that defendants in both cases obtained licenses for public performance. However, neither was licensed for reproduction. The US federal district court insisted on the doctrine of copyright divisibility and held that another license for reproduction is necessary. On the other hand, the German court approached this issue from an economic perspective and ruled that additional license for reproduction is pointless. Some scholars suggest that the case of CELAS presented the different practice of CMOs in continental-European countries and Anglo-American jurisdictions.[85] Continental-European CMOs normally require right holders to license both the reproduction right (or mechanical

[82]R.M. Hilty / S. Nérisson (2013), 229.

[83]J. Drexl (2014), 483.

[84]*Id.*

[85]J. Drexl / S. Nérisson / F. Trumpke / R.M. Hilty (2013), 328-329.

right) and public performance right; whereas Anglo-American CMOs typically only request public performance right.[86]

4 Possible Solutions to the Problem of Overlapping Rights

The enormous transaction costs for copyright clearance in a single use of any given work are not only bothersome for users but may also stifle new and innovative business models.[87] Startup companies may hesitate to develop innovative technologies or businesses if it is too costly to clear various exclusive rights. Therefore, it is worthwhile to explore the alternatives of bundling the fragmented rights in order to alleviate the tragedy of the anticommons.

4.1 Integration of Rights

Some scholars have criticized the overlapping layers of different rights as unnecessary and suggested that those rights should be consolidated from a policy perspective.[88] These reform proposals contained the redesigning of copyrights into one single right of commercial exploitation by eliminating divisibility.[89] Some others proposed to abolish divisibility in cyberspace while maintaining it in the real world.[90] However, incumbent copyright owners in the copyright market have opposed the reform of integrating the bundle of rights into one single right just to ensure their interests.[91] In fact, the U.S. Copyright Act adhered to the indivisibility principle before 1976, where copyright was "only a single incorporeal legal title or property."[92] In evaluating the reform proposal regarding rights integration, we need to reevaluate the factors influencing the change from indivisibility to divisibility in the 1976 Copyright Act.

[86] *Id.*

[87] J. Litman (2007), 1917; M.A. Heller / R.S. Eisenberg (1998), 700; J. Litman (2010), 20.

[88] P.B. Hugenholtz / M. van Eechoud / S. van Gompel / L. Guibault / N. Helberger (2006), 164; T. Lüder (2007), 26; *see also* J. Litman (2010), 43.

[89] J. Litman (2006), 180-186; J. Litman (2010), 43-45.

[90] J.W. Natke (2007), 505.

[91] J. Litman (2007), 1917; *see also* J.W. Natke (2007), 504.

[92] H.G. Henn (1955), 418.

4.1.1 Evaluating Integration as a Solution

The main reason for the 1976 reform regarding divisibility is that indivisibility created a problem for the standing to sue for infringement. If copyright owners would like to transfer part of his right to a transferee, such transaction would mostly be viewed as a license by the court, rather than as an assignment.[93] Consequently, the licensee would not have standing to sue third-party infringers.[94] Even if the license were an exclusive one, he would still have difficulties in joining the copyright owner as a necessary party in the infringement litigation.[95] Moreover, the indivisibility principle could not reflect the real copyright practice, which demanded varieties of contractual arrangement.[96] It was also believed that CMOs with the expertise in one specific subdivision of right may operate more efficiently.[97] Indeed the indivisibility rule has created some negative impact on the flexibility and efficiency of copyright transactions.

However, the problem of standing, which is the main concern in the 1976 Copyright Act, can be easily solved by slight revision of the Federal Rules of Civil Procedure[98] that allows exclusive licensees to join the copyright owner as a necessary party in the infringement. Moreover, some scholars raise concerns about the introduction of the divisibility rule in the 1976 Copyright Act. For example, Nimmer suggested that divisibility may produce difficulties for copyright notice, *i.e.* whose name should appear on the published copies of the work.[99] However, such concerns do not seem to have been realized in the last few decades, not to mention the fact that current rights management information,[100] marking multiple right holders has become easy, clear, and costless. Therefore, the difficulty of copyright notice may not be a strong reason for the elimination of the divisibility rule.

The real challenge faced by the proposal to reassemble different exclusive rights into an indivisible mass is how to cope with the status quo, in which different rights holders hold individual sub-rights, and international treaties, such as the Agreement on Trade-Related Aspects of Intellectual Property Rights (TRIPs), WCP, and WPPT, recognize a number of economic rights. Lastly, even if all exclusive rights were integrated into one single right of commercial exploitation, policymakers and the courts would still need to delineate a reasonable boundary of such right and decide whether such right is infringed whenever there is any new technological use.

---

[93] J.W. Natke (2007), 493-494.

[94] *Id.*, 494.

[95] *Id.*

[96] *Id.*, 492.

[97] J.W. Natke (2007), 503; R.C. Cooter / T. Ulen (2012), 165.

[98] J.W. Natke (2007), 505.

[99] M.B. Nimmer / D. Nimmer (1992), 14-121.

[100] 17 U.S.C. §1202(c).

4.1.2 Implications from the Anticommons Theory

Transaction costs are the main obstacles for market players to bundle the anticommons property through private ordering.[101] Bundling multiple rights by new laws, therefore, has been the most straightforward way to solve the anticommons problem.[102] With the integration of exclusive rights, users only need to seek one copyright holder, not several. The holdup problem can thus be avoided. However, whenever there is an anticommons problem, the integration of existing fragmented rights is "brutal and slow"[103] because it is difficult to deal with current rights holders and the existing contractual relationship. Just like rights holders who had "invested in reliance on current property regime" in post-Soviet Russia,[104] holders of any subdivision of the copyright may refuse to give up their rights, not to mention those who run their businesses primarily based on one particular right. Therefore, policymakers must design mechanisms to share the economic gain with existing rights holders or find other ways to adequately compensate them.[105] Given the high transaction costs in the anticommons scenario, copyright lawmakers should nevertheless try to simplify the variety of exclusive rights, although this may be hard to implement, and to avoid creating new exclusive rights for new technological use.[106]

4.2 Implied License

Another more modest proposal is to adopt the "implied license" approach to solve the fragmented copyright problem while maintaining the multiple exclusive rights regime.[107] By making an analogy to the concept of easement in property law, some researchers propose that if each distinct exclusive right in copyright is conveyed to separate entities, a licensed right should also include other rights incidental to the subject of use.[108] In other words, if licensee X only obtains the license of right A, but right B is incidental to the exercise of right A, then X should also get an implied license of right B, even though right B is not listed in the license agreement.[109] Implied license is not a new concept in copyright or IP law. Courts occasionally use

[101] M.A. Heller / R.S. Eisenberg (1998), 700.

[102] M.A. Heller (1998), 626, 640.

[103] M.A. Heller / R.S. Eisenberg (1998), 698.

[104] M.A. Heller (1998), 641.

[105] M.A. Heller (1998), 655.

[106] R.C. Cooter / T. Ulen (2012), 166.

[107] J. Litman (2007), 1917.

[108] *Id.*

[109] Copyright reform can even go further to implement the concept of "implied license" in other transactions concerning any single exclusive right, *see* J. Litman (2010), 46-47.

this concept to cope with disputes where contracts do not explicitly regulate whether licensees were licensed for a specific use of the work.[110]

The approach adopted by German courts in the CELAS case is, to some extent, similar to the "implied license" theory. Although the courts did not mention "implied license" in the decisions, they held that it did not make any economic sense if users need to secure another license for reproduction.[111] In other words, we may interpret such rules as: in the digital environment, reproduction of copyrighted work is incidental to its public performance. Therefore, users shall be deemed to have obtained an implied license for reproduction if they are licensed for public performance. Any additional request for license would be redundant.

Different from the integration approach based on legislation, the "implied license" represents the approach that the judiciary is capable of solving the anticommons problem. Implied license can avoid the legislative costs of pushing through the bundling of various exclusive rights.[112] Nonetheless, there are some problems underlying the implied license approach. First, compared to some bright-line rules, there are always some uncertainties regarding whether specific rights should be covered by implied licenses.[113] Second, it would be natural for holders of specific rights to object to this approach if their exclusive rights are covered by previous transactions with implied licenses. Some CMOs and rightholders have been relying on one single or a few types of exclusive rights. Implied license may thus impose negative effect on their revenues. Therefore, some commentators suggest that courts should consider the commercial reality and adopt a minimalist approach to grant the least amount of rights in implied licenses.[114]

4.3 Collaborations Between CMOs

The problem related to overlapping fragmented copyrights can also be addressed from a downstream perspective by the standardization of practice and cooperation between copyright collecting organizations. CRM has been conceived as a solution to the inefficiency caused by copyright enforcement on an individual basis.[115] CRM help users save an enormous amount of transaction costs in obtaining permission from copyright owners for the use of the latter's work.[116] CRM has also become a

[110]*See, e.g.,* Effects Associates, Inc. v. Cohen, 908 F.2d 555 (9th Cir. 1990).

[111]*See* text accompanying note 87.

[112]G. Calabresi (1982); R. Oman (1994), 21-22, n.8 (describing the difficulty of changing the IP law).

[113]D.J. Bainbridge (2007), 87.

[114]*Id.*

[115]D. Gervais / A. Maurushat (2003), 15.

[116]M. Heller (2008), p. 72; R. Aoki / A. Schiff (2008), 199; S. Dusollier / C. Colin (2011), 817-818; J. Drexl / S. Nérisson / F. Trumpke / R.M. Hilty (2013), 18-19; R.P. Merges (1996), 1295.

practical way for authors to be compensated appropriately.[117] Although some commentators believe that CRM is the most workable solution for copyright enforcement amid new technologies,[118] CRM does face new challenges in clearing rights in digital products and new business models with divided copyright ownership,[119] such as Internet radio, webcasting, podcasting, and pay-per-download services. If CMOs are not able to grant the complete set of rights that users need, the value of their services will decrease markedly.[120]

4.3.1 Evaluating CRM as a Solution

CRM is organized based on the traditional divisibility of copyright.[121] Among others, one of the most challenging tasks for CMOs and users in the digital age is to identify various rights associated with different right holders.[122] If different CMOs can agree that one CMO is to grant licenses on behalf of all other CMOs,[123] copyright users may save a great deal of costs in copyright clearance. In countries like the U.K., different collective societies have started to cooperate to provide a "one-stop" shop for clearing various copyrights.[124] From a policy perspective, governments or lawmakers may consider forcing CMOs to work together to solve the copyright anticommons problem. For example, the Copyright Board in Canada is empowered to legally force CMOs to work together to offer a single license fee.[125]

In addition to the cooperation agreements between CMOs, some researchers propose that various rights on one single object, especially the public performance rights and mechanical reproduction rights, owned by different right holders should be administered by one entity and under one license.[126] Moreover, the Canadian Private Copying Collective (CPCC) was incorporated in Canada as an umbrella collective for the benefit of other CMOs.[127] However, it should be noted that given the difficulty of harmonizing the differences between different works and the

[117] D. Gervais / A. Maurushat (2003), 16.

[118] J.H. Cohen (2001), 135; M.A. Lemley (1997), 571.

[119] M. Heller (2008), 190.

[120] M.A. Lemley (1997), 571.

[121] D. Gervais (2010), 11; M. Bouchard (2010), 311.

[122] D. Gervais / A. Maurushat (2003), 20; J. Litman (2010), 20.

[123] D. Gervais (2010), 12.

[124] S. Stoke (2002), 169-170.

[125] M. Bouchard (2010), 320.

[126] A. Gowers (2006), 45; R.P. Merges (1996), 1377.

[127] However, CPCC only focuses on royalties associated with music works. M. Bouchard (2010), 314.

interests of various right holders,[128] the centralized umbrella model has not yet become a widespread success.

4.3.2 Implications from the Anticommons Theory

Collaboration between CMOs represents a market route to solve the tragedy of the anticommons. Such an approach may fail if the transaction costs exceed the gains from collaboration.[129] Just like kiosk merchants who want to assemble fragmented rights by transactions, while reducing the pressure to overcome anticommons by *ex post* contracting, collaboration between CMOs does not change the property regime itself.[130] Similar to the problem caused by copyright divisibility, the free or open source software (F/OSS) and Wikipedia communities also encounter the tragedy of the anticommons concerning copyright management. Because contributors to F/OSS or Wikipedia are always scattered and the number of contributions is huge, the transaction costs of IP clearance for those commons projects are enormous.[131] Robert P. Merges proposed to solve such problem by having representatives administer multiple IP rights on behalf of the communities by contractual arrangement.[132] In reality, a number of commons organizations, such as the Free Software Foundation, Apache Software Foundation, and Wikimania Foundation, have aggregated scattered IP rights and alleviated the anticommons problem effectively.[133] Akin to the role of those F/OSS and Wikimania foundations, if CMOs can cooperate with each other, they shall be able to help ease the anticommons tragedies resulting from copyright divisibility. Ronald H. Coase has argued that organizations function to internalize the transaction costs stemming from imperfect markets and, as a result, firms increase the market's overall efficiency.[134] The theory can be applied in the context of commons organizations and CMOs as well. By internalizing the transaction costs of assembling fragmented copyrights, both commons organizations and CMOs provide solutions to the tragedy of the anticommons.

Empirical research has indicated that close-knit communities may develop norms and institutions to manage resources efficiently and avoid the tragedy of the anticommons.[135] Communities of IP owners with repeat-play features have also developed "institutions to reduce transaction costs of bundling multiple licenses,"

---

[128]*See* text accompanying *supra* note 139 and note 21.

[129]*Cf.* R.C. Cooter / T. Ulen (2012), 140; M.A. Heller (1998), 760; *Id.*, 657.

[130]M.A. Heller (1998), 642-643.

[131]J.-A. Lee (2010), 291-292.

[132]R.P. Merges (2008), 1187-1188.

[133]J.-A. Lee (2010), 292-293.

[134]R.H. Coase (1937), 386.

[135]R.C. Ellickson (1991), 64-166; E. Ostrom (1990), 182-184; M.A. Heller / R.S. Eisenberg (1998), 698; C. Rose (1986), 711.

such as patent pools.[136] Traditionally, different CMOs focus on different types of exclusive right and may not cooperate with one another frequently. Nonetheless, as the overlapping rights issue becomes increasingly common, CMOs that used to operate on different subdivision of rights may be forced to develop into a closer community. Consequently, the holdup problem becomes less important in the repeat-play setting.[137] In other words, by creating an environment with more overlapping rights, digital technologies may also push various CMOs to form a close-knit community, which will eventually develop a private-ordering solution to the anticommons problem.

4.4 Summary

The proposed solutions may help reduce transaction costs and correct market failure resulting from overlapping rights. They represent different approaches to the tragedy of the anticommons in the context of copyright divisibility. The integration of rights needs legislative action,[138] whereas implied license denotes a judicial treatment of the fragmented copyright. However, for regular incidental use of relevant exclusive rights in the digital realm, policymakers may consider legislating implied license as statutory license. It should also be noted that some other copyright reform proposals may alleviate the anticommons problem as well, for example, the extended collective licensing used in Nordic countries, a centralized one-stop-shop licensing agent, or compulsory licensing.[139] Different from those public initiatives, the collaboration between CMOs exemplifies how the market responds to the fragmented and overlapping copyright system. Nonetheless, these three proposals are not mutually exclusive. It is possible for these solutions to work together to ease the tragedy of the anticommons.

In addition to the proposed solutions analyzed above, private copyright practice has started to address the costs associated with royalty collection in new business models. As clearance of various rights involves enormous transaction costs, some users of multimedia works would rather use the materials in the public domain if they have such a choice, or even create everything from scratch, than obtaining permission to use other people's work.[140] On the other hand, copyright owners may rely on sophisticated digital rights? management (DRM) technology, rather than

[136] M.A. Heller / R.S. Eisenberg (1998), 700; R.P. Merges (1996), 1319, 1340-1342.

[137] R.P. Merges (1996), 1321.

[138] J.W. Natke (2007), 504 (predicting that "the Supreme Court is not likely to revive indivisibility in the absence of legislative action").

[139] D. Gervais / A. Maurushat (2003), 23-25; D. Gervais (2010), 17.

[140] D. Gervais / A. Maurushat (2003), 24.

various CMOs, to collect royalties.[141] The combination of those public and private orderings may, to some extent, reduce the transaction costs brought by copyright divisibility.

5 Conclusion

Although divisibility has provided flexibility for copyright owners' utilization of their works, it creates significant costs for copyright transactions and enforcement. The fragmentation of copyright occurs on various levels, such as national laws, the nature of copyrighted works, market structure, licensing practices, the interoperability of rights clearance systems, etc. The anticommons problem has become more serious in the Internet arena as digital technologies have enabled new ways of exploiting and distributing copyrighted works. Such new development has led to controversy over how new technological use should be classified into copyright law's traditional taxonomy of entitlements. A number of approaches have been suggested or implemented to solve the overlapping or fragmented issues in copyright clearance from a policy perspective.

A streamlined licensing process can not only reduce transaction costs for right holders and users, but also foster innovative business models.[142] CMOs may cooperate to facilitate streamlined copyright clearance, although not all of them have incentive to do so. Nonetheless, a centralized approach or collaboration between CMOs is not always easily implemented. Given that the nature, duration, and royalty rates of different rights cannot be easily harmonized, it is very likely that various rights holders may challenge the neutrality of the centralized authorities or mechanisms. Therefore, another yet-to-be-explored policy question is how to balance the diverse interests of rights holders and stakeholders of various copyrighted works.

References

Aoki, R. / Schiff, A. (2008), Promoting Access to Intellectual Property: Patent Pools, Copyright Collectives, and Clearinghouses, R&D Management 38(2), 189-204

Bainbridge, D.I. (2007), Intellectual Property, 6th ed., Pearson Education Limited

Beyer, K.E. (2014), Taking the "Hype" Out of Hyper-Linking: Linking Online Content Not Grounds for U.S. Copyright Infringement, IDEA: The Intellectual Property Law Review 55, 1-29

[141] M. Ricolfi (2007), 297-301; R.P. Merges (1996), 1298 (proposing the "electronic clearing-houses" where all copyright transactions can take place in one electronic marketplace).

[142] T. Lüder (2007), 19.

Bouchard, M. (2010), Collective Management in Commonwealth Jurisdictions: Comparing Canada with Australia, in: D. Gervais (Ed.), Collective Management of Copyright and Related Rights, 307-338, Kluwer Law International
Calabresi, G. (1982), A Common Law for the Age of Statutes, Harvard University Press
Coase, R.H. (1937), The Nature of the Firm, Economica 4, 386-405
Cohen, J.H. (2001), The Future of Copyright Collective Societies, E.I.P.R. 23(3), 134-139
Cooter, R. / Ulen, T. (2012), Law and Economics, 6th ed., Pearson Education Limited
Cornish, W.R. / Llwelyn, D. / Aplin, T.F. (2013), Intellectual Property: Patents, Copyright, Trade Marks and Allied Rights, Sweet & Maxwell
Drexl, J. (2014), Collective Management of Copyrights and the EU Principle of Free Movement of Services after the OSA Judgment—In Favour of a More Balance Approach, in: K. Purnhagen, P. Rott (Eds.), Varieties of European Economic Law and Regulation, 459-488, Springer
Drexl, J. / Nérisson, S. / Trumpke, F. / Hilty, R.M. (2013), Comments of the Max Planck Institute for Intellectual Property and Competition Law on the Proposal for a Directive of the European Parliament and of the Council on Collective Management of Copyright and Related Rights and Multi-Territorial Licensing of Rights in Musical Works for Online Uses in the Internal Market COM (2012)372, 44 IIC, 322-350
Dusollier, S. / Colin, C. (2011), Peer-to-Peer and Copyright: What Could Be the Role of Collective Management?, Columbia Journal of Law & Arts 34(4), 809-835
Elkin-Koren, N. (2005), What Contracts Cannot Do: The Limits of Private Ordering in Facilitating a Creative Commons, Fordham Law Review 74, 375-422
Ellickson, R.C. (1991), Order Without Law: How Neighbors Settle Disputes, Harvard University Press
Fisher III, W.W. (2004), Promises to Keep: Technology, Law, and the Future of Entertainment, Stanford University Press
Gervais, D. (2000), Electronic Rights Management Systems, Journal of World Intellectual Property 3, 77-95
Gervais, D. (2010), Collective Management of Copyright: Theory and Practice in the Digital Age, in: D. Gervais (Ed.), Collective Management of Copyright and Related Rights, 1-28, Kluwer Law International
Gervais, D. / Maurushat, A. (2003), Fragmented Copyright, Fragmented Management: Proposals to Defrag Copyright Management, Canadian Journal of Law & Technology 2, 15-33
Goldstein, P. (2003), Copyright's Highway: From Gutenberg to the Celestial Jukebox, Rev. Ed., Stanford University Press
Goldstein, P. / Hugenholtz, P.B. (2010), International Copyright: Principles, Law, and Practice, 328, Oxford University Press
Gowers, A. (2006), Gowers Review of Intellectual Property, 45, available at: www.hm-treasury.gov.uk/media/6/E/pbr06_gowers_report_755.pdf
Heller, M.A. (1998), The Tragedy of the Anticommons: Property in the Transition from Marx to Markets, Harvard Law Review 111(3), 621-688
Heller, M.A. (2008), The Gridlock Economy: How Too Much Ownership Wrecks Markets, Stops Innovation, and Costs Lives, Basic Books
Heller, M.A. / Eisenberg, R.S. (1998), Can Patents Deter Innovation? The Anticommons in Biomedical Research, Science 280, 698-701
Henn, H.G. (1955), "Magazine Rights"—A Division of Indivisible Copyright, Cornell Law Quarterly 40, 411-474
Hilty, R.M. / Nérisson, S. (2013), Collective Copyright Management, in: R. Towse, C. Handke (Eds.), Handbook of the Digital Creative Economy Cultural Economics, 222-234, Edward Elgar
Hugenholtz, P.B. / van Eechoud, M. / van Gompel, S. / Guibault, L. / Helberger, N. (2006), The Recasting of Copyright & Related Rights for the Knowledge Economy, University of Amsterdam

Information Infrastructure Task Force, Intellectual Property and the National Information Infrastructure (1995), The Report of the Working Group on Intellectual Property Rights
Kohn, A. / Kohn, B. (2000), Kohn on Music Licensing, 4th ed., Aspen Publishers
Leaffer, M.A. (2010), Understanding Copyright Law, LexisNexis
Lee, J.-A. (2010), Organizing the Unorganized: The Role of Nonprofit Organizations in the Commons Communities, Jurimetrics Journal 50(3), 275-327
Lessig, L. (2004), Free Culture: How Big Media Uses Technology and the Law to Lock Down Culture and Control Creativity, Penguin Books
Lemley, M.A. (1997), Dealing with Overlapping Copyrights on the Internet, University of Dayton Law Review 22(3), 547-585
Litman, J. (2004), Sharing and Stealing, Hastings Communications & Entertainment Law Journal 27, 1-48
Litman, J. (2006), Digital Copyright, 2nd ed., Prometheus Books
Litman, J. (2007), Lawful Personal Use, Texas Law Review 85, 1871-1920
Litman, J. (2010), Real Copyright Reform, Iowa Law Review 96(1), 1-55
Loren, L.P. (2003), Untangling the Web of Music Copyrights, Case Western Reserve Law Review 53, 673-721
Lüder, T. (2007), The Next Ten Years in E.U. Copyright: Making Markets Work, Fordham Intellectual Property Media & Entertainment Law Journal 18, 1-60
Merges, R.P. (1996), Contracting into Liability Rules: Intellectual Property Rights and Collective Rights Organizations, California Law Review 84(5), 1293-1393
Merges, R.P. (2008), Locke for the Masses: Property Rights and the Products of Collective Creativity, Hofstra Law Review 36, 1179-1190
Mysoor, P. (2013), Unpacking the Right of Communication to the Public: A Closer Look at International and EU Copyright Law, Intellectual Property Quarterly 2013(2), 166-185
Natke, J.W. (2007), Collapsing Copyright Divisibility: A Proposal for Situational or Medium Specific Indivisibility, Michigan State Law Review 2007, 483-532
Nimmer, M.B. / Nimmer, D. (1992), Nimmer on Copyright, LexisNexis
Oman, R. (1994), Intellectual Property after the Uruguay Round, J. Copyright Society U.S.A. 42, 18-38
Ostrom, E. (1990), Governing the Commons: The Evolution of Institutions for Collective Action, Cambridge University Press
Pessach, G. (2014), The Beijing Treaty on Audiovisual Performances—The Return of the North?, IDEA: The Intellectual Property Law Review 55(1), 79-104
Ricolfi, M. (2007), Individual and Collective Management of Copyright in a Digital Environment, in: P. Torremans (Ed.), Copyright Law: A Handbook of Contemporary Research, 283-314, Edward Elgar
Rose, C. (1986), The Comedy of the Commons: Custom, Commerce, and Inherently Public Property, University of Chicago Law Review 53, 711-781
Stoke, S. (2002), Digital Copyright Law and Practice, Hart Publishing
Vanheusden, E. (2007), Performers' Rights in European Legislation: Situation and Elements for Improvement, Association of European Performers' Organisations

One or Several Super-Rights? The (Subtle) Impact of the Digital Single Market on a Future EU Copyright Architecture

Guido Westkamp

Contents

Abstract The 2001 Directive on Certain Aspects of Copyright and Related Rights in the Information Society has often been criticized as being too rigid, and also for affording too powerful rights to exploiters, rather than emphasising the relationship between author's rights and the public interest. Recent CJEU jurisprudence has, very arguably, introduced more flexibility and shifted the focus, perhaps in a subtle anticipation of a digital single market. This contribution explores that jurisprudence and its potential impact, with an emphasis on uses of works by institutions such libraries. More generally, the role of limitations and exceptions to copyright in the broader framework of a novel (yet of course evolving) construction of key concepts is examined—in particular the notion of a new public and the advent of a digital exhaustion doctrine.

Guido Westkamp, LL.M. holds the Chair in Intellectual Property and Comparative Law, Centre for Commercial Law Studies, Queen Mary University of London and is Co-Director, Queen Mary Intellectual Property Research Institute.

G. Westkamp (✉)
Queen Mary University of London, London, UK
e-mail: g.westkamp@qmul.ac.uk

K.-C. Liu, R.M. Hilty (eds.), *Remuneration of Copyright Owners*, MPI Studies on Intellectual Property and Competition Law 27, DOI 10.1007/978-3-662-53809-8_2

1 Introduction

Traditional copyright doctrine manifestly understands the enumerated exclusive rights, such as reproduction and communication to the public, as individually enforceable and insulated property rights. Digital technology facilitates hypertextual access, from digitising "analogue" content to providing valued-added services—onsite consultations in libraries, email transmissions, hyperlinking, digital archiving, print-outs, or digital storage on digital tablets, smartphones or USB sticks. Current copyright regulates such uses under the constituent elements of its traditional self-contained system, mirroring different economic and social realities. The traditional notion of insulated exclusive rights drastically impacts upon the freedom to use works. Any digital use inevitably comprises acts of copying and acts of communication and transmission. Consequentially, there are difficulties, and especially so for institutions such as libraries, archives and educational establishments. The ensuing problems concern the entire spectrum of copyright doctrine—starting from the question of how limitations must be interpreted, and the scope of insulated exclusive rights to, ultimately, issues concerning extrinsic principles such as exhaustion. Exceptions and limitations, in particular, still stand isolated and hardly permit, by and large, more purposive modes of interpretation.

But at least to some extent the more recent jurisprudence of the Court of Justice of the European Union (EU) appears to be increasingly informed by—subtle—reflections of needs for a more flexible approach to copyright law, and thus may anticipate future concerns of a digital single market.[1] The principal legislation in EU—the 2001 Directive on Copyright and Related Rights in the Information Society (hereinafter "EUCD")[2]—evidently appears too one-sided, rigid[3] and vague, and is therefore subject to reform.

Copyright law, it may be surmised, no longer fully mirrors the interests and realities that have emerged with diverse digital use models.[4] The rigidity embedded in the EUCD is currently subject to political review, one emphasis being a possible re-conceptualisation of the communication to the public right and, it is hoped, a reconsideration of exceptions and limitations applicable to libraries and similar interests in the remit of science, research and education. Library uses—which this chapter focuses upon—require broader limitations so as to fully embed divergent use modalities, from permitting users to print digitised documents to more crucial issues such as e-lending or digitising library holdings such as books and journals.[5]

[1]See Communication from the Commission, "Towards a modern, more European copyright framework", Doc. COM (2015) 626 final, 9. December 2015.

[2]Directive 2001/29/EC of the European Parliament and of the Council of 22 May 2001 on the harmonisation of certain aspects of copyright and related rights in the information society, OJ L 167, 22. June 2001, 10-19.

[3]See *infra*, at 2.

[4]See K.-N. Peifer (2010), 641.

[5]See *infra*, 3.1.1.

Rather surprisingly, however, the Court of Justice seems to be developing what may be called a "commercial communication right". The conception of rather new concepts—a pan-European level of originality in the sense of an "own intellectual creation"[6] rather than the UK investment protection approach, the notion of real harm,[7] the concept of a new public,[8] and a commercial implication ("profit-making") as elements of construing communication rights[9] and, perhaps most importantly, the extension of the exhaustion doctrine to downloads—will drastically affect conventional notions of normative copyright. These assertions appear to considerably reshape the structure and architecture of digital copyright law, by re-conceptualising traditional copyright standards understood as a body of rules at odds with the digital single market aim. Although there is no express reference in that jurisprudence to the digital single market yet, most of the more recent decisions refer to a balancing of interests[10] as a pivotal point of departure.

Thus, one progressively finds an emerging, and novel, pattern of construction anticipating the needs of a digital single market. In essence, copyright may well become entrenched in a flexible balancing approach that defies the general statement that a high level of protection[11] will produce incentives for right holders to set up new business models benefitting the union citizens. In short, the digital single market aim may thus become the predominant benchmark against which interests of copyright owners are to be pitted. This move towards a stronger emphasis upon extrinsic principles[12] can, however, lead to further collisions with traditional copyright thinking as enshrined in international convention law.

---

[6]Infopaq International A/S v. Danske Dagblades Forening (C-5/08) ECR I-6569 (2009).

[7]Padawan SL v. Sociedad General de Autores y Editores de España (SGAE) (C-467/08) E.C.D.R. 1 (2011); Copydan Båndkopi v. Nokia Danmark A/S (C-463/12) E.C.D.R. 9 (2015); ACI Adam BV v. Stichting de Thuiskopie (C-435/12) E.C.D.R. 13 (2014); Entidad De Gestión De Derechos De Los Productores Audiovisuales (Egeda) v. Hostelería Asturiana Sa (Hoasa) (Case C-293/98) E.C.D.R. 231 (2000); Amazon.com International Sales Inc v. Austro-Mechana Gesellschaft zur Wahrnehmung mechanisch-musikalischer Urheberrechte Gesellschaft mbH (C-521/11) E.C.D.R. 12 (2013).

[8]See, for example, Padawan SL v. Sociedad General de Autores y Editores de España (SGAE) (C-467/08) E.C.D.R. 1 (2011); Ochranny svaz autorsky pro prava k dilum hudebnim os (OSA) v. Lecebne lazne Marianske Lazne as (C-351/12) European Court of Justice (Fourth Chamber) E.C.D.R. 25 (2014).

[9]Phonographic Performance (Ireland) Ltd v. Ireland (C-162/10) 2 C.M.L.R. 29 (2012); Societa Consortile Fonografici (SCF) v. Del Corso (C-135/10) European Court of Justice (Third Chamber) E.C.D.R. 16 (2012). See further below, 3.2.1.

[10]See particularly Productores de Música de España (Promusicae) v. Telefónica de España SAU (C-275/06) E.C.R. I-271(Grand Chamber) (2008); Case C-580/13 (2015); Nintendo Co. Ltd v. PC Box Srl. Case C-355/12 ECR, 23 January 2014 (2014). See further Scarlet Extended SA v. Societe Belge des Auteurs, Compositeurs et Editeurs SCRL (SABAM) (C-70/10) European Court of Justice (Third Chamber) ECR I-11959 (2011); Coty Germany GmbH v. Stadtsparkasse Magdeburg ECR, 16 July 2015 (2015).

[11]See Recitals 4, 9 and 11 EUCD.

[12]See also the contributions in G. Dinwoodie (2015).

2 Normative Rigidity

The collision of interests here goes far beyond a reflection of the degree of legitimate expectations claimed by publishers as owners of copyright and libraries as institutions. Indeed, the collisions of interest are manifold, depending on the specific system they are entrenched in. That insight requires some initial explanation. At the broadest level, the notion of a digital single market as a policy aim clashes with two relevant features of copyright law, namely territoriality and the highly rigid and one-sided character of the most important piece of European copyright legislation. The cause of that problem lies in the EUCD, and its underlying policy objective, itself. The EUCD is certainly not a mere tool for harmonisation. It is a piece of legislation which, at the time, was drafted predominantly around the anticipated demands of exploiters—and potentially primarily the music and film industries. Although the EUCD seems generally based on a balanced approach,[13] the European lawmaker concurrently ensured that, as far as digital uses (broadly understood) were concerned, national legislators and courts should exercise caution. Hence, claims for "fair" digital uses were perceived predominantly as threats to right holders and as obstacles to yielding the desired business models. Indeed, it may well be argued that the central aim underlying the policy rationale was to incentivise the establishment of online services.[14]

The solution thus foresaw and preferred direct licensing arrangements based on technological protection measures (TPM). In other words, there are clear tendencies to allocate control rights preferably to "right holders". This diminishes arguments favouring authors and user rights potentially in a drastic manner. The EUCD, in that sense, does not distinguish between the respective interest groups of authors, owners of neighbouring rights and, arguably, owners of licensed rights, but it very directly directs user rights—or, more generally, public interest concerns to privately ordered systems based on contracts. The real "turn" thus is that individual users generally are subject to individual negotiations and that the conventional dogma of a—more or less extensive—protection of the private sphere of individual users is renounced.

It is centrally that legislative approach to conceptualise copyright as a tool for incentivising new online business models which caused the multiple policy and legal problems that have surfaced in the more recent decade and which has led to new policy initiatives under the rather long-winded caption of a digital single market as a future "fifth freedom".

Although much of what the Court of Justice asserts is certainly subject to further debate and qualification, a tendency to overcome that rigidity seems certainly present. This is, as will be discussed, visible both as regards a more rationale-based construction of limitations and exclusive rights, as well as perhaps an incrementally developing self-perception of the Court as innovator of copyright doctrine through the lens of

[13]See Recital 31 EUCD.

[14]See Article 6(4)(4) EUCD.

European harmonisation and primary aims concerns. This, one would expect, would have a direct impact upon the interface between limitations and exclusive rights, towards a more rationale-based interpretation of limitations that allows, holistically, a transcension of the difficulty of diverse exclusive rights applying concurrently to a homogenous use. However, this is very arguably not the case.

In Article 5 EUCD, limitations have been—more or less—concocted without much conceptualisation, and drawn from diverse national legal traditions.[15] Many, such as the limitations for private copying and for transient copies, are the result of compromise solutions, and further a problematic distinction was made between limitations relating to the reproduction right and limitations covering both reproductions and communication rights. Importantly, then, uses such as by a library—which may require preparatory or incidental copies—may be controlled on the basis of isolated and sole-standing exclusive rights.[16]

From a normative or dogmatic perspective, the strictures embedded in the EUCD have not only prevented a broader and more involved debate[17] concerning a veritable re-conceptualisation of copyright law doctrine at the European level so far. Attempts to do so have, so far, mainly included discussions relating to individual and separate aspects such as originality, the scope of exclusive rights, the "proper" mode of interpreting limitations[18] or, conversely, the impact of legal principles and regulatory areas extrinsic to copyright, such as human rights law[19] and competition law.[20] The rigidity implicit in the architecture of the Directive, still, complicates the formulation and conceptualisation of the impact of balancing factors and policy aims into the normative assessment.

The prime example is the notion of the new public, which conceptually appears proximate to notions of exhaustion, and, even more importantly in this context, the notion of a commercial implication as an element of construing the term "public",[21] and in doing so the Court of Justice introduced a fundamental collision clause. Likewise, exhaustion was accepted as a concept applicable to the making available of computer programs, instigating a more general debate on whether copyright might be subject to broad extrinsic limitations.

As will be seen later in this contribution,[22] the combined effect of these advances may have the potential to significantly impact the tri-polar matrix of interests. Specifically the notion of a commercial use, which may arguably become applicable

---

[15]See P.B. Hugenholtz (2000), 501, 502.

[16]Cf. Recital 23 EUCD, noting that the concept of the communication to the public right does not include any other act.

[17]See, for example, R.M. Hilty (2006), 103; J. Cohen (2006), 121.

[18]See A. Ohly (2009), 212.

[19]See European Court of Human Rights, Ashby Donald and others v. France, Appl. No. 36769/08 = 45 (2014) IIC 354; C. Geiger (2006), 371; C. Geiger (Ed.) (2015).

[20]See A. Brown (2010), 51.

[21]See *infra*, 3.2. See further G. Westkamp (2004), 1057, 1061.

[22]See *infra*, 3.2.1.

more fully with regard to the rights of exploiters,[23] has the capacity to fundamentally alter the normative strictures and establish two separate and principled approaches that allow courts to make fundamental distinctions between the "legitimate" interests of authors and exploiters respectively. That said, there is nothing in the jurisprudence of the Court of Justice that clearly indicates how, and which, more general topoi may be integrated into what may become a novel system of balancing interests—specifically, the Court never mentioned the digital single market as a parameter for construing (and limiting) exploiter rights. But a (perhaps premature) attempt to conceptualise the overall matrix of interests should be revealed.

The incremental destabilization that might follow from the typically apodictic assertions of the Court may be placed conceptually at divergent levels. Previously, the system of "digital" copyright regulation was considered as highly self-contained and self-referential. The term destabilisation denotes that new arguments are incorporated which reflect an increasing awareness of more holistic and nuanced concepts that may more accurately and precisely be adapted to emerging and growing needs of individual interests. To be more precise, the evolution that is taking place contemporaneously—through the formulation of new normative elements—is rooted in probably rather diverse implications stemming from distinct systems. This may be more clearly illustrated as follows: at the level of normative copyright, the construction of individual statutory elements (such as the "public") is certainly constrained by methodical strictures that, in the EU, deviate from one member state to another, and here the EUCD sets limits with regard to, for example, an approach which would allow incidental uses to be absorbed.

A decision by a Swiss court[24]—not bound by secondary EU copyright law—shows how, at the level of normative construction, a broad and rationale-based approach can inform the assessment of limitations so as to fundamentally overcome an isolated understanding of exclusive rights and thus to establish rather generous access rules. If such an approach is considered improper as a matter of EU law, the perspective must turn from the normative and mostly intrinsic approach (i.e. limited by the "wording" of individual EUCD norms or by an approach informed by the initial values of the EUCD) to a principled approach—an illustrative example concerns the question of how far notions of recognising competition aspects may be considered at the level of normative interpretation, especially in the context of institutional uses clashing with interest of publishers.[25] These principles are manifold, as they may reflect rather divergent aspirations.

---

[23] *Id.*, 1064.

[24] See *infra*, 3.1.2.

[25] See BGHZ 151, 300, 311—"In-House Press Clippings Archive". Here, the BGH concluded that the extension of limitations to cover digital in-house archives was permissible; it was asserted that there was no danger of an over-extensive use outside the privileged entity. See also ProLitteris v. Aargauer Zeitung, AG, 4C.73/2007 (June 26, 2007), 133 Entscheidungen des Schweizerischen Bundesgerichts [BGE] III 473, 485: the defendant offered a service for delivering media items to third parties, rather than for in-house use, which the Swiss Federal Court held to be compliant with the limitation on media monitoring services.

I will, in the following paragraphs, first present an analysis of the treatment of annex use in relation to existing limitations privileging those institutions acting as grocers of knowledge dissemination such as libraries or archives, arguing that there still is a rigid approach towards the construction of exclusive rights and consequential maintenance of control rights that must (and can) be overcome by way of a proper teleological interpretation. Emphasis is placed on the relationship between (academic) publishers and beneficiaries of—broadly—limitations serving research and education.

3 Libraries, Publishers and Copyright

Libraries have persistently, and justifiably, claimed more freedom.[26] Against this, publishers have regularly objected, claiming a loss of important markets. Within this clash of interests, European copyright law provides, under Article 5 EUCD, four limitations that are potentially applicable to using digital copying and transmission technology by libraries, plus, in most member states, limitations allowing the making of copies for private purposes that may be relied upon by individual users. The reality shows a diverse and highly heterogeneous picture.

It is therefore uncertain whether library exceptions privilege the library as an institution or whether these uses are understood as an extension of "personal" privileges to make reproductions for research and related purposes. In fact, there exists only one permissible limitation that was formulated specifically for onsite consultations. Article 5(3)(n) EUCD permits member states to implement privileges for libraries, museum, archives and educational establishments covering onsite consultations by making available in the physical premises, i.e. on dedicated terminals. The provision is further limited where licensing agreements exist and also constrained to materials that have been purchased. The limitation for educational and scientific uses according to Article 5(3)(a) is worded extensively but applies only under further conditions—that is, to the extent justified by the non-commercial purpose. This means that educational or scientific purposes are usually restricted to parts or portions of works, and that libraries therefore cannot easily rely on that privilege, since a commercial dimension—one that would detrimentally impact on the commercial expectations of right holders—would usually not be justified. At the national level, there exist significant disparities which cannot be covered here.[27]

The following will cover illustrative examples from jurisdictions which, comparatively, allow libraries to permit certain digital uses, and these examples will be analysed on the basis of existing or decided disputes. The essential question which

---

[26] See European Bureau of Library, Information and Documentation Associations (EBILDA), available at: www.eblida.org/news/modernisation-of-eu-copyright-rules-yes,-but.html.

[27] See, in relation to film, G. Westkamp (2015), 55-74.

arises as regards the normative assessment of institutional limitations concerns the issue of whether or not, at a normative level, a purposive construction is capable of producing, ultimately, access privileges. Here, a Swiss decision will be contrasted with the approach under EU and German law. Further, the impact of exclusive rights and their construction will be analysed following recent jurisprudence. In this regard, existing statutory copyright law creates the (general) difficulty that any digital use may have impact upon diverse exclusive rights—for example, permitting users to have digitised documents emailed requires the making of reproductions, as do use modalities such as printing or digitally copying protected materials. Also, preparatory reproductions will be required.

3.1 Public Consultations of Works

The current structure of isolated yet overlapping exclusive rights poses problems especially in the context of limitations and statutory licenses as regards uses by libraries. The situation is highly heterogeneous, and the EUCD does not reflect a clear systematic structure of limitations. Unsurprisingly, therefore, the two regulatory levels—exclusive rights and limitations—present a muddled and incongruous picture; their combined application under national laws leads to a plethora of possible solutions with many complexities and grey areas.

3.1.1 Libraries and Incidental Uses

For a long time, libraries and other institutional users have demanded greater freedom based on general limitations for research and educational uses that would cover digital uses—including, for example, establishing digital archives from existing repositories, providing (digital) document delivery services or establishing electronic reading terminals.

These claims for freedom of use are currently not generally reflected in the EUCD.[28] Libraries may, as mentioned, be permitted to digitise their holdings, in general, only under Article 5(2)(c) EUCD—a clause that limits such use to reproductions and therefore would exclude any further use by making available. In addition, some member states have taken steps to allow libraries (and other institutions) to set up electronic consultation terminals following Article 5(3)(n) EUCD. That provision marks the sole permission to member states to permit digital technology to be used—in effect, a provision that transforms an "analogue" constellation of library users into digital consultations of works. The general educational limitation under Article 5(3)(a), derived from the Berne Convention, is in fact rather limited under national laws, would usually only apply where the use is

[28] Specifically on research exceptions *cf.* C. Engel (2004), 35; R.M. Hilty (2006), 107.

justified by the "non-commercial purpose", and is usually limited to only portions of works.[29] In conclusion, the fact that diverse limitations addressed to institutional users apply to divergent exclusive rights specifically under national laws shows how undesirably complex the legal assessment of the permissibility of such uses may be. Apart from the more specific wording of each of the limitations mentioned above, their application is of course subject to diverse uses. These range from preparatory uses (such as digitising copies) to concerns over whether libraries may offer certain annex uses, such as modalities to email documents to individual users or to permit them to make copies or print-outs.

A more general problem in the vexed relationship between institutions, users and right holders then concerns the relationship between online access services offered by right holders and the extent to which these may remove limitations. Thus, do right holders enjoy a general privilege to offer licenses that would replace reliance on any of the institutional limitations? This is expressly so for the limitation dedicated to electronic terminals but may as well follow, as regards the limitation for educational use, from the reference to a justified use. As mentioned, it was very much a policy expectation to incentivise right holders to do just that—create workable online services based on licenses and TPMs in order to establish and enhance online markets. Recent (and pending) litigation shows that this idea has not come to fruition as expected. In addition, divergent approaches between member states and the principle of territoriality generally mean that it is impossible to create cross-border access to repositories established in other member states. Overall, can there be a solution specifically for library uses that would offer the highest degree of access?

Fundamentally, as regards a potential European solution, it is unfortunate that the EUCD remains entirely uncertain as to the relevant public interest rationale underlying each limitation. However, one avenue towards an initial rationalisation may lie in the differentiation that the Court of Justice has—subtly—expressed as regards the criterion of the public,[30] and herein especially the important distinction between rights of exploiters and authors. It will be remembered that the Court of Justice now demands some commercial impact upon exploiters, a criterion that was not formulated with regard to authors in the context of the communication rights. To this aspect I will return later.

3.1.2 Three Disputes: *Ratio Legis* or Narrow Interpretation?

As far as the permissible extent of institutional limitations as such is concerned, three recent examples may illustrate the degree to which interpretational approaches may diverge as regards attempts by libraries to offer additional services

---

[29]See, on Article 5(3)(a) EUCD in particular, R. Xalabarder (2007); S. Ernst / D. Haeusermann (2006).

[30]See *infra*, 3.2.

to users. The first example concerns the litigation in *Ulmer*,[31] where two relevant issues arose under Article 52b of the German Authors Right Act, which implements the limitation for uses on dedicated terminals.[32] A German university library had digitised various books from their collection in order to make those available on dedicated terminals on their premises, and also permitted users to copy journal articles or extracts from books (i.e. on USB sticks) and to print such extracts out. The claimant, a publisher, asserted that such use would go beyond the express wording of the limitation and that, in addition, they had offered a licensing arrangement which should take precedence and thus disallow the defendant to rely on the limitation at all. The Court of Justice was, consequentially, asked to clarify the extent to which Article 5(3)(n) EUCD permitted such annex uses and whether the claimant could find comfort in proposing licensing arrangements.

As to the former, the Court of Justice replied that in general a limitation should not be interpreted so as to allow uses that are not expressly mentioned, and that therefore Article 5(3)(n) EUCD would have to be limited to acts of making available on screen; neither Article 5(3)(n) nor Article 52b of the German Authors Right Act mentions copying. Additional uses, such as making copies on digital storage media, could however be covered under applicable limitations in national laws, specifically as regards limitations for—broadly—private and/or personal research uses. The Court of Justice, more importantly perhaps, also held that the restriction to licenses referred only to existing licensing schemes rather than to mere offers—a position at odds with that of the German Federal Court of Justice.[33]

The German Federal Court of Justice[34] closely followed the reasoning of the Court of Justice. It held that preparatory digitisations would be covered by the limitation for the purpose of educational and scientific uses, combining the two limitations for dedicated terminals and educational and research purposes. Article 52a(3) of the German Authors Right Act, which permits acts of communication for educational or scientific purposes by educational establishments, additionally privileges preparatory and necessary copies; consequently, the German Federal Court of Justice applied that provision by way of analogy. Annex reproductions made by users were covered under the limitation for own research purposes, which allows the making of copies of entire works; here lies the bone of contention, because the Court of Justice had previously asserted that such annex reproductions may be covered by national limitations insofar as these comply with the respective private

[31]Technische Universitat Darmstadt v. Eugen Ulmer KG (C-117/13) E.C.D.R. 23 (2014).

[32]Article 5(3)(n) EUCD.

[33]BGH (2014) GRUR 549—"Meilensteine der Psychologie". The BGH asserted that library uses in universities were not "justified" according to Article 52a of the Authors Rights Act by the non-commercial purpose of research and educational uses in case a digitised textbook was offered to library users provided that the publisher had offered a reasonable licensing agreement. It is more than doubtful whether that position is consistent with the approach by the Court of Justice according to which the educational limitation is pre-empted only where agreements have actually been concluded.

[34]German Federal Court of Justice (BGH) (2015) GRUR 1101—"Elekronische Leseplätze II".

copying provision under the EUCD and the three-step test. Previously, the German Federal Court of Justice had contended that permitting users to make copies on digital carriers such as USB sticks would not be in compliance with the test, whereas permitting print-outs would. An important overall effect is that libraries and related institutions have a choice of whether to accept licensing conditions or not, an outcome that will certainly create competition.

In a Swiss litigation,[35] a university library provided a document delivery service by email upon the request of users, to which various publishers objected. The limitations framework under Swiss law differs from that of the EUCD: Article 19 of the Swiss Authors Right Act permits any personal use done for private or educational purposes, and the acts necessary may be carried out by a third party acting as an "agent" for individual users. The contentious issues were whether, in particular, the library was allowed to offer a general document delivery service including photocopying and forwarding documents by email. The Swiss Federal Court held that forwarding documents (for books, limited to extracts) by email was irrelevant, as such act would not violate the communication to the public rights. The Court did not address the question of whether any reproduction necessary for forwarding documents was captured by the own use limitation as well. For the uses in question, under both Swiss and German law, a statutory claim for compensation payable to authors is foreseen.

The approaches taken in the decisions discussed reveal entirely divergent patterns of statutory interpretation. Since Swiss law does not need to calibrate national concepts with assumedly more rigid EU pretexts, a solution to annex uses was found by relying on simple mechanisms of interpreting statutory law in accordance with established modes of interpretation. Incidental copies appear to be effortlessly consumed. That approach allowed the Swiss court to argue on the basis of the legal rationale supporting the limitation, and therefore perhaps the fact that the subsequent transmission of works by email would require that the making of additional copies was irrelevant, that the rationale would thus absorb the technical existence of further copies.

In contrast to the approach taken under the EUCD—which unfortunately does not designate a particular rationale to each limitation but leaves this largely to national laws—the approach taken under Swiss law could largely rest upon the consideration that the uses in question were basically personal uses, rather than uses to which liability is ascribed to an institution. Indeed, most member states make a distinction between uses for personal purposes, which may be covered by the private copying limitations, and uses privileging institutions such as libraries. The overlap between these purposes is not reflected in the structure of Article 5 EUCD, and therefore the idea of "combining" different limitations so as to exceed the scope of each according to the written wording of its elements is not permissible. The EUCD thus does not allow an assessment of limitations based upon fundamental legislative rationales, which in any case are hardly detectable in Article 5 EUCD. It

[35] Swiss Federal Court, BGE 140 III 616 (herein referred to as "ETH Zürich").

followed that copies necessary for digitising materials were within the scope of the onsite consultation provision, but annex uses were not. This is probably the reason why both the Court of Justice and the German Federal Court of Justice had to revert to limitations privileging private copying. In short, the EUCD does not permit annex reproductions to be covered by a limitation privileging libraries. However, such uses may be covered by limitations privileging the making of copies for private purposes (Article 5(2)(b) EUCD) if domestic law permits so, for example under the German limitation for private use or the UK defence for research purposes.

3.1.3 The Scope of Norm-Based Solutions: Expropriating Publishers?

The decision by the German Federal Court of Justice in *Ulmer* has been criticised for removing exclusive control rights in violation of the three-step test and the guarantee for property rights under constitutional law.[36] This is unpersuasive. Indeed, permitting students to copy entire books may cause dangers, since no further control over their dissemination via Internet can be established, unless technical solutions are available that may prevent the making of further copies. But this is not a problem of how limitations are to be construed. In that sense, the position is the same as in the Swiss decision; in both cases users acquire at least extracts of works in a digital form that may be easily distributed or uploaded. But this is a general danger, and the interpretation of the scope of a limitation should not be confused with questions of liability. It may thus well be that a library could, in general, be held liable for future copyright violations by users (to be sure, the privilege to make copies for private purposes does, of course, not permit the beneficiary to make these materials available online).[37] This, however, is a matter of national (tort law) concepts and not of secondary EU copyright law.

In Germany, a conclusion permitting increased access was achieved by standard legal methodology, that is, through an application of different limitations by way of analogy so as to allow one individual use modality to be justified by, ultimately, assimilating the personal and institutional use rationales that are expressed in different provisions under the EUCD. However, the degree to which broader rationales may be transplanted from one limitation to another though employing

[36] T. Dreier (2015), 1905, 1907.

[37] The same concern arises, of course, in relation to any other use where a user acquires a digital copy, whether on the basis of an end user license agreement or through services provided by a privileged institution. Right holders can prevent this by using TPMs. In general, the scope of protection for the TPM then depends upon whether the national private copying limitation can be enforced vis-à-vis TPM protection (Article 6(4) EUCD). There is no space here for discussing these implications in detail.

such methodology should not be overemphasised—the onsite consultation exception is obsolete if preparatory copying is prohibited.[38] Conversely, the rationale of the "own use" limitation under Swiss law was placed very much at the forefront of the assessment; the court made it unequivocally clear that it reserves to itself a broad methodical spectrum informed by the overall *ratio legis* of the own use provision. The Swiss Federal Court, in contrast to the approaches taken by the Court of Justice and the German Federal Court of Justice, referred expressly to a purposive mode of interpretation and mentioned that no one method could claim priority, thus allocating to itself much flexibility to proceed from a *ratio legis* basis. Certainly, the Swiss decision covers a different situation and centred on whether the library may make copies for personal use, rather than reflecting a situation where copies are made following an act of making available. However, much seems to suggest that a *ratio legis* approach would have allowed the defendant to succeed in the *Ulmer* dispute. It should be noted, however, that the *ratio legis* to which the Swiss Federal Court referred is principally the personal use of individual users, and in that sense acts done by a library must be understood as an extension of the "own use" rationale underlying Article 19 of the Swiss Authors Right Act.[39]

3.1.4 Summation

The decision of the Court of Justice to leave the applicability of different limitations to one singular use to domestic courts is certainly not ideal. It cements disparities between member states. Effectively, the *Ulmer* decision only applies where a member state has implemented both the limitations for onsite consultation and for private copying. The decision by the German Federal Court of Justice shows that national law can arrive at the desired conclusion—albeit by employing techniques, such as analogies, which may not be part of the arsenal of judicial interpretation in other member states. In essence, a solution based upon interpreting existing limitations under the EUCD on, broadly speaking, a "fair use" concept, by weighing up factors and mirroring legislative rationales, certainly has limits. In contrast to the highly purposive approach taken under Swiss law, Article 5 EUCD merely refers to individual purposes but otherwise leaves the recognition of what supports these privileges entirely to national laws. Therefore, the broader issue of how access rights can be established must be addressed in other contexts and at different levels of judicial assessment. The first context, discussed below, concerns the shift in the understanding of the communication to the public rights as formulated by the Court of Justice more recently, particularly the novel elements of a new public and a

[38] Otherwise, it could be argued that the limitation for educational purposes applies generally to uses in university libraries. Article 5(3)(a) EUCD only mentions educational establishments as beneficiaries, whereas Article 5(2)(c) and 5(3)(n) allow libraries to make copies for their own purposes and for making available for onsite consultation respectively.

[39] See R.M. Hilty (2010), 191 et seq.

commercial impact. Whilst this jurisprudence will have a more immediate impact upon national legal construction, many aspects that have been addressed here—in particular the potential impact of a more holistic statutory interpretation—must, at least at present, be relegated to considerations based on a new understanding of the exhaustion doctrine.[40]

3.2 *The "New Public" and Commercial Bearings*

The more recent jurisprudence of the Court of Justice introduced the concept of a "new" public as the perhaps most important element for interpreting the scope of control rights. The new public criterion appears to denote that at least one factor in the assessment depends on the declaration of the right holder and his or her legitimate expectations.

3.2.1 The New Public Criterion and Exploiter Rights

The new public[41] criterion assures, to a greater extent than an ontological formulation of the public could achieve, legal certainty by relying upon the first act of exploitation as a watershed. It is only where the defendant actively interferes with an act of communication by using a different technology that the new public criterion is fulfilled. This differs from the accepted understanding of the notion of the public in international convention law, where such a criterion is absent. The traditional view holds that a communication is to the public where it is targeted to a majority of persons who are not personally related to the entity responsible for communicating the work. Indeed, from the "new public" criterion an entirely novel structure of the exclusive right follows—where there is no active interference, the right holder factually is constrained to exploiting his or her first market. The proximity of that approach to exhaustion is apparent. For example, as far as the making available right is concerned, the decision in *Svensson* asserts that a hyperlink only constitutes an act of making available where indeed a new audience is targeted[42]—where an existing page is linked to, no new public is reached. It should further suffice to point out that the Court of Justice has not yet been asked how the new public criterion applies to uses that are potentially covered by copyright limitations. As regards the scenarios described above, however, the new public criterion

[40]See *infra*, 4.

[41]Svensson v. Retriever Sverige AB (C-466/12) E.C.D.R. 9 (2014); C More Entertainment AB v. Sandberg (C-279/13) E.C.D.R. 15 (2015); Societa Consortile Fonografici (SCF) v. Del Corso (C-135/10) E.C.D.R. 16 (2012); Phonographic Performance (Ireland) Ltd v. Ireland (C-162/10) 2 C.M.L.R. 29 (2012).

[42]Svensson v. Retriever Sverige AB (C-466/12) E.C.D.R. 9 (2014); C More Entertainment AB v. Sandberg (C-279/13) E.C.D.R. 15 (2015). See further the criticism in ALAI (2015), 9.

would usually apply to uses such as on dedicated terminals. It remains uncertain, however, whether a new public is also established where, for example, previously digitised works are subsequently made available in university intranets.

The new public criterion effectively eradicates the dichotomy between private and public uses. Therefore, it allows the Court of Justice to establish a rather novel pattern of argumentation which rests upon, it may be argued, fundamental notions of good faith—a new public is only established where there is no interference by a third party with an act of communication. The essential question is, therefore, whether the public in question had been taken into account by the right holder. Thus, hyperlinking to existing sources, or setting up television sets in hotel guest rooms without creating a technical interference do not violate the communication to the public right.[43] Conversely, linking to unpublished sources or relaying broadcasts via television aerials affixed by an hotelier would.

That notion of a new public necessarily will affect those limitations related to the communication right. The criterion certainly may have the capacity, if rationalised, to privilege additional uses such as in libraries—for example, it may be more effortlessly concluded that the use of works on dedicated university library terminals could also cover subsequent uses such as in university intranets accessible to a group of researchers, since here such a group of recipients may be classified as private according to the new public criterion. Notably, this criterion, in the context of university and similar uses specifically, may also well influence disputes on the scope of existing licensing agreements and respective framework agreements. Overall, the criterion thus may allow a fuller calibration of hyper textual uses as one of the central complexities as regards integration under a true digital single market.[44]

The effect is, further, to largely eradicate divergent national preconceptions of the public.[45] For example, Article 5(3)(a) EUCD, which allows rather generously uses for educational and scientific purposes, remains highly heterogeneous under national laws.[46] An institution wishing to make use of works for classroom and related uses is therefore faced with a complex legal situation. The use of works in "online" classrooms requires the making of copies, as well as of making those available by publicly performing works directly in a physical classroom. The previous assessment of whether such classroom use was to be considered public was dependent on the volatile question of whether, for example, a group of pupils shared personal relationships. That question may of course be answered differently. But where the institution is permitted to digitise materials and store these

---

[43]And thus remains a neutral activity. See, for a similar reasoning, the decision by the German Federal Court of Justice in BGH GRUR 153—"Paperboy", (2001).

[44]K.-N. Peifer (2010), 641, 643.

[45]For example, German courts have expressly rejected a "new" public concept in relation to the broadcasting right. See Munich Higher Regional Court, (1985) GRUR 537, 542—"Breitbandkabelanlage II"; see further German Federal Court of Justice (BGH) (2000) GRUR 699, 700—Cable Retransmission.

[46]G. Westkamp (2007b), 67 et seq.

permanently, for example on a central school server, the new public criterion eradicates any such issue and would largely leave the final classroom use, including in an online learning environment, arguably free.

In that sense, the traditional approach to communication rights, which is based on where the audience is in terms of place or time, as well as distinction between different and technically dissimilar modes of communication, becomes irrelevant. The criterion thus essentially institutes technological neutrality. Further, and perhaps most importantly, the new public criterion establishes a clear link between an implied license concept[47]—a concept alien to the EUCD—and the statutory elements delineating exclusive rights. Evidently, this denotes a shift in the centre of gravity. It places the construction of statutory copyright law much closer to an approach based on recognising conflicts between primary EU law (i.e. the body of rules establishing fundamental freedoms under the Treaties) and domestic copyright laws as harmonised on the basis of secondary EU law—ultimately, as will be discussed in more detail *infra,*[48] by conjuring up a new exhaustion paradigm that concurrently connects to the conventional approach of employing exhaustion as a collision clause used for delineating regime collisions between—now—secondary and primary EU law.

3.2.2 A Broad Division Between Authors and Exploiters?

Perhaps these anticipated difficulties are overrated. This is because—if taken seriously—the decisive criterion in the future will be whether the use in question is, apart from reaching a new public, additionally conditioned on a further requirement. In two cases, the Court of Justice formulated that a communication to the public required a profit-making nature with regard to claims for compensation of sound recording makers under the Rental and Lending Directive.[49] In *OSA*, then, the Court of Justice asserted that such commercial dimension does not apply to the right of communication to the public by broadcasting of *authors* as such, since such requirement would be incompatible with the high degree of protection afforded them.[50]

[47]See G. Westkamp (2012), 38 et seq.; M. Leistner (2014a), 417.

[48]See *infra*, 4.4.

[49]Article 8(2) Directive 2006/115/EC of 12 December 2006 on rental right and lending right and on certain rights related to copyright in the field of intellectual property, OJ L 376, 27. December 2006, 28-35. See Societa Consortile Fonografici (SCF) v. Del Corso (C-135/10) E.C.D.R. 16 (2012); Phonographic Performance (Ireland) Ltd v. Ireland (C-162/10) 2 C.M.L.R. 29 (2012). The provision was initially introduced in the Rome Convention, against the will of authors who feared a loss of income, E. Ulmer (1961), 569.

[50]Ochranny svaz autorsky pro prava k dilum hudebnim os v. Lecebne lazne Marianske Lazne as (C-351/12) 4 C.M.L.R. 19, at para. 19 (2014).

Because the condition of a "profit-making nature" was established,[51] expressly, only in relation to the claim for equitable remuneration owed by users for communicating sound recordings under Article 8(2) of the Rental and Lending Directive,[52] it has been argued that the condition of a new public must be exclusively constrained to such claims, and therefore to the remit of the Rental and Lending Directive.[53] Accordingly, it would not be applicable to the communication to the public right as a property right of *exploiters*. That is certainly debatable, and it seems more predictable that the notion of a profit-making nature may inform the construction of limitations based on statutory licenses, all the more so because the Court of Justice has clearly indicated that compensation must principally flow to authors.[54]

The contours of that requirement are, however, far from clear. Nevertheless, one may speculate—indeed, the requirement of a commercial dimension or a profit-making nature may ultimately lead to a dogmatically sound differentiation between rights of authors and exploiters, with drastic implications for evaluating their respective legitimate expectations. It arguably does not, according to the Court of Justice, apply to the construction of communication rights vis-à-vis author's rights. Strictly speaking, the application of that criterion may be considered constrained to that Directive,[55] and hence only to the rights of makers of sound recordings. Thus, whether it applies to owners of neighbouring rights, and to exclusive licensees, is open in the context of the EUCD.

But if so, the concept can have significant implications that may inform not only the scope of exclusive rights, but also annex uses in particular. It may indeed inform a new debate on the proper relationship between payments due to authors and those due to exploiters.[56]

3.2.3 "Actual" Harm

Given that the Court of Justice has also invented an "actual harm" element in the context of interpreting the meaning of fair compensation,[57] an entirely new matrix of assessment emerges. What is meant precisely by a real harm remains open; however, the Court of Justice has given some valuable guidance. First, harm does

[51] Societa Consortile Fonografici (SCF) v. Del Corso (C-135/10) E.C.D.R. 16 (2012); Phonographic Performance (Ireland) Ltd v. Ireland (C-162/10) 2 C.M.L.R. 29 (2012); ITV Broadcasting Ltd v. TVCatchup Ltd (C-607/11) European Court of Justice (Fourth Chamber) Bus. L.R. 1020 (2013); 3 C.M.L.R. 1 (2013).

[52] Ochranny svaz autorsky pro prava k dilum hudebnim os v. Lecebne lazne Marianske Lazne as (C-351/12) 4 C.M.L.R. 19 (2014).

[53] A. Lucas-Schloetter (2013), 84, 95.

[54] Hewlett-Packard Belgium SPRL v. Reprobel SCRL (C-572/13) E.C.D.R. 2 (2016).

[55] See further M. Leistner (2014b), 1145, 1149 et seq.

[56] Indeed, under German law payment for private uses is shared between publishers and authors.

[57] Copydan Båndkopi v. Nokia Danmark A/S (C-463/12) [2015] E.C.D.R. 9.

not equal any loss of a hypothetical and imaginable licensing income. Second, it depends on whether markets exist and whether consumers would be willing to pay for discrete uses.

For authors, the fact that they may still prohibit certain uses addressed to a "new" public remains a dogmatically important assentation since it elevates the rights of authors above the interests of exploiters. In reality, authors—at least those of academic work—have an interest in both a wide dissemination of their works and, perhaps to a modest degree, some payment. This is usually achieved where a statutory license is in place, as is the case with most institutional limitations, and therefore compensatory payments allow—from a legislative point of view—the scale to tip in favour of such licensing arrangements rather than in permitting exploiters to reserve any potential market found in education and science systems. It follows that exploiters would—pursuing this line of thought—rather logically not be able to claim that a statutory license for compensation payable to authors alone would cause them "real harm", since such argument is excluded by the fact that limitations in the realm of education and science are by definition intrinsically constrained to non-commercial purposes.

This insight consequentially eliminates a debate that unfortunately materialised much as a consequence of the general references to any "right holders"[58] (including, arguably, exclusive licensees such as publishers who do not enjoy neighbouring rights) which appeared to purport that the interests of authors and exploiters had to be considered equivalent and thus excluding attempts to differentiate—as was asserted by the Swiss Federal Court in the *ProLitteris* decision[59]: here, the court rejected the argument purported by a collecting society that the interest of publishers in having markets reserved to themselves under the three-step test was admissible, since the test would not apply to them at all. The position under EU law may then well be the same, at least in terms of a functional equivalence: where the conclusion is that no commercial dimension to the detriment of exploiters can be established, that qualification absorbs the exclusive right, and no room for manoeuvre under any of the conditions of the three-step test under Article 5 (5) EUCD is left. In this sense, the requirement of a commercial impact may well establish a broad watershed, or collision clause delineating the divergent spheres of legitimacy between author and exploiters.

From a policy point of view, there are certainly advantages. First, exploiters do not necessarily lose out, even though effectively limitations are broadened and potential future markets are lost. Indeed, many disputes between publishers and institutions such as libraries centre on claims for having potential sources of income reserved. It is certain that in such case the enforcement of exclusive rights—to which the EUCD, as mentioned, gave abundant enticement—leads to market failure especially where relevant institutions find it hard to meet the price expectations of

---

[58]See G. Westkamp (2004), 1057, 1065.

[59]ProLitteris v. Aargauer Zeitung, AG, 4C.73/2007 (26. June 2007), 133 Entscheidungen des Schweizerischen Bundesgerrichts [BGE] III 473.

publishers.[60] Thus, overall exploiters must offer online access services based on increased qualitative features as a consequence of competition with intra-institutional solutions. Incorporating a commercial dimension into the construction of the communication rights, it follows, downgrades the exclusivity drastically, and may eradicate claims for absolute protection entirely—publishers, in short, will find it difficult to claim such markets which are privileged because of non-commercial uses, such as educational and research. This does not mean a loss of such markets, but creates competition—the markets must be conquered. Thus, the notion of a commercial communication right may indeed create competition between publishers on the one hand and institutions on the other. and third parties wishing to offer value-added services to institutions on the other. In essence, it does not follow as an axiomatic rule that relying on the benefits of institutional limitations forecloses any market to exploiters.[61]

3.2.4 The Status of the Reproduction Right

This invention of commercially informed communication right does not, as such, affect the reproduction right, and incidental or annex copies cannot simply be absorbed by a permitted act of making available. The making of permanent copies then must be excused under a limitation. In the *Ulmer* decision, the fact that reproductions had to occur prior to making works available for allowing access at terminals meant that the Court of Justice was hesitant to establish an approach based on a purposive interpretation, and thus maintained that the rights of reproduction and communication to the public stood isolated and in mutual exclusivity—in contrast to the decision in *ETH Zürich,* which remained silent on the status of reproductions necessary for transmitting documents by email. Although the final outcome in *Ulmer* permitted the uses in question, the pathway towards such a conclusion remains vexed and depends ultimately on which limitations exist in domestic law.

The status of temporary copies was considered in *Infopaq*, which interpreted the scope of the mandatory limitation relating to transient copies under Article 5 (1) EUCD. Thus, the temporary copying of protected material in a scanner was ultimately subject to the test of whether these ephemeral copies had their "own economic significance", which the Court of Justice thought they did.[62] Again, the distinction between exploiters and authors may allow the Court of Justice in the future to consider the notion of "economic significance" as an element that may be more informed by the divergent interests. In summation, the reference to a commercial dimension has the capacity of broadly reordering how copyright norms are to be applied, both at the level of exclusive rights and respective limitations.

[60] R.M. Hilty (2006), 116; G. Westkamp (2008), 401, 420 et seq.

[61] See further C. Engel (2004), 35; R.M. Hilty (2006), 107.

[62] See Infopaq International A/S v. Danske Dagblades Forening (C-5/08) E.C.R. I-6569 (2009).

However, no such normative escape clause is available where the copies are permanent or temporary, since Article 5(1) EUCD only applies to "certain transient or ephemeral copies".[63] However, the concurrent presence of copies—at least in the context of annex uses as discussed herein—should probably not be overestimated. It is certainly true that the reproduction right still represents the central right of the exclusive rights from which other exclusive rights may have, to some extent, developed.

This is certainly unsatisfactory. In essence, a solution on the basis of judicial development seems difficult, but it is all the more important to gain clarity. There are numerous arguments that speak against a concurrent application of the reproduction right in settings where, from a functional perspective, the occurrence of copies is arguably covered by the purpose of the limitations or is necessary as a preparatory step. As far as incidental or annex uses are concerned, the *Ulmer* decision as rendered by the Court of Justice has for the time being foreclosed a more flexible treatment on a normative basis. In contrast to Swiss law, the limitations under Article 5 EUCD apply to the institution as such, and arguably publishers may also invoke the three-step test.[64] From here, it is only a small step to finding some commercial impact: though the use by an individual user remains for a non-commercial purpose, institutions pursuing educational or research aims operate at a level that creates direct competition.[65]

This, however, is not necessarily conclusive—it appears imaginable that the Court of Justice will shift that jurisprudence in the future towards a purposive approach, and such approach may well follow some of the contentions expressed in relation to "online" exhaustion. It will be recalled that in *UsedSoft*, the Court of Justice was able to overcome the issue of reproductions (to which exhaustion does not apply expressly) by designating the acquirer of respectively exhausted programs as "lawful users" under Article 3(1) of the Computer Program Directive. The approach much resembles that in *Ulmer*—one use may be governed by different "limitations"—but in *UsedSoft* the main issue was exhaustion of rights. As will be discussed *infra*, the "fate" of necessary and incidental reproductions can then arguably be contended with by applying broader principles including the exhaustion rule.[66]

[63]This excludes, however, a "reproduction" on a television screen; see Football Association Premier League Ltd v. QC Leisure (C-403/08) E.C.R. I-9083 (2011).

[64]Which does not apply to publishers (or other exclusive licensees) under Swiss law, cf. ProLitteris v. Aargauer Zeitung, AG, 4C.73/2007, 26 June 2007, 133 Entscheidungen des Schweizerischen Bundesgerichts [BGE] III 473.

[65]BGH (2014) GRUR 549—"Meilensteine der Psychologie" (asserting that libraries cannot rely on the limitation for educational and research purposes where reasonable licensing offers exist, a conclusion based upon the term "justified" in Article 52b of the German Authors Rights Act and Article 5(3)(a) EUCD).

[66]See *infra*, 4.1.

4 Exhaustion: A Final Clause for Access Claims?

The exhaustion doctrine had, starting in the 1960s, been employed as a metaphorical collision clause[67] to delineate single market interests and national, territorial IP rights. The specific subject matter test[68] thus advanced much flexibility to allow primary aims of EU law—in those days, overcoming the territorial effect of IP rights as an obstacle to creating an internal market without borders—to prevail, and in that sense exhaustion poignantly reveals how national IP rights had to succumb to primary aims. It is easy to see how attractive such meta-rule is for those claiming access rights. For example, in a litigation pending at the time of writing, a Dutch court presented a question to the Court of Justice[69] concerning the impact of the exhaustion rule on the lending right[70] in accordance with the findings in the *UsedSoft* decision,[71] that is, where payment had been made under a license to lend books and other works to users.[72] The defendant wanted to digitise and store books on a server accessible to users, who would then be able to download an eBook version for a limited period of time.

4.1 *Surmounting Normative Strictures: Exhaustion as a Guiding Principle*

Exhaustion is not merely a matter of free trade. It is also linked to notions of free circulation, incentive and an ensuing loss of control rights explained by the fact that the use in question had been compensated. It is then a small step from arguing in favour of exhaustion where tangible goods have been placed on the market towards an application of the principle, at least where the use had been paid for. This applies, broadly, to uses agreed upon in licensing agreements for online and related digital uses, and the exhaustion principle may develop into a meta-rule that is functionally equivalent to a broad purposive approach to construction, and may even go beyond so as to become a tool that can be employed to foster access rights.

---

[67]G. Westkamp (2007a), 291, 302 et seq.

[68]See, in particular, Coditel SA v. Cine Vog Films SA (C-262/81) E.C.R. 3381 (1982); LC Nungesser KG v. Commission of the European Communities (C-258/78) E.C.R. 45 (1981); Musik-Vertrieb Membran GmbH v. GEMA (C55/80) E.C.R. 147 (1981).

[69]Request for preliminary ruling, Case C-174/15, Vereniging Openbare Bibliotheken v. Stichting Leenrecht & Nederlands Uitgeversverbond and Others, 17. May 2015, (2015) OJ C 213, 17.

[70]Article 3(1)(a) Rental and Lending Directive = Directive 2006/115/EC of the European Parliament and of the Council of 12. December 2006 on rental right and lending right and on certain rights related to copyright in the field of intellectual property (codified version), OJ L 2006 376, 28.

[71]UsedSoft GmbH v. Oracle International Corp (C-128/11) E.C.D.R. 19 (2012).

[72]See *infra*, 4.1.

The debate concerning the exhaustion principle certainly brings up multifaceted and complex questions in detail. The considerations here focus only upon the appropriateness and aptitude of a broader exhaustion *principle* emanating from (primary) EU law rather than a limited normative *rule*.

Thus, exhaustion—as a principle displaying, today, certain needs of the digital single market in analogy to the market integration aims mirrored in the existing fundamental freedoms—may develop into a predominant principled rule for the construction of copyright norms. Thus, the discourse on enhanced access privileges—currently much concentrated upon considerations of human rights and competition law as extrinsic balancing arguments—will in all probability be supplemented by a third template, appending arguments based on market integration needs.

The recent line of decisions proves that tendency. The new public criterion integrates, very arguably, certain rationales of the exhaustion doctrine.

First, because it allows enhanced legal certainty vis-à-vis control rights over digital uses, especially considering the insistence by the Court of Justice on showing that a different technology must be used so as to define the notion of "communication". That condition eradicates the problem that digital transmissions can be severed into diverse acts of communication over each of which the right holder would have control—in essence, the requirement of a different technology brings the making available right in line with the right of distribution, and both rights apply only to the initial and principal act to which the right owner consented.

Second, the new public criterion is defined ultimately by the question of whether the public in question had been taken into account by the right holders, thus identifying the relevant group of recipients from the perspective of the right holders' first expressed intention—here, the Court of Justice effectively guides national courts to a test very proximate to notions of an implied license, which historically preceded the formulation of a general exhaustion principle as envisaged by *Josef Kohler* in the nineteenth century.[73] The new public criterion is thus functionally equivalent, to a large extent, with the underlying rationales of the exhaustion doctrine as providing a general boundary between the interests of right holders and freedom of use, with clear proximity to fundamental legal principles such as legal certainty and good faith.

Therefore, this extended understanding of exhaustion serves as a principle enlightening the construction of insulated control rights. From that perspective, the main criticism that was voiced against the decision in *UsedSoft*[74]—which concerned the application of the exhaustion rule to computer programs downloaded for payment—becomes flawed.

[73]J. Kohler (1880), 131.

[74]UsedSoft GmbH v. Oracle International Corp (C-128/11) E.C.D.R. 19 (2012).

4.2 Digital Exhaustion and Normative Criticism

That criticism held that the Court of Justice erred in applying the rule of exhaustion for two predominant reasons. First, that exhaustion could only occur in relation to tangible copies, which relies much on the wording of Articles 3(3) and 4(2) EUCD, and second that the *UsedSoft* approach would dilute the scope of application of the exhaustion doctrine by extending it from an application to the single copy towards an application to the exclusive right as such—in other words, exhaustion could only occur with regard to a specific physical copy, and not to the exercise of the right in general. This argument excludes any application of the exhaustion rule to anything but a concrete copy embodying a work or subject matter, and consequentially asserts that there cannot be scope for an application by way of analogy.

But this arguably misinterprets the notion of exhaustion under EU law and confuses the two areas of normative interpretation of (harmonised) copyright law and the development of union law as the prime task of the Court of Justice. As has been pointed out correctly,[75] the decision levels out differences in the legal treatment between online and physical markets[76] and thus permits the creation of new aftermarkets by effectively removing digital territorial borders.[77] The question of whether exhaustion can apply to "digital" copies, and whether it can apply outside of the remit of the distribution right[78] was therefore irrelevant[79] given that the Court of Justice—without, unfortunately, clarifying so—was certainly motivated by concerns over the single market. This confirms that the term "exhaustion" has a dual meaning and that its applicability in different regulatory systems—statutory copyright law on the one hand and European law on the other—is split. However, as a matter of EU primary aims, the decision falls perfectly in line with the traditional jurisprudence as regards the relationship between proprietary control rights and fundamental freedoms. The difference perhaps lies in the fact that the application of the exhaustion rule to a right of communication[80] (if the act of downloading forms part of such right) is not necessarily and primarily concerned with, strictly speaking,

---

[75]R.M. Hilty / K. Koklü (2013), 263; it may also tentatively be argued that data can constitute a type of property which is capable of being owned, see T. Hoeren / J. Voelkel (2014), 11 et seq.; T. Hoeren / M. Foersterling (2012), 642, 644.

[76]Therefore, the European Commission notes that the digital single market aim "requires rapidly removing key differences between the online and offline worlds to break down barriers to cross-border online activity". European Commission, available at: ec.europa.eu/priorities/digital-single-market/access/index_en.htm.

[77]See generally C. Reed (2006), 248. On the notion of equal treatment see UsedSoft GmbH v. Oracle International Corp (C-128/11) E.C.D.R. 19, para. 61 (2012): see generally T. Tridimas (1999), 46; T. Hartley (2014), 145.

[78]See C. Stothers (2012), 787.

[79]M. Stieper (2012), 668; H. Haberstumpf (2013), 470, 482; E. Linklater (2014); O. Rognstad (2014).

[80]Which was previously held not to apply to the right of public performance; see Coditel SA v. Cine Vog Films SA (262/81) E.C.R. 3381 (1982).

overcoming territorial restrictions. It goes further in informing the construction of harmonised copyright law through the lens of EU primary aims.

4.3 Exhaustion and Personal Freedom

There exists a more than tangential connection between exhaustion and evolving access rights. Indeed, it may be contended that a broader understanding of an exhaustion *principle* will resurrect the basic dichotomy between commercial rights and the exclusion of the private sphere.[81] The development of digital copyright law has removed that distinction and thus naturally led to precisely the problems addressed herein, that is, the fact that digital technology makes it increasingly impossible to demarcate the boundaries between exclusive rights and thus significantly has impact upon any use imaginable.

The exhaustion rule, in a traditional and analogue environment, ensured that end users (as well as traders) would not be affected by copyright claims. Both the enjoyment, or normal use of works and the ability to resell copies (in most EU jurisdictions coupled with a limitation permitting private copying) sheltered the private consumer from copyright claims—no right holder could exert any control over end users. At the level of the EUCD limitations and exceptions, any such distinction between personal and other uses is relinquished since, as noted, the perception is that it is the institution itself that is privileged. The concept underlying Article 19 of the Swiss Authors Right Act is a compelling counterexample, since here the "own use" rationale is doctrinally extended to uses such as by libraries. On that basis of such "agency"-rule, Swiss law can probably react better to technological and social change.[82] This provides a further insight. The broad own use rationale under Swiss law can be described as nearly identical to a general exhaustion principle as a mechanism to exclude, broadly speaking, the private or personal sphere from interventions by right holders. In sum, there is no reason to distinguish between the types of subject matter—from a broader perspective; there is no compelling argument why exhaustion should apply only in the context of software copyright.

4.4 Exhaustion, the Digital Single Market and International Obligations

But whilst considerations favouring an extended scope for applying the exhaustion doctrine may well provide a basis for a different line of attack onto the rigidity of

[81]See further J. Litman (2007), 1871, 1892; A. Perzanowski / J. Schultz (2010), 889, 894.

[82]See generally N. Elkin-Koren (1996), 215, 254 et seq.; O. Bracha (2007), 1799; P.S. Menell (2007), 1013; N. Netanel (2008), 54; L. Lessig (2001), 277.

current copyright law, rather serious problems must still be overcome. At present, as indicated, Article 4(2) EUCD simply prohibits the application of exhaustion to any right except for the distribution right. The reason for that express exclusion of exhaustion lies, again, in the central policy objective of the EUCD as a tool to incentivise online services to be pioneered by right holders, and hence "online" exhaustion certainly was seen as incompatible with that aim, as it would provoke a sweeping diminution of control rights.[83] It is certainly not conceivable, however, that a national court can deviate from that express wording based on the argument that this policy objective (i.e. the desired shift from territorial licensing schemes[84] to direct end user access contracts) did not materialise, or that the control rights afforded to right holders are too dense and burdensome so as to prevent the realisation of digital market aims. In the cold light of day, the jurisprudence thus appears to be conflict prone because it coerces national judges to apply secondary EU law—i.e. the normative rules under the EUCD—*contra legem*.[85] If it is true that the new public criterion, and a potential application of the exhaustion rule to communication rights, are incompatible with secondary law such as Article 3(3) and 4(2) EUCD,[86] the jurisprudence by the Court of Justice can only be understood as saying that secondary and harmonising rules under EU law can be incompatible with primary EU law, denoting that the original—inflexible and biased—concept that supported the EUCD in the infancy of digital technologies has been made redundant, surpassed by the speed of technological development and at odds with a digital single market aim. As far as the constituent elements under these rules have a different meaning under international copyright convention—and this affects both the allegedly novel understanding of the term "public" and the criticism as regards an erroneous application of the distribution right under Article 6 WPPT—the jurisprudence is out of touch with international obligations of the EU itself[87] and possibly subject to WTO sanctions under the TRIPs Agreement. This is certainly a novel implication and raises complex concerns as to which system should prevail; but it is ultimately caused by the inflexibility of the international convention system, coupled with conflicting EU policy aims incrementally enforced through the application of fundamental freedoms.

[83]As is also reflected in Recitals 4, 9 and 11 EUCD, which assert that copyright law must provide a high level of protection, arguably so without distinguishing between authors and right holders.

[84]See Recital 35 EUCD, which purports that divergent national remuneration schemes affect the functioning of the internal market.

[85]Article 216(2) Treaty on the Functioning of the European Union (TFEU) (formerly Article 300 (7) EC Treaty); Recital 15 EUCD. Article 216(2) TFEU states that agreements concluded by the union shall be binding on both the union and the member states. There is much debate on the meaning and scope of this provision. See generally G. Conway (2002), 679.

[86]See, in more detail G. Westkamp (2016) (forthcoming).

[87]ALAI (2014), 12.

5 Summation

Certainly, it can be argued that EU copyright law, as it currently stands as a statutory right under secondary legislation, is, to some extent, debilitated—the concept upon which the EUCD was drafted creates collisions with European aims, and its rigid texture appears to come apart at the seams. There are vibrant signals that the current jurisprudence as regards the status of exploiters, with all its doctrinal inventions and revelations, moves towards a purposive interpretation that takes as a starting point tests based on a differentiated balancing of interests as between authors, exploiters and the interests of third parties. As far as the normative interpretation of secondary (domestic but harmonised) copyright law in the EU is concerned, the interests of exploiters have already been severely reduced, whereas the interests of authors have been reinforced. This is likely to be considered an almost revolutionary transformation, accomplished through a rationale-based approach. The new public criterion, including the "different technology" test, ensures additionally that copyright is construed in a neutral and thus value-oriented manner.

Hence, there is much to be derived from this jurisprudence for the current debate on re-conceptualising copyright, and this should further inform the debate on limitations. The main problem in this regard is not only that the individual and self-contained limitations must be interpreted more adaptably, but that the concept underlying Article 5 EUCD is structurally flawed. At present, limitations are construed not purposively but mostly literally. The uncertainties surrounding the rationales underlying the privileges individually ascribed can hardly be overcome at a purely normative level. The same is true as regards the unresolved problem of how a more rationale-based approach may be calibrated with the three-step test.

The EUCD compels courts to make inconsistent distinctions between privileges ascribed to institutions and to individual users respectively, and between limitations covering reproductions only and those covering both the reproduction and communication rights. The proscribed methodology under the EUCD thwarts a perception that such institutional limitations, especially as regards research and education, ultimately have been fabricated for the benefit of creating spheres of personal freedom that are axiomatically defined as non-commercial. The Swiss approach, in relying on a personal use perspective, shows how a rationale-based approach can overcome the strictures of a narrow interpretation approach. It deals with incidental uses with ease—which under EU law may be accomplished, at present, only by transplanting elements derived from relying on primary law guided by extrinsic principles.

If correctly understood as a *principle* consuming control rights generally, the application of the exhaustion principle can develop into such broad principle, and this can be translated back as a means of construing limitations. This is already evident—the "new public" benchmark effectively establishes a functionally equivalent rule. The rule integrates, therefore, many concepts including notions of personal freedom, implied licenses and market freedom. The balancing mechanism emanating out of the current jurisprudence—that is, to predominantly focus on the collision of interests between authors and the public interest—can proliferate access rights and strengthen competition much in the same way as the exhaustion rule incapacitated territorial boundaries in the past. In essence, the jurisprudence by the Court of Justice may have ultimately introduced a notion of a commercial communication right potentially subject to exhaustion; and certainly this pleases neither exploiters nor proponents of an unfettered property right. However, copyright law has always been subject to constant review.[88]

References

ALAI (2015), Report and Opinion on the making available and communication to the public in the internet environment – focus on linking techniques on the Internet, available at: www.alai.org/en/assets/files/resolutions/making-available-right-report-opinion.pdf

Bracha, O. (2007), Standing Copyright Law on its Head? The Googlization of Everything and the Many Faces of Property, 85 Texas Law Rev., 1799-1869

Brown, A. (2010), Access to essential technologies: The role of the interface between intellectual property, competition and human rights, 24 Int. Rev. Law, Comp. & Tech. 51-61

Chafee, Z. (1945), Reflections on the Law of Copyright (Parts I and II), 45 Columbia Law Rev., 503-529 and 719-738

Cohen, J. (2006), Copyright, Commodification and Culture: Locating the Public Domain, in: L. Guibault / P.B. Hugenholtz (Eds.), The Future of the Public Domain, Kluwer Law International

Conway, G. (2002), Breaches of EC Law and the International Responsibility of Member States, 13 European Journal of International Law (EJIL), 679-695

Davies, G. (2002), Copyright and the Public Interest, 2nd ed., Sweet & Maxwell

Dinwoodie, G. (Ed.) (2015), Intellectual Property and General Legal Principles: Is IP a Lex Specialis?, ATRIP Intellectual Property Series, Edward Elgar

Dreier, T. (2015), Elektronische Leseplätze in Bibliotheken – Ein Urteil zum Nachteil von Autoren und Verlagen, NJW, 1905-1909

Elkin-Koren, N. (1996), Cyberlaw and Social Change: A Democratic Approach to Copyright Law, 14 Cardozo Arts & Ent. Law J., 216-295

Engel, C. (2004), Give the Journals Back to Scientists, 160 J. Inst. & Theoretical Econ., 35-38

Ernst, S. / Haeusermann, D. (2006), Teaching Exceptions in European Copyright Law – Important Policy Questions Remain, Berkman Center Research Publication No. 2006-10, available at: ssrn.com/abstract = 925950

European Bureau of Library (2014), Information and Documentation Associations (EBILDA), available at: www.eblida.org/news/modernisation-of-eu-copyright-rules-yes,-but.html

Geiger, C. (2006), 'Constitutionalising' Intellectual Property Law? The Influence of Fundamental Rights on Intellectual Property in the European Union, 37 IIC, 371-406

Geiger, C. (Ed.) (2015), Research Handbook on Human Rights and Intellectual Property, Edward Elgar

Haberstumpf, H. (2013), Josef Kohler und die Erschöpfungslehre, ZGE/IPJ, 470-496

Hartley, T. (2014), The Foundations of European Union Law, 8th ed., Oxford University Press

[88]See Z. Chafee (1945), 45; G. Davies (2002), 244.

Hilty, R.M. (2006), Five Lessons About Copyright in the Information Society: Reaction of the Scientific Community to Over-Protection and What Policy Makers Should Learn, 53 J. Copyr. Soc'y of the USA, 103-138
Hilty, R.M. (2010), Urheberrecht, Stämpfli
Hilty, R.M. / Köklü, K. / Hafenbrädl, F. (2013), Software Agreements: Stocktaking and Outlook – Lessons from the UsedSoft v. Oracle Case from a Comparative Law Perspective, 44 IIC, 263-290
Hoeren, T. / Foersterling, M. (2012), Onlinevertrieb gebrauchter Software – Hintergründe und Konsequenzen der EuGH-Entscheidung 'UsedSoft', MMR, 642-647
Hoeren, T. / Voelkel, J. (2014), Eigentum an Daten, in: T. Hoeren (Ed.), Big Data und Recht, 11-19, C.H. Beck
Hugenholtz, P.B. (2000), Why the Copyright is Unimportant, and Possibly Invalid, EIPR, 501-503
Kohler, J. (1880), Das Autorrecht: eine zivilistische Abhandlung; zugleich ein Beitrag zur Lehre vom Eigenthum, vom Miteigenthum, vom Rechtsgeschäft und vom Individualrecht, Fischer
Leistner, M. (2014a), The German Federal Supreme Court's judgment on Google's Image Search – a topical example of the "limitations" of the European approach to exceptions and limitations, 45 IIC, 417-442
Leistner, M. (2014b), Urheberrecht an der Schnittstelle zwischen Unionsrecht und nationalem Recht, GRUR Int., 1145-1155
Lessig, L. (2001), The Future of Ideas, Random House
Linklater, E., (2014), UsedSoft and the Big Bang Theory: Is the Exhaustion Meteor About to Strike? 5 JIPITEC, 12-22
Litman, J. (2007), Lawful Personal Use, 85 Texas Law Rev., 1871-1920
Lucas-Schloetter, A. (2013), Das Recht der öffentlichen Wiedergabe in der Rechtsprechung des Europäischen Gerichtshofs, 5 ZGE/IPJ, 84-102
Menell, P.S. (2007), Knowledge Accessibility and Preservation Policy for the Digital Age, 44 Houston Law Rev., 1013-1047
Netanel, N. (2008), Copyright's Paradox, Oxford University Press
Ohly, A., (2009), Economic Rights, in: E. Derclaye (Ed.), Research Handbook on the Future of European Copyright Law, 212-241, Edward Elgar
Peifer, K.-N. (2010), A legal view of selected aspects and the development of Digital Europe, GRUR Int., 671-677
Perzanowski, A. / Schultz, J. (2010), Digital Exhaustion, 58 UCLA Law Rev., 880-946
Reed, C. (2006), Online and Offline Equivalence: Aspiration and Achievement, 18 International Journal of Information Law and Technology, 248-273
Rognstad, O. (2014), Legally Flawed but Politically Sound? Digital Exhaustion of Copyright in Europe after UsedSoft, 1 Oslo Law Rev., available at: www.journals.uio.no/index.php/oslawreview/article/view/977
Stieper, M. (2012), EuGH, Urt. v. 3.7.2012, Rs. C-128/11 – UsedSoft, ZUM, 668-671
Stothers, C. (2012), When is Copyright Exhausted by a Software Licence? UsedSoft v. Oracle, 11 EIPR, 787-791
Tridimas, T. (1999), The General Principles of EU Law, Oxford University Press
Ulmer, E. (1961), Das Rom-Abkommen über den Schutz der ausübenden Künstler, der Hersteller von Tonträgern und der Sendeunternehmungen, GRUR Ausl., 569-594
Westkamp, G. (2004), Transient Copying and Public Communications: The Creeping Evolution of Use and Access Rights in European Copyright Law, 36(5) George Washington Int. Law Rev., 1057-1108
Westkamp, G. (2007a), Intellectual Property, Competition Rules and the Emerging Internal Market: Some Thoughts on the European Exhaustion Doctrine, 12(1) Marquette Intellectual Property Law Rev., 291-335
Westkamp, G. (2007b), Study on the Implementation and Effect in Member States' Laws of Directive 2001/29/EC on the Harmonisation of Certain Aspects of Copyright and Related Rights

in the Information Society: Part II – Implementation of Directive 2001/29/EC in the Member States, Brussels: European Commission
Westkamp, G. (2008), The Three-Step Test and Copyright Limitations in Europe: European Copyright Law between Approximation and National Decision Making, 55 J. Copyr. Soc'y of the USA, 1-64
Westkamp, G. (2012), Emerging Escape Clauses? Online Exhaustion, Consent and European Copyright Law, in: J. Rosén (Ed.), Intellectual Property at the Crossroads of Trade, ATRIP Yearbook 2011, 38-66, Edward Elgar
Westkamp, G. (2015), The Legal Framework, in Showing films and other audiovisual content in European Schools – Obstacles and best practices Report 2015/0091, European Commission, 55-74, available at: ec.europa.eu/digital-agenda/en/news/schools-europe-are-not-using-films-and-audiovisual-material-full-concluded-eu-study
Westkamp, G. (2016), Exhaustion and the Internet as a Distribution Channel: the Relationship Between IP and European Law in Search of Clarification, in: I. Calboli / E. Lee (Eds.), Research Handbook on Intellectual Property Exhaustion and Parallel Imports, Edward Elgar
Xalabarder, R. (2007), On-line teaching and copyright: any hopes for an EU harmonized playground?, in: P. Torremans (Ed.), Copyright Law, A Handbook of Contemporary Research 373-401, Edward Elgar

Simplification of Tariff Structures

Raquel Xalabarder

Contents

Abstract Any simplification of tariff structures is inherently related to the legal design of rights and to the existing licensing mechanisms (either mandatorily set by law or voluntarily offered by copyright owners). In this chapter we will examine and comment on some comparative law examples attempting to simplify tariff structures, either voluntarily developed by copyright owners or mandatorily established by legislators, and point out some issues to be considered when trying to successfully simplify these structures.

Raquel Xalabarder is Professor of Intellectual Property at the Universitat Oberta de Catalunya (UOC).

R. Xalabarder (✉)
Universitat Oberta de Catalunya, Barcelona, Spain
e-mail: rxalabarder@uoc.edu

K.-C. Liu, R.M. Hilty (eds.), *Remuneration of Copyright Owners*, MPI Studies on Intellectual Property and Competition Law 27, DOI 10.1007/978-3-662-53809-8_3

1 Introduction

Simplification of licensing structures may be easily done by looking at the needs of copyright owners; in fact, this is the kind of simplification traditionally achieved by collective management organizations (CMOs) and collective licensing structures. Simplification and licensing efficiency has always been the *raison d'etre* for CMOs and also the reason they have been requiring exclusivity from their members and then securing a monopoly position in each territory by means of reciprocal representation agreements—as "non-aggression" pacts.

However, simplification may also come from the users' end: licensing according to what the user needs. Furthermore, simplification should also aim at **improving and maximizing efficiency** of the licensing process so that authors, artists and producers are better remunerated in a fairer and more equitable manner, and so that private and commercial users' needs are correctly addressed. A **win-win situation** (for users and authors) is always the best outcome.

CMO licensing already offers some degree of simplification, by means of centralized-clearance facilities, which help cut licensing transaction costs, improve compliance with copyright law and thus increase revenues for right holders. CMOs serve authors and right holders, clearly, but indirectly also serve users and, in the long run, the general public interest by facilitating lawful access to copyrighted works. A CMO can offer one single license, for its national territory for all works and authors in its repertoire, as well as for a worldwide repertoire when reciprocal agreements with other CMOs are in place. CMOs already function as "one-stop shops".

So, do we need further simplification? On the one hand, quite often, the license granted by a CMO only covers some specific rights (or modalities of exploitation), while the user requires several licenses from different CMOs to cover the entire acts of exploitation. An act of exploitation (of a work or subject matter) usually involves **several exclusive rights** (reproduction, distribution, communication to the public, and transformation) and sometimes also results in various rights such as **remuneration rights or compensation rights**. On the other hand, an act of exploitation usually involves several rights of **several right holders** (authors, performers, producers, publishers, etc.) which are managed by different CMOs. In addition, the fees (tariffs) in these licenses (even when granted by one single CMO) are often calculated based upon different parameters. Furthermore, the CMO licensing system is based on **territorial markets** which is at odds with the multi-territorial licensing structure that is needed for digital markets.[1]

In short, there is room for further simplification and improvement of licensing and tariff structures for the analogue, as well as for the digital world.

Some further simplification has already been attempted by copyright owners and CMOs on a voluntary basis. Yet, as we will see, they fail either to fully meet the needs of users[2] or to clear competition law requirements. CMO's reluctance to move

---

[1]Any online use of a phonogram or an audiovisual recording involves different overlapping economic rights, several right holders as well as several territories. Furthermore, some of these activities may be differently exempted by limitations and exceptions under each national law.

[2]Usually, these solutions tend to be a mere aggregate of territorial licenses.

away from what they do, and do well, is understandable but shortsighted. And, in the end, some kind of state action (**government or parliamentary**) is not only justified but also necessary to achieve greater simplification: either by restructuring the legal design of rights (making them less fragmented or jointly owned, so that they are easier to exercise and license) and/or by imposing simplified mechanisms for their exercise (joint/single licenses or one-stop shops). We will examine examples of both voluntary and non-voluntary simplification efforts in the following Sects. 3 and 4.

2 A Few Questions Before Simplifying

Simplification may result from two different sources: the scope and nature of the license, as well as the setting of the fees and calculating criteria.

The scope of the license refers to which rights and right holders are covered by the license. Simplified licensing structures could be designed around an exploitation activity conducted by a collective of users so as to efficiently meet their needs (e.g. one single license per exploitation activity, gathering all rights necessary for it). This may involve several exclusive rights and remuneration rights from different owners, and—when necessary—for several territories.[3] Although for users the line between primary (exclusive) and secondary (remuneration) rights is blurred, in practice, simplification is easier when dealing with exclusive rights—which are subject to voluntary licensing and are to a large extent harmonized, e.g. through the EU InfoSoc Directive[4] or, indirectly, via the Berne Convention—than when dealing with remuneration rights or equitable compensation rights, e.g. in exchange for limitations, which are hardly harmonized and present significant differences among national laws.

The **nature** of the license may also be an issue for simplification: for instance, **a joint-single license**, a **mandatory assignment** of the license to one CMO or an **aggregate of independent licenses** available at a **one-stop-shop.** The former, in its turn, poses several questions, such as: how will the fees be negotiated? Which CMO or CMOs will grant the license: only one or either one of them? How will fees be collected and distributed among CMOs or directly to right owners?

The last issue that may also have a significant impact on simplification is the **fees.** Regardless of the scope and nature of the license, we still need a "price tag", so as to obtain the final licensing price to remunerate copyright owners for the licensed rights. Due to **the inherent difficulties** in pricing intellectual property (IP), fees are usually calculated on the basis of external criteria (such as business revenues, usage capacity, number of rooms, etc.) that have nothing to do with the value of IP and sometimes with little or no uniformity among different licenses.

---

[3]Simplification may be achieved by converging all rights from all right holders required to license a specific activity under one single license. Simplification may also be achieved by overcoming territoriality when the exclusive rights and remuneration rights of several right holders are licensed by one single CMO for several territories.

[4]Directive 2001/29/EC of the European Parliament and of the Council of 22 May 2001 on the harmonisation of certain aspects of copyright and related rights in the information society.

The following example, from Spain, for the licensing of the online exploitation of phonograms and movies, shows the complex interaction of these three issues: multiplicity of rights (exclusive rights and remuneration rights) and owners (hence, CMOs) as well as the lack of uniformity in the pricing criteria and the resulting fees.

Musical works/Phonograms

CMO	Owners	Object	Rights	Fee for streaming	Fee for downloading
SGAE	Authors Performers (musicians)	Phonograms	Equitable remuneration right[5] Equitable remuneration right	10 % of gross revenues *(7.25 % of gross revenues)*	12 % of gross revenues *(0.98 % of gross revenues)*
AIE—AGEDI[6]	Producers (authors & performers)[7]	Phonograms	Exclusive rights (reproduction and making available online)	14.79 % of gross revenues *(7.54 % of gross revenues)*	1.99 % of gross revenues *(1.01 % of gross revenues)*
AGEDI	Producers	Phonograms	Exclusive right of reproduction[8]	2.20 % of gross revenues	15 % of gross revenues

Audiovisual works/recordings

CMO	Owners	Object	Rights	Fee for Downloading
SGAE	Authors	Movies	Equitable remuneration right	2.5 % of gross revenues
AISGE	Performers (actors)	Movies	Equitable remuneration right	1.5 % of gross revenues
AIE	Performers (musicians)	Movies	Equitable remuneration right	0.76 % of gross revenues
EGEDA	Producers (authors & performers)	Movies	Exclusive rights	6.95 € per user/month

Licensing structures depend, to a large extent, upon the statutory design of rights (whether the exploitation affects exploitation rights and/or remuneration rights) and

[5]These rights of equitable remuneration are set in favor of authors and performers, as inalienable and unwaivable, and are subject to compulsory licensing by CMOs.

[6]AGEDI and AIE offer a joint license (on a voluntary basis, not mandated by statute) covering the phonogram performers' equitable remuneration right for making available online and the exploitation rights (of performers and producers) for making available online. Amounts in brackets (above and below the license fees) show the amounts distributed amongst both CMOs.

[7]The exploitation rights of authors and performers have been transferred to the producer.

[8]AGEDI also licenses the reproduction done for streaming purposes as "instrumental reproduction"; one wonders whether these acts could be exempted as temporary copies to enable a lawful use under Art. 5.1 InfoSoc Directive.

owners (who are entitled to these rights); however, right holders (and CMOs) and users also have a lot to say in the success or failure of any simplifying efforts.

3 Some Bottom-Up Simplification Efforts

In some cases, rights holders and/or CMOs have joined efforts to license certain activities by forming "licensing hubs" or "clearance centers." These hubs basically help connect users with the relevant CMOs, and offer an **aggregated service of territorial licenses** (each license according to different fees set by CMOs). Successful examples include SDRM-SESAM[9] (France) and CEDAR[10] (Netherlands). These efforts are to be welcomed to the extent they facilitate the clearance of rights, although they still work on a territorial basis. In reality, they simplify the "appearance" (the window of a shop) but hardly affect the licensing and tariff structures. Even ARMONIA,[11] which appears to be something more than a clearance center, is essentially an aggregation of territorial licenses. CMOs' efforts are being stalled as more and more music publishers are withdrawing from CMOs' management to directly license their catalogues online.[12]

Other examples of bottom-up simplification efforts involve cooperation among big players, which needs clarification from competition law. For example, on 16 November 2000 the International Federation of the Phonographic Industry (IFPI) applied to the European Commission for negative clearance or, alternatively, for exemption under Article 81(3) of the EC Treaty (currently Article 101(3) of the

[9]SDRM-SESAM was created in 1995 as a federation of several CMOs (ADAGP, SACD, Sacem, Saje, Scam, and SDRM) to license multimedia online uses (CD, DVD, mobile, streaming, and download). CMOs entrust their rights of reproduction and making available online of repertoires to SESAM, which negotiates and manages the rights, and collects and distributes royalties. Rights managed by SESAM are exclusive rights and belong to several rights holders, available at: sdrmsesam.wordpress.com/sesam. However, SESAM does not appear to be active anymore, as it is not included in the Rapport annuel 2014 de la Commission permanente de contrôle des SPRD, available at: www.ccomptes.fr/Publications/Publications/Rapport-annuel-2014-de-la-Commission-permanente-de-controle-des-SPRD (accessed on 30 March 2016).

[10]CEDAR (The Centre for Service to Authors' and Related Rights) was created in 2005 for the clearance of multimedia rights. CEDAR manages the repertoires of several CMOs by collecting fees and subsequently distributing amongst them, available at: www.cedar.nl/ (accessed on 30 March 2016).

[11]ARMONIA was initiated by SACEM, SGAE, and SIAE and later joined by others, to license universal music products. ARMONIA manages the aggregated repertoires of authors and publishers, to license music to online service providers and telecom platforms such as YouTube, Google Play, Deezer, etc., available at: www.armoniaonline.eu (accessed on 30 March 2016).

[12]For instance, CELAS was a joint venture between the German GEMA and the British PRS for Music to offer Pan-European licenses of the Anglo-American mechanical rights repertoire of EMI Music Publishing in the field of online and mobile services. EMI's repertoire is now being licensed by SOLAR—Music Rights Management, available at: www.solar-music.com (accessed on 30 March 2016).

Treaty on the Functioning of the European Union), in respect of a reciprocal agreement between record producers' rights administration societies for the licensing of "simulcasting" (unaltered and simultaneous transmission via the Internet of a sound recording broadcasted by radio or TV). The **IFPI Simulcasting Agreement** allowed each participating CMO to grant for its repertoire simulcasting licenses to cover not only the territory of the licensing CMO but also all EU territories. Royalties were calculated on the basis of the fees that the participating CMOs would charge individually for their respective territories. The Commission granted the exemption on the grounds that the reciprocal agreement promotes technical and economic progress, improves the distribution of goods, brings benefits for the consumer, is indispensible and does not eliminate competition.[13]

Another example in point is **the Santiago Agreement** of October 2000. It consisted of an agreement amongst five organizations (UK's Performing Rights Society (PRS), Broadcast Music Inc. (BMI) from the US, SACEM, GEMA and BUMA) which was later joined by all other CMOs within the European Economic Area (EEA)—except for the Portuguese SPA and Swiss SUISA. According to this Agreement, each participating CMO could be the only one entitled to grant a non-exclusive license to the users established in its territory, which would be valid for all EU territories and would cover the whole music repertoires of all participating CMOs. Competition concerns are easily spotted: on the one hand, commercial users could only apply for a license from the CMO established in their own Member State, thus reinforcing the monopoly (territorial exclusivity) of each CMO within its jurisdiction (the CMO is the only one to grant this license within that state); on the other, based on the reciprocity agreements, licenses granted by CMOs would extend beyond their original jurisdictions. The EU Commission initially ruled that the Agreement was a concerted practice contrary to EU competition rules. On appeal, however, the General Court of the EU (GCEU) accepted the CMOs arguments and concluded—based on the presumption of innocence—that it had not been proved that CMOs were incurring in an anticompetitive behavior.[14]

4 Some Top-Down Simplification Efforts

Simplification of licensing structures has also been attempted by governments and legislators. Simplification schemes may range from the statutory design of one joint/single license to cover several rights and different owners, to the joint management of several licenses (one CMO license on behalf of other CMOs), or a mere aggregate of licenses (one-stop shop). We will now examine a few of these efforts.

[13] Commission Decision COMP/C2/38.014 (8 October 2002).

[14] See GCEU (6th ch.) T-392/08 *AEPI v. Commission* and the several rulings known as the CISAC cases (12 April 2013).

4.1 Joint/Single License

In the EU market, a good example of a joint/single license is the **fair compensation right for private copying** set in Art. 5.2(b) Directive 2001/29/EC. It is a good example of an effort to simplify tariff structures, and it is an easy one because it only involves one single remuneration (compensation) right, set by law, which is jointly owned and shared among all right holders. Yet, differences still exist at national level.[15] For instance, the fees for the equitable compensation are mostly set by law or by the government, but they are instead negotiated in Austria,[16] Germany and Croatia; usually fees are based on a percentage of the selling price of the support or device or on a fixed levy (which vary from one country to another), while in Spain the amount of compensation is annually fixed by the Government[17]; usually, all affected CMOs are entitled (*in solidum*) to license and collect fees from users; amounts collected are later distributed amongst affected CMOs, while in Belgium, compensation for private copying is managed by only one entity, REPROBEL, which aggregates 15 CMOs (in Belgium, fees are set by decree). Distribution schemes among right owners are mostly agreed among CMOs, while in Spain, France, Germany and Lithuania distribution is set by law or by decree.[18] In other words, the licensing structure to compensate for private copying in a EU harmonized context is simple (to the extent that it is a single license carefully designed by the national statute), but there is still plenty room for discretion when setting the fees and criteria to calculate them, and even when deciding who are the copyright owners entitled to it.[19]

More complex scenarios involve several rights from different owners, the more so when remuneration rights and exclusive rights overlap for the same act of exploitation. **Spain** provides some good examples of these complex scenarios, and shows how excellent endeavors may easily turn sour, when legal design is

[15]WIPO/IFRRO, International Survey on Text and Image Copyright Levies 2014, WIPO, available at: www.ifrro.org/sites/default/files/levies_2014_online.pdf (accessed on 30 March 2016).

[16]In Austria, there is only one CMO and one single license (which explains why it is feasible that fees are negotiated with users).

[17]In Spain, the levy regime was derogated in 2011; equitable compensation for private copying is calculated each year by the Government (and distributed among each category of works/authors). For 2014, the amount was 5.000.000 € and distributed as follows: Books and assimilated: 22.6 %; Phonograms and alike: 31 %; Videograms and alike: 46.4 %. Orden ECD/2226/2015, de 19 de octubre. A preliminary question (C-470/14 EGEDA) is pending at the Court of Justice of the European Union (CJEU) to see if the compensation regime based on the General State budget is consistent with EU law and clears the requirement of "equitable compensation" of Art. 5.2 Directive 2001/29/EC.

[18]For instance, in Spain, Art. 5 Royal Decree 1657/2012 the annual compensation amounts (set by the government) are distributed within each category of right owners as follows: Phonograms and alike: 50 authors, 25 % performers, 25 % producers; Videograms and alike: 33.3 % authors, 33.3 % performers, 33.3 % producers; Books and assimilated: 55 % authors, 45 % publishers.

[19]See, for instance, the CJEU ruling, 12 Nov. 2015 (C-572/13) REPROBEL, regarding the reprography limitation in Art.5(2)(a) Directive 2001/29/EC.

not done accurately. Under Spanish law (TRLPI),[20] producers and performers of **phonograms** share **a "single" joint remuneration right** for the public performance of their performances/recordings (Art. 108.4 and Art. 122.2 TRLPI); the same applies to producers and performers of **audiovisual works/recordings** (Art. 108.5 and Art. 122.2 TRLPI). In both cases:

- It is a "single" and equitable remuneration (which is sometimes licensed together with the license of the exploitation rights);
- It is shared by performers and producers;
- It is an ancillary right deriving from the right of communication to the public;
- It is managed and collected by either one of the CMOs involved;
- Monies collected are shared among them (as agreed by them).

However, these ancillary/remuneration rights accumulate with the exclusive (and independent) exploitation rights held by producers (owned *ab origine* or transferred by authors and performers)—and there is no statutory obligation to manage these rights jointly. Accordingly, a Spanish hospital must obtain **five different licenses** for the communication to the public by means of TV sets in private rooms, involving several exclusive and remuneration rights of authors, performers and producers.

The following table illustrates the five different licenses that the hospital needs to obtain.[21]

CMO	Owners	Works	Rights	Fee	Calculation (100 beds/ year)
SGAE	Authors	Movies and Music	Remuneration right	0.1949€ per bed/month	233€
DAMA	Authors	Movies	Remuneration right	0.55€ per bed/trimester	660€
AGEDI—AIE	Producers Performers (Musicians)	Phonograms	*Exploitation* + Remuneration rights Remuneration right	22.88€ (up to 50 rooms) / month + 10.35€ (every 25 rooms) / month	522€
EGEDA—AIE	Producers Performers (Musicians)	Movies	*Exploitation* + Remuneration rights Remuneration right	1.09 € per bed/ month	1308€
AISGE	Performers (Actors)	Movies	Remuneration right	1.68€ per room/ trimester	From 336€ to 672€[a]

[a]Depending on number of beds per room

[20]Texto Refundido de la Ley de Propiedad Intelectual, Real Decreto Legislativo 1/1996, April 12, 1996, as last amended by Act 21/2014, of 4 Nov. 2014.

[21]This is a theoretical comparative exercise based on CMOs' published fees. In practice, discounts and other modulating criteria may apply.

Each license is set and managed independently by each CMO. Notice that in addition to the remuneration rights of authors, performers and producers, the licenses granted by producers (AGEDI and EGEDA) also include the exclusive rights of communication to the public of all the former right holders Notice also that the fees are calculated based on different criteria (number of beds or number of rooms, monthly or quarterly) and the resulting annual amounts range from 233€ (authors of audiovisual works) to 1308€ charged by the producers of audiovisual works. We will come back to this issue in Sect. 5.

Furthermore, it is worth mentioning that AISGE (the CMO for movie actors) is offering its own license for a remuneration right of performers which is "jointly owned" by movie producers. This is because in 2006, the language of Art. 108.5 TRLPI (granting a joint/single remuneration right to performers and producers of audiovisual works/recordings) was amended and what used to be a "single" joint remuneration right is now perceived as two independent remuneration rights (despite that Art. 122.2 TRLPI remained unaltered and referred to a joint/single remuneration).[22] As far as phonograms are concerned, the remuneration is still "single" and shared by producers and performers.

[22]Producers of audiovisual recordings are granted an exclusive right of communication to the public of the audiovisual recording (Art. 122.1 TRLPI). In addition, they also have a right (Art. 122.2 TRLPI) to receive an equitable remuneration for the communication to the public of audiovisual recordings under Art. 20(2) (f) and (g) TRLPI. According to Art. 122.2 TRLPI, this equitable remuneration is shared with the performing artists (ex Art. 108.5 TRLPI) whose performances are included in the audiovisual recording. Art. 122.3 TRLPI confirms that it is a "single" equitable remuneration and it will be jointly managed (negotiated with users, calculated, collected and distributed) by the corresponding CMOs (AIE and AISGE for performers, and EGEDA for producers). The same applies to phonogram producers. Art. 116 TRLPI establishes a "single" equitable remuneration in favor of both the phonogram producers and the performers for its communication to the public (in any means, except for making available to the public online), which is subject to compulsory collective licensing. Unlike for audiovisual recordings, here the law expressly states that failing an agreement among the corresponding CMOs regarding how to share the remuneration collected, it will be shared in equal parts. And the same applies regarding performers of phonograms under Art. 108.4 TRLPI. So far, so good. After all, according to the Directive on rental and lending (Art. 8), the remuneration right in favor of phonogram performers and producers is expressly qualified as a "single equitable remuneration." However, when dealing with the performers of audiovisual recordings Art. 108.5 TRLPI not only fails to mention that it is "single equitable remuneration" but implies that each CMO is entitled to establish and collect the "applicable remuneration according to the general fees set by each collecting society." This text (which only affects Art. 108.5 TRLPI; Art. 122.2 TRLPI still refers to a joint/single remuneration right) was introduced by Act 23/2006. The CMOs support that this amendment put an end to the compulsory "joint management" of the remuneration right for communication to the public (of performers and producers) of audiovisual recordings. It is to be expected that this inconsistency (for audiovisual recordings) is someday solved by case law or by a revision of the Act. In practice, EGEDA and AIE currently collect the remuneration jointly, (i.e. EGEDA collects for AIE as well), whereas AISGE goes its own way. It is interesting to notice that the tariff applied by EGEDA (and AIE) remained the same as before, when it also included the remuneration right of the performing artists (AISGE). See also R. Xalabarder (2013), op. cit. 1-138.

In summary, a statutory effort to simplify the tariff structure for the communication to the public of phonograms and audiovisual recordings wasted because of poor drafting technique and little interest on the side of CMOs to collaborate.

The **Swiss** Copyright Act (LDA) of 1992 does a better job at simplifying tariff structures by providing for an obligatory **joint tariff** when several CMOs are licensing **"the same field of use"** (Article 47).[23]

1. *Where more than one collective rights management organization operates in the same field of use, they shall draw up a single and same tariff applying uniform principles for use of the same works or performances and shall designate one of their number as the joint office for payment.*
2. *The Federal Council may enact further provisions concerning their collaboration.*

Rather than an aggregate or a joint-management of fees and licenses set by several CMOs as seen in previous examples, this is a real and successful **single joint fee and license** ("*seul et même tarif*"). It is imposed on all CMOs which license the same field of use of any kind, which means that it affects exclusive rights as well as simple remuneration/compensation rights (i.e., resulting from a limitation) belonging to different right holders (authors, performers and producers). One of the CMOs must be designated as the office for payment. Furthermore, it is also an excellent example of good and earnest collaboration among CMOs, making it unnecessary for the Federal Council to enact any further provisions to enforce their collaboration. The websites of the Swiss CMOs, as well as the joint website (http://www.swisscopyright.ch), offer detailed information about these joint tariffs.

Through these joint licenses, users are able to obtain from one CMO, one single license and pay one single fee for all the rights involved in the exploitation activity of the repertoires of all CMOs affected. Fees are "single" for each license/exploitation activity (it is not an aggregate of fees from each CMO).

The specific joint licenses are not directly identified by the statute but agreed upon by CMOs and users following the statutory mandate. In fact, the majority of the licenses offered by Swiss CMOs are joint ones.[24] The number of joint tariffs has increased since 2007, when an amendment of the LDA introduced several remuneration rights in favor of authors and performers.[25] Currently, there are **13 joint**

[23]Swiss Federal Copyright Act—9 October 1992 (LDA). Art. 47 (Joint tariff). See also D. Barrelet / W. Egloff (2008), op. cit. 285-287.

[24]As explained on the Swiss copyright website, "If only one repertoire is used e.g. music at concerts, the society responsible generally produces its own tariff. If several repertoires are used, e.g. in the private copying of radio or television broadcasts or corporate photocopying, the societies draw up joint tariffs."

[25]Before then, only three joint tariffs existed: JT1 (cable retransmission), JT2 (retransmission of broadcasts) and JT3 (reception of broadcasts in public places).

tariffs shared by all 5 CMOs (ProLitteris,[26] SSA,[27] SUISA,[28] Suissimage,[29] Swissperform[30]) and **11 joint tariffs shared by SUISA and Swissperform**.[31] In turn, some of these joint tariffs are divided into in several sub-tariffs.

Each tariff (and sub-tariff) is designed on the basis of the specific acts of exploitation as well as the licensed users (which can be easily explained in order to facilitate negotiations). For instance, the rights involved in the rental of works and recordings is licensed under two different joint tariffs: one for general rental businesses (JT 5, managed by SUISA) and one for libraries (JT 6a, managed by ProLitteris); both cover the same rights and right owners but are subject to different fees and calculating criteria (see *infra* Sect. 5).

CMOs initially agree on the **uniform principles** to structure the license; then fees are negotiated with the users (usually, consumers' organizations and the DUN).[32] Fees will be later approved by the Federal Arbitration Board, an independent body with equal representation of users, CMOs and external experts.

CMOs must also agree on designating the CMOs that will be managing the license.[33] The designated CMO is not necessarily the one that gets a bigger share from the licensed activity but usually the one that is best located regarding the licensed users.[34] This CMO will be responsible for collecting the fees and distrib-

---

[26]Authors of literary and visual works, publishers, available at: www.prolitteris.ch/ (accessed on 30 March 2016).

[27]Société Suisse des Auteurs, available at: www.ssa.ch/ (accessed on 30 March 2016).

[28]Cooperative Society of Authors and Publishers (music), available at: www.suisa.ch/en/home.html (accessed on 30 March 2016).

[29]Swiss Authors' Rights Cooperative for Audiovisual Works, available at: www.suissimage.ch/ (accessed on 30 March 2016).

[30]Collecting Society for Neighboring Rights, available at: www.swissperform.ch/ (accessed on 30 March 2016).

[31]A list of all tariffs offered by Swiss CMOs, indicating which of them are joint tariffs and the designated CMO, available at: www.swisscopyright.ch/en/income-and-distribution/tariffs/overview.html (accessed on 30 March 2016).

[32]The DUN is an umbrella organization of users of authors' rights, see http://www.dun.ch (accessed on 30 March 2016). When the license affects the end consumer, consumer protection associations may also participate in the negotiations.

[33]The 13 joint tariffs participated by all 5 CMOs are managed as follows: ProLitteris is the designated payment office for 4 of them: JT6 (rental in libraries), JT8 (reprography), JT9 (internal networks) and JT10 (blind and handicapped people); SUISA for 3 of them: JT 3 (background broadcast reception and public viewing), JT 4 (private copying) and JT 5 (rental); SUISSIMAGE manages 4: JT 1 (cable redistribution), JT2 (retransmission via internet servers), JT 7 (school use), JT 12 (set-top-boxes); and Swissperform is the central managing office for 2: JT 11 (archive recording by broadcasters) and JT 13 (orphan rights).

[34]For instance, SUISA manages JT5 (rental) despite only getting 23 % of its revenues and ProLitteris manages JT 6a (rental in libraries) despite only getting a 35 % of its revenues, while SUISSIMAGE gets respectively 60 % and 38 % of these revenues. See the amounts distributed in 2014 for JT5 and JT6a, available at: www.swisscopyright.ch/en/income-and-distribution/money-flows/key-figures.html (accessed on 30 March 2016).

uting them between the CMOs, according to shares agreed among them.[35] The designated CMO will discount its administrative costs before distributing amounts to other CMOs.[36] Each CMO will, after discounting its own costs, distribute the remunerations to its right holders according to internal regulations.[37]

An example of joint license and distribution of fees under JT1 (cable distribution) may be found on the Swisscopyright.com website[38]:

> Multiple beneficiaries under Joint Tariff 1 (JT 1)
>
> Cable networks carry copyright works and services looked after by all collective rights management organisations. For this reason, their remuneration is governed by a joint tariff. All five collective rights management organisations are involved in the JT 1 and all distribute monies to their rightholders. Collecting monies from the cable networks is dealt with by SUISSIMAGE. In return, SUISSIMAGE retains 2 % for its work. The net distribution amount is allocated as follows:
>
> - ProLitteris 7.03 %
> - SSA 3.28 %
> - SUISA 17.25 %
> - **SUISSIMAGE 47.44 %** (managing CMO)
> - SWISSPERFORM 25 %
>
> Each society then covers its own distribution costs from the distribution amount and deducts a proportion for culture and welfare funds. The monies are then distributed among the entitled members.

CMOs must work together closely to draw up a license and fees **with uniform principles**. In principle, the amounts paid by the users (and received by right holders) should be the same as if they were licensing their rights individually (after all, Art. 60 LDA requires that the remuneration of authors be equitable). Furthermore, the nature of the right that is being remunerated, be it an exclusive exploitation right or a remuneration right or even a compensation right, must be taken into account when calculating the fees, and later, when distributing the amounts among right holders. The joint tariffs of SUISA and Swissperform offer some good examples: JT H (public performance of music in the hotel industry) combines two percentage fees (3.8 % fee for authors and a 1.14 % fee for performers) which apply on the basis of the same criteria: (entrance fee + beverage price) x number of persons every day (with a minimum fee of 6 CHF); and JT HV (public communication in private hotel rooms) sets a fee of 28 CHF for authors'

[35]Some examples of annual amounts distributed among CMOs for several joint tariffs, available at: www.swisscopyright.ch/en/income-and-distribution/money-flows/key-figures.html (accessed on 30 March 2016).

[36]Administrative costs of Swiss CMOs for 2014 range from 4 % (Suissimage) to 23 % (ProLitteris) depending on the number of licenses managed, customers, members and employees, available at: www.swisscopyright.ch/en/income-and-distribution/money-flows/administrative-costs.html (accessed on 30 March 2016).

[37]The distribution criteria (regulations) for each CMO are approved by the Swiss Federal Institute of Intellectual Property (IGE).

[38]Available at: www.swisscopyright.ch/en/income-and-distribution/money-flows/example.html (accessed on 30 March 2016).

rights and 22 CHF for performers' rights per room per month. As we can see, the licensing of this act of exploitation is far better than the Spanish licensing example displayed above (Sect. 2).

This system of joint licensing mandated by law is clearly beneficial for users since it avoids individual negotiations with different CMOs which are subject to different calculating criteria and fee regimes. Although it may seem that it imposes a duty of sacrifice upon the right holders, the joint tariff regime is ultimately also beneficial for them, since it simplifies and reduces the costs of their licensing activity and increases the number of licenses issued to users.

4.2 *One-Stop Shops*

The 2014 amendment to the **Spanish TRLPI** introduced an obligation of **"*ventanilla única*", (literally, a "single window")** for all CMOs.[39]

According to Art. 157.1 TRLPI, CMOs are obliged to:

> (e) Participate in the creation, management, financing and maintenance of a "one-stop shop" for billing and payment, accessible over the Internet, within the terms and conditions set by the applicable norms, through which the users of the CMOs' repertoires may have updated information on the individual and total cost to be paid to these CMOs, as a result of applying the general fees for their activities, and make the corresponding payment.

This obligation is further explained in the Additional Provision n. 1 Act 21/2014, entitled "Means for reducing transaction costs":

> 1. The Government will foster measures to reduce transaction costs among owners of intellectual property rights and the users of such rights, taking specially into account the opportunities afforded by technological developments, including measures aimed at a more efficient way to interact between rights owners, their representatives, and users.
>
> 2. The lawfully established Collective Management Organizations of intellectual property rights shall create a one-stop shop through which to centralize the operations of billing and payment of the amounts that the users owe them, according to the obligation set in 157.1.e TRLPI. Within five months from the entry into force of this Act, CMOs have an obligation to agree on the terms of creation, financing and maintenance of this one-stop shop. Failing an agreement among CMOs, the First Section of the Commission of Intellectual Property may issue –within the next three months, and this term cannot be further extended– such terms and it may solve any existing controversies and establish any instructions that are necessary for the correct functioning of this one-stop shop, in addition to the sanctioning procedure that will be open against CMOs for failing to comply with their legal obligation.
>
> The one-stop shop will be managed by a private legal person and no CMO will have the power to control its decision making process.
>
> The one-stop shop must provide its services in an objective, transparent and non-discriminatory manner, and in accordance to these rules:

[39] Act 21/2014 of 4 November 2014, amending the TRLPI and implementing Directive 2012/28/EU on orphan works and Directive 2011/77/EU on phonograms term extension; BOE 268, of 5 November 2014.

(a) It must provide services to any lawfully established CMO.

(b) It must incorporate the general applicable tariffs for each user group and for all lawfully established CMOs.

(c) It must facilitate the payment of the amounts owed by users to lawfully established CMO.

The Ministry of Culture and the National Commission on Markets and Competition, within their respective competences, will supervise that this is complied with, including the control of the Statutes of the legal person that will manage the one-stop shop before it starts its activity.

The Government may develop all that has been provided in this paragraph by means of a regulation.

3. The CMOs, when complying with the obligation provided for in Art. 154.5 (d) TRLPI,[40] will devote the amounts deriving from such obligation to the financing of the one-stop shop for billing and payment provided for in the previous paragraph.

This is basically **an aggregate of independent CMO licenses** through **one single website**. It is not a joint (let alone, single) tariff, but a one-stop shop of aggregated licenses available online: all information regarding the applicable tariffs for each CMO can be obtained, and the user can calculate the fees to pay and also make the payment online. It is structured as a private business, independent from CMOs, most of which in Spain are non-profit associations. It will be created, financed, managed and maintained by all the Spanish CMOs. None of them has control over it (it must be an independent business) and all CMOs must be granted services by it. This business has no ability to negotiate any fees; fees are set (as usual) independently by each CMO. It has been questioned that this provision is unconstitutional, because it is contrary to the freedom of association and of conducting private business.[41] It remains to be seen if this *ventanilla única* will help reduce transactions costs at all (and, if any, whose costs?). For the user, of course, the website will help identify the CMO and provide information regarding all the licenses needed to carry out a specific use. However, the user will still need to apply and pay for all of them, according to the criteria and fees established by each CMO.

In this context, Directive 2014/26/EU[42] also deserves to be mentioned as a simplification effort, by imposing on CMOs and copyright owners of musical works a duty to ensure their contribution to the development of the Single Market. Under this Directive, CMOs are allowed to license multi-territorial licenses (MTL) at the pan-EU level provided that they have sufficient capacity to process electronically (in an efficient and transparent manner) data needed for the administration of such

[40] According to Art. 154.5 TRLPI, any amounts collected but undistributed (not claimed within 5 years) shall be used for several purposes (assistance, education, and re-distribution), including financing the one-stop shop; the minimum of 15 % set for each does not apply to the one-stop shop.

[41] A claim of unconstitutionality against this *ventanilla única* is pending at the Spanish Constitutional Court (# 681-2015) (BOE 58, 9 March 2015), submitted by the Socialist Parliamentary Group.

[42] Directive 2014/26/EU of the European Parliament and of the Council of 26 February 2014 on collective management of copyright and related rights and multi-territorial licensing of rights in musical works for online use in the internal market. OJEU L 84/72, 20 March 2014.

licenses, including for the purposes of identifying the repertoire and monitoring its use, invoicing users, collecting rights revenue and distributing amounts due to right holders. A CMO which does not fulfill these criteria or does not wish to grant MTL may mandate another CMO to grant an MTL for its repertoire, and the latter is obliged to accept it and manage it in a non-discriminatory manner;[43] representation agreements between CMOs will be concluded on a non-exclusive basis. Royalties are later distributed to each participating CMO.

Right holders have the choice to decide to which CMO (in any EU country) to mandate their rights. In practice, this means that a few CMOs may acquire a stronger position within the EU market. Furthermore, nothing in the Directive precludes copyright owners from withdrawing their rights from collective management and creating management "operators" which are subject to less scrutiny than CMOs, thus fragmenting rights management in the EU market and at the same time weakening the position of CMOs.

The MTL that the Directive foresees only deals with the exclusive rights of music authors, not of performers and producers. It fails to address the management of any remuneration rights accruing to these authors (as well as, in many cases, performers) for the making available of their works online. It is unlikely that the Directive will be fully efficient in simplifying the granting of MTL by CMOs for the making available online of music contents within the EU; instead, it may simply strengthen direct licensing by copyright owners.

In other words, digital service providers will still need to apply for several licenses from multiple CMOs and operators to operate in the EU market.[44] Some obstacles deriving from territoriality may have been cleared for licensing music online, but we are still far from any real simplification of the tariff structures.

4.3 Extended Collective Licensing and Compulsory Collective Management

Extended collective licensing (ECL) refers to the system of licenses granted by a CMO representing a substantial number of rights holders in a given category of works, which are extended by virtue of the law to cover all rights holders in the same category, including those who have not mandated their rights to that CMO. Similarly, compulsory collective management (also by virtue of the law) amounts to granting a CMO a universal and exclusive mandate to license and collect on

[43] A duty to contract (Article 29) is set on two conditions: there must be a request from a CMO that is not offering MTL, and the requested CMO must be representing the same category of online rights in musical works in one or more CMOs.

[44] For instance, it is unlikely that the implementation of this Directive alone will simplify the Spanish licensing scenario—as sketched in Sect. 2—for the online exploitation of phonograms and audiovisual recordings.

behalf of all affected owners (regardless of its catalogue).[45] Despite the fact that both systems expedite and facilitate the licensing, neither ECL nor compulsory collective management simplifies tariff structures, since each CMO retains its own licenses and fees.

5 Simplification of the Fees?

As we have seen, simplification may be achieved by redesigning the scope and the nature of the licensing structures, but another important element in any simplification effort is the fees and the criteria used to calculate them.

Setting a price tag for IP has never been an easy task. We cannot use an approach based on production costs, because on the one hand the artistic creation in most cases is invaluable and, on the other, the making of copies (especially digital ones) requires very low costs. So CMOs tend to rely on either flat fees or on a percentage based on indirect means such as business revenues, exploitation incomes or advertising budgets, etc.[46]

On top of the inherent pricing difficulty, CMOs have a tendency to issue standard licenses with internally pre-approved (not always negotiated) fees. Furthermore, any simplification efforts tend to repeat these patterns.[47] National laws usually require that authors be **"proportionally" remunerated** when transferring their exclusive rights to a producer or publisher[48]; when dealing with **remuneration rights, and (fair) compensation (for limitations) copyright laws usually require that the fees be "equitable"**.[49] However, national laws tend to be less specific

---

[45]In Israel, the equitable remuneration of performers for communication to the public of their performances is subject to compulsory collective management of several CMOs, which is assigned exclusively to one CMO, namely the one that represents the largest number of performers. This organization "shall also transmit the royalties to performers and holders of performers' rights who are not members in it" (sec. 3 Performers' and Broadcasters' Rights Law, 5744-1984), thus formally working as extended collective licensing. Courts have come to recognize de facto the Representative Organization of Performers in Israel as holding this status. See T. Greenman (2013), op. cit. 1-126.

[46]In its 11-12-2008 ruling (case C-52/07, *Kanal 5 and TV4*), the CJEU accepted that the application of a percentage of fees on these items was not per se contrary to Article 102 TFEU.

[47]For instance, the fees in the licenses granted by "clearance centers" are not negotiated, but simply calculated for each client, and based on the pre-existing licensing structures and fees of the CMOs. Any negotiation is done a posteriori through discounts and favored prices.

[48]For instance, Art. 46 Spanish TRLPI.

[49]The CJEU (C-192/04, C-245/00, C-572/13) has been establishing criteria to modulate the concept of "equitable remuneration"—especially when it is based on a percentage of gross revenues—such as the intensity and volume of use, the effective use of works, the amount of use, the audience indexes, and even by comparing the fees to other CMOs fees or to the remuneration agreed in exploitation contracts. See also C-467/08, regarding the meaning of "fair compensation" under the private copying limitation.

regarding the price of copyright licensing, in general. Only regarding the fixation of fees by CMOs do some national laws require that they be **equitable**,[50] **non-discriminatory**,[51] **efficient**[52] and **non-abusive.**[53]

Once again, Swiss law seems to be doing a better job than the rest. According to Art. 60 LDA, collective licensing fees must be **equitable** and must take into account the **proceeds** obtained from the use; on top of that, the law establishes a maximum amount of 10 % for authors' rights and of 3 % for neighboring rights.[54] Despite these statutory constraints, Swiss CMOs still have ample discretion when setting their licensing criteria and fees. In fact, these may diverge even when licensing the same kind of rights and works to different users. An example is that the rental of works and recordings (licensed under two different joint tariffs: JT 5, managed by SUISA, and JT 6a, managed by ProLitteris) is subject to different fees and calculation criteria. JT5 applies different fees for phonogram and audio-visual recordings: for phonograms, a total fee of 0.33 CHF for each rental (0.25 CHF for authors and 0.08 CHF for performers), with a minimum fee of 60 CHF every 3 months; for audiovisual recordings, a single fee of 7.30 CHF is paid for each audiovisual recording acquired for rental purposes, with a minimum of 18.40 CHF every 3 months (minimum fees increase according to the number of recordings acquired up to over 1030 CHF). Instead, JT 6a applies the same criteria for all supports (a on the rental price paid by the user): 11 % for phonograms (9 % for authors and 3 % for performers), 11 % for audiovisual recordings (9 % for authors and 3 % for performers) and 9 % for books.

In similar terms, the **Spanish TRLPI** (as amended in 2014) also requires that the fees for CMO licensing be "*reasonable (equitable), taking into account the economic value of the copyright use within the user's activity, and seeking a fair*

[50]For instance, Belgium: équitables et non discriminatoires (Art. XI.275).

[51]Fees cannot be applied differently without an objective justification, and especially not in a manner that has a negative impact on competition (when it causes a competitive disadvantage for the client).

[52]Management costs to be deducted from collected fees should be reasonable.

[53]For instance, Germany and Italy; National Reports ALAI International Congress 2015, available at: www.alai2015.org/en/national-reports.html (accessed on 30 March 2016).

[54]Swiss LDA Art. 60 "*Principle of equitableness*

a. When determining remuneration, account will be taken of:
b. the proceeds obtained from the use of the work, performance, phonogram or audiovisual fixation or broadcast, or alternatively the costs incurred in such use;
c. the nature and quantity of the works, performances, phonograms or audiovisual fixations or broadcasts used;
d. the ratio of protected to unprotected works, performances, phonograms or audiovisual fixations or broadcasts as well as to other services.
e. Remuneration normally amounts to a maximum of 10 per cent of the proceeds or costs incurred from the use of the copyright and a maximum of 3 per cent for related rights; however, it is determined in such a way that entitled persons receive equitable remuneration conditioned upon sound financial management for the administration of rights."

balance among both parts" (Art. 157.1b TRLPI).[55] However, nothing is said about a maximum percentage of remuneration. Once again, it is interesting to revisit the Spanish example used above (Sect. 2), and compare it with the Swiss text. In Spain, a service provider of music (phonograms) online must pay Spanish CMOs a total of 56 % of its gross revenues (27 % for streaming and 29 % for downloading) for all exclusive and remuneration rights involved; notice also the gap existing between the Swiss limits (10 % and 3 %) and the Spanish fees (12 % for the authors' remuneration right, or some 16 % for neighboring rights). These fees are now being revised by Spanish CMOs, but lacking any statutory guidance similar to that offered by the Swiss legislator, it is unlikely that the Spanish collective licensing structures will ever be close to the Swiss ones.

6 Conclusions

Any actual simplification of tariff structures requires a combined effort from governments and legislators as well as from CMOs and copyright owners. On the one hand, structural changes that could significantly help simplify licensing require some kind of statutory action: either by redesigning the rights in the copyright statute (making them less fragmented and easier to exercise and license) and/or by imposing simplified mechanisms for their licensing (be it joint/single rights and licensing structures, mandatory one-stop shops or ECL set by law). On the other, CMOs and copyright owners need to move away from their comfort zones and redesign their licensing criteria and fees also in favor of users. CMOs serve authors and right holders, clearly, but they also serve users and, ultimately, the general public interest, by facilitating lawful access to copyrighted works. From this perspective, simplification of tariff structures should be a duty imposed on all collective licensing.

[55] Art. 157.1b TRLPI adds: "... *account will be taken of at least the following criteria:*

a. the effective use of the repertoire within the whole activity of the user;
b. the intensity and relevance of the repertoire used within the whole activity of the user;
c. the amount of repertoire managed by the CMO;
d. the economic proceeds obtained by the user for the commercial exploitation of the repertoire;
e. the economic value of the service provided by the CMO to enforce the licensing fees;
f. the fees set by the CMO to other users for the same kind of use;
g. the fees set by similar CMOs in other EU member States for the same kind of use."

References

Barrelet, D., / Egloff, W. (2008), Le nouveau droit d'auteur, 3rd ed., 285-287, Stämpfli

Greenman, T. (2013), *Chapter 20: Israel*, in: S. von Lewinski (Ed.), Copyright throughout the World, 1-126, Thomson Reuters

Xalabarder, R. (2013), *Chapter 35: Spain*, in: S. von Lewinski (Ed.), Copyright throughout the World, 1-138 Thomson Reuters

Remaining Scopes for Collective Management of Copyright in the Online World

Sylvie Nérisson

Contents

Abstract The online world seems to enable creators and other rights holders to know who the users of their works are as well as to control their use. This may involve a shift of the role of collective management organizations towards a decrease of their scope of activity. This chapter defines collective management of copyright as it developed until today, and questions the decrease of the role of collective management of copyright considering the current developments.

Sylvie Nérisson is associate professor at IRDAP (Université de Bordeaux) and IUT métiers du livre Bordeaux-Montaigne, Bordeaux, France and affiliated to the Max Planck Institute for Innovation and Competition.

S. Nérisson (✉)
Université de Bordeaux, Bordeaux, France
e-mail: Sylvie.Nerisson@u-bordeaux.fr

K.-C. Liu, R.M. Hilty (eds.), *Remuneration of Copyright Owners*, MPI Studies on Intellectual Property and Competition Law 27, DOI 10.1007/978-3-662-53809-8_4

1 Introduction

In order to state which scopes remain for collective management of copyright in the online world, this chapter firstly defines collective management as it developed until today (in the second section). The third section then questions the decrease of the role of collective management of copyright considering the current developments. For this it presents the advantages of collective management in order to assess in which areas and under which conditions this way of exercising copyright is a solution to questions raised by the digitization and the Internet. The fourth section presents the current role of collective management in the online world, and the open questions. Taking these questions into account, the fifth section proposes the introduction of a statutory presumption of collective management for online uses, as a way toward easier and more peaceful relations between creators, intermediaries and users on the Internet.

2 Collective Management of Copyright: An Old Tool

Collective management organizations (hereinafter "CMOs") appeared as legislators recognized new copyrights covering mass distribution (first public performances, then radio, then terrestrial, satellite and cable television) or as new technologies gave rise to new uses of copyrighted works and consequently new royalties to be received by right holders from new users.

2.1 The Contractual Origins of Collective Management

Beaumarchais, a famous playwright of the eighteenth century, realized that Parisian theatres abused their power towards playwrights so to avoid paying royalties to authors. He invited his colleagues to join him in order to pool their rights and handle and negotiate together against theatres. This was the birth of the *Bureau de lé gislation dramatique*, which became SACD,[1] the oldest CMO, still active today.[2] The scheme repeated itself in the musical field with SACEM[3] in France, AKM[4] in Austria, and the historic form of GEMA[5] in Germany, as composers needed to act

[1]"Société des auteurs et des compositeurs dramatiques", Society of theatrical writers and composers, available at: www.sacd.fr/A-society-for-and-by-authors.750.0.html.

[2]J. Boncompain (2015), 747.

[3]"Société des auteurs, compositeurs et éditeurs de musique", Society of lyricists, composers and publishers of music, available at: www.sacem.fr/en.

[4]Autoren, Komponisten, Musikverleger, Authors, composers, music publishers, available at: www.akm.at/Service/Forms_and_Infos_in_English/.

[5]"Gesellschaft für musikalische Aufführungs- und mechanische Vervielfältigungsrechte", Society for musical performing rights and mechanical reproduction rights. https://www.gema.de/en/home/.

together to enforce their performing rights against restaurants and bars. In other words, collective management appeared as an initiative of creators for the purpose of acting together vis-à-vis users reluctant to pay royalties. In a nutshell, the origins of CMOs are contractual.

2.2 *The Shift Towards State Intervention: Statutory Collective Management*

In the second half of the twentieth century, legislatures worldwide started to introduce a new scheme. Until then, states recognized new exclusive rights but left the enforcement to the private sector. Creators chose to establish associations, cooperatives, corporations or any kind of group in order to enforce, in a collective manner, those of their rights that were not enforceable on an individual basis. Indeed, collective negotiations and enforcement were, in many cases, the only efficient way to monetize the rights granted by law. Reciprocally, CMOs also were successful because they met the need of users for a licensing one-stop shop. Neither a discothèque, nor a bar, nor a TV channel are happy about spending time and money on identifying all the rights holders of works they use in the course of their activities, and then individually negotiating with each one of them.

Since the German vanguard Copyright Act of 1965[6] introduced a private copying fee whose management and enforcement were statutorily collective, numerous legislators have overtaken the scheme of "limitation-based remuneration rights".[7] Especially when legislators associated the introduction of a limitation-based remuneration right with statutory collective management, it appears as the best known way to achieve a balance between the interests of users to access works and the interests of creators and investors to recoup investment.

This historical reminder[8] has two objectives: first, to highlight that collective management is originally a contractual tool, created by authors and rights holders, meeting the needs of users for an efficient solution to clear licenses; second, to recognize that collective management is *per se* protean, be it a contractual creation of rights holders or a punctual solution of legislature to achieve a balance of conflicting interests. There are therefore as many collective management schemes as there are CMOs, or specific rights to clear or remunerate, or applicable laws. In other words, the definition of collective management has to be flexible since it always has been employed to enable legal use of copyrighted works and facilitate payments, as an answer to specific environments. It always represents a specific

[6]Cf. sections 53, 54, and 54 h of the German Copyright Act, available at: www.gesetze-im-internet.de/englisch_urhg/englisch_urhg.html.

[7]Cf. the chapter by C. Geiger.

[8]For a more detailed presentation of the historical background of collective management, see J. Boncompain (2015) about its roots, and R.M. Hilty / S. Nérisson (2013) about the second half of the twentieth century and the last decade in Europe.

adaptation to specific needs. In order to assess the future of collective management for online uses, we need a definition of this way of exercising copyright.

3 A Definition of Collective Management of Copyright

Three sources help us to define collective management: Directive 2014/26/EU of the European Parliament and of the Council of 26 February 2014 on collective management of copyright and related rights and multi-territorial licensing of rights in musical works for online use in the internal market, issued by the European Union (EU); a report for WIPO in 2002 by Mihaly Ficsor[9]; lastly a report for the EU Commission conceived as a guidebook for multimedia producers in 1996 by Gilles Vercken.[10]

The Directive 2014/26/EU gives no definition of collective management but one of organizations processing this kind of copyright management:

> 'Collective management organisation' means any organisation which is authorised by law or by way of assignment, licence or any other contractual arrangement to manage copyright or rights related to copyright on behalf of more than one rightholder, for the collective benefit of those rightholders, as its sole or main purpose, and which fulfils one or both of the following criteria: (i) it is owned or controlled by its members; (ii) it is organised on a not-for-profit basis. (Article 3(a) Directive 2014/26/EU).

Key points of this definition are the following: the dual foundation of collective management (authorization by law or by contractual arrangements); the management of copyrights has to be on behalf of a community of rights holders and for the collective benefit of this community; a legal form shall ensure either that rights holders, whose rights are managed by the CMO, administer the CMO, or that the CMO is organized on a not-for-profit basis.

Ficsor defines collective management by describing their activities:

> Owners of rights authorize collective management organizations to monitor the use of their works, negotiate with prospective users, give them licenses against appropriate remuneration on the basis of a tariff system and under appropriate conditions, collect such remuneration, and distribute it among the owners of rights.[11]

Vercken gives two definitions, one descriptive and the other synthetic:

> Systems of pooling the management of copyrights were gradually introduced (. . .) for the purpose of controlling the use of works, issuing comprehensive authorizations for their use, collecting the remuneration for the authorization to disseminate, and distributing to the authors the monies received: collective management.[12]

---

[9]Mihaly Ficsor a former judge and high level official of the World Intellectual Property Organization and CISAC (the international confederation of CMOs).

[10]Gilles Vercken is an attorney and former in-house lawyer of two French CMOs and the first French pay-TV.

[11]M. Ficsor (2002), 21.

[12]G. Vercken (1996), 10. In the following paragraphs, Vercken explains functions and specificities of CMOs.

and

> Collective management is a method of exercise of rights.
>
> Narrowly defined, collective management is where the author's rights are included in the repertoire of a society of authors and the society authorizes a user to have overall access to that repertoire, the payment of the remuneration not being directly linked to the use of a particular work.
>
> Strictly speaking, therefore, the term 'collective management' should be reserved for the issue of a blanket authorization where no price is set for the use of an individual work.[13]

Compared to the definition found in these older reports for the WIPO or EU Commission, the Directive did not mention an essential point of the definition of collective management: the tariff system (that appears in the Directive,[14] but not in its CMOs' definition) and blanket licenses. These two aspects concern the relationships between CMOs and users. Tariffs and blanket licenses provide the legal security to users regarding the cost of use of works belonging to the repertoire, in other words, the portfolio or the works of registered rights holders. They are therefore the most attractive features of collective management from the users' point of view. They are of great relevance for emerging business models as long as the price asked by the CMO is affordable for the user.

4 Benefits of Collective Management of Copyright

Overall speaking, collective management of copyright is successful. As of today, CISAC, the International Confederation of Societies of Authors and Composers, has 230 members in 120 countries.[15] The reasons for this growth[16] are numerous; I focus on three aspects (Sect. 4.1). Later I will pay attention to the preconditions for these positive effects of collective management (Sect. 4.2).

4.1 Benefits of Collective Management

First, collective management of copyright is the precondition for creators to be remunerated for secondary uses (as opposed to primary uses that depend on

[13] G. Vercken (1996), 106. In the following paragraphs, Vercken explains different schemes of blanket licenses.

[14] See Recitals 6, 31 and 35, and Articles 16.2 and 21.

[15] www.cisac.org/Cisac-Home/Our-Members.

[16] CISAC was founded in 1926 by 18 CMOs.

individual negotiations[17]) as long as there is no need for exclusivity regarding the uses intended.[18] This is due to the economies of scale and to the strength of the group.[19] Collective management of copyright materializes the shares due to creators and artists.

Second, collective management helps users to obtain licenses on a world repertoire[20] and to solve the problems caused by rights fragmentation. This is for example necessary for radio broadcasters to offer the broadest repertoire available[21] and not to be limited by contracts they have signed with specific publishers or distributors and their respective portfolio.

Third, collective management of copyright is useful to rights holders because CMOs enable them to act together vis-à-vis users[22] and to mitigate their inner conflict, such as the conflict between publishers and writers when it comes to the distribution of royalties.[23] Similarly, CMOs help movie producers distribute what they owe to all the participants of a work they market.

4.2 *Preconditions for Effective Collective Management*

4.2.1 A World Repertoire

The collective management system relies on the network of reciprocal representation agreements (hereinafter RRAs) for cross-border management of rights. How does this work? For example, a German CMO and a Taiwanese CMO contractually agreed to represent each other in their respective territories. The German CMO will represent the members of the Taiwanese CMO in Germany, and vice versa. Thanks

---

[17]Individual contracting in relation to copyrighted works is traditionally possible in the primary market only: the writer contracts with a publisher; the lyricist, the composer and the performer of a song deal with a music publisher or a record company, etc. These are the primary uses. In contrast, single licensing on the secondary market for copyrighted works, related to the use of products of the primary market (for example, public performance of phonograms or DVDs, lending books or broadcasting), is generally not feasible. The uses involved in this secondary market are the secondary uses.

[18]There is, for example, a need for exclusivity on the specific secondary uses of a novel, when it is used as the script of a movie.

[19]Even if the single authorization for the audiovisual adaptation will be contracted on an individual basis (mostly between the publisher, not the creator) of the novel and the film producer, the shares of the creator for performing, broadcasting, private copying (etc.) of the film are mostly distributed by a CMO. The idea is, briefly: that if cherry-picking were possible, most commercial users would concentrate on the mainstream works, and this would raise the price to access niche repertoire.

[20]Cf. EU Commission, COMP/38.014—IFPI "Simulcasting", Decision 2003/300/EC of 8 October 2002, and US ASCAP, BMI, and SESAC consent decrees.

[21]US Consent decree in the case CBS / BMI, 441 U.S. 1 (1979).

[22]Cf. EU Court of Justice BRT / SABAM, C-127-73, ECLI:EU:C:1974:25.

[23]Cf., however, the German case BGH Vogel / VG Wort, I ZR 198/13, 21 April 2016.

to this, Taiwanese users are not deterred from playing German music because of the difficulty of identifying and contacting a German-speaking rights holder, and Taiwanese rights holders are effectively represented in Germany and vice versa. Since the RRAs' network is so well developed, all CMOs that are part of the network are able to grant licenses to a world repertoire (the sum of all repertoires of CMOs of the network). This grants overall access to this world repertoire for a unique price. Therefore the monopoly position of CMOs and the fact they only grant licenses on their complete repertoire (in other words, refuse cherry picking) encourage cultural diversity.[24]

4.2.2 Effective Control

In 2014, CMOs collected €7.9 billion the world over.[25] There is consequently a need for control of the money flows, especially in order to ensure that users get licenses and that CMOs help rights holders get their fair shares and, obviously, avoid that the only true beneficiaries are the chairmen of CMOs.

Efficient control requires that sufficient means be allocated to the assessment of all the practices of the CMOs, including the tariff setting, the distribution keys among groups of registered right holders, the effective distribution (among rights holders and considering allocations of some percentage of the fees received to social funds), the amount of administrative costs, and the relations to the users, to their members, and to all their debtors, especially the non-members. The control of CMOs relies not only on their members and contractors but also on the respective states where CMOs are active. Such efficient control requires a sizeable staff with the necessary skills and knowledge in copyright and antitrust law and accounting. It also requires independence of the monitoring body. It means independence from the government in order to avoid any interference that would amount to cultural censorship and from the industry. At last, effective control also requires legal means for oversight bodies to, at least, obtain information from CMOs.[26]

5 Collective Management and the Online World

This section will summarize the impact of the Internet and digitization on the collective management of copyrights, and then draws up an inventory of the current state of affairs.

[24]On this monopoly position, and the antitrust concerns that it raises, see J. Drexl (2013), at Chapter 11, 210-264. More specifically on the promotion of cultural diversity, see A. Dietz (2014).

[25]Available at: www.cisac.org/Who-We-Are/Key-Figures.

[26]Cf. the chapter by R.M. Hilty and T. Li.

5.1 *The Questions Raised by the Internet Regarding Collective Management of Copyright*

The need for economies of scale and for pooling actions of rights holders towards multiple users grew rather than diminished with the development of the Internet. In this regard, collective management still has a role to play, actually more than ever.

The big shift that raises questions about the practice of CMOs is the multiterritorial aspect of anything happening online: the territorial scope of licenses traditionally granted by CMOs doesn't fit anymore. This precisely causes questions about the national scope of licenses: a CMO only granted licenses for the national territory in which it had its seat. This limitation is due to the need for local monitoring,[27] and has its roots in the fact that until the last decades of the twentieth century (as satellite broadcasting appeared) the use of copyrighted works was not multiterritorial.

Thanks to the adaptation of their RRAs, CMOs grant licenses for multiterritorial online use in the fields of visual arts[28] and neighboring rights in music.[29] But the achievement is only partial in the field of music. Regarding authors' rights, a recommendation issued by the European Commission in 2005,[30] together with the decision of the European Commission in the CISAC case in 2008,[31] dismantled the network of RRAs regarding authors' rights as opposed to neighbouring rights covered by RRAs that passed the review of the European Commission.[32] Due to the lack of publicity of RRAs, one may only assume that RRAs *most probably* also exist regarding performing rights of creators, administered by traditional CMOs. What we know about the field of mechanical rights, namely the secondary rights to reproduce works (mostly owned by publishers) is that it is complicated, at least in Europe. The reason for this is that major publishing companies withdrew their rights from the traditional CMOs and their network of RRAs and founded new

---

[27]EU General Court, International Confederation of Societies of Authors and Composers (CISAC) / European Commission, T-442/08, and EU General Court, OSA—Ochranný svaz autorský pro práva k dílům hudebním o.s. / Léčebné lázně Mariánské Lázně a.s., C-351/12.

[28]See OnLineArt, http://www.onlineart.info/.

[29]See European Commission, COMP/C2/38.014—IFPI "Simulcasting", Decision 2003/300/EC of 8 October 2002. For a presentation of the developments in Europe, see R.M. Hilty / S. Nérisson (2013), and for an overall presentation of the interplay with competition law, J. Drexl (2013), Chapter 11.

[30]Commission Recommendation 2005/737/EC of 18 May 2005 on collective cross-border management of copyright and related rights for legitimate online music service.

[31]European Commission, COMP/C2/38.698—CISAC, Commission Decision of 16 July 2008.

[32]European Commission, COMP/C2/38.014—IFPI "Simulcasting", Decision 2003/300/EC of 8 October 2002.

"independent management entities" (cf. Article 3(b) of the Directive 2014/26).[33] There *most probably* are some RRAs regarding mechanical rights. But due to the enhanced competition between CMOs, these new independent management entities and publishers, the provisions of such RRAs are not available. The only sure thing is that the actual licensor for multiterritorial licenses of mechanical rights of the UK-US repertoire of multinational publishers is difficult to identify.[34]

The Internet should change the business models of CMOs for at least two reasons, first because of the new technologies available,[35] and second, because of the new intermediaries, the most visible of which being the search engines. Here, the difficulty is that the most important regulation regarding these bridges (or essential facilities...?) to access information consists of the liability exemption provisions (more famously known as "safe harbor") for these intermediaries.[36] But how different are these new intermediaries really from cable operators or copy shops, both kinds of intermediaries that owe royalties to CMOs for the use of copyrighted works they facilitate, as they have no editorial control over the works used in their pipes or venues but make money out of the possibility they offer?

5.2 An Inventory of Collective Management of Online Copyright Today

Collective management of online uses is effective and successful in the fields of visual arts for all uses that don't involve moral rights (e.g. thumbnails in Google image[37] and the OLA network[38]), mass digitization,[39] and non-interactive uses.[40]

[33]Such as CELAS, a joint venture of EMI Publishing and music CMOs from Germany (GEMA) and UK (PRS for Music), see Munich Court of Appeal (Oberlandesgericht), MyVideo, IIC 2014, 97, 29 April 2010—Case No. 29 U 3698/09. Meanwhile Sony/ATV Music Publishing acquired EMI Music Publishing, the joint venture became SOLAR, in which GEMA and PRS for Music grant pan-european licenses on the repertoires of both Sony/ATV Music Publishing and EMI Music Publishing.

[34]About these developments, see R.M. Hilty / S. Nérisson (2013), and L. Guibault / S. van Gompel (2015).

[35]See for instance, S. Wilson (2016).

[36]Cf. section 512 of 17 U.S. Code and articles 12-14 of EU Directive on electronic commerce (Directive 2000/31/EC of 8 June 2000) and CSPLA (French high council for literary and artistic property)'s report of P. Sirinelli / J.-A. Benazeraf / A. Bensamoun (2014) about the interplay of two directives, the directive on copyright and the directive introducing the safe harbour for internet intermediaries, following the report of P. Sirinelli / A. Bensamoun / C. Pourreau on the review of the 2001/29 directive, available in English.

[37]France recently introduced a mandatory collective management of the rights for the reproduction of images in the results of the search by images by search engines, cf. new articles L. 136-1 to L. 136-4 of the Code de la propriété intellectuelle.

[38]Available at: www.onlineart.info/.

[39]Cf. the international overview of such projects in the report of the US Copyright office, Orphan Works and Mass Digitization, June 2015, 18-33.

[40]Cf. the extensions of radio broadcasters' licenses to online uses.

Regarding authors' rights in music, the scope of activity of CMOs is unclear. The European Directive 2014/26 mandates all CMOs to streamline their practices towards more transparency, diligence and accountability, which can only be beneficial to all players involved. It also contains a part that is dedicated only to authors' rights (as opposed to neighboring rights) in music for online uses,[41] which encourages CMOs to abandon the reciprocity models and promotes the emergence of "licensing hubs". In other words, CMOs that comply with the highly demanding conditions set by the third Title of the Directive 2014/26 are allowed to grant multiterritorial licenses. The International Copyright Enterprise[42] (ICE), a joint venture of the German, British and Swedish CMOs (GEMA, PRS for music, and STIM respectively) was approved by the European Commission in June 2015.[43] We can only wait and see what will come out of this.

Again, only one thing is sure: the application of antitrust law to CMOs[44] and especially to RRAs makes the future role and form of collective management in the music field uncertain. Such agreements indeed raise concerns for antitrust authorities, since they may restrain competition among CMOs on the licensing markets. The European CISAC case showed two forms of reluctances. First, authors' rights CMOs in the field of music refuse to abandon the condition that users may only get a multiterritorial license from the CMOs of their economic residence. With this clause in the RRAs, CMOs commit themselves to only deal with users active on their territory. Consequently, if a user wishes to obtain a license from a non-domestic CMO, the RRA constrains the latter to refuse to grant the license and to tell the user to contact the CMO of its economic residence. Second, the European Commission[45] and the European Court of Justice[46] don't agree: after the European Commission prohibited 24 European CMOs from restricting competition, in particular by limiting their ability to offer their services to commercial users outside their domestic territory,[47] the European General Court annulled the Commission's decision in respect of the finding of the concerted practice because "the evidence relied on by the Commission is not sufficient to render implausible the explanation – other than the existence of concertation – for the collecting societies'

---

[41]Title 4 of the Directive.

[42]See icerights.com/.

[43]Cf. the case before the European Commission, M.6800, and the press release regarding the approval, available at: europa.eu/rapid/press-release_IP-15-5204_en.htm.

[44]In this regard, generally, see J. Drexl (2013) Chapter 11. On the specific impact of European case law on collective management and the consequences on the CMOs' activities regarding online licenses, R.M. Hilty / S. Nérisson (2013), 7-9.

[45]The European Commission is the first instance in EU for anti-trust cases.

[46]The European Court of Justice is the appellate body against decisions of the European Commission.

[47]European Commission, COMP/C2/38.014—IFPI "Simulcasting", Decision 2003/300/EC of 8 October 2002.

parallel conduct put forward by the applicant, based on the need to ensure the effectiveness of the fight against the unauthorised use of musical works".[48]

Considering that legal certainty is the reason why both rights holders and users contract with CMOs, there is a need for some state intervention as suggested in the following section in order to keep collective management fit for the swiftly changing landscape of business models in the online world.

6 Statutory Presumption of Collective Management of Copyrights for Online Uses

Considering the need for legal certainty and the current legitimacy crisis of copyright law, I suggest, for online uses, to turn the copyright paradigm on its head. The point would be to further use collective management as a tool fixing copyright law and to consider the silence of rights holders not as a prohibition of use, but as a tacit assent to the collective management of their online rights—in other words, to introduce a statutory presumption that online rights are managed by CMOs, which would grant non-exclusive licenses. The silence of rights holders would therefore enable the public to access copyrighted works and ensure fair remuneration of rights holders. Creators and other rights holders would be free to opt out of the presumed collective management. With such a scheme, professionals planning a commercial exploitation and therefore requiring exclusivity, as well as creators choosing to disseminate their works for free (for example via open access licenses) could do so after opting out. Users would be able to obtain broad licenses from CMOs for non-disputed repertoire. Also, since states would, with such a scheme, endorse CMOs, it would be necessary to strictly regulate their activities and to enhance their efficiency and transparency.

The need for legislative action, in order to introduce such a presumption, is on an international scale, since this would turn the copyright paradigm on its head and violate the current applicable international law.[49] As a matter of fact, a question is currently pending before the CJEU regarding a French law that entrusts an authorized CMO with management of online rights in "out of print books" (*livres indisponibles*) to grant licenses to publishers for commercial uses. The question reads:

> Do [Articles 2 and 5, regarding reproduction rights, the list of limitations and exceptions and the three step test] of the Directive 2001/29 of 22 May 2001 preclude legislation that gives approved collecting societies the right to authorise the reproduction and the representation in digital form of 'out-of-print books', while allowing the authors of those books,

---

[48]Judgment of the European General Court of 12 April 2013, T-442/08, 181.

[49]Mainly the Berne Convention. Two key principles could be violated by such a presumption: the need for prior consent (as shown in the opinion of Advocate General Wathelet in his opinion delivered on 7th July 2016 in the case C-301/15), and the prohibition of formalities conditioning enjoyment and exercise of copyrights, cf. discussions of J. Ginsburg (2016), M. Ficsor (2015), D. Gervais (2015).

> or their successors in title, to oppose or put an end to that practice, on the conditions that it lays down?[50]

The legislation challenged in this case differs from my proposal since the French scheme entrusts the CMO with the rights for the commercial exploitation of out-of-print books. Beyond this European dimension, the French regime could also be considered a violation of the prohibition of formalities (indeed, the writer willing to exploit his works has to opt out of the CMO management) of Article 5.2 of the Berne Convention for the protection of literary and artistic works.[51]

7 Conclusion

Internet and digitization constrain CMOs to further adapt their activities to the uses of copyrighted works. The online world doesn't change the fact that creators need to act together against users in order to enforce copyright effectively, and that no one is willing to pay for goods or services if they are accessible for free. Considering the swiftly changing business models, the most efficient and secure way to provide legal certainty would be that legislatures intervene to anchor the beneficial role of CMOs in the online world. The EU Directive of 2014 about collective management goes in the right direction since it requires transparency and efficiency in the management, both indispensable tools for involved players to trust CMOs and the market. Indeed, two facts may not be forgotten. First, the new possibilities given by technical progress don't help only users; they also provide CMOs with better means to monitor uses and adapt to the needs of all players involved. Second, CMOs are not the intermediaries most endangered by the Internet and digitization. In this regard, Professor Daniel Gervais, an international specialist of collective management, says it very clearly:

> Let me suggest a simple view of the aims of copyright:
>
> Authors want their books to be read (and songwriters their music to be heard etc.) and users want to access and read/listen to them. Hence in the grand copyright policy equation, only authors and users are, in fact necessary. Beyond this, only CMOs, as agents of the authors, also may have some claim to being necessary: without them, many users would find it impossible to conduct their business. By contrast, commercial intermediaries, whether they be publishers, record companies or online service providers of various kinds, are all contingent, because no individual intermediary or business model is essential.
>
> Yet, commercial intermediaries of all stripes seem to dominate the policy and scholarly discourse. My hunch is that this is so precisely because commercial intermediaries know they are replaceable. They have an incentive to use judicial, regulatory and other processes to artificially heighten their importance and to protect and increase their position and market shares.[52]

---

[50] See the question lodged on 18 June 2015, in the case C-301/15.

[51] P. Samuelson (2015), 10, F. Macrez (2012), 9, S. Nérisson (2015), 1427.

[52] D. Gervais (2013), 394.

References

Boncompain, J. (2015), La Révolution des auteurs – Naissance de la propriété intellectuelle, Fayard

Dietz, A. (2014), The European Commission's Proposal for a Directive on Collecting Societies and Cultural Diversity – a Missed Opportunity, International Journal of Music Business Research, April 2014, vol. 3 no. 1, available at: musicbusinessresearch.files.wordpress.com/2012/04/volume-3-no-1-April-2014_dietz_end1.pdf

Drexl, J. (2013), Copyright, Competition and Development, for the WIPO, available at: www.wipo.int/export/sites/www/ip-competition/en/studies/copyright_competition_development.pdf

Ficsor, M. (2002), Report for the WIPO, Collective management of copyright and related rights, WIPO, available at: www.wipo.int/edocs/pubdocs/en/copyright/855/wipo_pub_855.pdf

Ficsor, M. (2015), Collective Rights Management from the Viewpoint of International Treaties, with Special Attention to the EU 'Acquis', in: D. Gervais (Ed.), Collective Management of Copyright and Related Rights, 31-80, Kluwer Law International

Gervais, D. (2013), The Internet Taxi: Collective Management of Copyright and the Making Available Right, after the Pentalogy, in: M. Geist (Ed.), The Copyright Pentalogy How the Supreme Court of Canada Shook the Foundations of Canadian Copyright Law, University of Ottawa Press, 373-401, available at: www.press.uottawa.ca/sites/default/files/9780776620848_12.pdf

Gervais, D. (2015), Collective Management of Copyright: Theory and Practice in the Digital Age, in: D. Gervais (Ed.), Collective Management of Copyright and Related Rights, 3-30, Kluwer Law International

Ginsburg, J. (2016), Berne-Forbidden Formalities and Mass Digitization, Boston University Law Review, Vol. 96, 2016; Columbia Public Law Research Paper No. 14-510, available at: ssrn.com/abstract=2772176

Guibault, L. / van Gompel, S. (2015), Collective management in the European Union, in: D. Gervais (Ed.), Collective Management of Copyright and Related Rights, 139-174, Kluwer Law International

Hilty, R.M. / Nérisson, S. (2013), Collective Copyright Management and Digitization: The European Experience, in: C. Handke and R. Towse (Eds.), Handbook on the Digital Creative Economy, 222, Edward Elgar; Max Planck Institute for Intellectual Property & Competition Law Research Paper No. 13-09, available at: ssrn.com/abstract=2247870

Macrez, F. (2012), L'exploitation numérique des livres indisponibles: que reste-t-il du droit d'auteur ?, 747-755, Recueil Dalloz, available at: franck.macrez.net/?p=210

Nérisson, S. (2015), La gestion collective des droits numériques des «livres indisponibles du XXe siècle» renvoyée à la CJUE: le Conseil d'État face aux fondamentaux du droit d'auteur, 1427-1432, Recueil Dalloz

Samuelson, P. (2015), Answer to the request for comment of the US Copyright office about a Mass Digitization Pilot Program, available at: copyright.gov/policy/massdigitization/comments/Samuelson,%20Pamela%20University%20of%20California,%20Berkeley%20School%20of%20Law.pdf

Sirinelli, P. / Benazeraf, J.-A. / Bensamoun, A. (2014), for the CSPLA (French high council for literary and artistic property) Rapport sur l'articulation des directives 2000/31 et 2001/29, 2015, available at: www.culturecommunication.gouv.fr/content/download/130608/1420306/version/2/file/Rapport%20articulation%20directives%202000-31%20et%202001-29.pdf

Sirinelli, P. / Bensamoun, A. / Pourreau, C., Report of the mission on the revision of Directive 2001/29/EC on the harmonisation of certain aspects of copyright and related rights in the information society, available at: www.culturecommunication.gouv.fr/content/download/108377/1263731/version/3/file/CSPLA%20Report%20-%20Directive%202001-29-C-1.pdf

Vercken, G. (1996), Practical guide to copyright for multimedia producers, EU bookshop, available at http://bookshop.europa.eu/en/practical-guide-to-copyright-for-multimedia-producers-pbCDNA16128/

Wilson, S. (2016), PRS and Google working on a "Shazam for music licensing", available at: www.factmag.com/2016/02/03/prs-for-music-google-licensing-fees-device/

Effects and Potential of Extended Collective License Systems

Felix Trumpke

Contents

Abstract Extended collective license systems (ECL systems) have drawn increasing interest from researchers and policymakers in recent years. They are deemed a future solution to create a licensing framework for copyrighted works in mass-use situations. But is this growing interest in those systems really justified? This chapter tries to illuminate the functioning of ECL systems in general and to elucidate why the most elaborated model of them—the **ECL regime** from the Nordic countries—has worked so smoothly for such a long time. Certain prerequisites are necessary for those systems to "work", i.e. to facilitate the necessary acts of use by collective agreements and to safeguard

---

Felix Trumpke is Trainee Lawyer, Higher Regional Court Frankfurt/Main.

F. Trumpke (✉)
Higher Regional Court Frankfurt/Main, Frankfurt/Main, Germany
e-mail: cftrumpke@web.de

K.-C. Liu, R.M. Hilty (eds.), *Remuneration of Copyright Owners*, MPI Studies on Intellectual Property and Competition Law 27, DOI 10.1007/978-3-662-53809-8_5

the interests of right holders and users. In view of the promising experiences from Scandinavia, it would not be unreasonable to increasingly consider the introduction of ECL systems in order to create a proper legal framework for the digitisation and dissemination of works.

1 Introduction

Extended collective license systems (ECL systems) are primarily aimed at including the rights from non-represented right holders (so-called "outsiders"), in order to create a complete repertoire for the user. By doing that ECL systems improve the collective rights management (CRM). As a form of "blanket paying mechanism" the CRM and, in particular, ECL systems have worked quite well in the past. Whether those instruments could also succeed under new conditions, i.e. within the fast-changing online markets, is, however, debatable. More than any other ECL systems, a certain legal model, which applies in the Nordic countries,[1] has attracted international attention within legal research[2] and among legislators all over the world in recent years.[3]

Against this background, the question arises as to whether and under what conditions ECL systems might be utilized as a mechanism in the future to simplify the licensing practice and to adequately reward right holders. As a prerequisite to finding an answer to this question, a thorough understanding of how ECL systems actually work nowadays seems to be indispensable. With a special focus on the Scandinavian **ECL model**, this chapter is an attempt to illuminate the functioning of those systems as well as to discuss their suitability for the future.[4]

The chapter first gives a brief introduction of the term "ECL system" (Sect. 2). The functioning and application of the Scandinavian **ECL model** are presented in Sect. 3. In Sect. 4 the potential of ECL systems is elaborated in more depth, while in

[1]"Nordic" resp. "Nordic countries" shall be understood as the countries of Denmark, Sweden, Norway, Finland and Iceland. "Scandinavia"—although rather imprecise—shall be used as a synonym.

[2]See e.g. J. Wang (2010); Y. Jiang (2013); J. Axhamn / L. Guibault (2011); T. Riis / J. Schovsbo (2010).

[3]See e.g. in the UK, 1 October 2014, a new "Extended Collective Licensing Scheme" which came into force (Copyright and Rights in Performances (Extended Collective Licensing) Regulations 2014); see also the draft legislation in China, where an ECL-scheme has been proposed in favour of karaoke bars (Article 63 of the 3nd version of the draft is available at: www.chinalaw.gov.cn/article/cazjgg/201406/20140600396188.shtml).

[4]See generally and in more depth on ECL systems the doctoral thesis Exklusivität und Kollektivierung—Das skandinavische Modell der Erweiterten Kollektiven Lizenz (Extended Collective Licensing) by the author of this chapter (forthcoming).

Sect. 5 challenges and risks which might accompany those systems are discussed. Section 6 concludes the chapter.

2 The Term "ECL System"

2.1 The Origin of the Term

The term "ECL" has been in use to primarily describe a specific legal instrument applied in the Nordic countries since the 1960s. In this context, ECL refers to a licensing model, which allows the agreement between a collective management organization (CMO) and a user to be extended by law to all works and subject matter whose right holders are not represented by the CMO in question ("outsiders").

The original expression for "ECL" is in Swedish: "avtalslicens".[5] The English translation "extended collective license" was made by a Swedish law professor in 1985 who was then comprehensively introducing this instrument to a non-Scandinavian readership for the first time.[6]

It is worth noting that the term "ECL" has also found its way into European law. In Recital 18 of Directive 2001/29/EC (InfoSoc-Directive),[7] in Recital 24 of Directive 2012/28/EU (Orphan Works)[8] as well as in Recital 12 of Directive 2014/26/EU (Collective Rights Management)[9] the "extended collective licenses" are explicitly named and categorized as "arrangements concerning the management of rights". It was the Scandinavian countries that were responsible for the inclusion of the term into the final version of the InfoSoc-Directive.[10] However, neither in the Directives nor in the preparatory works is a thorough definition of the term given.

---

[5]The expression "avtalslicens" simply means "contractual license". In the beginning, the term only referred to a usual collective agreement between a CMO and a user. It later became the name for this specific legal model of the Scandinavian countries.

[6]G.W.G. Karnell (1985-86).

[7]Directive 2001/29/EC of the European Parliament and of the Council of 22 May 2001 on the harmonisation of certain aspects of copyright and related rights in the information society.

[8]Directive 2012/28/EU of the European Parliament and of the Council of 25 October 2012 on certain permitted uses of orphan works.

[9]Directive 2014/26/EU of the European Parliament and of the Council of 26 February 2014 on collective management of copyright and related rights and multi-territorial licensing of rights in musical works for online use in the internal market.

[10]See also below, at Sect. 5.2.

2.2 ECL Systems in the Context of CRM

The basic principle of collective management is well known: Right holders authorize a CMO to monitor the use of their works. The CMO then negotiates with prospective users and grants them licenses for the use of the works, which are part of the CMO's repertoire. The CMO also collects the remuneration paid by the licensee for the use and distributes the money among the right holders. In this field, collective licensing agreements are an everyday phenomenon.

Interestingly, most of the licensing agreements concluded by CMOs are characterized as not only being "collective", but also being "extended". It is a matter of fact that even in areas where CMOs manage the rights of many right holders, such as in the field of musical works, a CMO is hardly ever able to grant all necessary rights to a user. However, judging from practical experience, CMOs do grant all rights even though they are in fact not authorized to do so.[11] In order to bypass the problem, CMOs often work with "indemnity clauses": The risk for the user to be liable for using works of right holders, who have not authorized the CMO, is contractually transferred to the CMO. Apart from those indemnity clauses there are also some other "ECL systems" such as "mandatory collective administration" or "legal presumptions" in favour of CMOs, which, however, differ greatly from the Nordic system.

3 The Nordic ECL System

3.1 Main Elements

As said above, Nordic copyright law allows the extension of collective agreements to all right holders in a specific field.[12] This is accomplished by a statutory provision in the copyright acts of the Nordic countries, which states that as soon as the CMO and the user have concluded an agreement on the basis of voluntary negotiations, this agreement is extended to all works and other subject matter in a specific field (the "extension effect").[13] However, only those organisations are entitled to these special extended agreements, which already represent a substantial number of right

[11]M. Ficsor (2002), para. 379, 380.

[12]For an excellent overview and introduction of the Nordic ECL system and its main issues, see T. Riis / J. Schovsbo (2010).

[13]Sec. 42a (1) s. 1 of the Swedish Copyright Act (CA); Sec. 50 (1) of the Danish CA; Sec. 36 (1) s. 1 of the Norwegian CA; Sec. 26 (1) s. 1 of the Finnish CA; Sec. 15a (1) s. 1 of the Icelandish CA.

holders of works used in the country in question.[14] That means that the CMO has to possess a certain level of representativeness. Moreover, apart from Sweden all Scandinavian countries provide some kind of approval system for CMOs.[15]

Once the agreement is concluded and extended, the user may use not only works of the repertoire of the CMO, but also works of non-represented—national and foreign—right holders (world repertoire). In order to diminish the unfavourable role of outsiders to some extent, it is provided by law that those outsiders shall be treated like members of the CMO.[16] As a result, they have an equal right to remuneration and other benefits granted by the CMO. Moreover, they enjoy the right to individual remuneration[17] and sometimes even the right to opt out from the agreement.[18]

3.2 *Beneficial Effects*

If there is no market for individual licensing or if the use of a huge amount of works is uncontrollable, collective licensing seems to be one (if not the best) possible solution. However, collective management can hardly play out its strength when it runs the risk of fragmentary repertoire. The **ECL model** supports the collective management by "completing" the repertoire. The effects of this model are without doubt quite appealing: The user gets a licence covering all necessary rights he needs. At the same time, right holders are assured of remuneration for their works.

With regard to right holders who are not represented by the CMO, the Nordic model offers a number of advantages too. Outsiders are not only treated in the same way as members, but also enjoy remuneration for the use of their works that they would hardly have obtained by means of individual licensing.

---

[14]Sec. 42a (1) s. 1 of the Swedish CA; Sec. 50 (1) of the Danish CA; Sec. 38a (1) s. 1 of the Norwegian CA; Sec. 26 (1) s. 1 of the Finnish CA; Sec. 15a (1) s. 1 of the Icelandish CA.

[15]Sec. 50 (4) of the Danish CA; Sec. 38a (1) s. 1 of the Norwegian CA; Sec. 26 (2), (3) of the Finnish CA; Sec. 15a (1) s. 1 of the Icelandish CA. See J. Axhamn / L. Guibault (2011), 30.

[16]Sec. 42a (2) s. 1 of the Swedish CA; Sec. 51 (1) of the Danish CA; Sec. 37 (1) of the Norwegian CA; Sec. 26 (4) of the Finnish CA; Sec. 15a (2) s. 3 of the Icelandish CA.

[17]Sec. 42a (2) s. 3 of the Swedish CA; Sec. 51 (2) of the Danish CA; Sec. 37 (2) of the Norwegian CA; Sec. 26 (5) of the Finnish CA. The right to individual remuneration allows the author to claim compensation based on the individual use of his work—regardless of the agreement or the distribution plan. However, the right holder has the burden of proof to show that his work has been used to greater extent, which is, in practice, hardly ever possible.

[18]See e.g. Sec. 42b (2) of the Swedish CA; Sec. 30a (2) of the Danish CA; Sec. 32 (2) s. 2 of the Norwegian CA; Sec. 16d (2) of the Finnish CA; Sec. 15a (1) s. 2 of the Icelandish CA. If the right holder opts out, the user is not entitled anymore to use the work on the basis of the ECL agreement.

3.3 Application

Today, the Nordic countries have the broadest application of ECL systems. Originally designed for broadcasting of music in the 1960s,[19] now specific **ECL provisions** also apply to reproduction in private and public institutions and organizations, reproduction for educational purposes, to the cable retransmission right as well as to specific uses made by libraries, museums, archives and broadcasting organizations.[20]

Until recently, only in certain areas (e.g. re-use of archives) and only in favour of specific users (such as broadcasters) were the extension of collective agreements allowed. However, a new phase has started in 2008, when Denmark adopted a "new type" of ECL system. According to the new provision, every agreement between a representative CMO and a user may get an extended effect, provided that both parties agree on the extension of the contract.[21] With regard to every use and every exclusive right in copyright, the collective licensing of world repertoires by CMOs to users is—at least theoretically—possible. Such a "general clause" has also been introduced in Sweden in 2013[22] and is currently the subject of discussion in Norway.

3.4 The Uniqueness of the Nordic Model

Compared to other extended collective licensing solutions, which all aim at the incorporation of outsiders such as indemnity clauses, legal presumptions or mandatory collective management, there are some interesting features that make the Nordic model unique in this context.

3.4.1 Representativeness and Contractual Setting

In comparison to mandatory collective administration, where a right holder may only manage his rights collectively, the right holder under the Nordic ECL system is, as a matter of principle, free to manage his rights, be it individually or collec-

[19]Broadcasting organizations have always faced the problem of clearing rights due to the huge amount of works included in their programmes. However, at that time, broadcasting organizations had used unlawfully the works of right holders who were not represented by the CMO. In order to solve this unsatisfactory situation, an ECL provision was added in the Copyright Act.

[20]See J. Axhamn / L. Guibault (2011), 29, 43.

[21]Sec. 50 (2) Danish CA. See T. Riis / J. Schovsbo (2010), 476-477.

[22]Sec. 42 h Swedish CA.

tively. Moreover, if a right to opt out is provided, the right holder can even end the collective exploitation.[23]

However, probably the most distinctive element is that only under the Nordic regime is a CMO required to possess a certain degree of representativeness. If the CMO is not able to show that it already represents a substantial number of right holders, no ECL agreement can be legally constructed. That means that the CMO itself must endeavour to aggregate a large repertoire of rights. On the other hand, the representativeness requirement limits the effect of the ECL, since the more representative the CMO becomes, the fewer the number of outsiders and so the less effect the ECL will have.

Lastly, even if most ECL systems require a licensing agreement between a user and a CMO, there is a crucial difference to the Nordic model: The "extension effect" of all other types of extended collective licensing solutions is more or less closely related to the CMO itself: It is the collective organisation that is authorized by law to license rights from non-represented right holders. By contrast, under the Scandinavian **ECL model** the law addresses first and foremost the agreement, not the CMO: As long as parties do not enter into a contract, no use of the (extended) repertoire of works is allowed. It is the parties, the user on the one hand and (at least) a substantial number of right holders organized in a CMO on the other hand, who negotiate the terms of use. Since the inclusion of outsiders is inextricably linked to the collective agreement, the contractual component might play a much stronger role under the Nordic regime.

Both essential components of the Nordic **ECL regime**, namely the representativeness of the CMO and the fact that a contract is the point of departure, safeguard the smooth functioning of the model and respect the interests of all parties involved.

3.4.2 Structural Framework

Another important aspect to bring to mind is the structural "collective framework" in the Nordic countries. These countries are characterized by a high rate of unionization in the field of copyright.[24] Both original and derivative right holders are highly unionized. At the same time, remarkable coordination and cooperation between individual right holder organisations exist.[25]

In Scandinavia, three types of right holder organisations can be distinguished: professional organizations and associations (in terms of "interest groups"),[26] classic CMOs and the so-called "umbrella-organizations", which comprise both other organisations as members, coordinate and carry out the conclusion of ECL

[23]Similarly, under a presumption clause the right holder can rebut the presumption.

[24]H. Olsson (2009), 354; T. Koskinen-Olsson (2010), 283. On the beginnings of organisational collaboration in Denmark: H.L. Christiansen (1978), 279.

[25]T. Koskinen-Olsson (2010), 283, 289.

[26]H.L. Christiansen (1978), 280.

agreements and govern the distribution of money.[27] The very complex organisational structure might undoubtedly have contributed to the long-standing success of the Nordic system: The bundling of different right holders and the collaboration between several right holder organisations create a coordinated licensing, no less than a "one-stop shop". Furthermore, the cooperation between different right holder organisations ensures the acceptance and legitimacy of the **ECL model**, since the diverging interests of right holders with regard to licensing and distribution of money are given much greater attention.[28]

Without this framework, there is a risk that CMOs might not have the time, the capacity or the will to respect and safeguard the interests of all right holders (especially outsiders).

4 Potential of ECL Systems

4.1 Achievements So Far

The Nordic ECL model has not only worked considerably well in the countries of Northern Europe for quite a long time, but has also come into the consideration of many legislators worldwide.[29] This is hardly surprising, as the model has produced a number of remarkable results in solving (some) copyright problems. For instance, the problem of the so-called "orphan works", which has been discussed extensively,[30] has virtually been of no relevance in the Nordic countries due to the Nordic **ECL model**. In addition, the digital re-use of archive productions by broadcasting organizations as well as of collections in digitized form by cultural heritage institutions have been made possible quite easily as explained below.

4.1.1 Re-Use of Archives by Broadcasting Organizations

The Danish Copyright Act allows public-service broadcasters the re-use of their own or predominantly self-funded programmes by rebroadcasting them as well as by making them available to the public provided that the requirements of the ECL have been met.[31] Based on this provision, the Danish broadcaster DR has concluded

[27]See also Y. Jiang (2013), 741.

[28]T. Riis / J. Schovsbo (2010), 496.

[29]See for China: Y. Jiang (2013); J. Wang (2010). See for the U.S.: US Copyright Office (2015), 5, 82; see also P. Samuelson (2011), 697. See for Canada: D. Gervais (2003). See for the Netherlands: P.B. Hugenholtz / S. van Gompel / L. Guibault / R. Obradović (2014), 73.

[30]See e.g. S. van Gompel (2007), 669; T. Lüder (2010), 677; S. van Gompel / P.B. Hugenholtz (2010). See also European Commission (2011).

[31]Sec. 30a of the Danish CA.

two ECL agreements with Danish CMOs that manage the respective rights for right holders: The first contract enables the broadcaster to make its old productions available to the public,[32] whereas the other **ECL agreement** covers the re-broadcasting of old programmes by cable or wireless.[33]

4.1.2 The "Bookshelf Project"

In 2006, the National Library of Norway started an initiative with the objective of digitalizing its entire collection.[34] The whole digitalization process is supposed to take 20–30 years. The project covers works protected by copyright as well as public domain works.[35] With regard to copyrighted works that have been digitized, some of them can only be accessed within the premises of the library, while other parts of works can be accessed from anywhere by anyone with a Norwegian IP address. The latter use is covered by the so-called "Bookshelf agreement", which has been concluded between the National Library of Norway and Kopinor, an umbrella organisation representing several right holder organisations.[36] Again, a specific **ECL provision** in the Norwegian Copyright Act, which allows museums, libraries and archives the reproduction and the making available to the public of published works from their collections, serves as a basis for this contract.[37]

4.2 Future Application

Now we turn to the question in what way ECL systems may be utilized in the future. The Nordic **ECL model** provides an appealing solution when mass licensing of copyrighted works is concerned by facilitating the collective licensing through an appropriate mixture of contractual latitude for all parties involved and legal determination in form of the extension effect.[38] This instrument may also be used in a

[32]To that end, DR has launched a new website ("Bonanza") from which old newscasts, TV-shows, short films and other programmes can be accessed from any place at any time. Additional content is added every day. Available at: www.dr.dk/Bonanza/index.htm.

[33]For this purpose, DR has started two new television channels: While DR Ramasjang covers children's programmes, DR Kultur focuses on cultural and historical topics.

[34]M. Takle (2009).

[35]By 2014, 15 % of its collection of about 5 million newspapers, one third of its picture collection, 15 % of its collection of 2.8 million books and more than half of the radio programmes in the collection have been converted into digital format. See Nasjonalbiblioteket (2014), 7.

[36]Contract regarding the digital dissemination of books (Bokhylla/The Bookshelf), available at: www.nb.no/pressebilder/Contract_NationalLibraryandKopinor.pdf.

[37]Sec. 16a of the Norwegian CA.

[38]T. Riis / J. Schovsbo (2010), 472.

non-Scandinavian environment and in new areas where mass licensing by CMOs provides a possible solution.

4.2.1 ECL Systems in Favour of Cultural Heritage Institutions

Cultural heritage institutions such as libraries, museums, archives or broadcasting organisations are confronted with the problem of acquiring complete licenses. In order to fulfil their task for the public interest, namely preservation and dissemination of works, they need to digitize their collections and make them available. However, it is practically impossible to ask all right holders for permission individually, partly because they are unknown or untraceable, and partly because they might refuse that kind of use. Instead of looking for an individual solution addressed to granular problems such as the European regulation on orphan works, an ECL system would provide a more "holistic" approach.

4.2.2 ECL Systems Within New (Online) Markets

Certain market participants, often labelled intermediaries,[39] who create—within the scope of their own commercial service—an additional value by using a huge amount of works protected by copyright, could also benefit from an **ECL mechanism**. The range and variety of those intermediaries, however, seem to be vast: be it a market player who wants to use a particular segment of works (e.g. television programme) for its own commercial purposes, be it a market player who wants to build its own online media platform by using the content of a third party provider.[40] The wide range of potential market participants who could benefit from an ECL system would favour a broadly phrased **ECL provision**, if not in the form of a general clause.

When utilizing the ECL system in such a way, another impact of the model becomes visible: By facilitating access to and legal use of works by many, competition with regard to the exploitation of works might be fostered. The promotion of value-added services from intermediaries would probably lead to a greater choice

[39]The term "intermediary" is hardly self-explanatory, as it is used in different contexts, especially in connection with the liability of platform operators. However, for the purpose of this chapter the term "intermediary" shall be understood as a market player that enables decentralized acts that are copyright-relevant either in form of platforms for collaborative interactions between authors or by using copyrighted works while pursuing its own (commercial) objectives. In a similar sense D. Wielsch (2011), 665; see also R.M. Hilty (2010), 125.

[40]In the same sense Y. Jiang (2013), 736.

of services, to a broader dissemination of works and in the end to better remuneration for right holders.[41]

5 Challenges

ECL systems may only fulfil their promising task if certain indispensable conditions are met. This includes a CRM under a certain degree of regulation, in particular with regard to good governance, transparency and distribution of money. Moreover, additional rights that safeguard the interests of non-members must be provided. However, an ECL system always comes along with the risk that the lump sum that is paid by the user does not properly reflect the scope of the license and does not reach every right holder who is entitled to remuneration.

When it comes to the most elaborated model of ECL systems—the Nordic one—the (pre-) existence of a functioning CRM is a key part of the whole regime: Organisations which manage the rights of right holders must be in place, and right holders, on the other hand, must be willing to exercise their exclusive rights collectively. As the Nordic model is rooted in the free will of the parties and depends entirely on the willingness of the right holders to collectivize the exploitation of their rights, any kind of "forced promotion" would probably be counterproductive. It is precisely the decision of right holders to prefer collective management to individual exercise that justifies the extension of collective agreements to non-represented right holders.

5.1 Hold-Up Problems

If both parties cannot come to an agreement, no use of works may legally be made. The hold-up problems during negotiations can become a rather delicate matter when it comes to large-scale everyday use, which is in the public interest, such as the use of works for educational purposes. For good reason, most countries

[41]Even if collective management is not well developed in a certain field, in particular when it comes to new rights and uses in the digital age, the option for right holders and users to enter into an extended collective agreement should yet be provided. In the new evolving and fast changing online markets, the preferred way of exploitation is often not clear or still being sought. By introducing a general Nordic ECL provision, a voluntary instrument facilitating the collective licensing would be available, which the parties can make use of with regard to certain acts of use if they are willing to do so. As soon as individual licensing becomes the appropriate way of exploitation, the extension of collective agreements will lose their justification. Against this background, an ECL system might even help to explore the boundaries of individual and collective licensing.

therefore provide clearly defined limitations in those areas. In fact, ECL systems might only work in those environments which are characterized by a high density of CRM and where all parties involved are accustomed to licensing those uses by collective agreements.

The Scandinavian countries have hardly been confronted with the problem that agreements are not being concluded. One reason for this is that these countries provide different forms of measures that promote the conclusion of contracts, such as provisions on mediation and arbitration.[42] Another reason might be that the **ECL model** constitutes a fundamental part of Scandinavian copyright law nowadays. At the same time, the collectivization of significant parts of copyright has also been fostered by the **ECL model** itself.[43] Lastly, there is some sort of "pragmatism" inherent in the society that surrounds all parties involved when searching for legal solutions to copyright problems particularly, or when concluding collective agreements in order to facilitate the use of works.[44]

This unique environment, which has helped to build the fertile ground for the ECL system to work properly, has been described as "cultural background" in legal literature,[45] and it is fair to say that every attempt to understand this model has to take the cultural environment of the Scandinavian countries into account.

5.2 Compatibility with European and International Law

Copyright is based on the idea of exclusivity. That means that a copyright holder has the right to decide whether, when and how his work shall be exploited. However, non-represented right holders hardly have the right to decide the exploitation of their works. In fact, their works are legally being used not because of consent, but by virtue of the legal extension of the agreement. The only thing remaining is a right to remuneration. Thus, for outsiders the **ECL model** may constitute a restriction to their exclusive right.[46]

With the classification of the **ECL model** as "restriction", problems might arise, since national legislators are bound by international law when it comes to introducing new restrictions to the exclusive rights of right holders. On the international

[42]See e.g. Sec. 47 (2) and Sec. 52 (1) Danish CA. See generally J. Axhamn / L. Guibault (2011), 38.

[43]T. Riis / J. Schovsbo (2010), 495.

[44]*Id.*

[45]*Id.*, 495-496.

[46]This holds true even if the right to opt out is provided. If the right holder opts out, he may get his exclusivity back, but only for the future. See in more depth F. Trumpke (2012), 278.

level the so-called "three-step test" applies to all "limitations and exceptions".[47] Moreover, on the European level, only a closed catalogue of limitations and exceptions may be used by Member States to restrict the exclusive right under national law.[48]

In legal literature there has been an inconclusive debate about whether the Nordic ECL model constitutes a limitation or exception, which would result in this model being subject to the three-step test.[49] Against the background that the issue of compatibility of the Nordic model with superior law is, in fact, debatable and by far not settled, it might seem surprising that the Scandinavian countries have been able to broaden the application of their ECL system under their national law so constantly in the past decades. The main reason for that can be found in Recital 18 of the InfoSoc-Directive mentioned above, which simply states, "This directive is without prejudice to the arrangements (...) concerning the management of rights such as extended collective licenses". The Nordic countries have not only explicitly campaigned for the incorporation of this "grandfather clause", but have also defended their model since then as a mere "arrangement concerning the management of rights". Not being bound by the closed catalogue of limitations and exceptions in European law, they feel free to introduce new ECL provisions in their national law. In light of this, the unique structure of the ECL model and to some extent the successful lobbying by the Nordic countries have helped to keep their model untouched by European regulation.[50]

5.3 ECL Systems in a Borderless (Online) Environment

The legal use of works outside of a country on the basis of a national **ECL model** is not possible due to the principle of territoriality. Given the fact that creative content is increasingly distributed in non-physical formats across national borders through different networks and devices, it is questionable whether the national models of

[47] Article 13, Agreement on Trade-Related Aspects of Intellectual Property Rights (TRIPS); Article 8, WIPO Copyright Treaty (WCT).

[48] Article 5 Directive 2001/29/EC of the European Parliament and of the Council of 22 May 2001 on the harmonisation of certain aspects of copyright and related rights in the information society.

[49] F. Trumpke (2012), 265, 275 with further references. See also T. Riis / J. Schovsbo (2010), 482, 484. The same holds true with regard to mandatory collective administration, see S. von Lewinski (2004).

[50] At this point, another notable consequence becomes apparent. Thanks to this understanding of the ECL, the Nordic countries have been in the position for years to find answers to certain challenging questions in copyright by using their ECL model, whereas other countries are prevented from finding proper solutions that are in conformity with their legal traditions. See F. Trumpke (2012), 289-290.

ECL systems may have a future at all.[51] In other words, the suitability of ECL systems within these new online markets might be considerably reduced.

However, within a territorial-based framework combined with reciprocal agreements between national CMOs or by introducing a country of origin or transmission rule[52] ECL systems might continue to work on a national basis. Even within a true borderless copyright environment, an ECL system would be conceivable if it is tailored properly. With regard to a possible unitary European Copyright Code,[53] for instance, an ECL system might operate across borders provided that CMOs working on a pan-European basis are in place. The extension effect could then apply on a pan-European basis.

6 Concluding Remarks

There is not merely a remaining, but rather a growing scope for CRM in the online world.[54] Consequently, greater importance will probably be attached to ECL systems in the future. The Nordic **ECL model** in particular is an effective instrument that facilitates the collective licensing and adequate rewards for all right holders involved. However, ECL systems may only function if certain conditions have been met and if certain safeguards are present.

Given the different structure and intensity of collective right holder organisations in the world, a general (additional) **ECL provision** might be a better choice than forcing the parties into a system they are unaccustomed to. If there is one thing that we could learn from the Nordic **ECL model,** it is the fact that the system needs some time in order to run smoothly. And there is another thing history has shown us in Scandinavia: The Nordic ECL model has proven its flexibility and ability to develop and advance continuously—for more than half a century.

Acknowledgement The author wishes to thank Professor Dr. Kung-Chung Liu and Professor Dr. Reto M. Hilty for inspiration and support as well as Professor Dr. Xiuqin Lin and Professor Dr. Lucie Guibault for their valuable comments.

[51]As far as Europe is concerned this development has also been identified by the European Commission, which clearly strives to facilitate cross-border use of works by promoting transnational or pan-European licensing. See European Commission (2015).

[52]L. Guibault (2015) and (2014); J. Axhamn / L. Guibault (2011), 60. Under a "country of transmission rule" a user would only have to obtain a license from the country where the copyrighted work was made available, since the relevant act would be interpreted as taking place in the country of origin resp. transmission. A similar rule was introduced for satellite distribution in Europe (Article 1 Paragraph 2(b) Council Directive 93/83/EEC of 27 September 1993 on the coordination of certain rules concerning copyright and rights related to copyright applicable to satellite broadcasting and cable retransmission).

[53]See e.g. T. Dreier (2013), 296.

[54]See the chapter by S. Nérisson.

References

Axhamn, J. / Guibault, L. (2011), Cross-border extended collective licensing: a solution to online dissemination of Europe's cultural heritage?, IViR-Study, available at: www.ivir.nl/publicaties/download/292

Christiansen, H. L. (1978), Organisationernes betydning inden for ophavsretten, NIR, 279-291

Dreier, T. (2013), The Wittem Project of a European Copyright Code, in: C. Geiger (Ed.), Constructing European Intellectual Property. Achievements and New Perspectives, Cheltenham, Edward Elgar

European Commission (2011), Commission Staff Working Paper. Impact Assessment on the Cross-border Online Access to Orphan Works, Accompanying the document Proposal for a Directive of the European Parliament and of the Council on certain permitted uses of orphan works, SEC

European Commission (2015), A Digital Single Market Strategy for Europe, COM

Ficsor, M. (2002), Collective Management of Copyright and Related Rights, WIPO

Gervais, D. (2003), Application of an Extended Collective Licensing Regime in Canada: Principles and Issues Related to Implementation, Study Prepared for the Department of Canadian Heritage, Faculty of Law University of Ottawa, available at: works.bepress.com/daniel_gervais/29/

van Gompel, S. (2007), Unlocking the Potential of Pre-Existing Content: How to Address the Issue of Orphan Works in Europe, IIC 2007, 669-702

van Gompel, S. / Hugenholtz, P.B. (2010), The Orphan Works Problem: The Copyright Conundrum of Digitizing Large-Scale Audiovisual Archives, and How to Solve it, IViR-Study, available at: www.ivir.nl/publications/vangompel/the_orphan_works_problem.pdf

Guibault, L. (2014), D5.4: Report on the effectiveness of licensing systems for clearing content for Europeana use, Europeana Awareness, available at: pro.europeana.eu/files/Europeana_Profes sional/Projects/Project_list/Europeana_Awareness/Deliverables/EA%20D5_4%20EAwareness %20ECLcross-border.pdf

Guibault, L. (2015), Cultural Heritage Online? Settle It in the Country of Origin of the Work, JIPITEC 6 (3), 173-191

Hilty, R.M. (2010), Kollektive Rechtewahrnehmung und Vergütungsregelungen: Harmonisierungsbedarf und -möglichkeiten, in: M. Leistner (Ed.), Europäische Perspektiven des Geistigen Eigentums, 123-166, Mohr Siebeck

Hugenholtz, P.B. / van Gompel, S. / Guibault, L. / Obradović, R. (2014), Extended collective licensing: panacee voor massadigitalisering? Onderzoek in opdracht van het Ministerie van OCW, IViR-Study, available at: www.rijksoverheid.nl/binaries/rijksoverheid/documenten/rapporten/2014/09/01/extended-collective-licensing-panacee-voor-massadigitalisering/extended-collective-licensing-panacee-voor-massadigitalisering.pdf

Jiang, Y. (2013), Changing Tides of Collective Licensing in China, Michigan State Int. Law Rev. 2013, 729-750

Karnell, G.W.G. (1985-86), Extended Collective License Clauses and Agreements in Nordic Copyright Law, Columbia J. of Law & the Arts 1985-86, 73-81

Koskinen-Olsson, T. (2010), Collective Management in the Nordic Countries, in: D. Gervais (Ed.), Collective Management of Copyright and Related Rights, 2nd ed., Alphen aan den Rijn, Wolters Kluwer

von Lewinski, S. (2004), Mandatory Collective Administration of Exclusive Rights – A Case Study on its Compatibility with International and EC Copyright Law, e-Copyright Bulletin, UNESCO

Lüder, T. (2010), The "orphan works" challenge, GRUR Int. 2010, 677-685

Nasjonalbiblioteket (National Library of Norway) (2014), Årsrapport, available at: www.nb.no/content/download/11188/105430/file/Årsrapport%202014_nynorsk.pdf

Olsson, H. (2009), Copyright. Svensk och internationell upphovsrätt, 8th ed., Norstedts Juridik

Riis, T. / Schovsbo, J. (2010), Extended Collective Licenses and the Nordic Experience: It's a Hybrid but is it a Volvo or a Lemon?, Columbia J. of Law & the Arts, 471-498

Samuelson, P. (2011), Legislative Alternatives to the Google Book Settlement, Columbia J. of Law & the Arts, 697-729

Takle, M. (2009), The Norwegian National Digital Library, Ariadne, available at: www.ariadne.ac.uk/issue60/takle

Trumpke, F. (2012), The Extended Collective License – A Matter of Exclusivity?, NIR 2012, 264-294

US Copyright Office (2015), Orphan Works and Mass Digitization. A Report of the Register of Copyrights, available at: copyright.gov/orphan/reports/orphan-works2015.pdf

Wang, J. (2010), Should China Adopt an Extended Licensing System to Facilitate Collective Copyright Administration: Preliminary Thoughts, EIPR, 283-289

Wielsch, D. (2011), Die Zugangsregeln der Intermediäre: Prozeduralisierung von Schutzrechten, GRUR, 665-673

Reference Points for and Obligors of Levies in the Online-World: Should ISPs Be Obliged to Pay the Levies for Cloud Services and Private Copying?

Yasuto Komada

Contents

Abstract Private copying as limitation of copyright is well acknowledged in many countries, and some of them (especially European countries) have institutionalized a levy system that makes it possible for rights holders to obtain a certain amount of money as compensation. Then, should Internet service providers (ISPs) also be obliged to pay the levies for the reason that they make it possible for end-users to do private copying in the Cloud? To answer this question, we must know whether and to what extent reproduction taking place in the Cloud are to be regarded as private copying. Some exploratory discussion has already occurred in specialized commissions in France and Japan. But we must take note that the levy itself is now faced with challenges that make us reconsider thoroughly the rationale of the system.

Yasuto Komada is Professor at the Faculty of Law and Chairperson of Department of International Legal Studies at Sophia University.

Y. Komada (✉)
Sophia University, Tokyo, Japan
e-mail: komada-y@sphia.ac.jp

K.-C. Liu, R.M. Hilty (eds.), *Remuneration of Copyright Owners*, MPI Studies on Intellectual Property and Competition Law 27, DOI 10.1007/978-3-662-53809-8_6

1 Introduction

Should levies be assessed on ISP to build a sensible mechanism for paying for copyright? The term "levy system" is used in academia to mean generally a quasi-tax system (but not a tax in the strict sense) for private copying. The collective society of rights holders receives levies from manufacturers and importers (or retailers) of media or machines whose main function is to make it possible for consumers to do private copying. Therefore, the levies are charged on the prices of those products, and are ultimately born by consumers, who are presumed to be undertakers of that act.

The characteristics of the levy system are as follows:

(a) Levies are paid for private copying that enjoys the status of copyright limitation. What is paid for any commercial exploitation that the rights holders would have been able to forbid is not levy.
(b) The levy system is a government-mandated scheme. Neither negotiation nor any agreement is made between rights holders and consumers. The tariff is set by copyright-related law, Cabinet order, or regulations. Normally the amount of the levy varies according to the sort of media or machines concerned. The collective society receives the levies not directly from consumers but from the manufacturers and importers (or the retailers) of the media and machines in question.

The next question follows immediately: Does private copying take place in the online world? Of course, the terminals of the network (consumers' PCs, tablet computers or mobile phones etc.) must be the place where private copying (downloading) happens very frequently. Therefore the legal questions in the light of the above-mentioned theme must be as follows: Does private copying that justifies the passing of the burden of levies onto ISPs take place in the online world? If it does, to what extent?

These are very difficult questions. As is generally known, reproductions of copyrighted works occur very often in the course of services undertaken by ISPs, and some of them occur when end-users (consumers) take the opportunity to enjoy the services that make it possible to store and access data and programs over scattered devices all connected to the Internet. Recently, we very often call those services "Cloud services". If they are the reproductions whose undertakers are ISPs, they must be regarded as commercial exploitations, and have nothing to do with the levy system. If however they are the reproductions whose undertakers are end-users and made for their personal use, they can be regarded as private copying, and passing the burden of levies on to the ISP might be justified. But we must take note that national laws might require that additional conditions be fulfilled in order to apply private copying regime.

2 Does Private Copying Take Place in the Cloud, and to What Extent?

Let us have a look at some results of exploratory discussions that aim at influencing governmental policies.

2.1 *CSPLA Commission's Report*

First is the report submitted by the French Cloud computing special commission set up by the High Council for Literary and Artistic Property (*Conseil supérieur de la propriété littéraire et artistique*, hereinafter as "CSPLA").[1] The French Minister of Culture and Communication received this report on October 23, 2012.

The commission surveyed existing Cloud services by identifying the following three major service categories:

(1) Services known as "personal locker" intended to store contents that have already been held by the user and access to this content and its reproduction on a wide range of devices (e.g. Dropbox, OVH);

(2) Services involved in a legal downloading service, allowing the user, once the content has been acquired on the download platform, to play it, separately or simultaneously, on a wide variety of devices. Such services might be described as synchronization services associated with a sales service (e.g. iTunes in the Cloud, Google Play);

(3) Scan and match services allowing consumers that already have a copy of a copyrighted work, on the one hand, to access a replacement file (which is generally a better quality version than the file held and is accompanied by complete metadata) made available by the service provider and, on the other hand, to be able to make copies of this match on a wide variety of devices (e.g. iTunes Match).[2]

The question is, as mentioned above, which service is the one that falls into the realm of the exclusive right, or which service is the one that offers only the means of private copying that is exempted from that right? Interestingly enough, the commission could not reach a consensus on the legal status of all these categories, which shows the tremendous difficulty of resolving the question.

2.1.1 Synchronization Service

In the second category of service (iTunes in the Cloud type), two functional features of synchronization are to be found. One is the feature that allows a consumer to obtain a copy of the content on several connected terminals automatically and simultaneously with the purchase of that content. The other is the feature that allows a consumer to re-download from the Cloud a copy of the content that he or she purchased.

The report shows that some members of the commission think that the effect of the above-mentioned synchronizations is totally identical with cable-related

[1]The CSPLA is an independent advisory board, in charge of advising the Minister of Culture and Communication on matters concerning literary and artistic property. The CSPLA published a French version (full text and summary) and an English version (summary) of this report.

[2]CSPLA Commission's summary report (English), 2. See also, CSPLA Commission's report (French), 7-9.

synchronization, so that, thanks to the principle of technological neutrality, the private copying limitation should apply to both.[3]

The report also shows that some other members think that these synchronizations should be governed by the exclusive right. They say that in both synchronizations, the undertakers of making the copies should be regarded as ISPs, because they are the ones who materially reproduce copyrighted works, even though the persons who decide to take the opportunity to synchronize and enjoy the copies are the end-users. They also point out that the private copying regime cannot apply when the copier and the user of the copy are different.[4]

According to the report, there is a 3rd group of members suggesting that it is not provided for in French law explicitly that the copier in the material sense and the user must be the same person in order to apply the private copying regime. They think that if a reproduction is made commercially, such an act should be governed by the exclusive right, but it does not prevent the copy from being made for (the user's) personal use and subject to the private copying regime. In this regard, they distinguish the copy made in the provider's database from the copy made on the user's terminal (namely, on the end of the network), and think that only the latter can fall under the private copying regime.[5]

In this context, the report invokes a judgment by the Court of Justice of the European Union (CJEU), the *Padawan* case,[6] which ruled that "the activity of the person liable to finance the fair compensation, namely the making available to private users of reproduction equipment, devices and media, or their supply of copying services is the factual precondition for natural persons to obtain private copies". So, according to this judgment, the lack of identity between copier and beneficiary of the copy should no longer be an obstacle to applying the private copying regime, any more than the commercial nature of the actual reproduction.[7]

2.1.2 Personal Locker Service

As regards the first category of service (personal locker), the report confirms that it is similar to any service seen in the second category of service (storage, access and release of reproductions by ISP at the consumer's request, and the difference lies in

[3]CSPLA Commission's report (French), 14; CSPLA Commission's summary report (English), 4.

[4]CSPLA Commission's report (French), 15; CSPLA Commission's summary report (English), 4.

[5]CSPLA Commission's report (French), 16; CSPLA Commission's summary report (English), 4. The report calls this way of thinking "approche duale (dual approach)".

[6]CJEU (3rd Chamber), October 21, 2010, C-467/08.

[7]CSPLA Commission's report (French), 17; CSPLA Commission's summary report (English), 4-5.

the fact that the service is not supported by the sale of the content), and the reflections made for that category are to be applied.[8]

In addition, the report makes some remarks on the possibility of ISPs claiming the special liability regime for hosting providers. As is well known, hosting providers, defined as operators who have neither knowledge nor control over the information transmitted or stored in their space, can be exempted from civil and penal liabilities for illicit use of contents hosted if their activity is purely technical, automatic and passive.[9] The report shows two incompatible ways of thinking. On the one hand, it would be odd to regard the personal locker service provider which stores contents and only makes them available to a single person as a hosting provider.[10] On the other hand, there would be a paradox in recognizing the hosting provider status for service providers "that operate more sophisticated services, where contents are made available to the public, and not when these contents are only made available to a single person for her private use."[11] Here again the commission could not reach a consensus.

2.1.3 Scan and Match Service

As regards the last category of service (iTunes Match type), the report gives an observation that there is no guarantee of absolute identity between the matched file and the equivalent file made available by the provider. The latter may have better quality and be accompanied by complete metadata. So the report does not hesitate to conclude that the reproduction of a matched file taking place in the Cloud should not be regarded as private copying.

But, concerning the non-matched file, the copy is destined to be stored in a personal space in the Cloud, from which it could further be copied to feed different user terminals. Therefore, the identity between the original file and the copy is guaranteed at this stage, and some members do not exclude the application of the private copying limitation to the copy first made in the Cloud.[12]

---

[8]CSPLA Commission's report (French), 19; CSPLA Commission's summary report (English), 5. The report shows that some members think that the server-computers are managed by ISPs and the copy made in the course of this service is kept under the ISPs' control, which means that the application of the private copying limitation may be excluded under the traditional interpretation of the French law.

[9]Cf. Article 14 (1) of E-Commerce Directive (2000/31/EC), OJ L 178/1; CJEU (Grand Chamber), March 23, 2010, C-236/08 to C-238/08 (AdWords cases); CJEU (Grand Chamber), July 12, 2011, C-324/09 (eBay case). In this context, it should be reminded that the regime does not say anything about the infringement arising from illicit use of contents that the provider hosts, and cannot take the injunction relief away from rights holders whenever the infringement takes place on the service.

[10]CSPLA Commission's report (French), 20-21; CSPLA Commission's summary report (English), 5.

[11]CSPLA Commission's report (French), 21; CSPLA Commission's summary report (English), 5.

[12]CSPLA Commission's report (French), 22; CSPLA Commission's summary report (English), 6.

The report adds that a consensus was found within the commission to consider that if there is an illicit file at the starting point, the subsequent operations in the Cloud shall be illegal.[13]

2.2 CSPLA Opinions

On the same day that the commission's report was submitted, CSPLA adopted several opinions ("*avis*") by making reference to the report.

One of the opinions is that, as regards scan and match services, reproductions of a matched file with better quality are subject to the exclusive right.[14]

As regards personal locker services, CSPLA says that the service providers may enjoy the hosting provider status, and rights holders may not exercise their exclusive rights against them. It adds that the private copying limitation shall apply not only to this type of services but also to the synchronization services, the effect of which is totally identical to cable-related synchronization on the condition that the source of the copy is legal, and the use of it is strictly personal and compatible with the Three-step Test.[15][16]

2.3 JACA Commission's Report

Next I would like to focus on the report submitted by the Japanese Cloud computing special commission set up by the Japanese Agency for Cultural Affairs (hereinafter "JACA").[17] The report was published in February 2015.

It mainly examines the question of legal status of locker services. But it classifies the services into four types according to two axes (personal / common, distribution by the provider / uploading by the end-user).[18] They are as follows:

---

[13]CSPLA Commission's report (French), 22-23; CSPLA Commission's summary report (English), 6. As regards synchronization services, the source of the copy is always legal. The writer of the report considers this to be a big difference from scan and match services.

[14]CSPLA opinions, no. 6.

[15]CSPLA opinions, nos. 7 and 8. The test is provided for in plural international conventions (Berne Convention, Article 9 (2); TRIPs, Article 13; WCT, Article 10; WPPT, Article 16 (2); Beijing Treaty on Audiovisual Performances, Article 13 (2)) and Information Society Directive (2001/29/EC), Article 5 (5).

[16]CSPLA suggests the application of the levy system, but also introduces the objections made by cinematographic and audiovisual producers. See CSPLA opinions, nos. 9 and 10.

[17]The JACA is a special body of the Japanese Ministry of Education. It was set up in 1968 to promote Japanese arts and culture.

[18]JACA Commission's report, 7-8.

Type 1: Personal locker service in which each end-user has his or her personal space in the Cloud, and the provider makes contents available for the end-user (personal / distribution type)
Type 2: Personal locker service in which each end-user has his or her personal space in the Cloud, and the end-user must upload contents on the space (personal / uploading type)
Type 3: Locker service in which plural end-users can access a certain space in the Cloud and enjoy contents made available by the provider (common / distribution type)
Type 4: Locker service in which plural end-users can access a certain space in the Cloud and enjoy contents uploaded by any of the end-users (common / uploading type)

	Distribution by the provider	Uploading by the user
Personal	Type 1	Type 2
Common	Type 3	Type 4

The report explains that the above-mentioned iTunes Match type (scan and match service) should be qualified as Type 1 or Type 2 according to the sort of the relevant file. As far as matched files are concerned, the service should be regarded as Type 1. As far as non-matched files are concerned, the service should be regarded as Type 2.

2.3.1 Type 1 and Type 3

It is not difficult at all to say that, concerning Type 3, the undertaker of the reproduction and the transmission (communication) of contents taking place in the Cloud is the provider. Concerning Type 1, the provider should be regarded as the actor of those acts indeed, but the provider makes contents available by partitioning off the service into every single end-user. In this regard, Prof. Okumura, a member of the commission, invokes the recent Supreme Court case[19] in his article.[20] It held that even a single user can be the "public" when the provider is ready to make a contract with any user and thanks to the contract the user can enjoy the service.

In these services (Type 1 and Type 3), the current situation is that the providers are conducting their business by concluding license contracts with rights holders. In the light of this practice, the report points out that no legislation is necessary for them.[21]

[19]Supreme Court of Japan, January 18, 2012, Saikôsaibansho Minjihanreishû, Vol. 65, No. 1, 121.
[20]H. Okumura (2015), 25.
[21]JACA Commission's report, 9.

2.3.2 Type 4

Concerning Type 4 service, the report does not hesitate to conclude that the reproduction and the transmission of contents taking place in the Cloud constitute infringements of the exclusive rights. But who is the undertaker of these exploitations? The report seems to take the opinion that in most cases the undertaker is the end-user who uploaded the content.[22] And it adds that in the commission there was an opinion according to which the provider may enjoy the status of hosting service provider and be exempted from any liability for damage.[23]

2.3.3 Type 2

Type 2 service causes the biggest controversy. The report reveals that, in the commission, rights holders insisted that the undertaker of reproductions and transmissions of contents taking place in the Cloud is the provider, while the experts insisted that, in most cases, the undertaker is the end-user.[24] The report takes the latter opinion as its conclusion. It also makes clear that the existing private copying limitation in Japanese Copyright Act may cover the Type 2 service, so that no license contract is necessary for conducting such kind of business.[25]

Interestingly enough, concerning scan and match services, the CSPLA Commission's report pays attention to the possible difference in quality between the matched file and the equivalent file, while the JACA Commission's report emphasizes the fact that the provider makes the equivalent files available for every user. However, it should be pointed out that these different views come from the same fact (the provider owns the database of the equivalent files).

3 Should ISPs Be Obliged to Pay the Levies?

According to the discussions introduced in the previous sections, it may be said that not all but some reproductions taking place in the Cloud could be regarded as private copying.

Suppose that such reproductions are to be covered by the levy system. Should ISPs be obliged to pay the levies?

The levy system has been, in many countries' laws, the one whereby the collective society receives the levies from manufacturers and importers

---

[22]According to the report, the current situation is that certain providers actually make contracts with rights holders on behalf of the end-users.

[23]JACA Commission's report, 10.

[24]JACA Commission's report, 13-14.

[25]JACA Commission's report, 15.

(or retailers) of the media or the machines concerned. In the context of Cloud services, the server-computer seems to correspond to the machine concerned. Then, applying the same formula, the manufacturers thereof (rather than ISPs) appear to be obliged to pay the levies.

But it seems very strange to me that the burden of the levies would be passed on the manufacturers while the server-computers (unlike DVD recorders or printers) would not be purchased by consumers, which means that the levies would not be born ultimately by end-users. I think that the position of ISPs is very close to that of the persons who supply consumers with the copying services, and CJEU repeatedly concluded in its judgments that such persons as well as manufacturers (plus importers) may be obliged to pay the levies.[26] This conclusion of the CJEU is justifiable because the levies can be charged on the prices of the services and are ultimately born by consumers doing private copying.

Therefore, starting from the baseline set by the CJEU's remark, it would not be difficult to say that ISPs should be involved in the levy system, for they are supplying end-users with the private copying services taking place in the Cloud.

Indeed, in the case where only the copy made on the end-user's terminal can be subject to the private copying regime and the copy made in the ISP's database can fall into the realm of the exclusive right (see Sect. 2.1.1), the burden of the levies should be passed on not to the ISP but to the manufacturer of the terminal. ISPs should be obliged to pay the levies so long as the relevant copy made in the Cloud can be subject to the private copying regime.

And realizing such a system seems to be promising, especially in some EU member states that are very active in enhancing the existing levy system. But in other countries, especially outside the EU, realizing such a system would not be easy because there are still many countries that do not have the levy system at all; even in some countries having the levy system, the system itself is now faced with challenges.

4 Challenges to the Levy System

In Germany and France, receiving the levies is often qualified as one of the forms of exercise of intellectual property, and the levies are qualified as "royalties" (*Vergütung* in German and *rémunération* in French). Under this theory, mechanical private copying should in principle be regarded as an exploitation that cannot be

[26]This remark was originally issued in the Padawan case (*supra* note 6) and quoted repeatedly in the Stichting case (CJEU, 16 June 2011, Case C-462/09), VG Wort cases (CJEU, 27 June 2013, C-457/11 to C-460/11), Amazon case (CJEU, 11 July 2013, C-521/11) and Copydan Båndkopi case (CJEU, 5 March 2015, C-463/12).

done legally without a license.[27] Of course, it is unrealistic for rights holders to negotiate with end-users individually for such private copying, therefore it is thought that the Government must intervene in this legal relationship and the license must be constructive. In this context, the levy system can be regarded as one of the regimes of statutory license.[28]

Besides the above-mentioned "license theory", there is another theory according to which the levy system is needed as long as end-users' mechanical private copying brings certain negative effect to rights holders' market (sale loss). In other words, the levy system cannot be justified without a certain economic harm caused by such end-users' activities to rights holders. This "reparation theory" is concordant with the idea that the levy system stems from the last step of the Three-Step Test, namely, the idea that the levy should be paid when the private copying limitation prejudices unreasonably the legitimate interests of rights holders.[29]

But we have seen some empirical studies showing that even private copying from illegal sources has had no causal relationship with the decline of the sale of genuine contents.[30] The conclusion is shocking or embarrassing for the rights holders thinking that piratical activities such as file sharing surely reduce their market. Even the CJEU observed in a recent judgment that "to accept that such reproductions may be made from an unlawful source would encourage the circulation of counterfeited or pirated works, thus inevitably reducing the volume of sales or of other lawful transactions relating to the protected works".[31] But, the question here can be simplified as follows: do they (end-users) buy genuine contents if they cannot do private copying anymore? Though still contested, I have the impression that major opinion of economists in this field is relatively against the supposition that private copying has a definitive effect on the decline of the sale of copyrighted works. Another empirical study shows that, as regards certain products, the levies

[27]The Supreme Court of Germany once took the view that mechanical private copying infringes the author's exclusive right. BGH, 18 Mai 1955, BGHZ 17, 266; BGH, 29 Mai 1964, BGHZ 41, 393 (GEMA cases). The last case led the way to the levy system.

[28]Cf. M.M. Walter / S. von Lewinski (2010), 11.5.25. "Indeed, the concept of 'harm' is alien to the tradition of Continental European Member States, which provide for remuneration rights as a counterpart for the use being made, irrespective of whether this use has caused any harm to the right holders". See also A.E. Pardo / A. Lucas-Schloetter (2013), 466. "In (continental European) countries, it is assumed that the compensation system may provide for a lump sum, independent of any proof of prejudice, the only criterion being that of knowing the extent to which protected works are subject to reproduction for private use".

[29]As regards the relationship between the levy system and the last step of the Three-Step Test, see M.R.F. Senftleben (2004), 238. Senftleben examines the license theory and concludes that the theory "hardly portrays reality."

[30]The paper by Oberholzer-Gee and Koleman analyzes whether file sharing has reduced the legal sales of music and shows that their estimates are inconsistent with claims that file sharing is the primary reason for the decline in music sales during their study period. See F. Oberholzer-Gee / S. Koleman (2007), 1-42. The paper by Waldfogel makes almost the same observation. See J. Waldfogel (2012), 91-109. In the field of animation cartoon, T. Tanaka (2011).

[31]CJEU (Fourth Chamber), April 10, 2014, C-435/12 (ACI Adam), para. 39.

are almost absorbed by the manufacturers of devices and not ultimately born by consumers, which makes us wonder whether the system is still concordant with the premise that the debtor of the levy is the natural person doing private copying.[32]

We should also take note that these days more and more rights holders make contracts for private copying with end-users (not individually but collectively) through the Internet, and utilize technological protection measures (TPM) to restrict the freedom of private copying within the proper range. Accepting the idea that the legal nature of the levy system is a statutory license, the system should not apply so long as rights holders can give the permission to make private copies and this "contract and TPM model" functions, so that the unjustified double payment would be prevented.

The US seems to be the country in which rights holders have resorted to this contract and TPM model since they failed to impose the levies on a portable MP3 player in the famous "Rio" case.[33] Also in Japan there has been a big controversy about whether and to what extent the levy system is still needed when a contract and TPM model has emerged, and its use is on the rise. In these two countries, the levy system has come to a deadlock because levies are assessed only on the media and machines that are old fashioned and have nothing to do with the online-world.[34]

By the way, the CJEU adopts the reparation theory under EU law. Article 5 (2) (b) of the Information Society Directive (2001/29/EC) permits member states to introduce the private copying limitation into their national laws on the condition that rights holders receive "fair compensation". Recital 35 of the directive states that "a valuable criterion would be the possible harm to the right holders resulting from the act in question" and "[in] certain situations where the prejudice to the right holder would be minimal, no obligation for payment may arise". Citing this Recital, the CJEU repeatedly stressed that fair compensation is linked to the economic harm

---

[32]According to the empirical case study made by Kretschmer commissioned by the UK Intellectual Property Office, the costs of levies are not always passed on to consumers: In a competitive market (e.g. the market of printers), manufacturers appear to absorb the levy (M. Kretschmer (2011), 15-17, 57). The report also tells that, in non-levy countries (including the UK), certain forms of private copying are already priced into retail purchases (*id.*, 19). The report conceives of introducing the private copying limitation for the forms of "priced into purchases (no lost sale)" into UK copyright law as maintaining the status quo and introducing the limitation for other forms as creating statutory license. However such a distinction is misleading, because whether a valid license is issued or not does not depend on the harm which would arise if no license were granted.

[33]Recording Industry Association of America (RIAA) v. Diamond Multimedia Systems Inc., 9th Cir. 1999 (51 U. S. P. Q. 2d, 180 F. 3d 1072). RIAA brought suit to enjoin the manufacture and distribution of the Rio (a portable MP3 player), alleging that the Rio does not meet the requirements for digital audio recording devices under the Audio Home Recording Act of 1992, 17 U. S. C. § 1001 et, because it does not employ a Serial Copyright Management System (SCMS). RIAA also sought payment of the levies owed by Diamond as the manufacturer and the distributor of a digital audio recording device.

[34]For the current status of the levy system in the US and Japan, see WIPO (2013), 83-91, 145-147.

caused to rights holders due to the private copying limitation.[35] But the court has not yet clarified the way to measure the harm,[36] so this notion still remains uncertain, and not a few authors criticize the judgments in this regard.[37] At least we may assume that, for the CJEU, contract and TPM cannot substitute for the levy in principle. The CJEU held that:

> [T]he technological measures that rights holders have the possibility of using should be understood as technologies, devices or components which are capable of ensuring that the objective pursued by the private copying exception is achieved or capable of preventing or limiting reproductions which are not authorized by the Member States within the framework of that exception.[38]
>
> Having regard to the voluntary nature of those technological measures, even where such a possibility exists, the non-application of those measures cannot have the effect that no fair compensation is due.[39]
>
> [W]here a Member State has decided, pursuant to a provision in Article 5(2) and (3) of Directive 2001/29, to exclude, from the material scope of that provision, any right for the rightholders to authorise reproduction of their protected works or other subject-matter, any authorising act the rightholders may adopt is devoid of legal effects under the law of that State. Consequently, such an act has no effect on the harm caused to the rightholders due to the introduction of the relevant measure depriving them of that right, and cannot therefore have any bearing on the fair compensation owed, whether it is provided for on a compulsory or an optional basis, under the relevant provision of that directive.[40]

Therefore, under EU case law, it is very difficult to establish that certain private copying causes no harm or no more than minimal harm to rights holders and that the levy system is not necessary. Perhaps this difficulty also comes from the fact that Recital 35 of the Information Society Directive uses the words "possible" harm.[41]

---

[35]This observation appeared first in the Padawan case (*supra* note 6) and is repeatedly used in the relevant CEJU judgments.

[36]Antonio Vitorino, former European Commissioner for Justice and Home Affairs, believes that, in order to achieve coherence in the levy system, it is necessary to define "harm" uniformly across the EU. See A. Vitorino (2013), 20. In this context, his remarks in "Recommendations resulting from mediation process on private copying and reprography levies" focus on the lost income opportunities via the license agreements that rights holders and consumers would have concluded if there were no private copying limitation. But Poort and Quintais criticize very adequately that Vitorino's definition of "harm" conflates the concepts of lost profit and lost licensing opportunities and ignores the fact that the harm arises not from one single copy but from a number of natural persons' activities. See J. Poort / J.P. Quintais (2015), 205.

[37]For example, M. Kretschmer (2011), 13-14; A.E. Pardo / A. Lucas-Schloetter (2013), 466; S. Karapapa (2012), 124.

[38]VG Wort case (*supra* note 26), para. 56.

[39]VG Wort case (*supra* note 26), para. 57. The equivalent ruling can be found in Båndkopi case (*supra* note 26), para. 71.

[40]VG Wort case (*supra* note 26), para. 37. The equivalent ruling can be found in Båndkopi case (*supra* note 26), para. 65.

[41]Cf. A.E. Pardo / A.E. Lucas-Schloetter (2013), 467. "...the Court of Justice in practice does not require right holders to give proof of their loss. In fact, it estimates that possible harm is sufficient and gives rise to a lump sum assessment".

Recently the UK introduced private copying limitation having very narrow scope in its copyright law with no levy system,[42] but the High Court quashed the relevant regulations, ruling that there is insufficient evidence that harm to rights holders would be no more than minimal.[43]

Thus the notion of "fair compensation" in EU law might have become very close to that of a "tax" that can be imposed irrespective of the harm or the contracts.

5 Conclusion

Which reproduction taking place in the Cloud can be regarded as private copying?

It seems to me that some of it should be qualified as private copying. Otherwise the prosperous future of Cloud services will be shaded by the force of the exclusive right.

My opinion is that, starting from the baseline set by the CJEU, it is possible and just to oblige ISPs to pay the levies, as they are the ones who supply end-users with private copying services in the Cloud.

But I think that empirical research is warranted in order to know to what extent the contract and TPM model functions in the digital environment including the Cloud. As long as this model functions, the levy as the reparation or the consequence of the constructive license (statutory license) is theoretically not necessary, despite what the CJEU has said.[44] There is no doubt that rights holders have the incentive to develop a contract and TPM model, for they can flexibly adjust the model to various conditions and forms of private copying. In contrast, the levy system cannot but remain "rough justice".[45] We should go back and reconsider the rationale of the levy system and find the right timing to let rights holders and end-users solve the question of payment by themselves.

---

[42]The Copyright and Rights in Performance (Personal Copies for Private Use) Regulations 2014 provide an exception limited to the personal use and to the owners of a personal copy, available at: www.legislation.gov.uk/ukdsi/2014/9780111116036/regulation/3.

[43]The decision of 19 June, 2015 (CO/5444/2014), available at: www.bailii.org/ew/cases/EWHC/Admin/2015/1723.html.

[44]M.M. Walter / S. von Lewinski (2010), 11.5.25 refers to the case where TPMs are used and allow the rights holder to receive remuneration directly from the user in exchange for removing the TPM and allowing use, and concludes that in that case, "additional statutory remuneration would amount to a double remuneration".

[45]C. Karapapa (2012), 128. "The fact that it is only the possibility of harm that should be taken into account...means that fair compensation can be seen as imposing a form of rough justice".

References

CSPLA Publications (2012), available at: www.culturecommunication.gouv.fr/Politiques-ministerielles/Propriete-litteraire-et-artistique/Conseil-superieur-de-la-propriete-litteraire-et-artistique/Travaux/Commissions-specialisees/Commission-du-CSPLA-relative-au-cloud-computing-informatique-en-nuage

CSPLA Commission's summary report (English), Cloud Computing specialized commission Report summary

CSPLA Commission's report (French), Rapport de la commission spécialisée 'Informatique dans les nuages'

CSPLA opinions, Avis

JACA Commission's report, Kraudo Sâbisu to Chosakuken ni kansuru Hôkokusho [Report on Copyright, Cloud and Other Services] (2015), available at: www.bunka.go.jp/seisaku/bunkashingikai/chosakuken/hogoriyo/h26_10/pdf/shiryo_1.pdf

Karapapa, S. (2012), Private Copying, Routledge

Kretschmer, M. (2011), Private Copying and Fair Compensation: An empirical study of copyright levies in Europe 2011, available at: www.gov.uk/government/uploads/system/uploads/attachment_data/file/310183/ipresearch-faircomp-201110.pdf

Oberholzer-Gee, F. / Koleman, S. (2007), The Effect of File Sharing on Record Sales: An Empirical Analysis, Journal of Political Economy, Vol. 115, No. 1, 1-42

Okumura, H. (2015), Kraudo Sâbisu to Chosakuken [Cloud Services and Copyright], Law and Technology, No. 68, 25-33

Pardo, A.E. / Lucas-Schloetter, A. (2013), Compensation for Private Copying in Europe: Recent Developments in France, Germany and Spain, E. I. P. R., 463-471

Poort, J. / Quintais, J.P. (2013), The Levy Runs Dry: A Legal and Economic Analysis of EU Private Copying Levies, JIPITEC, No. 3, 205-224

Senftleben, M.R.F. (2004), Copyright, Limitations and the Three-step Test: An analysis of the Three-step Test in International and EC Copyright Law, Kluwer Law International

Tanaka, T. (2011), Nettojô no Chosakukenhogokyôka ha Hitsuyôka – Animedôgahaishin wo Sozai toshite [Is More Protection of Copyright Necessary on Internet? A Case Study of Video Streaming of Animation Cartoons], RIETI, 1-28, available at: www.rieti.go.jp/jp/publications/dp/11j010.pdf

Vitorino, A. (2013), Recommendations resulting from mediation process on private copying and reprography levies 2013, available at: ec.europa.eu/internal_market/copyright/docs/levy_reform/130131_levies-vitorino-recommendations_en.pdf

Waldfogel, J. (2012), Music Piracy and Its Effects on Demand, Supply, and Welfare, Innovation Policy and the Economy, Vol. 12, 91-109

Walter, M.M. / von Lewinski, S. (2010), European Copyright Law: A Commentary, Oxford University Press

WIPO (2013), International Survey on Private Copying: Law & Practice 2013, available at: www.wipo.int/edocs/pubdocs/en/copyright/1037/wipo_pub_1037_2013.pdf

Mechanisms to Make End-Users of Copyrighted Works Pay Through Levy and DRM

Raman Mittal

Contents

Abstract In order to compensate the copyright owners for use of their works by end-users, a levy system has been implemented in various countries which seeks to tax certain copying equipment and operators. The same system has been proposed for cloud storage and Internet services. The levy system tries to balance the social

---

Raman Mittal is Associate Professor at the Faculty of Law of the University of Delhi.

R. Mittal (✉)
University of Delhi, New Delhi, India
e-mail: mittalraman@gmail.com

K.-C. Liu, R.M. Hilty (eds.), *Remuneration of Copyright Owners*, MPI Studies on Intellectual Property and Competition Law 27, DOI 10.1007/978-3-662-53809-8_7

norms of file sharing with the legal norm of copyright enforcement. The licensing mechanisms that could be used to give effect to the levy systems are built on the model whereby the owner forsakes some of his rights in order to gain fair remuneration. For the levy system to play a more meaningful role in the future, it has to be made more uniform and widespread in its application. Together with the levy system, various managerial goals and tools also aim at ensuring payment to rights owners by regaining and retaining control over copyrighted works in the digital environment. For the convenience of end-users, a single window service and a single fee license could be experimented with. Digital Rights Management (DRM), which mostly relies on technological protection measures, rights management information and electronic documentation to implement the controls and restrictions necessary for the overall management of digital works, has become a major mechanism for exploitation. While both DRM and a levy system aim at the same objective of ensuring payment to rights owners, the mechanisms to achieve the objective are different. If levies and DRM are implemented together, there is a danger that the user ends up paying twice for the same work. Therefore, DRM and levies can co-exist only when the practice of DRM has been taken into account when the levies are being set up.

1 Introduction

The possibility of consuming copyrighted works in privacy together with the promises of digital technology have led to a loss of control over the use of works by their owners. This loss of control is, in part, an outcome of failure to track and monitor the works, which results in usage of works without any compensation to the rights owners. In search of fair remuneration to the rights owners, this chapter focuses on the analysis of two sets of mechanisms. The first set can be used to ensure fair remuneration to the rights owners where it is not possible to exactly track and monitor the use of works by end-users. The second set can be adopted to track and monitor the use of works by end-users so as to regain and retain the control over works.

Accordingly, Sect. 2 of the chapter analyzes the levy system as it has been implemented, and examines the online situations where this system can be extended. Section 3 further explores various licensing mechanisms together with their jurisprudential requirements to implement the levy system. Section 4 examines managerial goals and various technical and legal mechanisms through which the use of digital works could be tracked so that payment for such use could be obtained from end-users. Section 5 highlights the reconciliation between the levy system and DRM in the implementation of these mechanisms before concluding with Sect. 6.

2 The Levy System

A 'copyright levy' is a form of indirect compensation made to the owners of copyright in order to recompense them for the harm caused by use of their works by third parties. Copyright levies are similar to taxes; the difference being that taxes are received by a government, while levies are received mostly by a private body, such as a collective management organization (CMO). The levy system is founded on the following three postulations:

1. the use of certain copyrighted works and/or their distribution cannot be tracked, monitored or controlled in certain cases;
2. there is a need to compensate rights owners for a supposed loss as a result of such use and/or distribution;
3. the default copyright licensing systems are not workable in such cases.

The application of these postulates could result in a levy system being adopted in the following four situations. In the first two, the levy system has already been adopted in many countries around the world and is being examined in some others; while in the last two, the levy system has only been proposed, without being experimented with.

2.1 Equipment Levy

Reproduction for private use is a special case under copyright law where practices differ amongst countries quite noticeably. In many countries, private copying is not permitted by law, or is permitted only to a limited extent by way of fair use exceptions. In such cases, in order to legally indulge in private copying beyond the permitted limits, a user would have to rely on some sort of voluntary licensing arrangement with the rights owners. On the other hand, the countries implementing the levy system are those countries where copying for private use is permitted by law, and compensation to the copyright owners is sought through a system of equitable remuneration or fair compensation by imposing levies.

Although all copyrighted works could be subject to private copying, the levy system has developed mainly in the music, audiovisual and publishing industries because there the impact of private copying is realized the most. Consequently, a copyright levy is imposed on the following two types of equipment:

- Copying equipment such as photocopiers, fax machines, reader printers, scanners, multifunctional devices, CD, DVD and Blue-Ray burners, MP3 players, mobile phones, tablets, etc.

- Copying media such as CDs, DVDs, Blue-Rays, memory sticks, external hard drives, photocopy paper,[1] etc.

In *Nokia* v. *CopydanBandkopi*,[2] Copydan, a Danish collecting society, demanded payment of levies from Nokia Denmark A/S for detachable memory cards as contained in some of Nokia's mobile phones. Those 'multifunctional' memory cards allowed users to store copyrighted works such as music and video files, as well as other non-copyrighted data. Nokia disputed its liability for payment of copyright levies. The Court of Justice of the European Union (CJEU) took the view that, in principle, it is irrelevant whether a medium is uni-or multi-functional. Copyright levies may be imposed, if at least one function allows for private copying, even if this function is of ancillary nature. However, the primary function of the carrier is to be taken into account whilst assessing what might be fair compensation. The CJEU stated that countries may further distinguish between storage media which are detachable and media which are non-detachably integrated in a device.

The equipment and media subject to levy and the rates of levy often differ significantly from country to country. These rates are determined either by national legislators, governments, courts or specialized bodies appointed by the government. In some countries the determination of levies is done after consulting stakeholders such as CMOs, the IT industry, consumers, etc. Remuneration by means of levies is indirect, as it is imposed on manufacturers, importers or distributors of equipment or media that allow consumers to copy. Ultimately the levy is included in the final purchase price of the equipment or media to be paid by the consumer. Manufacturers, importers and distributors of such equipment or media are liable for paying the levies to the CMO, which then is tasked with the distribution of collected revenue amongst the rights owners.

2.2 Operator Levy

Under the system of operator levy, all persons copying copyrighted works on a machine under the supervision or control of operators of such a machine are made to pay a levy proportional to the number of copies made of the copyrighted works. Such persons could be natural or legal and would include copy shops, schools, universities, libraries, government institutions, research institutions, business enterprises, etc. which usually make a large number of photocopies or require such photocopying by persons who are associated with them within the ambit of their work. The levy to be paid by such persons depends on the number of copies made by them, which is estimated statistically based on their volume and the nature of the

[1]Levy is imposed on photocopy paper in Greece, Nigeria and Poland in principle, but the system is not operational as yet.

[2]Nokia *v*. CopydanBandkopi (C-463/12) CJEU.

work. In some countries, an operator levy is applied cumulatively with an equipment levy, and in others only an operator levy is applied.[3] Within operator levies, there is variation about which operators should pay the levy.[4] In many ways, an operator levy resembles the 'site license' of voluntary licensing systems.

2.3 Levy System Vis-à-Vis Cloud Computing Services

In cloud computing content is stored in a centralized database accessible to consumers whenever and wherever they need it on a range of devices, and consumers can switch to whichever device is best suitable for them at a particular point of time. The use of cloud services in the music industry has already started to take off.[5] In countries where the levy system is in place, demands have been made to introduce the levy for cloud storage as well, because it shares many of the same characteristics as the electronic devices and hardware to which the traditional levy system does apply.[6] In 2014, the European Commission consulted on the imposition of private copying levies on cloud services.[7]

A cloud-based service could possibly translate into three different kinds of services to the consumers, i.e. streaming service, download service and private lockers. The attributes of these are explained below.

2.3.1 Streaming Service

In cloud-based streaming services, copyright-protected content is delivered to the consumer on-demand. Streaming services make it possible to measure authorized uses of creative content for precise, license-based remuneration to rights owners. In this case there is no right to private copying, and therefore no necessity to automatically extend exceptions to copyright for private copying.[8] For example, some cloud storage services that allow users to synchronize their content for different devices, such as iTunes Match, Spotify's Local Music Files and Kindle, already remunerate the rights owners directly.

[3]For example, in Czech Republic, Greece and Romania only an equipment levy is payable.

[4]For example, the German operator levy excludes businesses and public administration, although the Belgian operator levy includes these sectors, while in Poland, the operator levy is confined to copy shops. WIPO (2014), 9.

[5]Apple, Google and Amazon are now offering consumers cloud-based storage and retrieval of music files.

[6]A. Vitorino (2013), 5, 16.

[7]European Commission (2014), question 66; M. Horten (2014).

[8]National Rugby League Investments Pty Ltd. v. Singtel Optus Pty Ltd. (2012) FCAFC 59; Metropole Television v. Wizzgo, Tribunal de Grande Instance (2008).

2.3.2 Download Service

Download services allow consumers to make copies on their devices by legally downloading copyrighted content. Such services cannot be considered as falling under the levy system based on private copying exception, as they are akin to buying a new DVD from the market. It is only the subsequent copies, if made by the consumer himself from one medium and/or device to another which could qualify as private copies, and so the question of imposition of levy would arise. However, this situation has nothing to do with cloud service as such, because only after obtaining the first copy has the consumer chosen to make other copies on different devices/media. So, in this situation the traditional levy system for copying media could continue to apply.

2.3.3 Private Lockers

Cloud services could also be used by consumers to store content copied from legal sources on a so-called 'private locker',[9] wherein consumers rent capacity on the cloud by entering into a renting contract with the cloud service provider. The consumer thereby deems the rented capacity part of his private sphere. If such service does not permit sharing of stored content with others, it could be considered equivalent to private copying—the only difference being delocalization of something which was localized. In other words, instead of having a physical device, the consumer has remote access to similar capacity in the cloud. Therefore, cloud-based 'private lockers' could be treated as an externalized and delocalized storage device where the levy system could be made applicable. However, it would be difficult to map the levy system to the circumstances of a cloud. While the levy system is based on the storage capacity of the copying media, there is no limit to the memory capacity available in the cloud to a user; therefore it would be difficult to work out the value of the levies that should be applied. Further, one of the main features of cloud computing is their global nature, therefore trying to impose territorial and national levy systems on global services would certainly be challenging.

New business models based on technological developments like cloud-based services would have a significant impact on the private copying levy system. The cloud is the new way to exploit copyrighted content. As consumers increasingly adopt and use cloud-based services, they tend to replicate less content on their physical local devices, which in turn would make the private copy levy concept less relevant even in its traditional sphere. Though the applicability of the levy system to cloud-based services is being studied and it is too early to say anything

[9]For example services like "Drop Box".

conclusively, it seems that it is difficult and challenging to apply the existing levy system to cloud computing for most of its attributes.[10] The more appropriate way to deal with the challenges posed by cloud computing would be to ensure the working of direct licensing of copyrighted content between content provider and consumer.

2.4 *Levy System Vis-à-Vis P2P Networks*

P2P networks come in various hues and forms. However, a common feature of all P2P networks is that they allow searching for files on other people's computers; meanwhile, other users on the network can search for files on your computer, but typically only within a single folder that you have designated to share. People have by and large been able to share audio and audiovisual works through such P2P networks. While P2P networks make file sharing easy and convenient, they also have led to prevalent piracy of copyrighted works.[11]

Copyright owners the world over have resorted to copyright law in order to respond to the challenge posed by P2P networks. Countries have tried to counter the growth of P2P networks by enacting specific laws corresponding to P2P networks,[12] and declaring the use of P2P networks an infringement of copyright leading to primary and secondary liability. Such infringement proceedings have been launched against three different actors in the operation of P2P networks:

2.4.1 Developers and Hosts of P2P Networks

In order to check the harm caused by P2P networks, copyright owners have sued those who make such sharing possible, i.e. the developers and hosts of P2P networks. Some courts have held such developers and hosts liable for secondary copyright infringement, as they are responsible for aiding and abetting the sharing of copyrighted files.[13] Some have found that sharing of copyrighted works without authorization is the primary purpose of P2P technology and held it infringing, despite the fact that P2P technology has some possible lawful uses as well. One of the most famous cases in this regard is the Pirate Bay case, in which the hosts of a P2P network, the torrent tracking website The Pirate Bay, have been found guilty for promoting copyright infringement. The prosecutor successfully claimed that the

---

[10]Bureau Européen Des Unions De ConsommateursAisbl (2015).

[11]Pioneering P2P network Napster and its successors like Gnutella, and more recently, BitTorrent have been alleged to have cut into profits of the music and movie industries.

[12]France, the United Kingdom, Ireland and Thailand among others have enacted such specific laws.

[13]A&M Records, Inc. v. Napster, Inc., 239 F.3d 1004 (9th Cir. 2001); Metro-Goldwyn-Mayer Studios Inc. v. Grokster, Ltd., 545 U.S. 913 (2005); Tokyo ChihoSaibansho (Tokyo Dist. Ct.), 29 Jan. 2003, H17.3.31, No. 16 Ne 446 (Japan).

four organizers of 'The Pirate Bay' worked together to administer, host and develop the website and thereby facilitated other people's breach of copyright law. As a result, the four operators of the website were convicted by the Stockholm district court and sentenced to imprisonment and payment of fine.[14]

2.4.2 Uploaders and Downloaders

Uploading works on P2P networks is certainly an infringement of copyright, as it makes available protected works without authorization from copyright owners.[15] Downloading of copyrighted files through P2P networks can be considered an act of reproduction, and if unauthorized by the copyright owner and not covered by fair use[16] amounts to infringement. However, pursuing the downloaders of music and films through P2P networks presents many challenges for the rights owners. First, they are the consumers of the copyright industry, so suing them runs the risk of antagonizing them. Second, they have the protection of numbers—as they are in the millions and scattered around the globe—against how many could rights owners or CMOs pursue legal actions? Third, they can hide behind IP addresses due to national data protection laws. Still, hundreds of lawsuits have been filed against individual uploaders[17] and downloaders.

2.4.3 Internet Service Providers (ISPs)

ISPs usually hold a passive conduit position in respect of information sent or received by their subscribers using P2P networks where actual knowledge of the transmission of infringing material is usually absent. An ISP may be held primarily liable for copyright infringement where it temporarily reproduces, stores or distributes infringing material in the course of transmitting it to a subscriber engaged in

[14]Case no. B 13301-06, Stockholm District Court (2009). The Swedish Court of Appeal confirmed the criminal liability of the defendants, and the Supreme Court of Sweden refused to hear it when the matter was appealed before it.

[15]It has been held so in different jurisdictions across the world. See Metro-Goldwyn-Mayer Studios, Inc. v. Grokster, Ltd., 545 U.S. 913 (2005), in which the court held in essence that secondary liability could only be found where there has been affirmative encouragement of copyright infringement; Le Havre, Tribunal de Grande Instance, (2005), available at: www.juriscom.net/jpt/visu.php?ID=748.

[16]Fair use would also require that the copy should have been downloaded from a legal source. Therefore, if the P2P folder was not legal then a copy made from it could not be termed legal.

[17]Chan Nai Ming v. HKSAR, FACC 3/2007 (2007), where the Hong Kong Court of Appeal sentenced a user to three months imprisonment for having uploaded three movies on a P2P file sharing site.

P2P file sharing. However, such primary liability is rare and ISPs are often charged with secondary liability. In the architecture of the Internet, ISPs hold such a position where their cooperation is required to identify the P2P users and are often made parties in lawsuits for copyright infringement, in order to protect the ISPs that transmit infringing material but do not positively engage with it, exceptions to their liability have been incorporated in the laws of many countries. Such laws condition the ISP's liability on either the presence of knowledge or absence of due diligence.[18] A system whereby rights owners could ask for a take-down of infringing material is also implemented under the laws of many countries.[19]

One of the approaches adopted by legislators of various countries has been oriented towards enhancing the range of penalties together with surety and ease of conviction of wrongdoers. Strict enforcement aiming at prevention of infringement has been the hallmark of numerous legislative initiatives; the most striking examples of which are the 'graduated response' systems such as the 'HADOPI' model adopted in France[20] and some other countries. These strategies, for a variety of reasons such as territoriality of law enforcement, multitude of offenders located around the world and the shield of privacy offered by technology and law, have not been able to satisfactorily check the instances of piracy. There have certainly been some victories in litigation achieved by rights owners, which however have been largely pyrrhic, impractical, unpopular and unproductive. Copyright infringement has not decreased, and successful legal actions have often led the free file sharers on the Internet to simply migrate from one infringement-facilitating technology to another.

Because the online mass of P2P users is a market that needs to be organized and not quashed,[21] and because of the failure of the current system of copyright infringement, demands have been made to adopt the levy system vis-à-vis P2P networks. Various approaches have been proposed for more than a decade now.[22] These schemes and systems recognize that it is not profitable to continue to fight the P2P users and networks, and that the solution lies in legalizing non-commercial P2P file sharing while ensuring fair remuneration for rights owners. Further, these schemes envisage entrusting CMOs with collecting and distributing levies which could be imposed in the following three instances:

[18]See, for example, s. 79, Information Technology Act, 2000 of India.

[19]17 U.S.C. § 512(c) is one example of such a law.

[20]The French HADOPI law was introduced in 2009, providing a graduated response as a means to encourage compliance with copyright laws. The part of it that allowed for suspension of Internet access to a repeat infringer was revoked in 2013 because that penalty was considered to be disproportionate. The power to impose fines or other sanctions on repeat infringers remains in effect.

[21]D. Gervais (2010), 17.

[22]W. Fisher (2004); J.D. Litman (2004); D. Gervais (2005); A. Peukert (2009).

2.4.3.1 Levy on Equipment/Media

Levy could be imposed on devices used to gain access to digital content like computers and mobile phones. Consumer electronic devices used to store, copy and listen to music files downloaded from P2P networks could also be brought within the scope of the levy. This levy applies the time-tested model of the levy system for private copying to P2P networks.

2.4.3.2 Levy on P2P Networks

P2P network service providers could be made to pay a certain sum of money to the CMO based on the subscription base of the P2P network. P2P network service providers could then charge the users who download files using their service. Users could then pay a monthly flat fee or pay per downloaded song or movie.

2.4.3.3 Levies on Internet Access

Every Internet user gets web access from an ISP who could charge P2P users for their downloads. This could be a monthly flat fee. Alternatively, ISPs could charge every Internet user, irrespective of whether he is a P2P user, a smaller fee and provide blanket protection against lawsuits for downloading copyrighted works.[23]

The levy so collected would then be distributed by CMOs amongst the rights owners based on consumption of the work which could be measured by a system of file-tracking. For such tracking William Fisher advocated that the owners of all such digital works should register their works with the copyright office and obtain a unique identification number.[24] The levy system represents a shift in focus from the system that minimizes unauthorized use to the one that maximizes authorized use.[25] The goal is to improve the accessibility and quality of digital copyrighted works so that they are more attractive to would-be 'infringers' upon payment than is searching for something free on the Internet.

The levy system could simplify the combat against piracy because the rights owners would then focus on fighting only those sites which indulge in illegal commercial file sharing. Moreover, such commercial services would also lose a large percentage of their users who would prefer legalized non-commercial file sharing. It would also decriminalize the entrenched habits of file sharers[26] while striking a balance between the social norms of file sharing and the legal norm of copyright enforcement.

---

[23] If it is possible technically for ISPs to charge only P2P users, then the method could be a monthly flat fee, and if it is not possible then all Internet users could be taxed, and in that case the monthly fee would be much smaller, as the number of people paying would increase.

[24] W. Fisher (2004), 9.

[25] D. Gervais (2004), 58.

[26] M. Harrop (2009), 65.

3 Requirements for the Levy System

3.1 Building on the Model Whereby the Owner Forsakes Some Exclusive Rights to Gain Fair Remuneration

The voluntary licensing mechanism is an outcome of exclusivity granted to the copyright owners by law, which means that it is the owner alone who can authorize the use of his work by others, and he alone can decide the conditions of such usage. However, for an individual owner it may be well-nigh impossible to identify the numerous users and enter into agreements with them. In order to overcome these deficiencies of individual licensing of copyright, collective management is born wherein multiple owners of copyright authorize a CMO to deal with end-users on their behalf. CMOs have the organizational competence to identify potential consumers, enter into contracts with them, monitor the extent and character of their usage, collect remuneration and distribute it amongst the rights owners.[27]

At the most basic level, collective management of copyright is voluntary, as owners can freely decide to entrust an organization of their choice with the exercise of their copyright. For the sphere of copyright exploitation in which levy system is to function, individual licensing and voluntary collective management are not practical, as the potential users of a work could be numerous and scattered, and copying takes place within the confines of users' privacy. What is required instead is to creatively utilize the flexibilities of contract and copyright and carve out innovative licensing mechanisms so as to ensure lawful use by consumers together with fair remuneration for the rights owners.

The copyright system can be represented by the following diagram, where circle *A* represents the 'exclusive right to use' and circle *B* represents 'exclusive right to alienate', and these two circles together constitute the exclusive right of the owner over a work. In the copyright system, an owner of copyright has both *A* and *B*, but still it may be of little help to him in certain situations of mass uses of works where he may not be able to generate income by licensing the works to users.

The following diagram represents the innovative licensing mechanisms for the levy system to operate where a copyright owner has neither *A* nor *B* in totality. The legal system takes away varying portions of *A* and *B* and instead gives the owner circle *C* which includes some aspects of *A* and *B* together with *X*.

[27]CMOs are traditionally said to reduce transaction costs in enforcing copyright; R.P. Merges (1996), 1293.

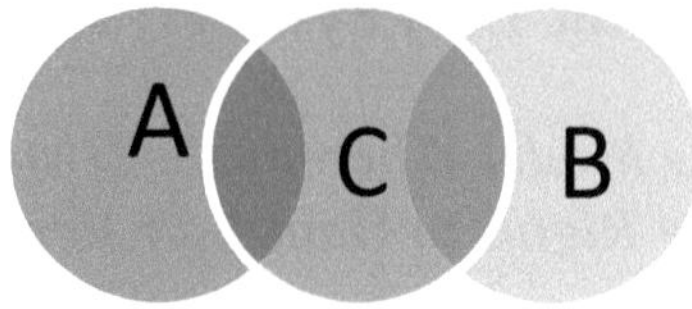

This system can be represented as:

$$C = A/N + B/N + X$$

In the above equation, N represents a variable value that depends on the kind of licensing mechanism chosen, and X represents a specifically created right of fair remuneration. Most innovative licensing mechanisms that could be used to give effect to the levy systems are built on this model whereby the owner forsakes some of his rights in order to gain fair remuneration. The two broad types of innovative mechanisms of licensing that have been proposed and used are mandatory collective management and non-voluntary licenses.[28]

3.1.1 Mandatory Collective Management

Under the laws of some countries, the levy system is implemented by making the collective management mandatory, where owners of rights have no choice but to commit the exercise of their rights to CMOs. In different mandatory collective management mechanisms, contractual freedom is eroded to variable extents. In the European Union certain Directives permit the use of mandatory collective management.[29] In France the right of reproduction, for example, by reprography is also subject to mandatory collective management.[30]

Another mechanism is the extended collective licensing (ECL) where an organization is authorized to manage certain rights by a sufficiently large number of rights owners, and the effect of such collective management is extended by law to the rights of those owners of rights who have not entrusted the organization to manage their rights.[31] This type of collective management is most widely practiced

[28]Many variants of these two mechanisms have been proposed and implemented in various countries for dealing with various instances of mass usage of works.

[29]Article 4, Council Directive 92/100/EEC on rental rights and lending rights and on certain rights related to copyright in the field of intellectual property; Article 9(1), Council Directive 93/83/EEC on the coordination of certain rules concerning copyright and rights related to copyright applicable to satellite broadcasting and cable retransmission.

[30]Article L. 122-10 of the French Intellectual Property Code.

[31]M. Ficsor (2003), 9.

in Nordic countries. Usually, some guarantees for outside right-owners are provided by law in such a system.[32] The ECL helps widen the repertoire of the CMO.[33]

3.1.2 Statutory and Compulsory Licenses[34]

In many countries, users can access and use copyrighted works by way of compulsory and statutory licenses. While in a compulsory license users need to apply to the designated authority to get a license, in case of statutory license the statute has already granted a license to all those who are willing to fulfill the prescribed conditions.[35] In case of these licenses the use of copyrighted works cannot be controlled or prevented by rights owners who are, however, compensated for such use. The rate of royalty could be decided by negotiation between the CMO and users or left to an administrative or judicial body.[36]

Certain obligations have been imposed by national law on the users before they can use the works; these are related to record keeping, payment of royalty, manner of use, etc. The CMOs should inspect and monitor the compliance of these conditions so as to check the instances of under reporting, improper use, etc.

3.2 Creation of a Right to Fair Remuneration

The levy system requires a shift in copyright law from a proprietary rights model to a model based on right to receive remuneration.[37] This shift is required vis-à-vis private copying, cloud computing and P2P networks. Therefore, the exclusive right of the owner is replaced by a right to equitable remuneration in countries which have implemented the levy system. The rights owners receive fair compensation or remuneration paid to a CMO in the form of a levy.

[32]Owners usually are given the right to claim individual remuneration from the organization concerned and sometimes the right to file individual prohibition of the use of their works under the agreement.

[33]For more on ECL please refer to the chapter by F. Trumpke.

[34]For more on statutory licenses and compulsory licenses please refer to the chapters by W.L. Ng-Loy and C. Geiger.

[35]This distinction between compulsory and statutory licensing is, however, not followed uniformly around the world.

[36]The private copy regime in Europe and Canada is mostly organized on the basis of such licenses.

[37]L. Lessig (2004).

3.3 Creation of Limitations and Exceptions That Comply with the Three-Step Test

Mandatory collective management, compulsory and statutory licenses require exceptions and limitations to be created to the principle of exclusivity, as they legally deprive rights owners of some control over use of their works.[38] These innovative licensing mechanisms will have to comply with obligations resulting from international conventions, particularly the three-step test set forth by the Berne Convention and the TRIPS Agreement.[39] The TRIPS Agreement provides that "members shall confine limitations and exceptions to exclusive rights to certain special cases which do not conflict with a normal exploitation of the work and do not unreasonably prejudice the legitimate interests of the rights holder".[40]

The levy system would pass the first test, as it is not general and is created only in respect of certain instances of use viz. private copying, cloud computing and P2P networks. The levy system is created only because normal exploitation has become impractical and nearly impossible in the situation of private copying. Therefore, the levy system does not conflict with the normal exploitation of works, but instead provides an alternative means of exploitation of works. The legitimate interest of the rights holder is to be able to exploit his work, and only when this becomes impractical does the levy system step in to enhance the interests of the rights holder. Therefore, the levy system should not fall foul of the mandatory requirement of the three-step test.

3.4 Clear Demarcation Between Limitations and Exceptions with and Without Compensation

The levy system is based on creation and recognition of limitations and exceptions, as is the case with the fair use system. However, in the case of fair use, no remuneration is payable to the rights owners, whereas fair remuneration to the rights owners is a requirement in the levy system.

Sometimes the right of the copyright owner or CMO to collect tariffs has to compete with a corresponding right made available to the public by way of fair use.

---

[38]These innovative mechanisms of licensing can be covered within the concept of limitations and exceptions, as all these mechanisms limit either the "exclusive right to use" and/or the "exclusive right to alienate", which together constitute the exclusive right granted to the owner, *supra* Sect. 3.1.

[39]Article 9(2), Berne Convention, 1886; Article 13, the TRIPS Agreement, 1994.

[40]Article 9(2) of the Berne Convention, however, does not confine the three-step test to limitations and exceptions, and simply states that "it shall be a matter for legislation in the countries of the Union to permit the reproduction in certain special cases...".

Fair use, of course, is an extremely important part of overall copyright philosophy which tries to strike a balance between the competing interests of the copyright owner and public with regard to access to copyrighted works. However, vaguely defined fair use can be a real hurdle and make the task of CMOs virtually impossible. A recent and ongoing case where CMOs' activities of collecting tariffs have come directly in conflict with fair use provisions under Indian law is presented below.

Photocopying is invariably the solution to the challenge of making materials available at low cost for students. University of Delhi is at the centre of a legal controversy which has engaged students, publishers, the university, and also the academicians.[41] The practice followed by a department of University of Delhi was that the faculty would prescribe a list of select readings for a particular course at the start of a new session. The list would usually contain a number of chapters to be read from different books. It was impossible for all the students to buy all the books. The students could individually get the books from the library and then photocopy themselves. Instead, the practice has been that the photocopy shop which operated from the premises of the department would get the books and do the photocopy work and prepare course packs in the required number. In 2012, leading publishers backed by the Indian Reprographic Rights Organization (IRRO) filed a suit against University of Delhi and its agent Rameshwari Photocopy Services.[42] Their claim was that the photocopied course-packs—bound sets of course material—sold by the shop infringed their copyright.

One of the solutions for this problem could be that University of Delhi procures licenses from the IRRO. However, this solution would place IRRO in a dominant position, as it has a virtual monopoly position under s. 33(3)(Proviso) of the Indian Copyright Act. A better solution would be to introduce a levy system whereby institutions could be made to pay a tariff to IRRO which could be determined by way of negotiations between the institution concerned and IRRO, and in case the negotiations fail, the Copyright Board could decide the tariff. For this arrangement to succeed, it is necessary that either the statute or the court decide the extent of fair use, as the calculation of the levy payable will depend on it.

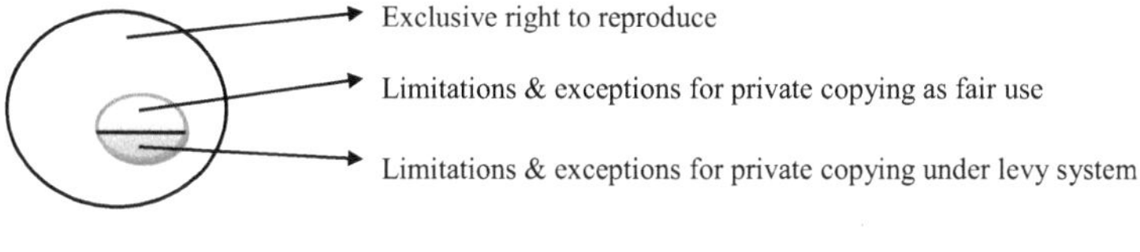

[41]S. Desikan (2013).

[42]University of Oxford and Others v. Rameshwari Photocopy Services and University of Delhi, IA No. 14634 and 14637/2012 (Delhi High Court).

4 Managerial Goals and Tools to Exploit Digital Works

The emergence of transmission of digital works by worldwide networks has also revolutionized the collective administration sector, which has to adopt new mechanisms. The managerial goals and tools that are discussed below aim at ensuring payment to rights owners by regaining and retaining control over copyrighted works in the digital environment.

4.1 Managerial Goals

4.1.1 International Collaboration Between CMOs

Because of the Internet, copyrighted works today are being used around the world on a scale they had never been used before. Therefore, in order to globally exploit the works, CMOs need to collaborate and cooperate to optimize the exploitation of their repertoires. For that to happen, contracts of mutual representation will have to be concluded with the societies of other countries.

The global use of creative works requires that vast amounts of information about works and uses need to be exchanged across borders. There is a need to enhance this information exchange by expanding the international network of CMOs and by setting standards and rules on the specifications for uniquely identifying creative works and their creators and on the architecture of a common system.

4.1.2 Single-Window Service or Single-Fee License

There is a section of users who are ready and willing to pay for the use but are unable to get the right easily and readily and also on clear and transparent terms. For the convenience of end-users, a single-window service in the form of the ECL could be started which takes the licensing requests from end-users and directs them to the concerned CMO. A further build-up on the single window service is a single-fee license issued to end-users with the royalty thereafter split between various CMOs representing different fragments of copyright. In this case the composite royalty could be determined by the copyright authority of the country concerned. This solution would serve end-users in terms of ease of access, and would also reduce transaction costs.

4.1.3 Efficient Dispute Resolution Between CMOs and End-Users

Often, end-users and the CMO will disagree on the terms of the license offered by the CMO, the extent of use of repertoire, payment of royalty, etc. In such situations, especially where a CMO enjoys monopoly position in the market, national laws must decide which type of state intervention is necessary, which of course varies to a great extent from jurisdiction to jurisdiction. In some jurisdictions, specialized copyright tribunals or boards have been empowered, while in others the matter is left entirely to civil courts.[43]

The most important aspect here is the establishment of an efficient dispute resolution mechanism. Dispute resolution through the court system can be costly and time consuming. In this regard, the utilization of an independent and impartial dispute resolution body, i.e. via mediation or arbitration, can be extremely helpful. Moreover, as the CMO's repertoire and its exploitation become increasingly international, the submission of related disputes to an alternative dispute resolution procedure becomes more attractive and prudent.

4.2 Technical Mechanisms to Achieve Managerial Goals: DRM

The managerial objectives discussed above are given effect by adoption of the DRM, which is a catch-all expression referring to the mechanisms used to enforce predetermined conditions on the use and transfer of copyrighted digital content. While first-generation DRM mechanisms merely sought to control copying, the second-generation DRM mechanisms seek to control viewing, copying, printing, altering and everything else that can be done with digital content.[44] DRM mostly relies on technological protection measures, rights management information and electronic documentation to implement the controls and restrictions necessary for the overall management of digital works.

DRM systems have the capacity to collect and compile precise details about individual use of works, and can help in controlling digital reproduction and dissemination of works by developing identification and tracking methods so that usage of and access to copyrighted works could be ascertained. DRM helps the development of new licensing models and new methods of monitoring and distribution of works.

An efficient DRM has to create robust mechanisms to identify works, performances, and rights owners, together with amassing information about conditions on the basis of which a work may be licensed.[45] DRM is slowly creeping into the legal

---

[43]In the United States a federal judge is empowered to decide the appropriate rate for the licenses by virtue of an agreement entered into between CMOs and the Department of Justice, while in Canada and Australia a specialized copyright tribunal/board has been established for that purpose. In India the Copyright Board, on an appeal, is empowered to remove any unreasonable element, anomaly or inconsistency in the tariff scheme. See s. 33A(2), of the Indian Copyright Act, 1957 and Rule 57 of the Copyright Rules, 2013.

[44]Available at: www.priv.gc.ca/resource/fs-fi/02_05_d_32_e.asp.

[45]J. Cunard (2001).

systems of many countries as they are signatories to the 1996 World Intellectual Property Organization Copyright Treaty which has already been ratified by ninety three countries to date.[46]

4.2.1 Rights Management Information (RMI)

RMI, which is also known as social DRM, is the electronic information that identifies the works protected by copyright, the rights owners of the work, and the terms and conditions of use associated with it. As the integrity of RMI is vulnerable to manipulation and removal, it is necessary to provide legal protection to it.[47] RMI could allocate a unique identification number to a work that could always be used to identify, monitor or track the work. This numbering system enables CMOs to administer the rights of their members more effectively. It also helps end-users to find information about a work easily and to obtain the necessary permission and to pay the royalty for its use. RMI forms the bedrock of DRM because it provides a fast and easy tool for users to buy licenses for the use of particular work, and for rights owners to collect information about such usage.

4.2.2 Technological Protection Measures (TPMs)

DRM can be used only inside a specific technological framework which is provided by TPMs. TPMs refer to technologies implemented on digital works that control and/or restrict the use of and access to the work. There are two categories of TPMs—access control and copy control. Access control TPMs prevent unauthorized access to works, while copy control TPMs prevent unauthorized copying of works. An adequate legal protection is also needed at the national level to prevent acts intended to circumvent technical protection measures.[48] With the growing use of digital technologies by end-users of copyrighted works, CMOs are facing ever new challenges in the exercise and management of rights that they administer. New technological solutions such as passwords, encryption, digital envelopes, etc. have been developed and implemented in response to these challenges. TPMs are mostly used in sound recordings, films and software, and digital artistic and literary works.

[46]Available at: www.wipo.int/treaties/en/ip/wct/.

[47]WIPO Internet treaties deal with obligations of member states concerning DRMs, and aim at ensuring that the owners of rights are protected when their works are disseminated on the Internet. These treaties have led to enactment of corresponding laws at the national level to combat the removal or alteration of any elements of DRMs.

[48]Art. 11, WCT, 1996.

4.2.3 Electronic Documentation

Documentation is the process of researching, substantiating and recording the fundamental elements of works' information undertaken by a CMO to carry out its task of licensing. All CMOs have databases both of their members and of the repertoire they represent.[49] Documentation is an important aspect of the process of an efficient system of collective management which is essential for the collection and distribution of royalties.

The documentation is built steadily by CMOs by encouraging authors and composers to declare all works created by them, accompanied by supporting documents. Publishers who are members of CMOs can also be obliged to declare works published by them. In such cases copies of the publishing contracts concerning works would form the supporting documents. Collaboration between various CMOs is also required to build an interlinked database of documentation.[50] Electronic databases will enable CMOs to precisely identify works and their owners together with the usage of the works, which are essential elements on which licensing by CMOs is based.

4.3 Legal Mechanisms to Achieve Managerial Goals: Obligations Concerning Reporting of Usage

With all the technological means to track the works, sometimes it may still not be possible to measure the extent of use by end-users. Therefore, in certain cases there are obligations imposed by law on end-users to report on record keeping, payment of royalty, manner of use, etc.[51] The CMOs, on behalf of their members, should actively inspect and monitor compliance with licensing conditions so as to check the instances of under-reporting, improper use, etc.

[49]Available at: www.cisac.org/Cisac-University/Collective-Management/The-Process.

[50]For example, the International Confederation of Societies of Authors and Composers has set up its Common Information System (CIS). This is a method for administering authors' rights using a set of linked databases. CIS is a series of tools that provide the building blocks to global copyright administration by standardizing and streamlining the exchange of information amongst member societies.

[51]See, for example, s. 31D, Indian Copyright Act, 1957 imposes obligation on the statutory licensees for proper usage, record keeping along with payment of royalty. Further, the statutory licensors have been empowered to inspect and check the records.

5 Reconciliation of Levy System with DRM

5.1 Shortcomings of the Levy System

The levy system has constantly been criticized and opposed over the years on the basis of shortcomings discussed below, and for the levy system to play a more meaningful role in the future it has to address these criticisms.

5.1.1 Increase in Price of Products and Services

The electronic equipment industry, ISPs and cloud computing service providers oppose the levy system, as it results in an increase in the prices of the products and services on which the levy is imposed, thereby placing an unjustified burden on the concerned industries. These stakeholders certainly stand to lose a part of their revenue because of imposition of levies; however, in the long run the demand for their equipment and services is likely to increase as a result of increased demand for the better quality content made available by content creators.

Consumers too stand to lose in the short run, as the equipment manufacturers and service providers will shift the burden of levy to the consumers. However, in the long run consumers too are likely to benefit from the availability of better quality of content. Moreover, any tax system would potentially threaten to increase the prices of taxed products or services, but this is no justification to abolish a legitimate tax.

5.1.2 Trade Distortion and Disparity in Practices

Levies are not applied uniformly in different markets. For example, consumers can easily get around the differences in the price of equipment and media from one European Union member state to another by buying online or otherwise. This creates distortions and inefficiency in the market. Even after half a century since its introduction,[52] the levy system has not been applied around the world. In those countries which have adopted the levy system, the practices differ in terms of rate levels, method of setting the rates, selection of products that can be levied, liability of market players, method of reporting, legal tools for monitoring and enforcement, etc.[53] For the levy system to play a more meaningful role in the future, it has to be made more uniform and widespread in its application.

[52]The levy system was first introduced in Germany in 1965 for audio/audiovisual private copying which was known as 'home taping' at that time, and extended to copying text and still images in 1985.

[53]World Intellectual Property Organization & de Thuiskopie (2013), 6.

5.1.3 Unfair Collection

Oftentimes, levy is imposed on all reproduction equipment regardless of whether the equipment is actually used for making private copies. However, much of the equipment and media can be and is often utilized for purposes which have nothing to do with the exploitation of copyright. For example, not all buyers of DVDs are indulging in private copying of copyrighted works,[54] and not all subscribers of the Internet are downloading files from P2P networks. So why should all buyers or subscribers be taxed for a thing they do not consume or for a service they do not avail themselves of, or for activities they do not indulge in? In the *Padawan-SGAE* case[55] the CJEU ruled that the indiscriminate application of the private copying levy to all types of digital reproduction equipment, devices and media, including cases in which such equipment is acquired by persons other than natural persons for purposes clearly unrelated to private copying, is incompatible with the 2001 Information Society Directive.[56] The decision of the CJEU recognizes the practical challenge of establishing whether or not individuals are using their recording media for purely private purposes.

It is, therefore, important for countries implementing the levy system to put in place adequate exemption schemes which allow manufacturers, importers or end-users to prove that the equipment is not intended to be used for private copying and hence to claim exemption from paying levy or claim reimbursement of levy paid.[57]

5.1.4 Inequitable Distribution

Distribution of the levies collected by CMOs amongst different categories of rights owners occurs according to the distribution schemes determined either by law or the designated authority or by CMOs. One of the major criticisms of the levy system is on account of the inequitable distribution of collected levies amongst the rights owners. It is alleged that only a small fraction of owners actually receive any significant revenue from these levies, and compensation received by rights owners is not in any way correlated to actual private use.[58]

---

[54]A DVD could be used for the storage of professional databases, manuals, client information, etc. or for such reproductions where a license would be required.

[55]Padawan SL v. SGAE, C-467/08 (2010).

[56]The judgment led to the abolition of the system of collecting levies through copying equipment and media in Spain, leaving Spanish rights holders with an amount determined annually by the government based on the harm caused to rights holders as a consequence of private copying.

[57]Nokia *v*. CopydanBandkopi (C-463/12) CJEU, para. 55.

[58]Many musicians feel they don't receive a fair share of levy revenues, and that the most famous (and richest) among them receive a disproportionately high share, to the detriment of lesser known artists, available at: www.digitaleurope.org/DesktopModules/Bring2mind/DMX/Download.aspx?Command=Core_Download&EntryId=815&PortalId=0&TabId=353.

5.2 *Shortcomings of DRM*

The potential of DRM as instruments for reducing copyright violations is uncertain, as the implementation of DRM is quickly undone by circumvention technologies. The ready availability of DRM has not been able to induce all the rights owners to use it, as they prefer alternate business models where DRM is a hindrance. Implementation of DRM technologies could result in inferior products with deliberately disabled features, and could also sometimes cause computers to crash even when no attempt was made to circumvent them. Consumers' rights to, for example, borrow books from each other or make backup copies are hampered once DRM is implemented. Privacy concerns are the largest non-technical argument against DRM, as its implementation could lead to a violation of consumers' privacy. DRM could be used in a way which allows only compatible digital material to play on a given device, thereby restricting competition. Though DRMs could be applied to digital content with some amount of success to restrict copying, they cannot exterminate all unlicensed copying.[59]

5.3 *DRM and Levy System: Whether Alternative or Complementary*

In an environment where both DRM and a levy system are implemented concurrently, a question arises as to whether DRM and the levy system are complementary to or alternatives of each other. Both DRM and the levy system are mechanisms to make end users pay for their usage of copyrighted works, and both are a response to the challenges faced in the process of enforcing the exclusive rights of rights owners. While both systems aim at the same objective of ensuring payment to rights owners, the mechanisms to achieve the objective are different. DRM tries to make private copying difficult or impossible for end-users so that they have to pay for every product or service they consume, and the levy system makes private copying a legitimate exception to exclusive rights subject to compensation for rights owners. Therefore, implementing both these systems for the same work would result in double payment: first by paying a license fee for the use of DRM-controlled content, and second by paying a levy on media or equipment.[60] As such double payment is wholly unjustified, the two systems in this sense are alternatives.

---

[59]Even when all digital music files bought from Apple's iTunes store implemented DRM, Steve Jobs still commented that DRM (systems) haven't worked, and may never work to halt music piracy. See R.K. Sinha / F.S. Machado / C. Sellman (2010), 40-54.

[60]P.B. Hugenholtz / L. Guibault / S. van Geffen (2003), 34; Recital, 35, Information Society Directive, 2001; VG Wort v. Kyocera, C-457/11 to C 460/11 (Joined CJEU cases).

The alternative nature of the two systems poses a problem far more complicated than picking one and dropping the other. The levy system predates DRM, which has also been around for more than two decades. Experience has shown that both systems are not perfect, as they have each received their share of opposition because of their inherent shortcomings. A full DRM-driven market has not developed, and a huge stock of copyrighted works is still subject to private copying, leading to continuance of the levy system together with demands for its expansion. In Europe the Information Society Directive tries to reconcile DRM with the levy system. On the one hand the Directive continues to provide not only for the levy system[61] but also for its expansion in the digital world.[62] On the other hand it provides for the protection of TPMs and RMI,[63] while adding that in arriving at the appropriate levy the applicability or non-applicability of DRM should be taken into account.[64]

The continuance and the level of levies are inversely proportional to the development and effectiveness of DRM, because the degree of use of DRM is regularly assessed when the levies are being set up. To the extent DRM enables the rights owners to restrict private copies of their works, the need for levies disappears. If DRM becomes more acceptable in the future levies could potentially be phased out. That could happen only if evolution and developments in DRM give the rights owners better control of private copying while at the same time successfully addressing the shortcomings of DRM for consumers and businesses. Till that time DRM and the levy system will have to be made complementary to each other by avoiding instances of double payment by end-users.

6 Conclusion

The quest to manage copyrighted works effectively and to make end-users pay for their consumption thereof so as to secure fair compensation to the rights owners has led the legal system to implement multiple mechanisms. In the situations in which it is not possible to track the works and monitor their usage by end-users, the legal system has experimented with the levy system, which creatively utilizes the flexibilities of contract and copyright and carves out innovative licensing mechanisms

---

[61] Article 5(2)(a), Information Society Directive, 2001.

[62] Recital 38, Information Society Directive, 2001.

[63] Article 6-7, Information Society Directive, 2001.

[64] The impact of implementation of DRM by a rights owner that would decrease the possible harm to him because of private copying has to be taken into account to arrive at the levies payable to him. So, each individual rights owner's claim to receive a share out of total levy collected would depend on whether or not his works were actually marketed in a technically protected format. Rights owners would thus be obliged to inform, on a case by case basis, their CMOs of the formats in which their works are being published. This places a heavy administrative burden on existing levy schemes, particularly on the CMOs that administrate them in practice. See P.B. Hugenholtz / L. Guibault / S. van Geffen (2003), 42.

so as to ensure lawful use by consumers together with fair remuneration for the rights owners.

On the one hand, there are suggestions to extend the levy system to newer areas. On the other hand, demands have been made to discontinue the levy system. The levy system is far from perfect; however, it is currently an effective mechanism which allows creators to be compensated for the widespread use of their works in private. Therefore, it is worth experimenting with the levy system in the sphere of the Internet. For the levy system to play a more meaningful role in the future, it has to be made more uniform and widespread in its application while putting in place adequate exemption schemes which allow manufacturers, importers or end-users to prove that the equipment or media is not intended to be used for private use and hence claim exemption from paying levy or claim reimbursement of levy paid.

The objective of tracking and monitoring the usage of works on the information superhighway has led to the adoption of DRM systems, which are given effect mainly through RMI and TPMs. DRM cannot possibly exterminate all kinds of piracy, and its application may hinder the efficiency of use and privacy of users. If DRM becomes more acceptable in the future by successfully addressing these shortcomings, levies could potentially be phased out. If DRM and the levy system have to be implemented together, they have to be made complementary to each other by ensuring that the simultaneous application of the two systems does not result in double payment by end-users.

References

Bureau Européen Des Unions De ConsommateursAisbl (2015), EU Cloud Computing Strategy, BEUC Position Paper 2015, available at: www.beuc.eu/publications/2013-00143-01-e.pdf

Cunard, J. (2001), Technological Protection of Copyrighted works and Copyrighted Management Systems: A Brief Survey of the Landscape, ALAI Congress

Desikan, S. (2013), Delhi University Students Impleaded on Copyright Row, The Hindu of 10 June 2013, available at: www.Thehindu.Com/Features/Education/Delhi-University-Students-Impleaded-On-Copyright-Row/Article4794919.Ece

European Commission (2014), Public Consultation on the Review of the EU Copyright Rules 2014, European Commission

Ficsor, M. (2003), Collective Management of Copyright and Related Rights at a Triple Crossroads: Should it Remain Voluntary or May it be "Extended" or Made Mandatory? Copyright Bulletin, The United Nations Organization for Education, Science and Culture

Fisher, W. (2004), Promises to Keep: Technology, Law and the Future of Entertainment, Stanford Law and Politic

Gervais, D. (2004), The Price of Social Norms: Towards a Liability Regime for File Sharing, Journal of Intellectual Property Law, 39-73, University of Georgia School of Law

Gervais, D. (2005), Use of Copyright Content on the Internet: Considerations on Excludability and Collective Licensing, in: M. Geist (Ed.), In the Public Interest: The Future of Canadian Copyright Law, 517-549, Irwin Law

Gervais, D. (2010), Collective Management of Copyright: Theory and Practice in the Digital Age, in: D. Gervais (Ed.), Collective Management of Copyright and Related Rights, 1-28, 2nd ed., Kluwer Law International

Harrop, M. (2009), Something for Nothing: Copyright, ISP Liability and P2P File Sharing, available at: www.otago.ac.nz/law/research/journals/otago036304.pdf

Horten, M. (2014), The Aereo Dilemma and Copyright in the Cloud, Internet Policy Review 2014, Alexander von Humboldt Institute for Internet and Society, available at: policyreview.info/articles/analysis/aereo-dilemma-and-copyright-cloud

Hugenholtz, P.B. / Guibault, L. / van Geffen, S. (2003), The Future of Levies in a Digital Environment, Institute for Information Law Amsterdam

Lessig, L. (2004), Free Culture: How Big Media Uses Technology and the Law to Lock Down Culture and Control Creativity, Penguin Books

Litman, J.D. (2004), Sharing and Stealing, Hastings Comm. & Ent. Law J., 1, 1-48

Merges, R.P. (1996), Contracting into Liability Rules: Intellectual Property Rights and Collective Rights Organizations, Calif. Law Rev. 1293-1393

Peukert, A. (2009), A Bipolar Copyright System for the Digital Network Environment, in: A. Strowel (Ed.), Peer-to-Peer File Sharing and Secondary Liability in Copyright Law, 148-195, Edward Elgar

Sinha, R.K. / Machado, F.S. / Sellman, C. (2010), Don't Think Twice, It's All Right: Music Piracy and Pricing in a DRM-Free Environment, Journal of Marketing, 40-54, American Marketing Association

Vitorino, A. (2013), Recommendations resulting from the Mediation on Private Copying and Reprography Levies, European Commission

WIPO (2014), International Survey on Text and Image Copyright Levies

World Intellectual Property Organization & de Thuiskopie (2013), International Survey on Private Copying Law & Practice, World Intellectual Property Organization, available at: www.wipo.int/edocs/pubdocs/en/copyright/1037/wipo_pub_1037_2013.pdf

Distribution Among Right Holders

Byungil Kim

Contents

Abstract The distribution of remunerations among rights owners is sometimes subject to detailed regulation at the national level, while the distribution scheme must be negotiated between the collecting societies and their members, subject to its approval by a public authority in some countries. In principle, CMOs must distribute the remunerations in proportion to the revenue derived from the individual works and performances. They must also make all reasonable efforts to improve efficiency in the collection and distribution of the CMOs for the benefit of all right owners and users.

Byungil Kim is Faculty Member of Hanyang University (School of Law).

B. Kim (✉)
Hanyang University, Seoul, Republic of Korea
e-mail: kimbyungil66@yahoo.com

K.-C. Liu, R.M. Hilty (eds.), *Remuneration of Copyright Owners*, MPI Studies on Intellectual Property and Competition Law 27, DOI 10.1007/978-3-662-53809-8_8

1 Introduction

With the development of digital technology and the global interactive network, the collective management of copyright and related rights has come far more essential for the right holders and the users in the digital world. One of the most relevant functions accomplished by collective management organizations (CMOs) has been to collect and distribute copyright remunerations to their members as right holders. The most critical issues among them are not only establishment of the mechanisms to ensure adequate remuneration for creators and performers, but also distribution of the collected remunerations in fair and equitable shares to them by CMOs.

It is therefore the focus of this chapter to discuss all possible mechanisms to guarantee right holders' fair remuneration. A first part of the chapter briefly analyses the practice of collective management of rights and the important roles these CMOs can play in addressing those issues. The second part is devoted to the analysis of some specific issues which the relevant CMO faces in distributing remunerations. Finally, some recommendations on how to improve efficiency in the collection and distribution of the CMOs for the benefit of all-right owners, users and the CMOs are presented and proposed.

2 Remuneration Schemes and Collective Management of Rights

Copyright law accords authors an exclusive right to authorize reproductions, performing, distribution, etc. of their works. The right holders can exercise their rights in person or can authorize CMOs to administer their rights in certain or all cases.[1]

Individual management of rights is practically impossible for certain types of use. For example, an author cannot contact every single radio or television station to negotiate licenses and remuneration for the use of his works.[2] Conversely, it is not practical for some users such as broadcasting organizations to seek specific permission from every author for the use of every copyrighted work.[3] The impracticability of managing these activities individually—both for the right holders and for the users—creates a need for CMOs.[4]

In the case of exclusive rights, the activities of a CMO are based on voluntary mandates from participating rights owners. However, copyright law does provide a number of exceptions and limitations to the general rule. The law has an exhaustive list of limitations on copyright and fair use. The law also grants some specific users

---

[1]M. Ficsor (2002), 16; T. Koskinen-Olsson / N. Lowe (2012), 20; v. S. Lewinski (2004), 2.

[2]D. Gervais (2010), 2-3.

[3]D. Gervais (2010), 2-3.

[4]D. Gervais (2010), 6; T. Koskinen-Olsson / N. Lowe (2012), 19; A. Waziri / S.O. Mohamed (2007), 2-4.

rights in favor of third parties subject to the payment of remuneration to the right holders.[5] In addition to a variety of limitations and fair use, the copyright law also provides for a compulsory license or a statutory license.[6] Collective management of rights is also very effective in the case of non-voluntary licenses in which there is no requirement of consent in use by the rights owners.[7]

Under a non-voluntary license, the remuneration may be a usage fee which right owners and users can negotiate (compulsory license), or the remuneration may be fixed by law (statutory license). In the cases of a mere right to remuneration, statutory licenses allow for certain uses of copyright material, without the permission of the right holders, subject to the payment of equitable remuneration.[8]

Furthermore, private copying remuneration is one form of non-voluntary collective management. The laws of most countries include an exception or limitation concerning private copying. Many countries have introduced special remuneration mechanisms to compensate rights holders for large amounts of private copying,[9] because the amount of private copies exceeds what is considered fair and legitimate use of works without compensating rights holders.[10]

The functions of CMOs are to administer the rights declared to them by the right holders.[11] CMOs have the authority to license copyrighted works and collect fees (royalties or remuneration) as part of non-voluntary licenses or individual licenses negotiated on behalf of its members.[12] The crucial function of CMOs is to guarantee that authors actually receive the fair remuneration they are entitled to.[13] CMOs do play an important role in terms of negotiating fees with the prospective users and then, through their effective and well-established mechanisms, collect the equitable fees from the users of copyrighted works and distribute fees to the right holders.[14]

---

[5]In Korea, specific user rights with remuneration are as follows: textbook privilege and utilization of works at higher education institutes (KCA Sec. 25); and some types of library privileges (KCA Sec. 31).

[6]Both statutory and compulsory licenses fall under the broader term of non-voluntary licenses. M. Ficsor (2002), 17-18.

[7]M. Ficsor (2002), 26.

[8]They are a type of compulsory license; where the license applies, rights holders cannot choose not to license their material.

[9]For example, Algeria, Austria, Belgium, Bosnia-Herzegovina, Burkina Faso, Cameroon, Croatia, Czech Republic, Dominican Republic, Ecuador, France, Germany, Ghana, Greece, Hungary, Japan, Kosovo, Lithuania, Luxembourg, Moldova, Montenegro, Nigeria, Paraguay, Poland, Portugal, Romania, Serbia, Slovenia, Turkey. However, Korean copyright law does not include a private copying remuneration system yet.

[10]A small copyright fee is added to the price of blank carriers and/or copying equipment. Producers, importers and retailers of equipment are liable for paying the fees to the CMO, which distributes collected revenue to right holders.

[11]D. Gervais (2010), 6-10.

[12]M. Ficsor (2002), 18-22.

[13]C. Handke / R. Towse (2007), 937; T. Koskinen-Olsson / N. Lowe (2012), 44-45.

[14]M. Ficsor (2002), 17-18. Some CMOs have amongst their functions social functions that aim towards the promotion of the recognition of the rights and interests of their members legislatively and socially and towards the promotion of creativity. T. Koskinen-Olsson / N. Lowe (2012), 20.

3 The Distribution of Remuneration by CMOs

3.1 Amount of the Fee and Licensing Conditions

Under a non-voluntary license, fees and licensing conditions are basically determined by contract.[15] In some countries competent authorities only intervene in case of conflict or to determine a ceiling[16] or minimum rate.[17] In Germany, Spain and Switzerland, the contractual determination of fees follows a legally prescribed process, relying on CMOs.[18] In some countries, the amount of fees can be determined by national law,[19] an administrative ad hoc commission,[20] an administrative institution[21] or ministers.[22]

Disagreements over tariffs and licensing conditions customarily arise between the representatives of users and CMOs. Special dispute settlement mechanisms, such as copyright tribunals, exist in some countries. Some countries have established mechanisms whereby tariffs are set or approved by a competent authority. Mediation or arbitration procedures are among the tasks of some copyright offices. In Germany, the arbitration tribunal of the Patent Office functions as an arbitration body in cases of disputes concerning legal licenses.[23] The decision may be deferred to ordinary courts.[24] Under UK law, licensees may refer a license or a licensing scheme to the Copyright Tribunal if they are dissatisfied.[25] The Tribunal's decisions are binding on both parties, but may be appealed before higher courts on questions of law.[26] In Australia, the Copyright Tribunal may determine the rate of payment for educational and government copying licenses in the event the RRO and the user fail to reach an agreement.[27] The Government has established guidelines for the Tribunal to take into account if it is called upon to set fees.[28]

---

[15]R.M. Hilty / S. Nérisson (2012), 61.

[16]Hungary for the reprography, Sec. 21 para. 4, Turkey Sec. 44.

[17]Belgium for the private copy (Royal Decree of March 28, 1996 about private copy remuneration for authors/composers, performing artists, and producers of phonograms and audiovisual works.).

[18]The German Copyright Administration Act Sec. 12, Spain Sec. 25, Switzerland Sec. 46 et seq.

[19]Private copying: Spain Sec. 25. Public lending fee: France Sec. L. 133-3. Reprography: Greece (Sec. 18 of Law 2121/1993 on Intellectual Property and Neighbouring Rights) and Portugal (Law 62/98, amended by Law 50/2004).

[20]France Sec. L. 311-5; India Copyright rules of 1958, Japan Sec. 71, Korea Sec. 25, etc.

[21]India for all remuneration.

[22]Private copying: Poland Sec. 20^1.

[23]The German Copyright Administration Act Sec. 14.

[24]Copyright, Design and Patents Act 1988 Sec. 149.

[25]The German Copyright Administration Act Sec. 14.

[26]T. Koskinen-Olsson / N. Lowe (2012), 31.

[27]The Copyright Tribunal of Australia is an independent body established under Sec. 138 of the Copyright Act 1968.

[28]T. Koskinen-Olsson / N. Lowe (2012), 31.

3.2 Distribution of Remuneration

In cases of remuneration rights, the consent of rights holders is not needed, but they have a right to equitable remuneration. In these cases, debtors are the legitimate users paying the fees to CMOs,[29] and the CMOs collect the remuneration and distribute it to copyright holders. An example of a right to remuneration can be performances of phonograms in broadcasting and other public performances. Holders of related rights have established CMOs to collect and distribute remuneration.[30] Remuneration is paid not only to right holders directly but also to representatives of authors, editors and publishers.

In cases where some rights holders authorize CMOs to manage their rights on the basis of individual tariffs and other conditions, the CMOs perform the role of an agent and offer licenses through a central source.[31]

A basic principle of collective administration is that the remuneration collected by CMOs should be distributed to those individual right holders whose works or objects of related rights have been used.[32] Irrespective of the method of distribution, the aim is to maximize the distribution to rights holders and minimize the costs, while maintaining sufficient accuracy.[33] The remuneration is distributed, on at least an annual basis, to copyright holders, after payment of administrative fees.[34]

The ideal distribution system would be one in which authors receive compensation based on the frequency with which their individual works are used.[35] Some countries have established rules whereby remuneration should be distributed to rights holders according to the actual use of their works.[36]

However, CMOs are not able to administer such a system because it cannot monitor with such detail scrutiny which individual works were being used.[37] Therefore, CMOs often base the collection and distribution of remuneration on

[29]R.M. Hilty / S. Nérisson (2012), 64.

[30]T. Koskinen-Olsson / N. Lowe (2012), 46.

[31]In the digital environment, licensees can check different conditions and buy their licenses online. This type of management is common among many CMOs that offer individualized services to their rights holders. In the field of analogue copying, they customarily continue to apply traditional collective management methods with uniform tariffs and conditions. T. Koskinen-Olsson / N. Lowe (2012), 46.

[32]T. Koskinen-Olsson / N. Lowe (2012), 50.

[33]C. Handke / R. Towse (2007), 943; T. Koskinen-Olsson / N. Lowe (2012), 50.

[34]IFRRO / WIPO (2014), 22.

[35]T. Koskinen-Olsson / N. Lowe (2012), 50; P.F. Burger (1988), 319, 334.

[36]For example, the Lithuanian copyright act provides that the remuneration collected by collective administration associations must be distributed among the authors and other owners of copyright and related rights as proportionately as possible to the actual use of their works and objects of related rights (sec. 48 para. 4).

[37]P.F. Burger (1988), 319, 335.

some form of statistically obtained data, either through a sampling system or through statistical surveys.[38]

In principle, two main options exist in distributing remuneration; (1) title-specific distribution based on full reporting, partial reporting based on sampling, or objective availability basis[39] or (2) non-title specific distribution on the basis of surveys.[40] Besides, the remuneration may be used for general purposes.[41]

In some countries and certain management areas, rights holders have opted for non-title specific distribution of remuneration. Under the distribution method on a non-title specific basis, remuneration is indirectly attributed to individual authors and publishers.[42] The CMOs using this method customarily obtain their mandates through rights holders' associations and not directly from individual rights holders.[43] The association then channels the revenue to their members and rights holders in their category.[44] Statistical surveys are used to collect generic, non-title specific information regarding the volume of copying in the type of material and category of publication, rather than identifying the specific publication, author and publisher.[45] Data is collected from a limited number of users covered by the agreement, for a limited period of time.[46] Surveys are conducted at intervals, normally every 4–5 years.[47]

In Korea, regarding the educational use privilege, KORRA conducted a survey sample design study on the distribution of remuneration for classroom education purposes in an effort to maintain transparency of remuneration distribution raised by universities, while completing the establishment of a system designed for simplification of contract signing and collection services. KORRA participated in a taskforce team set up to come up with standards for classroom education support purposes, which is another type of remuneration stipulated in Section 25(2) of the Copyright Act. In case of the library privilege, actual use is reported fully to the clearing body designated by the Minister of MCST by means of automated reporting systems that calculate compensation arising from those uses (reproduction and transmission), which is mandatory for users (Sec. 9 of KCA Enforcement Decree).

---

[38] IFRRO / WIPO (2014), 22. To find out what and how much is used, CMOs commission a reputable market research company to carry out surveys.

[39] Objective availability or possibility method is based on the assumption that all material that exists on the market can be used and at some stage probably will be used, see details, T. Koskinen-Olsson / N. Lowe (2012), 51.

[40] See details, T. Koskinen-Olsson / N. Lowe (2012), 51.

[41] IFRRO / WIPO (2014), 40.

[42] T. Koskinen-Olsson / N. Lowe (2012), 51.

[43] T. Koskinen-Olsson / N. Lowe (2012), 51.

[44] Reprography or photocopying is one example. T. Koskinen-Olsson / N. Lowe (2012), 51.

[45] IFRRO / WIPO (2014), 22; T. Koskinen-Olsson / N. Lowe (2012), 51.

[46] T. Koskinen-Olsson / N. Lowe (2012), 51.

[47] IFRRO (1998), 51.

3.3 *Determination of Distribution Schemes*

CMOs collect all the remuneration and distribute it to their members according to distribution rules and policies. These rules and policies are established by agreement between the CMOs' governing bodies and the membership to ensure they are fair, efficient, accurate and transparent.

Normally, the distribution schemes can be determined by national legislation, the regulations of the collecting society, and by agreements.[48] In most countries the distribution scheme is determined by the membership of the CMO,[49] usually subject to the approval of, or review by, a supervisory body.[50] In some countries, however, elements of the distribution scheme are fixed by law or detailed regulation or other state intervention.

The distribution scheme includes a number of requirements for the CMOs, including that all relevant copyright holders be entitled to membership, and that its rules include provisions to ensure its members' interests are adequately protected in relation to distribution of amounts collected by it. Thus, distribution policy is to be determined by the CMOs according to rules provided to the competent authorities. A similar approach has been taken in most countries to the collection and distribution of remunerations under other statutory licence schemes, such as those for educational copying and retransmission, etc.

In most cases, remuneration is paid not only to rightholders directly but also to rightholders via another CMO or rightholder organisation.[51] It is therefore necessary to determine how much of the levy remuneration belongs to authors, and how much to publishers.[52] Many countries provide that distribution of collected fees shall be fair or equitable.[53] German law refers to the internal proceedings within CMOs.[54] In case of statutory remuneration rights, does the law of some countries determine the percentage of the collected remuneration to be received by particular groups of right owners (e.g., the allocation between authors and producers, among different kinds of authors, performers, producers, etc.).

---

[48]R.M. Hilty / S. Nérisson (2012), 64.

[49]For example, Austria, Germany, and Slovakia. In Denmark, the statutes of COPY-DAN state that fees collected for photocopying shall be split 50/50 between the author and the publisher.

[50]For example, the Patent and Trademark Office in Germany or the Control Unit for Collecting Societies in Belgium.

[51]IFRRO / WIPO (2014), 40.

[52]This is known as the author-publisher split. IFRRO / WIPO (2014), 23.

[53]For example, section 49 of the Swiss Copyright Act requires that the proceeds are to be distributed in proportion to the revenue from the individual work or performance, and that the distribution among right holders in the same work applies according to *equitable shares*.

[54]According to the Article 7 of the German Copyright Management Act, disbursements made by CMO (thus regarding all remuneration rights) have to be based on a fixed disbursement scheme, thereby preventing arbitrary payments. Furthermore this Act allows CMOs to favor "culturally important works" and to allocate a part of the revenues to social funds benefitting their members (Secs. 7 and 8 of German Copyright Administration Act).

Table 1 Determination of distribution schemes

TI levy country (with operational levy system)	Determination by law or regulation	... by CMO	... subject to approval/ review by state body	Author-publisher split by law or regulation	Q-P split by CMO rules
Austria		×			50:50
Belgium		×	×	50;50	
Burkina Faso	×			65:35	
Cameroon	×	×		50:50	
Croatia		×		To be decided	
Czech Republic		×		60:40	
France	×	×		50:50	
Germany	×	×	×		70:30 for fiction and press works, otherwise 50:50
Ghana		×		60:40	
Greece		×		50:50	
Hungary		×		60:40	
Lithuania	×	×		60:40	
Poland		×		50:50	
Portugal		×		50:50	
Romania		×	×	50:50	
Slovakia		×			73:27
Slovenia		×		50:50	

IFRRO / WIPO (2014), 40

The laws of some countries provide exact shares for some of the remuneration rights.[55] Table 1 shows determination of distribution schemes in text and image levies (TI levies).

Some distribution schemes entitle "eligible" owners of copyright in sound recordings, and in works embodied in sound recordings, to participate in the distribution of remuneration from the scheme.[56] The other groups requiring consideration are performers and producers.[57]

[55]For example in Belgium, Cameroon, Poland, Portugal, Romania, and Slovenia, the law requires that half of the remunerations be assigned to authors and half to publishers in the case of private copy fee for text/images. In Korea, a distribution "schedule" must be negotiated between the CMOs and their members, subject to its approval by a public authority. Remunerations can be distributed to rights holders directly through the right holder's association. All collected remunerations on the basis of blanket licenses are paid to the member associations representing different categories of authors and publishers for further distribution. In cases where a license is granted on an individual basis outside the scope of the blanket license, proceeds are paid directly to authors and publishers concerned by KORRA. For details, R.M. Hilty / S. Nérisson (2012), 65-67.

[56]The following explanations, see R.M. Hilty / S. Nérisson (2012), 65-66.

[57]Broadcasters receive a share of private copying income in some, but not all, countries which currently have private copying compensation schemes. Broadcasters receive a share of video

Private copy fees for sound recordings shall be distributed as follows: 50 % for authors, 25 % for performers, and 25 % for producers in France,[58] Poland,[59] and Spain[60]; 40 % for authors, 30 % for performers, and 30 % for producers in Bosnia and Herzegovina, Lithuania and Russia[61]; 33 % each for the three groups in Israel; 45 % for authors (composers and writers), 30 % for performers, and 25 % for the phonogram producer in Hungary.[62] Private copy fees for recordings of audiovisual works shall be distributed as follows: 1/3 for authors, 1/3 for performers, and 1/3 for producers in Israel, France,[63] and Spain; 40 % for authors, 30 % for performers, and 30 % for producers in Russia[64]; 35 % for authors, 25 % for artistic performers and 40 % for producers of videograms in Poland[65]; 13 % for the producers of movie pictures, 22 % for the cinematographic creators of movie pictures, 4 % for creators of fine arts, designs and authors of artistic photographs, 16 % for script writers, 20 % for composers and lyricists, and 25 % for performers in Hungary.[66] Private copy fees for other works privately reproduced on digital carriers shall be distributed in equal shares to authors and publishers in France.[67] The Hungarian copyright law also provides for a mandatory distribution scheme in the case of the reprography. Of the *reprography remuneration*, 40 % shall be due to the publishers, 25 % to the authors of non-fiction and scientific works, 25 % to the authors of other literary works, and 10 % to the authors of works of fine arts and artistic photographs.[68] Remuneration for broadcasting and communication to the public of phonograms shall be distributed in equal shares among performers and producers in Bosnia and Herzegovina, Lithuania and Russia,[69] whereas Greece foresees 55 % for the intellectual creators, 25 % for performers and 20 % for producers[70]; and Hungary 45 % for authors, performers 30 %, and producers 25 %.[71] Hungarian law also states regarding movies: 22 % for filmmakers, 16 % for scriptwriters, 20 % for composers and lyricists, 25 % for performers, 4 % for fine artists, applied

---

royalties in Austria, Belgium, Denmark, France and the Netherlands. Australian Copyright Council (2001), 37-39.

[58]Sec. L. 311-7.

[59]Sec. 20 para. 2.

[60]Royal Decree 1434/1992.

[61]Bosnia-Herzegovina Sec. 22, Lithuania Sec. 21 of the government resolution n° 1106, Russia Sec. 1245 item 3.

[62]Sec. 20 para. 4.

[63]Sec. L. 311-7.

[64]Sect. 1245 item 3.

[65]Sec. 20 para. 2.

[66]Sec. 20 para. 5.

[67]Sec. L. 311-7.

[68]Sec. 21 para. 6.

[69]Bosnia-Herzegovina Sec. 22, Russia Sec. 1326 item 3.

[70]Greece Sec. 18.

[71]Hungary Sec. 20 para. 4.

artists and photographers, and 13 % for producers, unless the parties agree otherwise.[72]

Where the author-publisher split is not pre-determined by law, the distribution plan must address the split of remuneration.[73] The plan may provide for a uniform split, or for different splits for different types of work.[74] In most cases the remuneration split is fixed through the collecting society on the basis of agreements between the right holders or right holder groups concerned. However such distribution rules are normally subject to government supervision exercised by competent authorities.

The author/publisher split varies from one country to another. A 50/50 split is common. In some cases, factors such as the type of publication, type of material and copyright ownership are also taken into account. When the author-publisher split is being negotiated, authors generally claim their share of the money on the basis of the exclusive right granted to authors in copyright law to authorize any form of reproduction of their works.

One work has customarily several rights holders who may have participated in the creation of that work in different capacities.[75] In case of a musical work, the shareholders can be a composer, a lyricist and a music publisher. In case of photocopying a published work, the shareholders can be the authors of the literary, artistic and/or musical work (for printed sheet music) and the publisher.[76] Distribution rules of the CMO define how the remuneration allocated to one work is to be distributed among the shareholders of that work.[77] Distribution principles are normally decided by the General Meeting as the highest decision making body of the CMO.[78]

In Korea, the member organizations of KORRA have negotiated a more detailed scheme for the split between authors and publishers depending on the category of publication that has been photocopied. As of 2014, remuneration for both non-fiction works and fiction works is distributed 50/50 between authors and publishers by KORRA. Although standardized splits may assist in the administration process of KORRA & the MCST, publishers overwhelmingly expressed their opinion that contractual splits should be a matter for the publisher and the author to decide. Publishers may claim a share of the proceeds on the basis of protection given in copyright legislation. Such a legal basis is found in the Korean Copyright Act, which grants a 3-year period for the protection of the publishing arrangement.

---

[72]Hungary Sec. 20 para. 5.

[73]IFRRO / WIPO (2014), 23.

[74]E.g. in VG WORT, a 50:50 split applies to scientific works, and a 70:30 split in favor of authors applies to other cases. IFRRO / WIPO (2014), 23.

[75]T. Koskinen-Olsson / N. Lowe (2012), 52.

[76]T. Koskinen-Olsson / N. Lowe (2012), 52.

[77]T. Koskinen-Olsson / N. Lowe (2012), 52.

[78]T. Koskinen-Olsson / N. Lowe (2012), 52.

Furthermore, publishers base their claims on legislation designed to control unfair competition and/or on contractual agreements with authors.

A typical distribution scheme also allocates funds to foreign right holders on a non-discriminatory and objective basis.[79] The plan must also address the issue of what administrative costs will be applied, and whether any deductions will be made for social or cultural purposes.

3.4 *Disagreement on Distribution*

A CMO must establish procedures for the handling of disputes on the split of the proceeds between rights holders. Agreement on the split can, of course, be set as a condition for the payment of remuneration. However, many CMOs have developed dispute settlement procedures to resolve conflicts which may arise over the revenue split.

In Korea, the Administration Committee of KORRA elects a separate Distribution Board which only deals with the distribution of revenues. If negotiations between the rights holders' associations fail, the Distribution Board appoints two mediators from its members, usually one publisher and one author. Lack of success in the mediation process results in the case being sent to the Distribution Board, which eventually passes a resolution on distribution and payment. This decision may be appealed to an internal Arbitration Board, consisting of three copyright law experts, which makes the final decision. Even if a right holder is of the opinion that the determined amount is unreasonable, it cannot be contended legally according to any formality or by way of a lawsuit. The relevant problem should be solved politically.

3.5 *Deduction of Operational Costs Etc.*

3.5.1 Deduction of Administrative Fees

Administrative fees are deducted from total collection, and the rest is distributed to rights holders.[80] It should be noted that only reasonable and indispensable costs may be deducted from the collected remuneration by CMOs.[81] At the outset, the CMO needs to become self-financing so that its costs can be deducted from collected revenue, the bulk of which goes to the rights holders.[82] In some countries, the amount of costs that can be deducted from total revenue is defined by the law or

[79] IFRRO / WIPO (2014), 23.

[80] T. Koskinen-Olsson / N. Lowe (2012), 52.

[81] T. Koskinen-Olsson / N. Lowe (2012), 52.

[82] T. Koskinen-Olsson / N. Lowe (2012), 52.

regulations pertaining to collective management.[83] Where this is not the case, there are industry standards for defining maximum cost shares.[84]

Administrative fees vary among CMOs and from year to year. They may be set by the CMO annually, according to administrative costs in the year in question, as done, for example, by VG WORT in Germany; or the costs may be a set fee according to the law, as for example in Romania.[85] The maximum percentage administrative fee may also be prescribed in some legislation as between 20 and 30 %; in some countries, even lower.[86] It may also depend on the type of rights administered.[87]

3.5.2 Social and Cultural Deductions

What other deductions may be permissible from gross revenue before distribution to rights holders? A deduction for social/and or cultural purposes can be made. Deductions for such purposes are quite typical in the case of traditional collective management organizations. Cultural purposes mainly mean the use of certain amounts for the promotion of creativity (through prizes, competitions, fellowships, etc.), while social purposes usually involve the transfer of the money to health insurance or pension funds.[88] The CMOs concerned are usually obliged or authorised by law to make such deductions (often with a cap on the allocation for this purpose), although the amount deducted may vary from year to year and sector to sector, as determined by the governing bodies of the society.[89] Some CMOs apply this deduction for both social and cultural purposes, some only to one of these.[90] There is often a special body, such as a committee, in the CMO that is authorized to decide how money is used for social and cultural purposes.[91] In some countries, the law prescribes that a certain percentage be allocated for cultural purposes, in particular from remuneration for private copying.[92]

The maximum level of social and cultural deductions in the TI sector is normally 10 %, and in most subsectors the figure is much lower.[93] Nevertheless, it should be noted that in the *Amazon v Austro-Mechana* case,[94] which involved the private

[83]IFRRO & WIPO (2014), Id., 41 (Table 15: Administrative charge, and social and cultural deductions, as percentage of TI levy income).

[84]T. Koskinen-Olsson / N. Lowe (2012), 52.

[85]IFRRO & WIPO (2014), 23.

[86]For example, in Poland the limit is 20 %.

[87]T. Koskinen-Olsson / N. Lowe (2012), 53.

[88]See F. Melichar (1991), 47, 48.

[89]IFRRO / WIPO (2014), 24.

[90]For a more detailed explanation, see F. Melichar (1991), 50-53.

[91]T. Koskinen-Olsson / N. Lowe (2012), 53.

[92]F. Melichar (1991), 51-52; T. Koskinen-Olsson / N. Lowe (2012), 53.

[93]IFRRO / WIPO (2014), 24.

[94]C-521/11, 11/7/2013.

copying levy, the CJEU approved a social and cultural deduction of 50 % provided the rightholders benefit from the social and cultural funds on a fair and nondiscriminatory basis.[95]

3.6 *Non-distributable Amounts*

If the amount collected is extremely low and the costs associated with the distribution cannot be covered by a reasonable part thereof, it may be justified that the remuneration collected is not distributed and is used for common purposes. Several problems can occur which prevent distributions proceeding on time[96]:

- insufficient, unreliable or no data at all from users to allocate the money to a work or an author;
- in the case of compulsory collective management, CMOs collect both for members and non-members / non-represented right holders; constant efforts are made by CMOs to identify non-members. This requires human resources capacity and can be very time consuming.
- dispute over ownership, entitlement to receive royalties or on the split between co-authors.
- the estate of a deceased author has not been settled, etc.

It is therefore important that the money can be kept for a certain time, in order for the CMO, the user or the author himself to resolve the situation. CMOs have developed and apply procedures to address the most common problems (dispute resolution procedure for conflicts between authors, and international identifiers of works and authors), but some reasons fall outside their remit, or require the active cooperation of users for instance.[97] Once the issue is resolved, the society distributes the money with due diligence. However, there are situations which are never resolved. There is therefore a need for a time-limit after which CMOs are no longer obliged to hold on to the money. Generally provided for in national legislation, this period varies from 3 to 10 years.[98]

In the case of non-distributable amounts, it is important to find an answer to offer benefits to the active community of authors and their works. Firstly, the amounts are added to the rights revenue to be distributed.[99] The majority of CMOs add the non-distributable amounts to the rights revenue to be distributed at the end of the designated period. This is the choice made by the general assembly or the board of the societies. Secondly, the amounts are also allocated to cultural and social funds.

---

[95]IFRRO / WIPO (2014), 24.

[96]Society of Audiovisual Authors (2013).

[97]Society of Audiovisual Authors (2013).

[98]Society of Audiovisual Authors (2013).

[99]Society of Audiovisual Authors (2013).

In a few countries, the law or the statutes of societies provide that non-distributable amounts are allocated to cultural and social funds dedicated to the support of authors and cultural activities. However, under Korean law, it is not allocated for cultural or social funds created for the benefit of authors or performing artists. Regarding the privilege for educational use, "undistributed fees" (i.e. not received by right holders) may be used for the purpose of the public interest after a lapse of 3 years from the prior announcement of the remuneration distribution (KCA Sec. 25 (8)).[100] Lastly, a minority of CMOs use part of the non-distributed royalties to cover the management costs of the society, thereby reducing management fee deductions from members' royalties.

3.7 *Distribution of Remuneration to Outsiders and Foreign Right Holders*

The distribution rules of each CMO must allow for the fact that the collections relate to all works copied within the country concerned, not only to works written or published by members of the CMO. The rules must therefore address the issue of national non-members (sometimes referred to as outsiders) and foreign right holders.[101]

National treatment is one of the basic principles of collective management, and based on the provisions in international conventions, this means that foreign rights holders cannot be treated any less favorably than national ones. The share of the levy remuneration attributable to foreign works can be determined by statistical surveys, market availability or other objective data, and distributed through bilateral agreements with foreign CMOs.[102]

Non-represented rightholders have a right to individual remuneration on the basis of the law, and non-represented rightholders have also a possibility of prohibiting the use of their works. As to national non-members, it is important that an RRO's distribution of levy remuneration be publicly known within the country concerned, and that all national authors and publishers should have an equal opportunity of benefiting from it. Typically, national legislation or regulation has provisions to ensure that this is the case.[103]

The distribution rules may follow explicit provisions in national law,[104] or in the statutes of the RROs, or both. The following very general principles apply[105]:

[100]The announcement shall be carried out in a general daily newspaper registered with nationwide distribution and on the internet homepage of the KORRA (Sec. 7 Enforcement Decree KCA).

[101]IFRRO / WIPO (2014), 24.

[102]IFRRO has developed sample agreements. IFRRO / WIPO (2014), 24.

[103]IFRRO / WIPO (2014), 24.

[104]For example the German Administration of Copyright Act.

[105]IFRRO / WIPO (2014), 24.

1. Distribution should be in accordance with clear, published rules.
2. Distribution should be based on objective and non-discriminatory parameters.
3. The rules should be in accordance with the requirements of national law.
4. Insofar as not determined by national law, the rules should be democratically determined by the members of the RRO.

Revenue received for copied foreign works is distributed to sister organisations abroad in accordance with reciprocal agreements.[106] In absence of an agreement with a country, the payment is set aside in a separate bank account until an agreement has been signed. By KORRA's reciprocal agreements with foreign counterparts around the world, remuneration is distributed abroad to compensate for the copying of foreign works that takes place in Korea. Similarly, KORRA receives payment from foreign counterparts for onward distribution to Swedish copyright holders for the copying of Swedish works that takes place abroad.

4 Conclusion

In the past three decades, there have been dramatic changes in the copyright laws. Most countries have made dramatic reforms in the field of copyright law, with the result that the level of copyright protection has reached or even exceeded the reasonable level of protection. However, a strengthened copyright system has not led to a balance among holders of copyright and related rights in the field of collective management.[107] There are three principles in this field which should be applied and which may be significant from the viewpoint of compliance with existing international norms.[108] The first principle is that the monitoring of uses and the collection of remuneration should be as comprehensive as possible, provided that the costs of these activities can be kept at a reasonable level. The second principle is that rights owners should enjoy equal treatment in this respect. The extent and intensity of monitoring uses and collecting remuneration should be established in such a way that they do not prejudice the interests of particular categories of right owners.[109] Finally, the third principle is that appropriate legislative and administrative measures should facilitate the monitoring of uses and collection of remuneration by joint management organizations. Furthermore, the fullest possible cooperation of users in these fields should be prescribed as an obligation, and enforcement measures and sanctions should be available against users who create any unreasonable obstacles to such activities of CMOs.[110]

---

[106]There are two types of reciprocal agreement, the Type A Agreement and the Type B agreement. For details, available at: www.ifrro.org/sites/default/files/distributionof-remuneration-19981.pdf.

[107]I.H. Lee (2012), 605.

[108]M. Ficsor (2002), 147.

[109]M. Ficsor (2002), 147. This principle also applies to equal treatment of members and non-members (including right holders who are not members of CMOs).

[110]M. Ficsor (2002), 147.

Successful collective management inevitably leads to a harmonization of different values. That means that the copyright law should be fundamentally overhauled in the near future to establish certain appropriate standards to protect copyright holders and the need for appropriate remuneration for all categories of right holders. It is important that appropriate remuneration include all authors as well as performers. It should be noted that, subject to the non-distributable amounts, individual distribution may only be disregarded where the amount of remuneration is so small that distribution could not be carried out at a reasonable cost. The government or CMOs should establish rules about non-distributable amounts. It is also important that fair remuneration not just be tied to exceptions in exclusive rights, but actually cover contractual practice. It is hoped that the newly reformed copyright laws will remove the defects of the current laws, and contain a provision for improvements to a more harmonised definition of the remuneration requirement and transparency in what happens with the money collected through remunerations.

References

Burger, P.F. (1988), The New Photocopy Remuneration Provisions in the Federal Republic of Germany and Their Application to Foreign Authors under International Copyright Law, IIC, 319-336

Ficsor, M. (2002), Collective Management of Copyright and Related Rights, WIPO, available at: www.wipo.int/edocs/pubdocs/en/copyright/855/wipo_pub_855.pdf

Gervais, D. (2010), Collective Management of Copyright: Theory and Practice in the Digital Age, in: D. Gervais (Ed.), Collective Management of Copyright and Related Rights, 1-28, Wolters Kluwer

Handke, C. / Towse, R. (2007), Economics of Copyright Collecting Societies, IIC, 937-957

Hilty, R.M. / Nérisson, S. (Eds.) (2012), Balancing Copyright-A Survey of National Approaches, 1-78, 603-621, Springer

IFRRO (1998), IFRRO DETAILED PAPERS — Distribution of Remuneration, available at: www.ifrro.org/sites/default/files/distributionof-remuneration-19981.pdf

IFRRO / WIPO (2014), International Survey on Text and Images Copyright Levies, available at: www.ifrro.org/sites/default/files/levies_2014_online.pdf

Koskinen-Olsson, T. / Lowe, N. (2012), Educational Material on Collective Management of Copyright and Related Rights — Module 1: General Aspects of Collective Management, WIPO, available at: http://www.wipo.int/edocs/pubdocs/en/wipo_pub_emat_2014_1.pdf

Il Ho Lee, (in) Hilty, Reto M., Nérisson, Sylvie (Eds.), Balancing Copyright - A Survey of National Approaches, Springer, 2012.

von Lewinski, S. (2004), Mandatory Collective Administration of Exclusive Rights — A Case on its Compatibility with International and EC Copyright Law, e-Copyright Bulletin January – March 2004, 1-14

Melichar, F. (1991), Deductions Made by Collecting Societies for Social and Cultural Purposes in Light of International Copyright Law, IIC, 47-60

Waziri, A. / Mohamed, S.O. (2007), Collective Management of Copyright and Related Rights—Trends and Challenges for Developing Countries, available at: www.turin-ip.com/course-documents/documents-2007/archive/2007-edition/papers/papers-2003/WaziriOsman-1

Control Mechanisms for CRM Systems and Competition Law

Reto M. Hilty and Tao Li

Contents

Abstract There are basically two different mechanisms to control collective management organizations (CMOs), namely the general competition-law approach and the sector-specific regulation approach. This chapter explains the features of copyright management (CRM) systems in general and discusses up- and downsides of both approaches. In conclusion it suggests a primary focus on sector-specific regulation. This approach not only takes into account the particularities of two-sided markets in which CMOs act as intermediaries, but also allows the balancing of non-economic values and interests which are among the objectives

---

Reto M. Hilty is Director of the Max Planck Institute for Innovation and Competition; full Professor ad personam at the University of Zurich; Honorary Professor at the University of Munich.
Tao Li is Junior Research Fellow of the Max Planck Institute for Innovation and Competition.

R.M. Hilty (✉) • T. Li
Max Planck Institute for Innovation and Competition, Munich, Germany
e-mail: hilty@ip.mpg.de; tao.li@ip.mpg.de

K.-C. Liu, R.M. Hilty (eds.), *Remuneration of Copyright Owners*, MPI Studies on Intellectual Property and Competition Law 27, DOI 10.1007/978-3-662-53809-8_9

of CMOs. Sector-specific regulation is further capable of addressing governance issues of CMOs; above all, it promotes transparency for both right holders and users by providing ex ante guidance. General competition law, in contrast, applies ex post and is particularly likely to become a last resort to control CMOs.

1 Introduction

In pace with the development of network technologies and new possibilities of digital rights management (DRM), right holders largely retain the ability to individually control and manage their copyrights.[1] At the same time, business models of copyright and other culture-related industries are developing very dynamically and therefore increasingly require flexible licensing models.[2] Both the technological and market environments for traditional collective management organizations (CMOs) accordingly have changed over time. Copyright management (CRM) systems, in contrast, have basically remained as they were designed in the pre-digital era. Above all, the legal framework, the governance structure and the control mechanisms have not been adapted to this new environment and to new needs of the right holders and users.[3]

Most importantly, right holders may have an interest in choosing their own, possibly more efficient ways of adding value to their exclusive rights. CMOs, however, have special tasks and play a particular role, since they act as intermediaries between right holders and users. Users (the "clients" of CMOs), on the other hand, often complain about licensing conditions and royalty fees. In this respect, CMOs act in a "two-sided market"[4] which may require partial restrictions of contractual freedom and, with it, exclusive rights.[5] As a consequence, it may be impossible for right holders to withdraw certain of their rights from one CMO so as to assign them to anther CMO, or to manage their rights individually. Hence, since the CRM systems to a large degree have failed to adapt to the new reality,[6] right holders and users increasingly look for an alternative legal framework to achieve their—although quite often diverging—aspirations. On a regulatory basis, however,

[1] V. Vázquez-Lopez (2010), 689-695; D. Gervais (2010), 17-28; P. Gilliéron (2006), 952-956; R.M. Hilty, S. Nérisson (2013), 222-224.

[2] N. Searle, G. White (2013), 45-56.

[3] Recital 8 of Directive 2014/26/EU of 26 February 2014 on collective management of copyright and related rights and multi-territorial licensing of rights in musical works for online use in the internal market, 84 OJ L72-98.

[4] J. Drexl, S. Nérisson, F. Trumpke, R.M. Hilty (2013), 325-327; J. Drexl (2013), 11, 81.

[5] R.M. Hilty (2010), 151; R.M. Hilty, S. Nérisson (2013), 224-225.

[6] D. Gervais (2011), 591-617; about competitive deficit and its consequences, see R. Podszun (2014), 179-181.

not much has happened yet. Instead courts have repeatedly relied on competition law. Above all the Court of Justice of the European Union (CJEU) has in a number of cases intervened based on competition law.[7] Also the US jurisdiction has dealt with competition law in connection with the control of CMOs.[8] In view of these attempts, the question arises as to whether competition law may indeed create an appropriate legal framework to improve the functioning of CRM systems in the face of new technical realities and market conditions, in particular to provide effective remedies to lacking or inadequate governance and control mechanisms.

To answer this question, we first give an overview analyzing the features of CRM systems and the possible regulatory approaches (Sect. 2). Next, after discussing the prerequisites for interventions based on competition law and the range of application of competition law, the shortcomings and potential of the competition law approach will be explored (Sect. 3). Potential shortcomings of the competition law approach lead to another question, namely, to what extent other control mechanisms (especially sector-specific regulation) could be a more appropriate solution to re-align the CRM systems and encourage CMOs to adapt to the new environment (Sect. 4). In the conclusion it will be considered why improving the CRM systems only based on competition law would most likely be doomed to failure (Sect. 5).

2 Features of CRM Systems and Regulatory Approaches

2.1 CRM Systems, Monopolies and Consequences

Different from material property, intangible goods (such as copyright-protected works) can be used by many users at the same time without losing their quality. In the historical aspect, CRM systems were indeed established due to legal, technical and economic developments, which made it impossible for copyright holders to effectively control and prohibit mass uses of their works. The first and still existing CMO was the French *Société des Auteurs et Compositeurs Dramatiques* (SACD), founded in 1837.[9] The scope of its management encompassed the rights in

[7]See in particular CJEU, Case 78/70 Deutsche Grammophon v. Metro [1971] ECR 487; Case 127/73 BRT v. SABAM [1974] ECR 313; Cases 55/80 and 57/80 Musikvertrieb Membran GmbH v. GEMA [1981] ECR 147; Case 7/82 GVL v. Commission [1983] ECR 483.

[8]In 1941, the United States brought separate antitrust suits against Broadcast Music, Inc. (BMI) and the American Society of Composers, Authors and Publishers (ASCAP). Both suits were settled by Consent Decree. See *U.S. v. BMI*, 1940-43 Trade Cas. (CCH) paras. 56, 096, 381 (E.D. Wisc.1941); *U.S. v. ASCAP*, 1940-43 Trade Cas. (CCH) paras. 56,104, 402 (S.D.N.Y.1941). These Consent Decrees have been amended over time. For the latest amended Consent Decrees see *U.S. v. BMI*, 1996-1 Trade Cas. (CCH) paras. 71, 379 (S.D.N.Y. Nov. 18, 1994); *U.S. v. ASCAP*, 2001-2 Trade Cas. (CCH) paras. 73, 474 (S.D.N.Y. June 11, 2001).

[9]A. Schierholz (2010), 1151-1152.

dramatic-musical works, mainly stage performances and public performance of stage productions. At that time the demand for using the works was so great that the creators lost the ability to grant licenses and negotiate individually. Likewise, it became increasingly complicated for users to identify the original right holders and to negotiate licenses individually.[10] Such concerns from both sides prompted the emergence of CMOs.[11]

In the meantime, from an economic perspective, CRM systems can be seen as an example of an intermediary model, aiming at reducing high transaction costs and at enhancing transaction security to the benefit of both the right holders and the users.[12] In fact, it should be borne in mind that copyright law is not solely intended to protect authors and other right holders. Particularly, CRM systems help to benefit the society at large. The collectivization of thousands of individual right holders and millions of works make it possible for CRM systems to overcome unreasonably high transaction costs and turn "useless" individual rights into "useable" bundles of rights.[13] In other words, CRM systems increase trade in copyrights, especially the rights that individually would not be economic to trade.

At the same time—and even more importantly, at least in civil law systems, compared to the (more utilitarian-oriented) common law countries—CRM systems are deemed to fulfill non-economic values as well, notably with a view to certain social and cultural tasks.[14] Already at the birth of CMOs in France, CRM systems were seen as an issue of solidarity.[15] This means, firstly, that CMOs promote a strong bargaining position for all right holders (creators and companies—famous or weak) against users, and thereby make sure they receive their rewards. Secondly, amongst the right holders themselves, CMOs safeguard the remuneration right of authors and artists against powerful producers and publishers. Thirdly, solidarity also exists in the fact that some works of famous creators may cross-subsidize the costlier administration of less successful works.

Such non-economic objectives to a large degree contradict unrestricted competition in the market in which CMOs operate. In particular, the administration of minority cultures or economically less successful creators hardly can be carried out lucratively—and therefore could be omitted in an overly competitive environment. In view of that, restrictions of competition quite often go hand in hand with specific administration duties of CMOs in both civil and common law jurisdictions. In the US, for instance, case law of 1941 established the duty of ASCAP (American Society of Composers, Authors and Publishers, established in 1914) to accept all

[10]W. Herschel (1967), 26.

[11]R.M. Hilty, S. Nérisson (2013), 224-225.

[12]S. Besen, S. Kirby, S. Salop (1992), 383-411; R. Merges (1996), 1316-1317; G. Hansen, A. Schmidt-Bischoffshausen (2007), 461-463; J. Drexl (2007), 272.

[13]M. Heller (1998), 621-688; M. Kretschmer (2002), 126-137; J. Schovsbo (2012), 170.

[14]S. von Lewinski (2005), 401-407; J. Becker (2008), 33-41.

[15]P. Katzenberger, S. Nérisson (2011), 283-295; R.M. Hilty, S. Nérisson (2013), 225-226. For economic analyses of the risk-sharing in CMOs see A. Snow, R. Watt (2005), 23-35.

songwriters as members without discrimination.[16] In Germany, as well, Section 6 of the Act on the Administration of Copyright and Related Rights of 1965 (*Urheberwahrnehmungsgesetz, UrhWahrnG*) introduced an obligation of CMOs to accept all right holders under certain conditions.

Last but not least, some jurisdictions—especially in the European Union—explicitly protect and promote cultural diversity as one of the tasks of CMOs, which is in line with the aims expressed in Article 167 of the Treaty on the Functioning of the European Union (TFEU).[17] In practice, eleven member states provide in their legislation that collecting societies must set up social or cultural funds to help less fortunate creators and support cultural activities.[18] In France, for instance, all collecting societies together spent € 95 million on cultural activities in 2004.[19] Beyond that, Recital 3 of Directive 2014/26/EU confirms that "[c]ollective management organizations play, and should continue to play, an important role as promoters of the diversity of cultural expression, both by enabling the smallest and less popular repertoires to access the market and by providing social, cultural and educational services for the benefit of their right holders and the public."

On the other hand, due to certain economic features of the markets in which CMOs operate, they have the potential of forming monopolies.[20] In essence—according to antitrust theory—monopolies may arise from "economies of scale" or "economies of scope" and may increase through "network effects". Concretely, this means, firstly, that the fixed costs of a CMO are very high, but the marginal costs for CRM systems are digressive. In order to control and license the works collectively, huge control machineries (offices, platforms, databases, and employees) have to be set up at the beginning. After establishing and maintaining the administrative system, however, the more works a CMO manages, the more the variable costs (arising from expansion of the repertoires) will be reduced. As to the variable costs, there is almost no difference between managing 100,000 works and managing 100,001 works.[21]

Secondly, in terms of economies of scope, CMOs have different tasks (both economic and non-economic). CMOs can not only grant licenses in the light of different needs of users, but also exploit the rights in bundles. At the same time, granting different rights within a "blanket license" leads to more choices and perspectives for users.[22] In addition, due to the network effect, CMOs with larger

[16]See *U.S. v. ASCAP*, 1940-43 Trade Cas. (CCH) paras. 56, 104, 402 (S.D.N.Y.1941) (*supra* n. 8); R.M. Hilty (2012), 35-37.

[17]Recital 3 of Directive 2014/26/EU (*supra* n. 3); A. Schierholz (2010), 1152-1153.

[18]European Affairs (2006), 30.

[19]European Affairs (2006), 39; J. Becker (2008), 33-40.

[20]A. Katz (2005), 12-18.

[21]R. Podszun (2014), 181.

[22]G. Hansen, A. Schmidt-Bischoffshausen (2007), 470.

repertoires may act in a more cost-effective manner, and they are likely to attract more right holders and users over time—which, however, leads to barriers for potential competitors to enter the same market.[23] For all these reasons, some national legislations limit the number of CMOs directly or indirectly (e.g. through accreditation requirements), or they even stipulate legal monopolies, thus aiming at the widest possible efficiency.

Consequently, due to the above-mentioned functions and features of COMs, the mechanism of the market economy—that competition forces the competitors to improve their goods and services and to attract consumers—seems to be largely dispensed with in the field of CRM systems. Thus, a competitive deficit is the obvious consequence of the special treatment of CMOs by legislatures.[24] The consequences are the problems that all monopolistic markets are faced with: a lack of both downward pressure on prices and incentives to innovate business models and services—problems typically observed in the practice of CMOs.[25] In order to tackle such problems, and to promote a dynamic development of CRM systems as well as of licensing markets, basically two regulatory approaches are available, namely, general competition law and sector-specific legislation.

2.2 Competition Law Control for CRM Systems

Monopolies do not automatically have anti-competitive impacts. Competition law therefore generally only intervenes under certain conditions, in particular the (unilateral) abuse of a dominant market position (Sect. 3.2) or an agreement between competitors which limits competition (Sect. 3.3).[26]

In the case of an abuse of a dominant market position by a CMO, a monopolistic structure may have an impact on two markets: the market of collective management and the market of collective licensing. In both markets the existence of one contractual partner only is likely to lead to unfavorable conditions to right holders as well as to licensees. In the US, for instance, ASCAP was the only CMO at the beginning of the twentieth century. Because of discrimination against right holders and users, a second (SESAC, the Society of European Stage Authors and Composers) and a third CMO (BMI, Broadcast

[23] J. Drexl (2014), 263-268.

[24] R. Podszun (2014), 181.

[25] K. Viscusi, E. Joseph, M. John (2005), 401.

[26] Examples of agreements between CMOs to limit competition in this field are the Santiago and the Barcelona Agreement; see Commission Recommendation 2005/737/EC of 18 May 2015 on collective cross-border management of copyright and related rights for legitimate online music service, OJ L 276/54; see also Commission Decision of 16 July 2008 relating to a proceeding under Article 81 of the EC Treaty and Article 53 of the Agreement on the European Economic Area (Case COMP/C2/38.698—*CISAC*).

Music Inc.) were established in 1930 and 1939 respectively.[27] After that, in 1941 the Antitrust Division of Department of Justice (DOJ) brought a law suit against ASCAP for alleged violations of federal antitrust laws. This law suit was settled with the first Consent Decree, which was of great significance in the history of competition law control of CRM systems.[28] Based on this Consent Decree, ASCAP had to accept all songwriters as members, thereby putting an end to discrimination among right holders.[29] In addition, a duty to license was introduced in this Consent Decree; it allowed users to get non-exclusive licenses to perform all the works in the ASCAP repertory upon written request.[30] Many other jurisdictions followed suit, incorporating these principles into their sector-specific legislations for CMOs (Sect. 2.3).

The application of competition law to such cases, however, is a thorny path and does not necessarily lead to desirable results, especially because the general conditions usually are not met (Sect. 3). Moreover, if courts or competition authorities fail to take account of the specific nature of CMOs (Sect. 2.1), interventions based on competition law may generate negative effects on the specific objectives of CRM systems. For instance beyond the "duty to manage the rights of all right holders" and the "duty to license under the same conditions", established in the above-mentioned Consent Decree in 1941 and its revised versions of 2001, there are also other issues which continue being discussed under antitrust laws in the US till today. One example is the question of whether CMOs should be prevented from requiring an exclusive transfer of rights.[31] Another question is whether and to what extent the rate of a royalty should be controlled by courts (in terms of reasonable fees).[32]

As to the first question, freedom to license individually on the one hand may lead to more income for right holders; in some situations it also may lead to more flexibility for users who have individual concerns. On the other hand, the possibility of direct transactions between right holders and users weakens the bargaining power of CMOs. Additionally, powerful users could force certain right holders to grant licenses for free or at unfair prices. In the US, however, it remains possible to

[27]SESAC was established by the right holders from Europe whom ASCAP refused to accept as members; BMI was established by the radio broadcasters, for whom ASCAP tried to double its tariffs. See J. Drexl (2013), 217.

[28]In the US, most of the cases concerning cartel issues are settled by "Consent Decree"; for more details about the legal effect of a Consent Decree see R. Epstein (2007), 1-14; T. Lindstrom, K. Tighe (1974), IX.

[29]Para. X. A. of the ASCAP Consent Decree: *U.S. v. ASCAP*, 2001-2 Trade Cas. (CCH) paras. 73, 474 (S.D.N.Y. June 11, 2001) (*supra* n. 8).

[30]*Id.*, para. VI.

[31]*Id.*, para. IV. A.

[32]*Id.*, para. IX. D-E.

license rights individually as well, whereas most other jurisdictions prohibit this possibility in view of the above-mentioned drawbacks.[33]

The second question to a certain degree is rooted in particularities of the US system. In contrast to Copyright Royalty Judges (CRJ) from the Copyright Office of the US (who determine statutory remuneration rights),[34] judges from courts—determining contractual royalties—do not need to take into account special paragraphs of the American Copyright Act in making their decisions. In view of that, some scholars argue that contractual royalties should be set up either by the Copyright Office of the US as well or by a specialized decision body.[35] Viewed up close, the question is of a general nature and addresses the discretion courts should have to confine freedom of contract in support of the weaker party.

2.3 Sector-Specific Legislation for CRM Systems

Sector-specific legislation may be used as a legal instrument separate from general competition law. A number of jurisdictions have created such instruments to control CRM systems, which not (only) focus on issues of potential abuse of a dominant market position of CMOs, but also take account of the special features of the related markets, as well as of specific tasks of CMOs.[36] Sector-specific legislation may mean both a specific legislative act and specific provisions related to CRM systems

[33]There are only a few countries in the world that follow the US approach, for instance Ireland and Poland; see e.g. Irish Competition Authority, Decision No. 326 of 18 May 1994, Notification No. CA/2/91E—*Performing Right Society and individual creators/publishers* (Assignment of Copyright), para. 81; Poland: *UOKiK*, Decision of 16 July 2004, Case RWA-21/2004, Annual Report 2006, 20.

[34]The CRJ were set up under the Copyright Royalty and Distribution Reform Act of 2004. CRJ have to apply § 801(b)(1) of the US Copyright Act according to which "reasonable ... rates of royalty payments ... shall be calculated to achieve the following objectives:

(A) To maximize the availability of creative works to the public.

(B) To afford the copyright owner a fair return for his or her creative work and the copyright user a fair income under existing economic conditions.

(C) To reflect the relative roles of the copyright owner and the copyright user in the product made available to the public with respect to relative creative contribution, technological contribution, capital investment, cost, risk, and contribution to the opening of new markets for creative expression and media for their communication.

(D) To minimize any disruptive impact on the structure of the industries involved and on generally prevailing industry practices."

[35]D. Gervais (2011), 610-613; G. Lunney (2010), 333-334; NN (1978), Note CBS v. ASCAP, 802; G. Clark (1980), 749.

[36]A. Dietz (1978), 237-239; J. Fujitani (1984), 134-136.

within a general copyright act.[37] Generally, the subject matters of such legal frameworks are the functions, legal nature and way of establishment, governance structure, contracting duties, supervision or the legal liabilities of CMOs.

In this respect, the German approach may serve as a model.[38] In fact, the German Act on the Administration of Copyright and Related Rights of 1965 is deemed to be "the most comprehensive system" to regulate CMOs.[39] Recently, and particularly in order to implement Directive 2014/26/EU, the German government decided to enact an entirely new law, the Act on Collecting Societies (*Verwertungsgesellschaftengesetz, VGG*), amending the previous legislation on a large scale.[40]

The German arrangement of 1965, like some other European jurisdictions, is based firstly on the "principle of granting of concessions", and secondly on the "principle of continuous supervision of CMOs".[41] Accordingly, part one of the German Act on the Administration of Copyright and Related Rights details the rules, procedures and requirements to establish a CMO (Sections 1–5). The second part not only lays down the rights and duties of CMOs in order to prevent them from abusing their monopoly positions, but also works to benefit society at large (Sections 6–17a).[42] Above all, CMOs in Germany have the duty to set up social or cultural funds to help needy creators and support cultural activities (Section 8). Furthermore, special arbitration and lawsuit procedures have been established to resolve disputes between CMOs and contractual partners (Sections 14–17a), and a supervision authority, the German Patent and Trademark Office (DPMA), oversees the activities of CMOs (third part of German Act on the Administration of Copyright and Related Rights).

---

[37]In some jurisdictions, there are no substantive regulations or acts on CRM systems, but copyright act paragraphs concerning CMOs. For example, in Part IV of the British Copyright Act under the title "Performing Right Tribunal", in Part V of the Irish Copyright Act under the title "Jurisdiction of the Comptroller of Industrial and Commercial Property" and in Part VIII of the Copyright Ordinance of Hong Kong under the title "Copyright Licensing" (Articles 145-168).

[38]Although Germany was not the first jurisdiction to undertake such a specific regulatory framework related to CMOs and to provide special procedural rules in order to handle conflicts between the parties involved. As early as 1932, the Netherlands established a specific arrangement by introducing Article 30a and Article 35a to the Copyright Act and by a related regulation. For more details about the history of CMOs in the Netherlands see A. Dietz (1978), 234-237.

[39]J. Fujitani (1984), 132; A. Dietz (1978), 219.

[40]On 9 June 2015 the German Federal Ministry of Justice and Consumer Protection officially published a first draft and explanatory notes to seek public opinion, available at: www.bmjv.de/SharedDocs/Downloads/DE/pdfs/Gesetze/RefE_Richtlinie_Umsetzungsgesetz.pdf?__blob=publicationFile. The consolidated text of the draft has 6 chapters and 139 articles, while the law of 1965 has 4 chapters and 36 articles. This VGG amendment has been completed in May 2016 (BGBl. I S. 1190).

[41]A. Dietz (1978), 234; BT-Drucksache IV/ 271 (1962), 12.

[42]On the one hand, CMOs are obliged by law to contract with users under certain equal conditions (Section 11 of German Act on the Administration of Copyright and Related Rights); on the other hand, CMOs have the duty to contract with right holders under certain equal conditions (Section 6), and to disclose related information regularly (Section 9).

3 Competition Law in Particular

3.1 Excursus: Particularities of EU Competition Law

Since the 1970s, both the EU Commission and the CJEU have dealt with issues concerning CMOs from the perspective of competition law, which[43] practices are often mentioned as shining examples of how to control CMOs. Yet, that does not mean that the European experiences would equally help in other jurisdictions. There are several reasons for this.

First, the legislative competence of the EU is limited through the European Treaties. Competition law is one of the core competences of the EU (Articles 101 and 102 TFEU). Sector-specific regulation outside competition law, in contrast, not offhand falls under EU competence. Also from a political point of view it would be hard to reach consensus amongst the member states on sector-specific regulation beyond competition law.

Second, one of the underlying objectives of EU law is the establishment of the Internal Market (Article 26(2) TFEU). European competition law above all has to serve this objective[44] by e.g. eliminating obstacles to the free flow of goods, services or capital across the EU. For this reason, case law from the CJEU concerning CMOs as a matter of principle focuses on conflicts between parties located in different Member States. Under these circumstances, insights from EU law are not blindly transferable to national market situations—irrespective of whether or not an EU Member State is concerned. Above all Directive 2014/26/EU needs to be seen from that (limited) perspective. It focuses on collective management of copyright and related rights and multi-territorial licensing of rights in musical works for online use[45]; thereby it directly addresses only one core issue of the Internal Market.[46]

Third, the EU constitutes an exceptionally large market—larger than the majority of national markets in the world where competition among CMOs may indeed be useful to promote efficient administration. If several actors are operating in a market, full advantage of general competition law can be taken, in particular regarding cooperation amongst CMOs (Sect. 3.3). On the other hand, an integrated market related to CRM systems is by no means established in the EU. Competition law therefore applies in a rather singular manner that hardly serves as an example for other jurisdictions.

[43]Decision of the Commission: 71/224/EEC of the Commission of 2 June 1971; CJEU, Case IV/26.760—*GEMA*, [1971] OJ 134/15.

[44]D. Gerber (1994), 98.

[45]For further details see A. Schierholz (2010), 1164-1166.

[46]J. Drexl, S. Nérisson, F. Trumpke, R.M. Hilty (2013), 325-328. Indirectly, however, sector-specific competition law as established through Directive 2014/26/EU to a certain degree may also have harmonizing effects on substantive (national) copyright legislations.

Fourth, even in a large (and integrated) market, competition law will not suffice if we expect more than efficiency from CMOs.[47] Further-reaching expectations—e.g. regarding cultural diversity and other non-economic tasks of CMOs—however, seem to exist in most (at least continental) EU Member States (Sect. 2.1). This is indeed in line with Article 167(1) TFEU which mandates that "the Union shall contribute to the flowering of the cultures of the Member States, while respecting their national and regional diversity and at the same time bringing the common cultural heritage to the fore."[48] The promotion of culture on parallel layers in the EU and in the Member States, however, is a rather special setting and hardly comparable with the situation in other jurisdictions.

3.2 Prerequisites for Interventions Based on Competition Law

According to most standards (including the EU), there are basically three prerequisites for the application of general competition law.

First, the "relevant market" needs to be determined. This basically depends on the substitutability of products or services, be it demand-side substitutability (i.e. of customers), or be it—under certain conditions—supply-side substitutability (i.e. of suppliers).[49] In the context of CMOs, however, if a specific work can be licensed through one CMO only, the question arises as to whether or not (from an objective point of view) the need to use this work can be satisfied by licensing another work. If not, it might be doubtful to conclude what might be appropriate under general antitrust law, namely, that this work as such constitutes the relevant market; this hardly would lead to practical outcomes. In fact, the exclusivity provided by an IP right does not mean that "each copyright-protected work constitutes a proper market, in which the right holder is a monopolist".[50] In addition, individual tastes and preferences differ, a fact that makes it very speculative and unreliable to apply the concept of demand-side substitutability.[51] It should be further recalled that CMOs, as intermediaries, act in a "two-sided market" (Sect. 2.1) which impacts the

[47]For more about the tasks and functions of CMOs in the future, see K.-N. Peifer (2015), 34-35.

[48]R.M. Hilty (2010), 148.

[49]Supply-side substitutability is only taken into consideration when "its effects are equivalent to those of demand-side substitutability in terms of effectiveness and immediacy". See J. Drexl (2013), 75; The EU Commission notice on the definition of relevant market for the purposes of Community competition law (1997), OJ No. C 273, 5, para. 20.

[50]J. Drexl (2013), 75; M. Lamping (2015), 123-124; see also Case 89/205/EES, Magill TV Guide, 1989 ECR L 78/43, para. 20.

[51]J. Drexl (2013), 73, 75.

economic features—particularly the pricing structures and the business strategies[52]—in a way that complicates the definition of the relevant market.

Second, a dominant position in the relevant market needs to be determined. In relation to CMOs, however, complex questions may arise, especially if not only one CMO acts in a market, but if each of several CMOs manages only a specialized repertoire which cannot be found in other CMOs.[53] By general standards, each of them might have a dominant position, but this perception risks ignoring particularities of the related (two-sided) markets.

Third, the dominant market position must have been abused to justify an intervention of competition authorities. There are, however, a number of reasons why certain types of market behavior are not abusive, above all if economic parameters justify that behavior.[54] Price discrimination based on given necessities, for instance, may not be reproachable, especially with a view to characteristics of the two-sided market in which CMOs act.[55] More concretely, if solidarity among different right holders is required by the law, it may be justified for CMOs to subsidize the less successful by disadvantaging more successful authors. Generally speaking, not only the interests of one party, but an overall perspective needs to be taken into account.[56] This may justify, for instance, CMOs' restricting the freedom of contract of right holders to a certain degree in order to increase general welfare.

3.3 Range of Application of Competition Law

Competition law basically applies in two situations: unilateral conduct of one (dominant) market player, and cooperation amongst two or more market participants.

Unilateral conduct can be prohibited under antitrust law if the requirements mentioned under Sect. 3.2 are met. The examples given there, however, indicate the difficulties of applying competition law to CMOs acting under highly different market conditions. It is therefore unlikely that general competition law could adequately govern such two-sided markets.

Cooperation between the CMOs, on the other hand, is desirable and sometimes even required by law; it may be the only way to acquire licenses for works out of a

[52]D. Evans (2003), 325-354.

[53]In the US, although there are three CMOs which grant licenses for the public performance right for the musical works, each of them manages a special repertoire.

[54]In order to minimize the transaction costs, the "blanket licenses" found a basis for justification after a years-long dispute between the American collecting society ASCAP and commercial users CBS (Columbia Broadcasting System); see NN (1978), Note CBS v. ASCAP, 783-803; G. Clark (1980), 741-750.

[55]D. Evans (2003), 355-356; J. Drexl, S. Nérisson, F. Trumpke, R.M. Hilty (2013), 325-327; J. Drexl (2013), 11, 81; E. Arezzo (2015), 548-549.

[56]D. Evans (2009), 355.

repertoire not administered by the approached CMO. Through cooperation, transaction costs can be reduced, and to some extent the idea of a "one-stop shop" may be effectuated. On the other hand, cooperation may imply reciprocal agreements between the parties (e.g. on licensing terms and conditions) which possibly conflict with competition law.

General competition law, however, is hardly in the position to distinguish desirable from undesirable effects of cooperation in a differentiated manner. In the field of licensing agreements on technology, this challenge is addressed in the EU Regulation 316/2014[57] and in the US in the Guidelines for the Licensing of Intellectual Property of 1995.[58] Similar approaches might be conceivable in the context of CRM systems. In any case, the subject matter of regulation seems to be too specific to rely on general competition law, above all because issues outside of competition law need to be addressed.

3.4 Shortcomings and Potential of Competition Law

Competition law primarily focuses on economic efficiency. In view of that, the current CRM systems could be regarded as "second-best solutions" if individual rights management leads to more efficiency[59]—although different perspectives can be taken to evaluate efficiency.[60] In particular, if conflicting interests are involved, normative considerations beyond efficiency are necessary like solidarity amongst more or less successful right holders; this, however, is not a core feature of competition law understood as a primarily economic tool.

Sector-specific regulation, in contrast, is not limited to economic impacts of certain types of market behavior. Rather, other factors such as general welfare or cultural and social values (Sect. 2.1) may be taken into account. Furthermore, sector-specific legislation allows an ex ante perspective, whereas competition law

---

[57]Regulation 316/214 of 21 March 2014 on the application of Article 101(3) of the Treaty on the Functioning of the European Union to categories of technology transfer agreements, OJ L93/17.

[58]Antitrust Guidelines for the Licensing of Intellectual Property, issued by the U.S. DOJ and the Federal Trade Commission, 6 April 1995.

[59]See CJEU, Case C-52/07 *Kanal 5 and TV 4 v. STIM* [2008] ECR I-9275, para. 40: "However, it is conceivable that, in certain circumstances, the application of such a remuneration model may amount to an abuse, in particular when another method exists which enables the use of those works and the audience to be identified and quantified more precisely and that method is capable of achieving the same legitimate aim, which is the protection of the interests of composers and music editors, without however leading to a disproportionate increase in the costs incurred for the management of the contracts and the supervision of the use of musical works protected by copyright." See J. Schovsbo (2012), 185-187.

[60]In the US, after the case CBS v. ASCAP, 620 F.2d 930, 934 (2d Cir. 1980), some scholars have noted the relationship between technical development and management conditions and believe that "blanket licensing is maintained for only so long as is necessary for the minimization of transaction costs"; see NN (1978), Note CBS v. ASCAP, 802.

is doomed to wait passively for markets to develop in undesired directions.[61] On the other hand, the ex post framework of competition law provides substantially more freedom to market participants, especially freedom to develop new business models. For this reason, sector-specific regulation should not overly constrain CMOs. Above all it should not be overlooked that sector-specific regulation does not necessarily replace competition law; rather, there might be some overlap, for which reason sector-specific regulation may be limited to specific concerns of the markets involved without addressing issues of general competition law. Furthermore, different to sector-specific regulation, competition law—at least according to the review of the CJEU and other jurisdictions—fails to contribute much to a modern governance structure of CMOs, to the autonomy of right holders or to the increased transparency of a CMO vis-à-vis users.

4 Potential of Sector-Specific Regulation

4.1 Transparency and Autonomy of Right Holders

Under the umbrella of sector-specific regulation, control mechanisms for CMOs can be classified into two groups, namely, external control approaches (control by authorities or mechanisms outside the CMO) and internal control approaches (control by the members of the CMO).[62] Internal control mechanisms are of paramount importance in view of the fact that CMOs—no matter what kind of legal form they take, be it a non-profit organization, or a profit entity[63]—act mostly as a "trustee for the right holders".[64]

This suggests that it is fundamental that the autonomy of the right holders (in particular of the members of CMOs) have control over a CMO's activities. Important issues should be dealt with in general assemblies of the members, including innovative business models or new technological infrastructures. Yet, autonomy and internal control can only be exercised if right holders obtain sufficient information, which is premised on transparency.

More specifically, sector-specific regulation may foresee certain governance principles, a certain scale of transparency (such as financial information), details of the formulation of the tariffs, deductions made in respect of the management fees, and any revenue allocated to the right holders etc.[65] Moreover, sector-specific regulation similarly should provide transparency not only for members, but also for users, such as information about formulation of the tariff structures and licensing

---

[61] N. Dunne (2015), 43-44.

[62] Recital 49 of Directive 2014/26/EU (*supra* n. 3).

[63] Article 3 of Directive 2014/26/EU (*supra* n. 3).

[64] A. Schierholz (2010), 1154-1155.

[65] Recital 23-24 of Directive 2014/26/EU (*supra* n. 3).

conditions. Most importantly, imposing such duties on CMOs reduces information asymmetry and balances the bargaining power between users and CMOs, particularly with regard to tariff negotiations. In this respect, external control mechanisms gain importance.

4.2 External Control and Dispute Resolution

As opposed to internal control mechanisms exercised by right holders, external control is exercised by independent authorities or institutions. Such mechanisms are important to ensure the interests of right holders, but even more importantly to ensure the interests of users who are not in the position to exercise their influence through internal control mechanisms. In that respect, sector-specific regulation is the most appropriate way of setting up a legal oversight framework.

Disputes between right holders and CMOs usually concern the exercise of the right of membership, deductions of cost or the collection or distribution of royalty fees etc. Settlements may be achieved through internal resolution mechanisms, but also through external mechanisms such as mediation, arbitration or court proceedings.

Disputes between users and CMOs, on the other hand, regularly concern licensing terms and conditions, possibly breach of contractual restrictions etc. Such disputes can only be resolved through external mechanisms such as just mentioned.[66] In contrast to the proceeding based on competition law, such dispute resolution mechanisms have the potential to foster consistency and to settle disputes in a cost- and time-efficient manner.[67]

For all dispute resolution processes, swiftness, independence and impartiality are crucial.[68] Considering the particularities of such conflicts and the copyright-based markets, courts or any other dispute resolution bodies without specialized knowledge are likely to fail to decide appropriately. In particular, a limitation of the perspective to economic efficiency ignores other non-economic values, above all cultural diversity and other public policy goals.[69]

On the European level, Directive 2014/26/EU could have been the opportunity to go beyond a mere competition-oriented approach and to re-balance diverging interests between different groups of right holders. Admittedly, it might well have been difficult to find consensus amongst the Member States due to the number of stakeholders involved and pressure levied on the decision makers. The EU Com-

---

[66]W. Nordemann (1992), 584-589.

[67]J. Fujitani (1984), 135.

[68]Recital 49 of Directive 2014/26/EU (*supra* n. 3).

[69]R. Stewart (1983), 1567-1569; H. Hovenkamp (2005), 229-230.

mission, however, did not even attempt a more comprehensive approach, but confined itself to purely economic considerations.[70]

4.3 Ex Ante Control and Ex Post Regulation and Enforcement

Ex ante regulation is considered a "forward-looking" system focusing on an optimal structure and on a balance of the interests of the parties involved. Ex post enforcement, in contrast, focuses mostly on the identification and prosecution of past behavior—in the case of competition law, of anti-competitive behavior.[71] Generally speaking, ex ante and ex post policies may be used jointly in a wide number of areas.[72]

As regards CRM systems, a case review of the CJEU[73] and of US courts reveals that most decisions dealt with discrimination among right holders, restrictions of the economic freedom of right holders, the amount of management fees charged to right holders by CMOs, discrimination of users, licensing terms and conditions and especially licensing tariffs, but also breach of contract.[74] Related to CMOs, however, such conflicts are of a rather special nature. They therefore ideally are addressed by sector-specific regulation mirroring the particularities of CRM systems in general and especially the organization of CMOs.[75] An ex post approach as provided by competition law still may apply if specific legislation is missing. Nevertheless, general competition law hardly provides adequate guidance to improve markets in which CRM systems loom large.

---

[70]For more detail on this subject: J. Drexl, S. Nérisson, F. Trumpke, R.M. Hilty (2013), 332-334; J. Drexl (2014), 484-486.

[71]M. Hellwig (2009), 15, 212; D. Geradin, R. O'Donoghue (2005), 412; M. Cave, P. Crowther (2005), 487; N. Dunne (2015), 33.

[72]M. Lemley (2004), 129; C. Kolstand, T. Ulen, G. Johnson (1990), 888.

[73]See—regarding disputes between right holders and CMOs—e.g. CJEU, Case 127/73 BRT v. SABAM [1974] ECR 313; Case IV/29.971—GEMA-Satzung [1981] 82/204/EWG; M. Lichtenegger (2014), 104; regarding disputes between users and CMOs, CJEU, Case C-52/07 Kanal 5 and TV 4 [2008] ECR I-9275 (*supra* n. 59); Case C-395/87 Ministère public v. Jean-Louis Tournier [1989] ECR I-2521; see also M. Lichtenegger (2014), 109-110.

[74]CJEU, Case 78/70 Deutsche Grammophon v. Metro [1971] ECR 487; Case 127/73 BRT v. SABAM [1974] ECR 313; Cases 55/80 and 57/80 Musikvertrieb Membran GmbH v. GEMA [1981] ECR 147; Case 7/82 GVL v. Commission [1983] ECR 483 (*supra* n. 7). As to U.S. cases see U.S. v. BMI, 1940-43 Trade Cas. (CCH) paras. 56, 096, 381 (E.D.Wisc.1941); U.S. v. ASCAP, 1940-43 Trade Cas. (CCH) paras. 56,104, 402 (S.D.N.Y.1941); for their latest amended Consent Decrees see U.S. v. BMI, 1996-1 Trade Cas. (CCH) paras. 71, 379 (S.D.N.Y. Nov. 18, 1994); U.S. v. ASCAP, 2001-2 Trade Cas. (CCH) paras. 73, 474 (S.D.N.Y. June 11, 2001) (*supra* n. 8).

[75]Accordingly it has been suggested for the US, for instance, to introduce ex ante regulation in the field of collective management; see J. Fujitani (1984), 135; D. Gervais (2011), 610-613; G. Lunney (2010), 333-334; NN (1978), Note CBS v. ASCAP, 802; G. Clark (1980), 749.

With respect to emerging markets like China and India and other countries in Asia, South America or Africa, it is suggested to first focus on sector-specific regulation. Competition law has the advantage of indirectly facilitating market mechanisms with a view to the most efficient outcome. This, however, is a time-consuming process and presupposes sufficient experience and case law. Sector-specific regulation on the other hand bypasses such market processes and directly imposes concrete solutions.[76] The advantage of the latter approach is time-efficiency, which is of crucial relevance for less-developed countries. In the rapidly changing framework conditions of the digital environment under ongoing globalization, these jurisdictions have very little time to build up a legal framework to set up a relatively sound system to control the activities of CMOs with a view to bilateral or multilateral obligations. In other words, the ex ante approach based on sector-specific regulation may save valuable time in coming up with a workable CMO system.

5 Conclusion

An attempt to improve the CRM systems solely on the basis of competition law would be doomed to failure. The general setting of competition law is blind to a number of special features and objectives of CMOs, above all in legislations where CMOs are required to safeguard cultural diversity or the social security of creators. Although competition law may play a role in certain fields—for instance if independent CMOs cooperate—the particularities of the markets concerned usually prevail.

Consequently, it is advisable for legislatures to focus on sector-specific mechanisms to address the special concerns of the cultural and socio-economic environment of a country.

This insight does not exclude a complementary control based on competition law, especially if specific mechanisms fail to provide an adequate regulation or are not equipped with sufficient power. Competition law, however, was not designed with special concerns of those markets in mind in which CMOs play a crucial role and therefore should serve as the last resort.

References

Antitrust Guidelines for the Licensing of Intellectual Property, Issued by the U.S. Department of Justice and the Federal Trade Commission April 6, 1995: available at: www.justice.gov/atr/public/guidelines/0558.htm

[76] N. Dunne (2015), 46.

Arezzo, E. (2015), Competition and Intellectual Property Protection in the Market for the Provision of Multi-Territorial Licensing of Online Rights in Musical Works – Lights and Shadows of the New European Directive, IIC, 534-565
ASCAP Consent Decree: Second Amended Final Judgment entered in United States v. ASCAP (S.D.N.Y. 2001), available at: www.justice.gov/atr/cases/f6300/6396.htm
Becker, J. (2008), Verwertungsgesellschaften als Träger öffentlicher und privater Aufgaben, in: R. Kreile, J. Becker, K. Riesenhuber (Eds.), Recht und Praxis der GEMA, Handbuch und Kommentar, 33-43, De Gruyter
Besen, S., Kirby, S., Salop, S. (1992), An Economic Analysis of Copyright Collectives, Virginia Law Rev., 383-411
BT-Drucksache VI/ 271(1962): Entwurf eines Gesetzes über Verwertungsgesellschaften auf dem Gebiet des Urheberrechts (Verwertungsgesellschaftengesetz), available at: dipbt.bundestag.de/doc/btd/04/002/0400271.pdf
Cave, M., Crowther, P. (2005), Pre-emptive Competition Policy Meets Regulatory Antitrust, ECLR, 481-490, Sweet and Maxwell
Clark, G. (1980), Blanket Licensing: The Clash Between Copyright Protection and the Sherman Act, 729-750, The Notre Dame Lawyer
Commission Recommendation of 18 May 2005 on collective cross-border management of copyright and related rights for legitimate online music services, available at: eur-lex.europa.eu/legal-content/EN/TXT/?uri=uriserv:OJ.L_.2005.276.01.0054.01.ENG
Dietz, A. (1978), Copyright Law in the European Community, 19-21, 212-241, Sijthoff & Noordhoff
Drexl, J. (2007), Competition in the Field of Collective Management: Preferring 'Creative Competition' to Allocative Efficiency in European Copyright Law, in: P. Torremans (Eds.), Copyright Law. A Handbook of Contemporary Research, 255-282, Edward Elgar
Drexl, J. (2013), Copyright, Competition and Development (Report to the World Intellectual Property Organization), 1-284, available at: http://www.wipo.int/export/sites/www/ip-competition/en/studies/copyright_competition_development.pdf
Drexl, J. (2014), Collective Management of Copyrights and the EU Principle of Free Movement of Services after the OSA Judgment – In Favour of a More Balanced Approach, in: K. Purnhagen, P. Rott (Eds.), Varieties of European Economic Law and Regulation – Liber Amicorum for Hans Micklitz, 459-487, Springer
Drexl, J., Nérisson, S., Trumpke, F., Hilty, R.M. (2013), Comments of the Max Planck Institute for Intellectual Property and Competition Law on the Proposal for a Directive of the European Parliament and of the Council on Collective Management of Copyright and Related Rights and Multi-Territorial Licensing of Rights in Musical Works for Online Uses in the Internal Market COM (2012) 372, IIC, 322-350
Dunne, N. (2015), Competition Law and Economic Regulation, Cambridge University Press
Epstein, R. (2007), Antitrust consent decrees in theory and practice, 2007, 1-14, AEI Press
European Affairs (2006), The Collective Management of Rights in Europe The Quest for Efficiency, available at: www.europarl.europa.eu/meetdocs/2004_2009/documents/dv/study-collective-management-rights-/study-collective-management-rights-en.pdf
Evans, D. (2003), The Antitrust Economics of Multi-Sided Platform Markets, Yale J. on Reg. 2003, 325-381
Evans, D. (2009), Two-Sided Market Definition, in: ABA Section of Antitrust Law, Market Definition in Antitrust: Theory and Case Studies, Forthcoming, Global Econ., available at: SSRN: ssrn.com/abstract=1396751
Fujitani, J. (1984), Controlling the Market Power of Performing Rights Societies: An Administrative Substitute for Antitrust Regulation, California Law Rev., 103-137
Gerber, D. (1994), The Transformation of European Community Competition Law, Harvard Int. Law, 97-147
Geradin, D., O'Donoghue, R. (2005), The concurrent application of competition law and regulation: the case of margin squeeze abuses in the telecommunications sector, J. Comp. Law & Econ., 355-425

Gervais, D. (2010), Collective Management of Copyright: Theory and Practice in the Digital Age, in Collective Management of Copyright and Related Rights, 1-28, Kluwer Law International

Gervais, D. (2011), Keynote: The Landscape of Collective Management Schemes, Columbia J. of Law & the Arts, 591-617

Gilliéron, P. (2006), Collecting Societies and the Digital Environment, IIC, 939-969

Hansen, G., Schmidt-Bischoffshausen, A. (2007), Ökonomische Funktionen von Verwertungsgesellschaften – Kollektive Wahrnehmung im Lichte von Transaktionskosten- und Informationsökonomik, GRUR Int., 461-481

Heller, M. (1998), The Tragedy of the Anticommons: Property in the Transition from Marx to Markets, Harvard Law Rev., 621-688

Hellwig, M. (2009), Competition Policy and Sector-Specific Regulation for Network Industries, in: V. Xavier (Ed.), Competition Policy in the EU, 203-235, Oxford University Press

Herschel, W. (1967), Staatsentlastende Artigkeit der Verwertungsgesellschaften, UFITA Bd. 1967, 22-32

Hilty, R.M. (2010), Kollektive Rechtewahrnehmung und Vergütungsregelungen: Harmonisierungsbedarf und -möglichkeiten, in: M. Leistner (Eds.), Europäische Perspektiven des Geistigen Eigentums, 123-166, Mohr Siebeck

Hilty, R.M. (2012), Individual, Multiple and Collective Ownership – What Impact on Competition?, in: J. Rosén (Eds.), Individualism and Collectivization in Intellectual Property Law, 3-44, Edward Elgar

Hilty, R.M., Nérisson, S. (2013), Collective Copyright Management: The European Experience, in: R. Towse, C. Handke (Eds.): Handbook of the Digital Creative Economy, 222-234, Edward Elgar

Hovenkamp, H. (2005), The Antitrust Enterprise: Principle and Execution, Harvard University Press

Katz, A. (2005), The Potential Demise of Another Natural Monopoly: Rethinking the Collective Administration of Performing Rights, J. Comp. Law & Econ., 541-593

Katzenberger, P., Nérisson, S. (2011), Kulturförderung, Solidarität und Verteilungsgerechtigkeit in Recht und Praxis urheberrechtlicher Verwertungsgesellschaften, GRUR Int., 283-295

Kolstad, C., Ulen, T., Johnson, G. (1990), Ex Post Liability for Harm vs. Ex Ante Safety Regulation: Substitutes or Complements?, American Econ. Rev, 888-901

Kretschmer, M. (2002), The Failure of Property Rules in Collective Administration: Rethinking Copyright Societies as Regulatory Instruments, European Intellectual Prop. Rev., 126-137

Lamping, M. (2015), Refusal to License as an Abuse of Market Dominance – From Commercial Solvents to Microsoft, in: R.M. Hilty, K.-C. Liu (Eds.), Compulsory Licensing, Practical Experiences and Ways Forward, 121-145, Springer

Lemley, M. (2004), Ex Ante versus Ex Post Justification for Intellectual Property, Univ. of Chicago Law Rev., 129-149

von Lewinski, S. (2005), Gedanken zur kollektiven Rechtewahrnehmung, in: A. Ohly, T. Bodewig, T. Dreier, H.-P. Götting, M. Haedicke, M. Lehmann (Eds.): Perspektiven des Geistigen Eigentums und Wettbewerbsrechts, 401- 412, C.H. Beck

Lichtenegger, M. (2014), Verwertungsgesellschaften, Kartellverbot und Neue Medien, Mohr Siebeck

Lindstrom, T., Tighe, K. (1974), Antitrust Consent Decrees, Rochester

Lunney, G. (2010), Copyright Collectives and Collecting Societies: The United States Experience, in Collective Management of Copyright and Related Rights, 311-345, Kluwer Law International

Merges, R. (1996), Contracting into Liability Rules: Intellectual Property Rights and Collective Rights Organizations, California Law Rev., 1293-1393

NN (1978), Note CBS v. ASCAP: Performing Rights Societies and the Per Se Rule, Yale Law J. 1978, 783-803

Nordemann, W. (1992), Mängel der Staatsaufsicht über die deutschen Verwertungsgesellschaften?, GRUR, 584-589

Peifer, K.-N. (2015), Die Zukunft der kollektiven Rechtewahrnehmung, GRUR, 27-35
Podszun, R. (2014), Die Kontrolle der Verwertungsgesellschaften, in: M. Grünberger, S. Leible (Eds.): Die Kollision von Urheberrecht und Nutzerverhalten im Informationszeitalter, 173-210, Mohr Siebeck
Searle, N., White, G. (2013), Business models, in: R. Towse, C. Handke (Eds.): Handbook of the Digital Creative Economy, 45-56, Edward Elgar
Schierholz, A. (2010), Collective Rights Management in Europe – Practice and Legal Framework, in: M.M. Walter, S. von Lewinski (Eds.), European copyright law. A commentary, 1145-1190, Oxford University Press
Schovsbo, J. (2012), The necessity to collectivize copyright – and dangers thereof, in: J. Rosén (Eds.), Individualism and Collectiveness in Intellectual Property Law, 167-191, Edward Elgar
Snow, A., Watt, R. (2005), Risk Sharing and the Distribution of Copyright Collective Income, in: L. Takeyama, W. Gordon, R. Towse (Eds.), Developments in the Economics of Copyright: Research and Analysis, 23-36, Edward Elgar
Stewart, R. (1983), Regulation in a Liberal State: The Role of Non-Commodity Values, Yale Law J., 1537-1590
The EU Commission notice on the definition of relevant market for the purposes of Community competition law (1997), OJ No. C 273
Viscusi, K., Joseph, E., John, M. (2005), Economics of Regulation and Antitrust, MIT press
Vázquez-Lopez, V. (2010), Collective and individual exercise of copyright in the digital environment: An international perspective focused on development, GRUR Int., 689-695

Individual Licensing of Copyrighted Works

Kaya Köklü

Contents

Abstract Only some years ago right holders were increasingly losing control over their copyrighted works in the online world. But times have changed. Right holders are gaining back control over their works. Technological development allows right holders to individually license their works to users and retain control over the works even in cases of large-scale use in the online world. Individual licensing enables the right holders to individually determine the conditions of access to the copyrighted work as well as the scope of permitted use. Individual licensing and pricing are often much more lucrative to right holders than any collective remuneration system. Especially in the entertainment sector, users also benefit from the existing competition among right holders and intermediaries, which obviously leads to innovative services and products with more reasonable prices. However, this development is not free of problems. Particularly, limitations and exceptions are increasingly losing their relevance in the online world, which requires a certain intervention on the international level. In the area of scientific publications, there are major pricing problems. Scientific works are usually not substitutable, as scholars generally do

Kaya Köklü is a German qualified lawyer and a certified specialist in intellectual property law.

K. Köklü (✉)
Attorney at law, Munich, Germany
e-mail: kaya.koeklue@alumni.ip.mpg.de

K.-C. Liu, R.M. Hilty (eds.), *Remuneration of Copyright Owners*, MPI Studies on Intellectual Property and Competition Law 27, DOI 10.1007/978-3-662-53809-8_10

not have an alternative source of equal information available. This obviously causes a lack of competition, which leads to unreasonable pricing models by scientific publishers. The pricing problems could be tackled by introducing an obligation to grant fair, reasonable and non-discriminatory licenses and access conditions which need to be accompanied by efficient price-control mechanisms.

1 Introduction

Around 50 years ago the large-scale reproduction of copyrighted material started. Technological developments of affordable photocopiers, scanners and recording devices allowed private users to copy protected material en masse in an environment largely uncontrollable for right holders. At that time, it was predictable that right holders would increasingly lose control over the produced numbers of copies of their work. Absolute rights provided for in copyright laws suddenly became less efficient and were about to lose their practical relevance. They were hardly enforceable (like through injunction claims) against users reproducing copyrighted works in private with the help of the new technological opportunities.

Looking for an appropriate solution to solve the problem of uncontrollable reproduction of copyrighted works, the German legislature introduced in 1965 what was at that time a unique collective remuneration system. The idea behind was that bans on certain kinds of uses that could not be effectively enforced are of no practical value. Instead of prohibiting these uses, the German legislature permitted them, but only in exchange for remuneration to the benefit of the affected right holders. In practice this happened, for example, through the introduction of standardized copyright levies for storage media and reproduction devices. This approach turned out to be a major step in copyright law and has since been adopted by many other countries.

However, this approach was designed to solve problems specific to the analog world. For years now, many scholars worldwide have been trying to adapt efficient collective remuneration systems to use in the digital world as well. It is no surprise that the *Association Littéraire et Artistique Internationale* (ALAI) dedicated its annual congress in 2015 in Bonn precisely to the question of alternative mechanisms of remuneration for the use of works.[1] At this conference, scholars and practitioners from many countries discussed alternative remuneration schemes. Among the discussed options was again the idea of introducing a sort of Internet

[1]Information on the annual congress of ALAI, held on the occasion of the 50-year anniversary of the modern German Copyright Act (2015), available at: www.alai2015.org. The contributions by the panelists will be published in a conference volume in 2016.

levy or cultural flat rate for online uses of copyrighted works.[2] In a nutshell, the underlying idea is to establish a general levy for Internet uses and distribute the money collected among the right holders whose works are shared freely on the Internet.

However, many of these alternative remuneration systems are in one way or another based on a debatable judgment of the actual technological possibilities. The starting point of these alternative remuneration systems is often the misconception that a large-scale use of copyrighted works on the Internet is necessarily linked to a loss of control by the right holder. This might have been the case with the technological situation in the analog world, but it does not necessarily apply to the digital one. In fact, the situation within the digital world is significantly different, as the technological possibilities (flanked by the legal framework) allow right holders to effectively control online access, and dissemination and use of copyrighted works,[3] even there are a huge number of users involved.

In order to maintain the control over their copyrighted works in the online environment, right holders frequently make use of individual licensing models accompanied by technological protection measures (TPM). As both of these tools are applied throughout various online business sectors, it can be assumed that they are in general working efficiently.

Basically, there are no fundamental concerns about this trend as such. In fact, it is even gratifying that right holders are back in the position to manage the exploitation of their works in the online world by themselves without being dependent on (probably less lucrative) collective remuneration systems.

This chapter will focus on the pros and cons of individual licensing of copyrighted works chiefly from the legal perspective. Examples will be provided from mainly two areas where individual licensing plays an important role, namely, entertainment and scientific publishing.

2 Meaning and Types of Individual Licensing

In order to avoid misunderstandings, the term "individual licensing" as used in this chapter refers to any kind of individual permission to use a copyrighted work under specific terms and conditions. These licenses are granted directly by either the original or a derivative right holder.

It should be noted that individual licensing does not necessarily need to be a direct license granted to an end user. A licensee as understood in this context can also be an intermediary, for example the operator of an online platform. In

[2] J.P. Quintais (2015).

[3] An overview of the technological developments in the digital age, which can be categorized into three periods of decreasing relevance of tangible carriers, and their effects on the position of right holders is provided by R.M. Hilty / K. Köklü (2016), 2.1.

compliance with the specific licensing terms granted by the original right holder, these intermediaries are usually authorized to grant further sublicenses and apply access conditions to end users.

Whether the license fee is based on a pay-per-use or a flat-rate model does not affect the legal assessment within this chapter.

3 Beneficiaries of Individual Licensing

Individual licensing and pricing provides right holders with many advantages compared to collective remuneration regimes. Individual licensing particularly enables right holders to (more or less) freely determine the general terms and conditions for the use of the copyrighted works either in direct relation with the end users or indirectly via intermediaries like platform providers without being dependent on collective remuneration systems. It is no secret that individual licensing appears more lucrative to many right holders than collective remuneration systems, which are known for standardized tariffs and opaque allocation formulas.

Individual licensing further enables right holders to react more quickly to market changes by adapting the scope of their offers and the individual pricing accordingly. This even applies to cases in which right holders license their copyrighted works primarily to intermediaries, which happens quite frequently in the entertainment sector. There is even a reported case in which a right holder has become a shareholder of an intermediary that is his licensee at the same time.[4] This allows the right holder to participate in the revenue on more than one level of exploitation.

But there is also another trend. It seems that the benefits of individual licensing and pricing are so attractive that intermediaries or platform operators are now investing in the creation of copyrighted works themselves. This is particularly valid for internationally operating platforms offering movies and series like Netflix and Amazon.[5]

From a legal perspective, the hybrid status of some right holders and intermediaries described here does not affect the overall assessment. An intermediary will still ask for a license of copyrighted works if he is not the right holder himself. And a right holder will license his works to an intermediary, independent of whether he is a shareholder of that platform. Both intermediary and right holder have common

[4]It is reported that Sony Music received company shares from Spotify under some obscure conditions. More information, available at: www.theverge.com/2015/5/19/8621581/sony-music-spotify-contract. By the way, the contract between the two companies has been removed from the Internet for “copyright reasons”.

[5]Netflix, for example, originally started as a platform provider only. But it now produces many popular series itself, like “House of Cards”, “Orange is the New Black” and “Arrested Development”. A comprehensive list of series produced by Netflix, available at: en.wikipedia.org/wiki/List_of_original_programs_distributed_by_Netflix. A list of series produced by Amazon, available at: en.wikipedia.org/wiki/List_of_original_programs_distributed_by_Amazon.

interest in providing access to the copyrighted works to end users for payment. Users have various options to pay for access to the copyrighted works. These options include pay-per-use as well as subscription-based pricing models. Although there are even ad-financed free-of-charge models, the subscription-based models are getting more and more popular.

The entertainment sector makes extensive use of individual licensing. After a long dry spell, the movie and music sectors seem to be recovering. Particular access to copyrighted works by way of streaming is getting very popular, and obtaining one's own copy of the work by downloading is increasingly losing relevance.[6] The overall trend clearly goes to broad access to instead of permanent possession of individual works.[7] The success of the new online business models indicates that this kind of supply meets the demands and acceptance of end users.

Besides the entertainment area, there is also another sector that makes extensive use of individual licensing, namely, scientific publishing. The underlying business model of scientific publishers is quite simple. They provide online access to their publishing products via online databases, either on a pay-per-use basis or (more often) in combination with a large variety of subscription models. The profit margins of scientific publishers are indeed impressive. It is, for example, reported that the probably largest scientific publisher, Reed Elsevier, trading on the London Stock Exchange, has a market capitalization of around 11 billion GBP[8] and achieved a remarkable profit with its scientific, technical and medical publications of more than 1 billion USD in 2012.[9] Thus, the profit of Elsevier in 2012 was even higher than the profit made by Germany's largest bank, Deutsche Bank. Elsevier has also a breathtaking profit margin, which is reported to have been 37 % in 2013.[10] But Elsevier is not an exception. There are many other scientific publishers worldwide with similarly impressive revenue figures and profit margins of sometimes even more than 40 %.[11]

The reasons why this sector is highly profitable are diverse. A certainly relevant aspect is that scientific publishers usually obtain the content for free and pay—if at all—only a little to peer reviewers for quality control. In return they are granted exclusive exploitation rights and can claim high, sometimes even exorbitant prices

[6]Statistics show that that digital distribution has become more important for right holders than physical distribution, which was fairly standard only a few years ago. Available at: www.statista.com/statistics/272306/worldwide-revenues-of-the-music-industry-by-category/.

[7]This is also indicated by the great success of the sharing industry, which focuses on access and use instead of ownership. Examples are Airbnb, a platform for sharing flats, or the increasing number of car-sharing offers like Drive Now, etc.

[8]Available at: www.statista.com/statistics/324935/uk-lse-publishing-ranked/.

[9]Detailed information on Reed Elsevier's 2012 results is available at: www.relx.com/mediacentre/pressreleases/2013/Pages/reed-elsevier-2012-results.aspx.

[10]More information is available at: en.wikipedia.org/wiki/Elsevier.

[11]See for example "The obscene profits of commercial scholarly publishers", published on January 13, 2012 by SV-POW, available at: svpow.com/2012/01/13/the-obscene-profits-of-commercial-scholarly-publishers/.

for access to scientific journals.[12] Most of the subscribers to these journals are publicly financed institutions like libraries, universities and research institutes. They are paying high prices as they are actually given no other choice. This dilemma is due to the fact that scientific content is mostly not substitutable.[13] In contrast to access to works of fiction, a serious researcher can hardly afford to disregard a leading scholar's scientific work by simply reading a work by another scholar on a similar topic. Either the researcher gets access to the individual scientific publication or he will simply not be able to work on high-end research and development projects. That makes individual licensing of scientific works very attractive for scientific publishers.

In other words, individual licensing is good for scientific publishers, but bad for researchers and the public.

4 Problems and Solutions

It is obvious that a system that provides massive advantages for one stakeholder group often leads to disadvantages for another group. The economic attractiveness of individual licensing for right holders is closely linked to some severe problems for users. There are in particular two areas of concern: (1) relevance of limitations and exceptions in relation to technological protection measures (TPM) and licensing contracts and (2) pricing in the area of scientific publishing.

4.1 TPM and Contracts Versus Limitations and Exceptions

Right holders are gaining back control over the use of their works within the online environment. This development is to a large extent due to the possibility of being able to impose certain terms and conditions in license agreements in combination with the application of effective TPM. This is nothing bad per se. However, it leads to the problem that limitations and exceptions practically lose their relevance. The current legal setting in European Union (EU), for example, protects TPM from circumvention.[14] Article 6(4) para. 4 of the InfoSoc Directive even sets forth that beneficiaries of limitations and exceptions may not claim access to works based on Article 6(4) para. 1 of the InfoSoc Directive that are "made available to the public on agreed contractual terms in such a way that members of the public may access them from a place and at a time individually chosen by them". It does not need

[12]It is reported that in Germany, the subscription fee for Elsevier's journal "Cell" with 26 numbers a year amounts to around 15,000 EUR. Cf. J. Ludwig (2013).

[13]R.M. Hilty (2006), 179; also R.M. Hilty (2009), 633.

[14]Directive 2001/29/EC, Art. 6(4), para. 3.

detailed explanation that "making available to the public" is in fact the elementary way of exploiting works over the Internet, which is nowadays applied by almost any new business model. Consequently, TPM as well as terms and conditions of licensing agreements between right holders, intermediaries and (end) users deserve particular attention, as they may limit the scope of permitted uses more narrowly than the scope set forth by limitations and exceptions in copyright laws.[15] Furthermore, this development has also a negative impact on the remuneration of creators. In many jurisdictions, the use of works on the basis of limitations and exceptions is subject to mandatory remuneration for the benefit of the creator, usually collected by collecting societies. Depending on the kind of work, this remuneration can make a significant contribution to the creator's income. However, if the implementation of licensing terms and TPM prevents the use of works on the basis of limitations and exceptions, this important source of income will necessarily dry up over time. There is a non-negligible risk that this will lead to further imbalance of the involved interests to the disadvantage of particularly the creators.[16]

There are some conceivable options for solving this problem within copyright law. One of these options is the harmonization of mandatory limitations and exceptions to copyright on the international level, for example by way of an international treaty.[17] The current political situation, however, is not very promising in this regard, although there are recent examples like the WIPO Marrakesh Treaty of 2013, which already introduced a set of mandatory limitations and exceptions for the benefit of the blind, visually impaired, and otherwise print-disabled persons. It is in fact a striking situation that, for example, in the EU exploitation rights are to a large extent harmonized, whereas the existence and scope of limitations and exceptions still vary significantly among the Member States. This creates problems not only for the beneficiaries of limitations and exceptions, but also for internationally active intermediaries. While a specific kind of use may be permitted in one country, it may nevertheless constitute a copyright infringement in another. No wonder the current situation frustrates the establishment of new business models, particularly in the EU. Consequently, it would be a great achievement for the EU to establish a list of mandatory limitations and exceptions to copyright that remain enjoyable for the beneficiaries of limitations and exceptions, even in the online environment.[18] In order to achieve this goal, it is essential that any such mandatory limitations and exceptions will supersede contradicting licensing terms or TPM. This will ensure that limitations and exceptions will not lose their relevance in the online world.

---

[15]The legal possibility of contractually excluding statutory limitations and exceptions de lege lata is, however, controversial; see e.g. for German law: T. Dreier (2015), 653; M. Stieper (2009); J. Gräbig (2011); L. Guibault (2012).

[16]R.M. Hilty / K. Köklü (2016) 2.2; L. Guibault (2002), 197.

[17]R.M. Hilty / K. Köklü (2016) 3.

[18]L. Guibault (2002).

4.2 Pricing of Scientific Works

The pricing situation in scientific works gives reason for concern. Scientific publishers profit enormously from the fact that they actually get their scientific content for free and can nevertheless individually license this content for nearly any price, while users, particularly libraries, universities and research institutes, suffer from spending significant parts of their limited budget (which is most often publicly financed by taxes) to get online access to these scientific works. The situation gets even worse if one considers that the creation of these scientific works was already most often publicly funded. Hence, it is actually the tax payer who pays once for the creation of scientific works and a second time for obtaining access to them.[19] As scientific works are usually not substitutable, education and research institutions are forced to accept any terms and conditions set forth by scientific publishers. The institutions in fact depend on the access to scientific works if they want to provide reasonable research conditions to their scholars. So far, scientific publishers have made vigorous use of this predicament and continue to generate incredible profit margins.[20]

This imbalance should be improved for the future. There are various conceivable options to tackle this problem.

4.2.1 Promoting Open Access

An obvious solution could be to facilitate open-access publishing by scholars. There are two main methods of open-access publishing, namely the golden road and the green road.

The golden road covers works which are accessible online to anyone for free. The rationale of the golden road in open-access publishing is that research results can be published in freely accessible online databases without the need for direct or indirect involvement of commercial scientific publishers.[21] This is particularly interesting for research results that are publicly financed. The consequence is that the costs of publication are paid no longer by subscribers but by the publisher himself. These publishing costs for final formatting, quality control and operating an online database may be less than the price for the access to commercial databases provided by scientific publishers.

[19]C. Berger (2010), 1059; R.M. Hilty (2007), 128; K. Köklü (2012), 148.

[20]See for example "The obscene profits of commercial scholarly publishers", published on January 13, 2012 by S V-POW, available at: svpow.com/2012/01/13/the-obscene-profits-of-commercial-scholarly-publishers/.

[21]R.M. Hilty / K. Köklü / S. Nérisson / T. Hartmann / F. Trumpke (2013), para. 12.

And in fact, there are currently some promising projects ongoing to support this kind of open-access publishing.[22] However, scholars are reluctant to make use of this opportunity. It appears that according to the current academic system, scholars are still predominantly evaluated by the number of their publications that appear in established and respected journals. That is probably the reason why open-access publishing by way of the golden road is not yet very successful or accepted within the academic communities.

Another option is the green road to open-access publishing. Green-road publishing covers works that are first published within a closed-access journal and then—after the expiry of a certain embargo period—can be self-archived in open-access databases.[23] This option, however, is in terms of cost saving not very promising. Quite the contrary, the involved costs will likely even increase, as in addition to the costs for commercial publishing, the costs for establishing and operating an open-access repository for the subsequent second publication will be incurred.[24] Furthermore, it is not very likely that research institutions will wait until a work is freely accessible rather than paying for immediate access to the databases of the commercial publishers.

No doubt there is legitimate public interest in open access, but it is not likely that either of the two methods of open-access publishing will lead to the desired effects in the foreseeable future.

4.2.2 Establishing Price-Control Mechanisms in the Field of Scientific Publishing

Another more promising approach to decrease the costs for access to scientific works is a sort of price control. When assessing price-control mechanisms, regimes of antitrust law such as Article 102 of the Treaty on the Functioning of the European Union (TFEU) or the respective national provisions may first come to mind. However, applying mechanisms of antitrust law to copyright-related problems is

[22]The Max Planck Society, for example, has launched a major project to facilitate open-access publishing. Further information is available at: openaccess.mpg.de/2365/en.

[23]Cf. Article 38 (4) of the German Copyright Act: "The author of a scientific contribution which is the result of a research activity publicly funded by at least fifty percent and which has appeared in a collection which is published periodically at least twice per year has the right, even if he has granted the publisher or editor an exclusive right of use, to make the contribution available to the public in the accepted manuscript version upon expiry of 12 months after first publication, unless this serves a commercial purpose. The source of the first publication shall be indicated. Any deviating agreement to the detriment of the author shall be ineffective." See also comments of the Max Planck Institute for Innovation and Competition, R.M. Hilty / K. Köklü / S. Nerisson / T. Hartmann / F. Trumpke (2013), recital 14; C. Bruch / T. Pflüger (2014), 389; G. Krings / C.-H. Hentsch (2013), 909; a similar provision is about to be introduced in Art. 25fa of the Dutch Copyright Act, see D. Visser (2015), 534.

[24]Comments of the Max Planck Institute, R.M. Hilty / K. Köklü / S. Nérisson / T. Hartmann / F. Trumpke (2013), recital 15.

only possible to a limited extent, as it encounters difficulties in defining the relevant market and establishing the required dominant position.[25] Antitrust law proves particularly insufficient in the field of scientific publishing because each academic publication is most often not substitutable and, hence, creates its own market.[26]

But there are some sorts of price-control mechanisms that are already successfully applied in other fields of intellectual property law, for example in copyright contract law concerning the reasonable remuneration of creators, and also in patent law with regard to standard-essential patents (SEP). It is worth considering making use of the basic idea of these existing mechanisms to solve the problems in scientific publishing. There are in fact significant similarities between scientific works and patents essential to the standard. Both subject matters are actually not substitutable and users depend on access to them. There is usually no alternative available to the user—neither an alternative technology compared to an SEP, nor an alternative scientific work for one's own research.

In patent law, owners of SEPs usually commit to granting licenses on fair, reasonable and non-discriminatory terms (FRAND). The European Court of Justice (ECJ) has recently determined concrete requirements of a FRAND licensing offer in the context of Article 102 TFEU.[27]

It is worth thinking about applying some sort of FRAND licensing in copyright law too. An obligation of scientific publishers to grant licenses and access to scientific works according to fair, reasonable and non-discriminatory terms would probably lead to the desired reduction of the current high price level to a more reasonable one. Despite the generally applicable freedom of contract between licensors and licensees,[28] there are various options for how to introduce such an obligation into the current legal framework. It is, for example, conceivable to implement a claim for fair, reasonable and non-discriminatory licenses into a limitation or exception to the benefit of public research institutions. The beneficiaries of such a limitation or exception would then be entitled to claim access to scientific works under these more reasonable and, hence, preferable terms.

However, any such obligation needs to be accompanied by sufficient enforcement and control mechanisms in order not to be a toothless tiger. There are various options conceivable to ensure that any licensing and access terms imposed by scientific publishers are fair and reasonable.

A copyright tribunal, for example, might be an option to consider. Upon request of a user seeking online access to scientific works (e.g. a university or research institute), any such copyright tribunal could provide a binding assessment of whether the license and access terms offered by the scientific publisher comply

[25]R.M. Hilty (2009), 638.

[26]W. Fikentscher (1992), 137; R.M. Hilty (2009), 639.

[27]ECJ, Decision of 16 July 2015, C-170/13—Huawei v. ZTE. A comprehensive discussion as to the legal nature of FRAND patent licenses and their impact, R.M. Hilty / P.R. Slowinksi (2015), 787.

[28]*Id.*

with its obligation described above. Once applied in practice, experiences accumulated overtime will build a solid basis of decisions, which may serve as orientation for publishers and users for subsequent deals.

As an alternative to a copyright tribunal, there is also the option of establishing a provision in the copyright law stipulating that exploitation rights of scientific publishers in relation to libraries, universities and research institutes can only be exercised by way of mandatory collective management. Such an approach is nothing new in copyright law, as in many jurisdictions there are already several claims that right holders can only exercise through collecting societies.[29]

Any such approach will probably help to establish a certain level of price control in the area of scientific publications.

5 Conclusions

As indicated above, there are no fundamental objections to the trend that right holders more and more focus on individual licensing and access control of their copyrighted works in the online environment. They have good—particularly financial—reasons to do so. Especially in the entertainment sector, this trend seems to have predominantly positive effects not only for right holders, but also for users. Competition in this sector appears to be thriving, as there are a large number of internationally operating intermediaries offering access to various repertoires of music, movies and eBooks. It further appears that the prices in this sector have also reached a reasonable level, which apparently meets the acceptance of users. One of the remaining problems is, however, that limitations and exceptions are slowly but steadily losing their relevance in the online environment. This will lead to a further imbalance of the involved interests in copyright law, if the needed steps are not taken now. In this regard, one should consider establishing a list of mandatory limitations and exceptions (preferably at the international level), which remain enjoyable by beneficiaries of limitations and exceptions in the online world.

While the developments in the entertainment sector are certainly encouraging, there are major problems to be solved in the sector of scientific publishing. As shown above, individual licensing and access control are also used extensively by scientific publishers. However, the absence of competition and the lack of alternatives for users have led to price levels that are obviously unreasonable. There is an urgent need for action. An obligation to grant licenses on fair, reasonable and non-discriminatory terms, accompanied by the suggested price-control mechanisms, is a promising way to bring the prices charged for access to scientific works down to a normal and more reasonable level.

[29]See e.g. Article 54 h I German Copyright Act, which states that claims, according to Articles 54–54c, 54e II, 54f and 54 g, can only be exercised by collecting societies.

References

Berger, C. (2010), Die öffentliche Zugänglichmachung urheberrechtlicher Werke für Zwecke der akademischen Lehre, GRUR, 1058

Bruch, C., Pflüger, T. (2014), Das Zweitveröffentlichungsrecht des § 38 Abs. 4 UrhG – Möglichkeiten und Grenzen bei der Anwendung in der Praxis, ZUM, 389

Dreier, T. (2015), Überlegungen zur Revision des Schrankenkatalogs der Richtlinie 2001/29/EG, GRUR Int., 648

Fikentscher, W. (1992), Recht und wirtschaftliche Freiheit, Band 1: Die Freiheit des Wettbewerbs, Mohr Siebeck

Gräbig, J. (2011), Abdingbarkeit und vertragliche Beschränkungen urheberrechtlicher Schranken, Nomos

Guibault, L. (2002), Copyright limitations and contracts, Springer

Hilty, R.M. (2006), Das Urheberrecht und der Wissenschaftler, GRUR Int., 179

Hilty, R.M. (2007), Sündenbock Urheberrecht?, in: A. Ohly, D. Klippel (Eds.), Geistiges Eigentum und Gemeinfreiheit, 107, Mohr Siebeck

Hilty, R.M. (2009), Renaissance der Zwangslizenzen im Urheberrecht? – Gedanken zu Ungereimtheiten auf der urheberrechtlichen Wertschöpfungskette, GRUR, 633

Hilty, R.M., Köklü, K. (2016), Limitations and Exceptions to Copyright in the Digital Age, to be published in: The Future of Copyright, A European Union and International Perspective, I. Stamatoudi (Ed.) in 2016

Hilty, R.M., Köklü, K., Nérisson, S., Hartmann, T., Trumpke, F. (2013), Stellungnahme des Max-Planck-Instituts für Immaterialgüter- und Wettbewerbsrecht zur Anfrage des Bundesministeriums der Justiz vom 20. Februar 2013 – Zum Referentenentwurf eines Gesetzes zur Einführung einer Regelung zur Nutzung verwaister Werke und weiterer Änderungen des Urheberrechtsgesetzes sowie des Urheberrechtswahrnehmungsgesetz, available at: www.ip.mpg.de/fileadmin/templates/pdf/Stellungnahme-BMJ-UrhG_2013-3-15-def1_01.pdf

Hilty, R.M., Slowinski, P.R. (2015), Standardessentielle Patente – Perspektive außerhalb des Kartellrechts, GRUR Int., 781

Köklü, K. (2012), Innovation und Urheberrecht, in: R.M. Hilty, T. Jaeger, M. Lamping (Eds.) Herausforderung Innovation, 145, Springer

Krings, G., Hentsch, C.-H. (2013), Das neue Zweitverwertungsrecht, ZUM, 909

Ludwig, J. (2013), Streiten bis zum Access, in: ZEIT Campus no. 4/2013, available at: www.zeit.de/campus/2013/04/studieren-dwdd

Quintais, J.P. (2015), Alternative Compensation Models for Large-Scale Non-Commercial Online Uses, available at: papers.ssrn.com/sol3/papers.cfm?abstract_id=2625492

Stieper, M. (2009), Rechtfertigung, Rechtsnatur und Disponibilität der Schranken des Urheberrechts, Mohr Siebeck

Visser, D. (2015), The Open Access provision in Dutch copyright contract law, GRUR Int., 534

Music Individual Licensing Models and Competition Law

Xiuqin Lin

Contents

Abstract With the swift progress of Internet technology, the way to get access to copyrighted work is undergoing substantial change. A variety of licensing models, usually operated by intermediaries, such as Spotify or Pandora, have emerged. What are the impacts of such new models on the end users of the music? Will they generate anticompetitive concerns? The chapter examines the currently popular music licensing models from the perspective of competition law and concludes that the key players such as Apple and Tencent have a strong position in the music market. It is not certain whether such key players have a dominant market position, and this needs to be assessed on a case-by-case basis. However, some conduct of the

---

Xiuqin Lin is Professor and Director of the Intellectual Property Research Institute of Xiamen University.

X. Lin (✉)
Intellectual Property Research Institute, Xiamen University, Fujian, People's Republic of China
e-mail: xqlin@xmu.edu.cn

K.-C. Liu, R.M. Hilty (eds.), *Remuneration of Copyright Owners*, MPI Studies on Intellectual Property and Competition Law 27, DOI 10.1007/978-3-662-53809-8_11

licensing intermediaries may fall within the subject of antitrust scrutiny if the requirement of dominant position is satisfied. Particularly, in the new era of "crossover", high tech giants such as Apple, Tencent and Alibaba are building up content libraries, and pose serious threat to their rivals without synthesized platforms. (Synthesized platform refers to the online services that provide a wide range of services, which may cover instant messaging, information portals, online games, online music, e-business etc. Such synthesizing has significant impacts on consumers' switching cost.) Competition law should adopt a more flexible approach to define the "relevant market" in order to protect market competition.

1 Introduction

It is widely recognized that creative works (e.g. music, film, and literature) are culturally essential and economically important to the world we live in today. Thus, easy access to copyrighted works is essential to contemporary life. With the robust development of the Internet and information technology, the ways through which end users get access to copyrighted work are undergoing substantial change. In the case of music, online downloading and streaming, instead of purchasing music CDs, are becoming the dominating methods for users to gain access to music.[1] While physical music product markets are shrinking rapidly, online digital music markets are becoming ever more congested and competitive.[2] A variety of music licensing models (streaming, downloading, etc.) have emerged. It has become a trend that end users access music through intermediaries such as Spotify, iTunes, QQ Music, Pandora, Deezer, and Tidal. Virtually, these intermediaries become collective management organizations (CMO[3]). However, unlike the traditional licensed CMOs, which are subject to state control or regulation, the online intermediaries are usually unregulated and operating in a free competition market. If those undertakings have gained dominant market power and pose threat to competition by improper means such as tying or charging excessive or discriminatory royalties, competition law should intervene to police their behavior in relation to

[1]Digital downloading now accounts for 39 % of total industry revenues, and in three of the world's top 10 markets, digital channels account for the majority of revenues, IFPI, 2014 Annual Report.

[2]Available at: www.spotifyartists.com/spotify-explained/.

[3]CMO here refers to organizations approved and registered in accordance with the applicable law to manage certain categories of copyrights on behalf of right holders.

copyright owners, competitors or end users.[4] The licensing models operated by the Internet intermediaries are categorized as "individual licensing" as opposed to traditional CMOs.

This chapter focuses on individual licensing of music. Firstly, it will set the scene by analyzing three popular music licensing models, namely, the Spotify model, Apple music model and QQ Music model. Secondly, the chapter analyzes the conventional rationale and legislation on regulating intellectual property licensing in order to provide a theoretical framework for further discussion. Thirdly, it reviews the three licensing models and examines whether their questionable behaviour would result in antitrust concerns. It argues that the behavior by dominant Internet intermediaries of banning competitors' free music service is problematic and should be regulated.

2 Licensing Models by Major Players

With technological development, the uses of copyright-protected works are becoming more widespread and instantaneous than ever before. Copyright licensing is becoming more complex,[5] and new models of licensing are evolving. The way to deal with copyright licensing of music is undergoing tremendous change. Until the late 1990s, physical media, such as music CDs, remained the most common way for people to listen to music. Later in 2003, Apple and the major labels begun to offer an online music service and launched the iTunes Music Store, through which consumers in many jurisdictions can legally access digital music by purchasing[6] and downloading albums and individual tracks.[7] iTunes soon became popular and dominant. However, since 2010, iTunes has faced increasingly intense competition from various providers of music "streaming"; among them Spotify[8] in the world market and QQ in the Chinese market are the most popular two. Since streaming is the most popular model by which users "consume" music today, the following subsection will examine the three licensing models starting from Spotify.

[4]According to a study by French music industry trade group SNEP and accounting firm Ernst & Young, recording labels receive 46 % of streaming subscription revenues, while artists, publishers and songwriters share 17 %, with the rest going to streaming providers and taxes. Available at: www.spotifyartists.com/spotify-explained/.

[5]Recently, a report issued by the US Copyright Office states: "our rules for music licensing are complex and daunting even for those familiar with the terrain"; see US Copyright Office (2015), 16.

[6]In legal terms, a user, who "buys" a song, is granted a license by the licensor ("Apple") to use the song under the conditions specified.

[7]Available at: www.apple.com/itunes/music/.

[8]A. Klebanow / T. Wu (2015), 4.

2.1 Spotify Model

Spotify, which started in Sweden, is a music streaming service that offers DRM (digital rights management) streaming of licensed music since 2008. It soon gained popularity and became successful due to its extensive catalog of music and easy accessibility in different locations. In mid 2014, the company reported 40 million users and availability in 50 countries.[9] As of December 2014, it had over 60 million global users, among which more than 15 million users pay a monthly subscription of $9.99/ £9.99/ €9.99 respectively to subscribe to the service.[10]

Spotify has a two-sided market to deal with in order to form a virtuous circle in the market: on the one side, it must be able to obtain license from artists to create a vast catalogue of music, which is crucial to attract consumers; on the other side, it must attract a huge amount of customers.

In the relationship between Spotify and copyright holders, Spotify is not in a strong position. It is difficult for Spotify to obtain licenses from various right owners. As a matter of copyright law, different types of copyright co-exist in an album or track. Multiple licenses are required both for the musical work and the sound recording containing a performance of that musical work. Generally, a songwriter and his/her publisher own the copyright in the musical composition, and a record label owns the copyright or related rights in the sound recording. After gaining popularity in Europe and beyond, Spotify has negotiated and signed licensing agreements with major record labels (such as EMI, Universal, Sony and Warner), performing rights organizations (PROs, such as BMI,[11] ASCAP and SESAC) and other music distributors such as CD Baby[12] and Ingrooves.[13] Spotify had paid out over US$2 billion in royalties ($500 million was paid in 2013 alone).[14] However, artists are paid based on the royalty rate set in their contracts with record labels, which usually have the superior bargaining power. It is thus unlikely that Spotify would be able to impose unfair licensing terms on major record labels.[15]

In relation to users, Spotify offers three different tiers of service: Free, Unlimited, and Premium. Free users are given a 6-month trial period for initial registrants to evaluate the service, after which users are restricted to 10 h of free music

[9]"Spotify is Quickly Catching Up With Pandora", available at: www.forbes.com/sites/greatspeculations/2015/02/03/spotify-is-quickly-catching-up-with-pandora/.

[10]Available at: www.spotifyartists.com/spotify-explained/.

[11]The BMI is entrusted by 475,000 songwriters, composers and copyright owners with their public performance right. D. von Wiegandt (2013), 180, 187-188.

[12]CD Baby represents over 250,000 artists, so the agreement provides Spotify's users with access to over one million tracks.

[13]D. von Wiegandt (2013), 188.

[14]Available at: www.spotifyartists.com/spotify-explained/.

[15]European consumers, identified by the address on their credit card, paid the same price, 99 Euro cents, in Austria, Belgium, Denmark, Germany, Finland, France, Greece, Ireland, Italy, Luxembourg, Netherlands, Norway, Portugal, Sweden, Switzerland and Spain, while UK users paid 79 pence.

listening per month. Unlimited users, by paying five dollars per month, are able to stream music without advertisements or restrictions as well as listen to music offline, but only on their computers. The Premium service extends the Unlimited service to mobile devices such as iPods and Smartphones. In addition, to enhance its position in the market, Spotify established a strategic link with Facebook to bring its catalogue of music to the attention of millions of Facebook users. Also Premium users are able to see what their friends are listening to via Facebook and generate collaborative playlists with them as well.

2.2 Apple Model

Apple provides music service under two models: its iTunes model, which is a music downloading service, and Apple Music, which provides streaming service similar to that of Spotify. The iTunes Music Store allows users to purchase songs and download them into their iTunes music library, with one click.[16] Access to the iTunes Music Store and its song catalog is embedded in Apple's iTunes software. Apple's iTunes allows the users to "play" music on various Apple devices, including an iPhone, iPad, iPod touch, Mac, PC, or Apple TV.[17] Users may also pay $24.99 per year to buy the iTunes Match, which will enable them to store their music in the iCloud.[18] With iTunes Match, users can access their music from all devices[19] and listen to their entire library.

Different from Spotify, which charges a monthly subscription fee, Apple's iTunes model allows users to "buy" songs *à la carte* with no subscription fees. However, use of the iTunes service requires compatible devices, Internet access, and certain software (fees may apply) that may require periodic updates. Thus, the iTunes model offers a package deal to combine hardware, software and music. Consumers of iTunes are required to abide by Apple's complicated "Usage Rules" which may cut off or restrict the right or freedom of users entailed by copyright law or other laws. For example, Apple's Terms of Service require users not to circumvent, reverse-engineer, decompile, or disassemble the software. With a vast catalogue of over 40 million tracks, iTunes soon gained overwhelming popularity and became the largest music store in the world. At its peak, Apple took up 75 % of the digital music market.[20] Recently, Apple launched its music streaming service in 2015, when the trend of the digital music market shifted from downloading to

---

[16]Available at: www.justice.gov/atr/competition-and-monopoly-single-firm-conduct-under-section-2-sherman-act-chapter-1.

[17]*Id.*

[18]Available at: www.apple.com/itunes/music/.

[19]Available at: www.justice.gov/atr/competition-and-monopoly-single-firm-conduct-under-section-2-sherman-act-chapter-1.

[20]A. Klebanow / T. Wu (2015), 5.

streaming. To compete with its rivals, Apple has taken aggressive strategies. For example, Apple is increasing the use of exclusive licenses with particular artists to create "windows" in the music distribution. And it is reported that Apple has pressured music labels to ban "free" streaming options.[21]

2.3 *QQ Music Model*

China is a potentially lucrative market for music,[22] but the music service providers are struggling to get users to pay. In China, a long-standing "free culture" has developed under which users can access or download free music online easily, sometimes from pirated music websites. Notwithstanding, motivated by the prospective growth market, major Internet companies such as search service provider Baidu, e-commerce giant Alibaba, and Tencent (collectively referred to as "BAT") are competing for the online music market. Copyrighted music contents have become a strategic tool to lure potential customers. BAT is building up their music libraries to attract more than 600 million Internet users in China, by signing agreements with big music labels and artists. In addition, BAT is trying to offer movies, television shows, and games as well as their platforms to keep their users engaged and to prevent them from switching to rivals.

QQ Music, operated by Tencent, is one of the most popular music services, with more than 200 million users and more than 40 million active users. Somewhat similar to Spotify, QQ Music is operated under a 2-tier system: (1) Freemium (ad-financed) tier: users listen to online music provided by big labels for free while other businesses pay to put their advertisements on QQ Music's platform to expose their products to the users. (2) Premium Green Diamond Tier, under which users pay 10 RMB per month subscription to get access to high quality music and members-only concerts, and to enjoy chances to send gifts to their favorite stars. However, until very recently, paying subscribers have been extremely few, only "in single digits", as lamented by Dowson Tong, a Tencent senior vice president.[23]

To attract potential customers, Tencent has signed deals with big labels such as Sony Music Entertainment, Warner Music Group and South Korea's YG Entertainment to put their copyrighted works in its catalogue. In some cases, Tencent strives to become the exclusive online distributor of some big labels such as YG Entertainment Inc. in China.[24] Compared with its rivals, Tencent possesses obvious

---

[21] A. Klebanow / T. Wu (2015), 11.

[22] By the end of 2014, there were 478 million users listening to music online in China, but the revenue generated therefrom was US$ 91.4 million, ranked at 21st in the world. Source: IFPI, 2014 Annual Report.

[23] Available at: blogs.wsj.com/digits/2015/06/09/qa-how-tencent-plans-to-get-chinese-consumers-to-pay-for-music/.

[24] Available at: www.reuters.com/article/us-tencent-sony-music-idUSKBN0JU0UN20141216.

advantages to attract users because it operates China's most popular smartphone messaging apps, WeChat and Mobile QQ, each with more than 500 million active users.

2.4 *Summary*

Streaming has become the trend as smartphones become popular. Currently, competition within the streaming market industry remains congested as companies strive to differentiate from one another with variations in packaging, licensed music libraries, regions of operation, and features. However, switching costs[25] are quite high for customers, as there is limited compatibility between different streaming services. Moreover, streaming companies are trying to create network effects, which add value to their products among their services by including social media. As discussed above, all three music services have set up links with social networks such as Facebook or WeChat. What are the implications of such network links for competition law? In the following section, this chapter will analyze the rationale and legislation on regulating IP licensing to provide a theoretical framework for further examination of some questionable conduct of the three intermediaries from the perspective of competition law. Does Spotify have a dominant position in music streaming? Has conduct by Apple violated the antitrust law, or will it? How can one define the "relevant market" in the case of QQ Music?

3 Antitrust Intervention in Copyright Licensing: Rationale and Legislation

It has been controversial whether and to what extent antitrust law should intervene in copyright licensing. It is thus important to expound upon the theoretical foundation for antitrust analysis in this context.

3.1 *Principle*

Historically, intellectual property, including copyright, and competition law, were considered to be inherently in conflict ("theory of conflict"). However, the contemporary scholarship has the tendency to view intellectual property and competition law as complementary, instead of conflicting (theory of "complementarity"). Under

[25]Switching cost of consumers depends on various factors such as the coverage of a platform's service, a user's existing connection with a service and the devices used by a consumer.

the complementarity theory, both IP law and competition law are designed to promote innovation by creating incentives for dynamic competition for better and diversified processes and products. Accordingly, copyright law and competition law have to be understood in the sense of promoting complementary goals.[26]

As a general principle, IP licensing is considered beneficial and pro-competitive, as it can reduce transaction cost and the cost of introducing new products. Licensing arrangements raise antitrust concerns only if they are likely to adversely affect prices, quantities, qualities, or varieties of goods and services either currently or potentially available.[27] In the context of copyright licensing, antitrust lawsuits are rare, although collective trade group licensing practices do sometimes raise the issues of unlawful collusion or "refuse to license".

3.2 Overview of Legislation

A review of legislation in many jurisdictions finds few antitrust regulations on copyright licensing. As one comprehensive report by the Max Planck Institute for Innovation and Competition observes, "Copyright is practically never addressed in specific provisions. A considerable number of jurisdictions have adopted specific regulations or guidelines that deal with certain aspects of intellectual property from a competition law perspective. What is typical about such subrules is that they focus more on trademarks, namely, trademark licenses in the framework of vertical distribution agreements such as franchising agreements, or on agreements that are technology-oriented such as technology transfer agreements or research and development (R&D) agreements. Copyright issues may be covered by such rules to the extent that especially technology transfer rules also apply to software copyright licenses."[28] For instance, the European Commission states that it will not apply the Technology Transfer Block Exemption Regulations (TTBER) to copyright licences other than software copyright licensing agreement,[29] including those that deal with the performance or the reproduction and sale of works.

The US may be an unusual exception. In the USA, antitrust concerns have been the traditional rationale for government intervention into copyright licensing practice. Since the enactment of the 1909 Copyright Act, Congress was concerned about lack of competition in the marketplace, while it recognized copyright owners' exclusive right to make and distribute, and authorize the making and distribution,

[26]MPI Report (2013), 4-5.

[27]U.S. Department of Justice and the Federal Trade Commission, Antitrust Guidelines for the Licensing of Intellectual Property, 1995 (hereinafter "US 1995 Guidelines"), 7.

[28]MPI Report (2013), 27.

[29]The TTBER applies to agreements concerning the following IPRs: software copyright, designs and utility models, patents and know-how. The licensing of trade marks, copyright and other IPRs is not covered by the TTBER unless the licensing is ancillary to the licensing of the technology covered by the block exemption. Commission Regulation (EC) No 772/2004, Article 1(1)(b).

of phono records of musical works.[30] To address the monopoly concern, Congress simultaneously created a compulsory license for mechanical reproductions of musical works—the first compulsory license in U.S. copyright law history was at a rate of 2 cents per copy.[31] The compulsory licensing provisions, amended several times, remain a mechanism to safeguard competition in the copyright marketplace. Recently, the US Copyright Office observed that "The government's involvement in the music marketplace is unusual and expansive relative to other kinds of works created and disseminated under the Copyright Act. In many cases, it compels copyright owners to license their works at government-set rates. Regulation of music publishers and songwriters is particularly pervasive: the two most significant areas of their market (mechanical and performance licensing) are subject to mandatory licensing and government-set rate."[32] Additionally, the IP licensing guidelines (1995 Guidelines) of the US antitrust agencies apply to copyright licensing as well as patent licensing.

As the MPI Report points out, most jurisdictions do not provide for copyright-specific rules in their competition laws. At best, some mention copyright law along with other IP rights such as patents, while many jurisdictions do not mention IP at all in their competition laws. At worst, exemption provisions in the competition law lead to the misguided belief that competition law should never be applied to IP-related cases.[33] Thus, as the current laws stand, it is not easy to apply competition law to IP licensing.[34]

4 Competition Law Analysis of the Three Models

4.1 Spotify Model

In general, the digital music industry can be divided into two submarkets: the streaming market and the digital downloading market. The latter is dominated by iTunes and Amazon. In the streaming market, which is taking over "downloading", the industry still has many players, including Xbox Music, Tidal, Google Play Music and Apple Music. As discussed above, Spotify here faces a two-side market: the market to "sell" music to users, and the market to "buy" copyright contents from right holders. In the market with users, competition is fierce because there are many players in the market. Moreover, the users can shift to other services easily under the Spotify model. Compared with Apple music and QQ music, Spotify's platforms

[30]It was alleged that the Aeolian Company, a manufacturer of player pianos, was seeking to buy up exclusive rights from publishers to create a monopoly for piano rolls.

[31]US Copyright Office (2015), 26.

[32]*Id.*, 3.

[33]MPI Report (2013), 6.

[34]*Id.*

are less synthesized to enhance the loyalty of users. So far, there is no evidence to show that Spotify possesses dominant market power. Nor does it show that Spotify's licensing model will result in anticompetitive consequences, although it is a key player in the industry. In relation to users, Spotify has little leverage to impose unfair terms or engage in other abusive conduct.

In the relationship with right holders, Spotify has limited market power. In the highly competitive streaming market, content availability is fundamental to attracting customers: the larger the music library, the more customers will be attracted by the streaming service. Most key players, including Xbox, Spotify, Apple Music, and Google Music, have more than 30 million tracks in their catalogues. In order to build up its music library, Spotify strives to obtain authorizations directly from copyright holders such as songwriters and performers, who, however, can join or leave at their free will. When artists like British band Radiohead and US pop star Taylor Swift shifted their catalogues to Tidal—a competitor to Spotify—claiming that Spotify does not pay artists their fair share, Spotify came under great pressure to rethink the handsome copyright royalties it paid to big labels.

In order to increase its user and subscription base, Spotify signed an agreement with Facebook to make it compulsory for anyone trying to access Spotify to have a Facebook account. But such "tying up" with Facebook does not seem to cause antitrust concerns, not only because Spotify does not dominate the market. The "tying up" with Facebook may cause Spotify to fence off some potential users who did not have Facebook accounts, so it does not prevent or reduce competition in streaming service.

4.2 *Apple Model*

It is said that Apple's service has caused antitrust concerns in several aspects, which will be explored below.

4.2.1 Tying or Bundling

A tie-in arrangement is an agreement by a party to sell one product on the condition that the buyer also purchases a different (or tied) product, or at least agrees that he will not purchase that product from any other supplier. In the iTunes download model, Apple actually "ties" the use of the iTunes music service to compatible devices such as iPhone, iPad, iPod touch, and software, and this "tie-in" practice has generated antitrust litigation. In 2005, Thomas Slattery, an iTunes Music customer, sued Apple for trying to monopolize the online music market, arguing that he was "forced" to buy an iPod to hear the music he had purchased from the iTunes Music Store.[35] Apple was accused of violating U.S. and California antitrust law by restricting music purchased on iTunes from being played on devices other than iPods and by not allowing iPods to play music purchased from other digital music services. In early 2009, Apple removed DRM from iTunes and thus solved the antitrust claim against iTunes, so the remaining lawsuit covered iPods only. However, a federal jury decided in 2014 that Apple didn't breach antitrust law when it sold music players and songs with copyright-protection software that was incompatible with rival devices and music from competing online stores. The court rejected the expert opinion offered by the plaintiffs that Apple's design of its business model "raised the cost of switching from iPods to competing portable digital media players by eliminating the ability of consumers to collect a library of downloads that could be played on all players."[36]

The assessment of tying arrangements under U.S. antitrust law has undergone significant changes over time. For 40 years since the late 1940s, tie-in was found to be per se unlawful in the US.[37] However, more recently, courts acknowledged that "[m]any tying arrangements . . . are fully consistent with a free, competitive market."[38] Courts may use the rule of reason principle to analyze tie-in arrangements.[39] In the Microsoft case[40] where Microsoft combined two potentially separate products (an operating system "Window" and an Internet browser "Internet Explorer") into one, the court of appeals concluded that "the rule of reason, rather than per se analysis, should govern the legality of tying arrangements involving platform software products."[41] It added: "In fact there is merit to Microsoft's broader argument that Jefferson Parish's consumer demand test would 'chill innovation to the detriment of consumers by preventing firms from integrating into their products new functionality previously provided by standalone products--and hence, by definition, subject to separate consumer demand'."[42] The court thus reversed the decision of the trial court on the Microsoft's violation of the Section 1 of the

[35]In Apple iPod iTunes Antitrust Litigation, 96. Supp. 2d 1137—Dist. Court, ND California 2011.

[36]Court Order, in Apple iPod iTunes Antitrust Litigation, Case No.: 05-CV-0037 YGR, September 26, 2014.

[37]International Salt Co. v. United States, 332 U.S. at 396, the Court held, "it is unreasonable, per se, to foreclose competitors from any substantial market." In Standard Oil Co. v. United States 337 U.S. 293, 305-06 (1949).

[38]H. Hovenkamp / M.D. Janis / M.A. Lemley (2010), § 21.5, at 21-113-115.

[39]D.S. Evans / J. Padilla / C. Ahlborn (2013).

[40]United States v. Microsoft Corp., 253 F.3d 34 (D.C. Cir. 2001) [hereinafter Microsoft III].

[41]Microsoft III, part IV.

[42]Microsoft III.

Sherman Act.[43] In the view of the court of appeals in Microsoft III, the application of the per se rule that developed in the "old economy" to the "network economy" is backward-looking and ill-fitting.

By contrast, the EC competition law seems to take a more traditional approach to the issue of tying. Under EC law, "tying" has been addressed largely in the context of unilateral behavior of dominant firms, although tying may also fall within the scope of restrictive agreements.[44] In the Microsoft case, the Commission found that the "bundling" of Windows OS with Windows Media Player is illegal, because it satisfied four elements of Article 82(d) tying offense, which are the following: (1) the tying and tied goods are two separate products; (2) the undertaking concerned is dominant in the tying product market; (3) the undertaking concerned does not give customers a choice to obtain the tying product without the tied product; and (4) tying forecloses competition.[45] It is said that EC law in respect of tying is closer to the early U.S. cases under the per se approach than to the more recent U.S. cases under the rule of reason approach.[46]

In a summary, the treatments of "tying" vary substantially from one jurisdiction to another. The US antitrust law takes a more flexible and accommodating approach to "tying", especially in the area of the Internet. The rationale behind this is that the pace of innovation has become faster and competition has become more fierce, and a new technology could destroy previous business models overnight. So the court becomes more cautious about intervening, and it is more difficult to challenge "tying".

4.2.2 Maintenance of Monopoly

Apple's newly launched streaming service has been reported to have antitrust concerns on two aspects. The first concern is that Apple is alleged to have pressured labels to provide it with exclusive "windowing," that is, to exclusively launch their music first on Apple before making it available on other platforms.[47] This behavior may be incompatible with Article 2 of the Sherman Act According to long-standing principle, the requirement for monopolization is both (1) the possession of monopoly power in the relevant market and (2) anticompetitive conduct, which is defined as "the willful acquisition or maintenance of that power as distinguished from growth or development as a consequence of a superior product, business acumen,

[43]It reads: "every contract, combination in the form of trust or otherwise, or conspiracy, in restraint of trade or commerce among the several States, or with foreign nations, is declared to be illegal".

[44]European Commission, Guidelines on Vertical Restraints (2000/C291/01).

[45]Case COMP/C-3/37.792, 796-798, Microsoft Corp. v. Comm'n, (unreported, Mar. 24, 2004) (CEC), available at: europa.eu.int/comm/competition/antitrust/cases/decisions/37792/en.pdf.

[46]D.S. Evans / J. Padilla / C. Ahlborn (2013), 39.

[47]A. Klebanow / T. Wu (2015), 27-28.

or historic accident."[48] To determine whether Apple's exclusive "windowing" is unlawful, the first step would be to assess whether Apple possesses a dominant position in the "relevant market".

In this case, what is the proper scope of "relevant market"? The definition of relevant market mainly depends on whether the products are "substitutable" in the view of consumers. This is the "demand substitution" doctrine. Logically, there are three options: (1) the whole music industry, which includes physical media and the digital market; (2) the digital market, which includes music downloading and music streaming; (3) music streaming only. As a matter of substitutability, physical media and digital music should not be treated as being in the same market; but music downloading and streaming may be in the same market. Apple has undoubtedly established a dominant position in the music downloading business, but it is a newcomer to the streaming service, which is a more competitive industry. Nevertheless, Apple can ensure consumers continue to use their "downloaded" music products by integrating music with Apple's iOS operating system. Apple can also utilize its 850 million credit cards on file and integrate with its 1 billion iOS devices sold. This is the advantage that its rivals would find difficult to match.[49]

If Apple were found to have a dominant position in the music industry,[50] then the next question is whether Apple's exclusive "windowing" is compatible with antitrust law. Historically, windowing is a fairly common practice in the media industries other than music,[51] and Apple has brought exclusive windowing to the music industry in the last 5 years.[52] It has not formed a general pattern, and the duration for "windowing" has varied widely, from one week to one month. The "windowing" may be used as a way to attract new subscribers to Apple's music services and prevent consumers from defecting. The key question is whether it may reach a point where Apple is in a position to maintain its dominance by foreclosing competition in the industry, and whether Apple took improper means. Viewing the scope of Apple's "windowing" practice, which is restricted to some new songs, with the duration relatively short, the answer to the first question should be negative.

The second antitrust concern is that Apple is said to have placed pressure on the music labels to refuse to deal with streaming companies like Spotify who employ freemium.[53] In this aspect, Apple's behavior may result in serious antitrust concern

---

[48]Available at: www.justice.gov/atr/competition-and-monopoly-single-firm-conduct-under-section-2-sherman-act-chapter-1.

[49]A. Klebanow / T. Wu (2015), 17.

[50]The music market changes swiftly, so it is not clear whether Apple has a dominant market position. In the UK music retail market in 2014, Amazon overtook Apple as the UK's biggest music retailer last year, with 27 % of all spending, with iTunes accounting for 26.7 %. However, the newly launched Apple Music has attracted millions of subscribers; available at: www.musicbusinessworldwide.com/amazon-sold-more-music-than-apple-in-the-uk-last-year/.

[51]A. Klebanow / T. Wu (2015), 18.

[52]*Id.*

[53]For example, in November 2014, Taylor Swift's label, Big Machine Label Group, withdrew the entire Taylor Swift catalog from Spotify while keeping her music on other streaming services owned by Apple. A. Klebanow / T. Wu (2015).

if Apple has a dominant market position. Freemium has become a common practice in streaming service for two reasons. Firstly, some users will never become paid users, and the advertising-based service is therefore the only way to capture such users. If this service were not available, these users would likely shift to free music elsewhere, including pirate sites. Secondly, the ad-based service may attract potential consumers to try the service, and later become paid users.[54] Thus it is important for streaming services to develop a potential customer base. For example, 80 % of Spotify's 15 million paying subscribers started out as free users, before converting to be paid users.[55] If Apple were allowed to push big labels to ban freemium services, it would be able to force its competitors to abandon an entire business model (ad-share revenue), or even push them out of the music business. If Apple were found to have dominant market position, the successful elimination of a business model relied on by competitors would have serious consequences for competition in the industry. Apple's exclusionary conduct may harm consumers as well as the competition process. If other requirements of competition law were satisfied, Apple's conduct may fall within the category of "coordinated price manipulation".

Recently, it is said that Apple's aggressive practice has drawn the attention of the Free Trade Commission in the US[56] and EU Commission.[57] The EU Commission's main concern is that Apple will use its significant market power in neighbouring markets such as the smartphone (iPhone) market to force record labels to give its music service more favourable terms than those accorded to rivals, or even force labels to deal exclusively with Apple.

4.2.3 Discriminatory Pricing

It is not uncommon for licensors to charge different royalties based on consumer location. Usually, such practice depends on technological measures to detect location and enforce nation-specific access, and on legal measures to prohibit circumventing the technology and to validate market differentiation. It is not certain whether such differentiating practice constitutes the abuse of IP. In the US, the courts found a discriminatory royalty scheme to be patent misuse in a series of cases.[58] However, those decisions have received widespread criticism, and some

[54] A. Klebanow / T. Wu (2015), 20-21.

[55] *Id.*, 21.

[56] C. Kang (2015).

[57] EU Commission fears Apple may leverage its market power to corner the music streaming market, available at: eu-competitionlaw.com/eu-commission-fears-apple-may-leverage-its-market-power-to-corner-music-streaming-market/.

[58] See LaPeyre v. FTC, 366 F.2d 117 (5th Cir. 1966); Peelers Co. v. Wendt, 260 F. Supp. 193 (W.D. Wash. 1966); Laitram Corp. v. King Crab, Inc., 245 F. Supp. 1019 (D. Alaska 1965).

courts subsequently refused to find misuse or an antitrust violation based on licenses providing for differential royalties.[59]

In Europe, the 2007 Apple case shows that the European Commission is willing to intervene when a discriminatory price arrangement may generate anticompetitive effects. In that case, Apple operated an iTunes online store with different prices in the European Economic Area (EEA). The iTunes online store detected customers' country of origin through their credit card details, and consumers using a credit card issued by a UK bank were charged 6 % more than those in the rest of Europe.[60] Upon a complaint filed by a UK consumer group, the Commission began an antitrust investigation into Apple's business practices in 2007. Apple argued that it had been paying higher wholesale prices to UK music labels and was passing the cost along to UK customers. However, in 2008, Apple agreed to cut the prices for UK consumers to bring them in line with the rest of Europe, and the European Commission ended its antitrust investigation.[61]

4.3 QQ Music Model

The QQ music service model is somewhat similar to that of Spotify. However, different from Spotify, Tencent is notably an Internet giant and has strong power in multiple platforms and markets, just like Apple. Tencent may use its market power in other products and services, such as WeChat, to support the QQ Music platform, and some practices may result in anti-competition consequences. For instance, in February 2015, WeChat blocked its competitors' music services including Alipay "red envelope" (gift money circulated online among network friends), TTPOD Music Small Shrimp Music and Netease cloud music, to "punish" Alibaba for the unwelcomed "red envelope" distributed during Chinese New Year. Tencent felt that Alibaba took advantage of its WeChat platform to promote Alibaba's services, so it cut off Alibaba's two music Apps. The case didn't catch the government's attention, but generated public debate about the legality of Tencent's behaviour. Viewed from the perspective of antimonopoly doctrine, it is difficult for the "block" executed by Tencent to pass the "reasonableness" test, and it may well be found unlawful. Tencent's ban on its competitors' service may be considered "abusive". Basically, to establish an "abuse of dominant position", two elements are required: (1) a dominant position in the relevant market; (2) abusive behaviour. It is not clear whether Tencent dominates the music market. But Tencent's banning of

[59]See, e.g., USM Corp. v. SPS Techs. Inc., 694 F.2d 505 (7th Cir. 1982); see also, Akzo NV v. United States Int'l Trade Comm'n, 808 F.2d 1471 (Fed. Cir. 1986).

[60]European consumers in Austria, Belgium, Denmark, Germany, Finland, France, Greece, Ireland, Italy, Luxembourg, Netherlands, Norway, Portugal, Sweden, Switzerland and Spain paid the same price, 99 Euro cents, while UK users paid 79 pence.

[61]Available at: www.theregister.co.uk/2008/01/09/apple_cuts_uk_prices/.

competitors' music service was criticized as "irrational", "unreasonable" and "unacceptable". Such criticism is valid for several reasons. Firstly, the blocking adversely affects millions of consumers, who stored their music in the blocked services and were not able to use the blocked services. Secondly, Tencent's blocking in effect prevents its rival, Alibaba, from providing similar service to consumers and thus would have anticompetitive effects. Thirdly, Tencent's could not provide convincing reasons for its blocking.[62] However, if conventional principle in defining relevant market is applied, it is difficult to establish that Tencent possesses a dominant position in the online music industry. As discussed above, China's music market is not mature, there are few users who pay for music, and few music service providers make profit. In the meanwhile, there are many operating players in the online music market (including the services for downloading and streaming), and Tencent seems to face serious competition.

However, in today's cross-over era, we should take a more flexible and comprehensive approach to define "relevant market", because an Internet giant like Tencent has strong power in multiple markets given its vast user base. Tencent thus has unbeatable influence in the music individual licensing market. Tencent may employ the power of its social network to reduce or exclude competition in music service. As stated by analysts, "Whether Tencent can dominate online music in China—and get more users to pay—may depend on how well it can take advantage of the popularity of its messaging and social-networking services".[63] Also, as experience has shown, once major technology players with synergies across multiple platforms enter a market, it would be difficult for rivals without such cross-market coverage and resources to compete effectively. Thus, to define the "relevant market" of Tencent's QQ music service, one should take into account the company's power in a social network or other market which would have indirect impacts on the competition in the music industry.[64]

5 Conclusion

Application of competition law to copyright licensing practice poses many challenges for law enforcement bodies. It is particularly the case considering the intricate business structure in the Internet era. Although the overall competition implications of the new business models need to be further evaluated, a few observations can be drawn. First and foremost, while the methods for accessing

[62]Tencent claimed that the "blocking" was due to safety reasons, or malicious marketing on the part of Alibaba, but it lacks sufficient evidence to back up the claim.

[63]J. Osawa (2014), Tencent Customers Come for the Music, Stay for the Perks, http://www.wsj.com/articles/tencent-customers-come-for-the-music-stay-for-the-perks-1433869369.

[64]Cf. Qihoo 360 v. Tencent. China's Supreme Court took a "broad approach" to define the "relevant market", finding that the defendant did not have a dominant position in the relevant market.

and using copyright-protected work change radically with technology development, the channels for consumers to use copyrighted works are diverse, and the competition in the relevant market is intense. Secondly, several of Apple's actions such as "banning" its competitors' "freemium" services may fall within the category of "maintenance of monopoly", if Apple were found to have a dominant market position. Thirdly, we are experiencing a new era of "crossover": high tech giants with synergies across multiple platforms, such as Apple, Tencent and Alibaba, play an increasingly fundamental role in obtaining copyright and the build-up of content libraries. Some of their conduct poses a serious threat to their rivals without such synergies. By using their market power in other markets (e.g. hardware, software or social network), those giants are able to impose unfair terms on consumers or push their competitors out of the market. In order to protect market competition, we should adopt a more flexible approach to defining the relevant market in this crossover era.

References

Evans, D. S. / Padilla, J. / Ahlborn, C. (2013), The Antitrust Economics of Tying: A Farewell to Per Se Illegality. Antitrust Bulletin, 2003. available at: ssrn.com/abstract=381940

Hovenkamp, H. / Janis, M.D./ Lemley, M.A. (2010), IP and Antitrust: An Analysis of Antitrust Principles Applied to Intellectual Property Law

Kang, C. (2015), Everything to Know About the FTC's Antitrust Review of Apple's Music Business, available at: www.washingtonpost.com/news/the-switch/wp/2015/07/16/everything-with-know-about-the-ftcs-antitrust-review-of-apples-music-business/.

Klebanow, A. / Wu, T. (2015), Is Music the Next eBooks? An Antitrust Analysis of Apple's Conduct in the Music Industry, Columbia Journal of Law & the Arts, 14. July 2015, available at: ssrn.com/abstract=2633751

Max Planck Institute for Intellectual Property and Competition Law (2013), Copyright, Competition and Development ("MPI Report")

Osawa, J. (2014), Tencent Signs China Deal With Sony Music, available at: www.wsj.com/articles/tencent-signs-china-deal-with-sony-music-1418720584

US Copyright Office (2015), Copyright and the Music Marketplace

U.S. Department of Justice and the Federal Trade Commission (1995), Antitrust Guidelines for the Licensing of Intellectual Property

von Wiegandt, D. (2013), Spotify: Incentivizing Album Creation through the Facebook of Music, Berkeley J. Ent. / Sports L., 2013 (2), 180

Individual Licensing Models and Consumer Protection

Lucie Guibault

Contents

Abstract Copyright law is not primarily directed at consumers. Their interests are therefore only marginally accounted for, as the copyright rules exempt specific uses of works from the right holder's control. This chapter examines the impact of digital technology on the position of consumers of licensed copyrighted content. While ownership of the physical embodiment of a work does not entail the ownership of the rights in the work, how does copyright law deal with 'disembodied' works? How does digital technology affect the consumers' reasonable expectations in terms of workability and functionality of digital content? Do consumers have any recourse under consumer protection law for 'defective' content, for example for the impossibility to make a copy for private purposes, the lack of interoperability between devices, and the geo-blocking of their account? Does consumer protection

Lucie Guibault is Associate Professor of Intellectual Property Law at the Institute for Information Law, Universiteit van Amsterdam.

L. Guibault (✉)
Universiteit van Amsterdam, Amsterdam, The Netherlands
e-mail: L.Guibault@uva.nl

K.-C. Liu, R.M. Hilty (eds.), *Remuneration of Copyright Owners*, MPI Studies on Intellectual Property and Competition Law 27, DOI 10.1007/978-3-662-53809-8_12

law treat physical embodiments of works, digital downloads and streaming differently?

1 Introduction

The romantic idea of authors conveying their works to the enjoyment of individual members of the public has progressively evolved over the past century into a powerful creative industry geared to the demands of masses of eager consumers. That 'digital content', defined as any content protected by copyright and/or related rights which the consumer can access on-line or through any other channels as CDs and DVDs, are consumption goods is undeniable. Without consumers, mass entertainment products, like films, TV programs, songs, books and video games, would have no public. But the creative industry has gone through a rough transition period in recent years due to the constant development of digital technology: not only must the industry face the enduring threat of online piracy, but more importantly, it must counter this threat by offering innovative legal channels of digital content to the public. According to the 2015 edition of the International Federation of Phonogram Industry's (IFPI) *Digital Music Report,*[1] the music industry derived for the first time in 2014 the same proportion of revenues from digital channels (46 %) as physical format sales (46 %). In recent years, music subscription services like Spotify, iTunes, Tidal, and Pandora have gained tremendous ground worldwide. Of the revenues generated from digital channels, digital downloads still account for the bulk of the global digital revenues (52 %). These figures show that in the coming years, a further switch from a world of music primarily characterized by tangible goods to one primarily characterized by digital forms of distribution should be expected to take place.[2] The same phenomenon is unfolding as we speak, with respect to films and other types of content, as Amazon Prime, Netflix and other services give consumers access to a wide catalogue of audiovisual works.[3]

Whatever the channel of distribution, however, the digital content that is legally offered to the public on a commercial basis is usually 'packaged' so as to discourage any act of piracy with respect to that content. Such 'packaging' commonly entails a combination of contractual licensing conditions, conditional access measures and anti-copying devices. Measures enabling the industry to monitor the use made of copyrighted content by individual members of the public are often also part of the bundle. This type of 'packaging' does affect the general public's enjoyment of the content. Consumers complain about a lack of interoperability between

[1]IFPI Digital Music Report—Charting the path to sustainable growth, www.ifpi.org/downloads/Digital-Music-Report-2015.pdf.

[2]R.M. Hilty (2015).

[3]N. Fried (2015).

devices, the impossibility to make a copy for time or format shifting purposes, the lack of access to or the presence of restrictions on the use of the content in different territories, the limited possibilities to restore damaged or lost content, and data protection issues arising in relation to the monitoring of their use of copyrighted content.[4]

The intersection between copyright law, contract law and consumer protection law is increasingly attracting attention among legal commentators[5] and civil societies.[6] Many of the consumers' concerns when purchasing digital content, in fact, have their source in the way copyright law governs the exploitation and use of digital content. Some 'disruptive' features in the 'packaging' of content have been challenged before the courts in some countries.[7] But as digital technology evolves, together with the business models used to bring copyrighted content to consumers, the point of intersection between the three fields of law moves as well. What does the disembodiment of copyrighted content mean for consumers? Are the consumers' concerns the same if the film, song, book or game is distributed on a tangible medium or through a digital channel? Are the solutions different?

This chapter examines the question of the impact of digital technology on the position of consumers of licensed digital content. The analysis starts from the basic tenet in copyright law, according to which the ownership of the physical embodiment of a work does not entail the ownership of the rights in the work. The existence and exercise of the copyright owner's rights in an original work actually determine whether the lawful acquirer of a copy of this work has any rights in it. Qualifying the nature of the transaction between the copyright owner and the consumer constitutes a necessary step before enquiring whether the consumer has any claim against the copyright owner in respect of the lawfully acquired copy. Contract law plays a role in the copyright-consumer equation, inasmuch as copyrighted works are commonly accompanied by contractual terms of use. Do the contractual terms of use affixed to works qualify the transaction as a sale or a licence? What is the consequence of this qualification? Moreover, depending on the copyrights involved and their mode of exercise, consumers may or may not have a claim under consumer protection law against copyright owners for the lack of

---

[4]N. Helberger / L. Guibault / M. Loos / C. Mak / L. Pessers / B. van der Sloot (2012).

[5]S. Arnerstål (2015), 750-758; N. Helberger / L. Guibault (2012); N. Helberger / L. Guibault / M. Loos / C. Mak / L. Pessers / B. van der Sloot (2012); J. Schovsbo (2008), 393-408; T. Kreutzer (2011); G. Mazziotti (2007).

[6]J. Malcom (2015).

[7]Brussels Court of Appeal, 9 September 2005 (Test Achats v. EMI Recorded Music Belgium et al.); Cour de cassation, (1st chamber, civil section), 28 February 2006, (Studio Canal, Universal Pictures Video France and SEV / S. Perquin and UFC Que Choisir); Tribunal de Grande Instance de Nanterre, 6th chamber, Judgment of 24 June 2003, Association CLCV / EMI Muisc France; Tribunal de Grande Instance de Nanterre, 6th chamber, Judgment of 2 September 2003, Francoise M. / EMI Music France, Auchan France; Tribunal de Grand Instance de Paris, 3rd chamber, 2e section, Stéphane P., UFC Que Choisir/Société Films Alain Sarde et, Judgment of 30 April 2004.

interoperability between devices, the impossibility to make a copy for private purposes, and the geo-blocking of their account.

The chapter is further divided in three parts: the first part provides a brief description of what is to be generally understood throughout this part of the book by 'individual licensing'. The second part examines the nature of the transaction between the copyright owner and the consumer of digital content, from a copyright and contract law perspective. To see how digital technology affects the consumers' position in relation to online digital content, the act of licensing will be broken down in three separate instances: physical purchase, digital download and streaming. As will become apparent, the use of digital technology as a support for the distribution of digital content to the public does affect the way in which the rights are allocated and exercised by the rights holder, thereby affecting the position of the consumer. On the basis of the analysis of the nature of the transaction, the third part explores how consumer protection law responds, in each separate instance, to a number of recurring concerns expressed by consumers with respect to the digital copyrighted content that they have acquired. This part will show whether European consumer protection law treats the consumption of tangible goods differently from that of services.

For the purposes of this chapter, the rules in force in the European Union on copyright, contract and consumer protection serve as the legal framework of reference. Although international copyright conventions, such as the Berne Convention and the WIPO Copyright Treaty, ensure a certain degree of harmonisation of the concepts of copyright law, national legislation still shows too many differences in terminology and scope of protection to allow a high level comparison between countries or regions of the world. Moreover, the rules on contract and consumer protection law are not harmonised internationally, as a result of which the level of protection vastly differs between countries. Identifying the legal framework within which the analysis of the present chapter is conducted is all the more important knowing that the outcome would most probably differ if the analysis were conducted on the basis of the legal framework of any other jurisdiction. Be that as it may, the legal concepts discussed in this chapter are presented, as much as possible, in a jurisdiction-agnostic manner.

The expectations of consumers, defined as 'any natural person who is acting for purposes which are outside his trade, business, craft or profession',[8] with respect to the purchase and use of digital content are taken as a given. Moreover we assume that these expectations are reasonable. As this chapter focuses on copyright, contract and consumer protection law, data protection law remains outside the scope of the analysis. Finally, since the objective of the chapter is to describe a situation with a potentially global application, current legislative developments at the European level regarding the establishment of the Digital Single Market and the cross-border portability of online content services are mentioned only as an

[8]Directive 2011/83/EC of the European Parliament and of the Council of 25 October 2011 on Consumer Rights, L 304/64, O.J.E.U. 22 November 2011, Article 2(1).

example of how consumer concerns with regards to individual licensing practices for digital content can be addressed.

2 "Individual Licensing" of Digital Content to Consumers

The consumption of digital content forms an integral part of the daily life of consumers of all ages, professions and level of experience. More and more digital services are aimed at meeting consumer demand for information, education, entertainment and communication: music downloads, online gaming, online publishing and the purchase of e-books, subscription to podcasts, webcast and streaming services, et cetera. Business models enabling the exploitation of digital content come in an array of different arrangements, ranging from 'on-demand' offerings, 'near-on-demand' content, on-demand downloading, streaming, webcasting, and IP-based TV, to subscription for e-books, e-journals and newspapers, social broadcasting, cloud computing, and many more. Forms of payment are as diverse as the business models supporting them, including pay-per-download, pay-per-bundle, pay-per-use, pay-per-source (e.g. a specific title), pay-per-day, flat access fee, subscription, advertisement financed, or free of charge.

In comparison to more conventional means of exploitation of content protected by copyright and related rights, the online distribution of digital content involves the intervention of numerous intermediaries. While traditional rights owners, most notably publishers, (recording and film) producers, and collective rights management organisations (CRMOs) continue to take an active part in the licensing of digital content, new players have secured themselves a place in the chain: among them, content aggregators (like Spotify, Netflix, Amazon Prime or Apple iTunes) and Internet service providers (ISPs) (like Youtube, DailyMotion etc.) play an increasingly important role in the supply of digital content. The complexity of the chain of exploitation and the identity and role of the different intermediaries vary between sectors of the creative industry.[9] The very simplified licensing scheme for the exploitation of copyright content, shown in Fig. 1, indicates, in a generic manner, how rights are transferred (red arrows between the author and the publisher/CRMO or between the publisher and the CRMO) and licensed (blue arrows between the publisher/CRMO and aggregators/online services) from the initial author all the way down to the consumer.

At the bottom of the chain is the consumer. Content sold or communicated via conventional channels, e.g. the purchase of books, CDs, DVDs or the broadcast or transmission of songs or films, can generally be used without requiring consumers to abide by the specific contractual conditions (grey arrows). By contrast, digital content is commonly exploited through online channels along with licensing conditions that set restrictions on the possibility to use the content (blue arrow).

[9] Europe Economics / L. Guibault / O. Salamanca / S. van Gompel (2015); C. Cooke (2015).

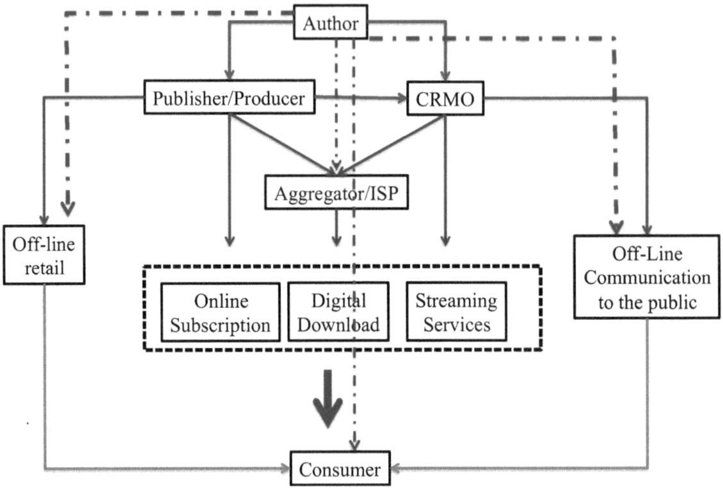

Fig. 1 Licensing scheme for the distribution of content

The model described above forms a complex web of individual licensing agreements for the exploitation of digital content, which can be either direct or indirect to consumers:

- Direct licensing from right holders to consumers, e.g. where a newspaper publisher offers an internet-based business models allowing for daily individual downloads by every single subscriber; or
- Indirect licensing through intermediaries, like Spotify, YouTube, or Amazon Prime, who provide services to consumers based on individualized licensing models; in this case, the intermediaries obtain a license from the right holder (publisher/producer or CRMO) to provide their service and to grant sub-licenses to consumers.

The form of payment associated with a particular individual licensing model does not affect the nature of the model: irrespective of the calculation of a licensing fee, a contract between individuals, which allows for the use of digital content, remains under all circumstances a licensing agreement.

Admittedly the more intricate licensing schemes in place for the exploitation of digital content could be qualified as hybrid, in that they involve both individual and collective licensing arrangements. The structure of a particular licensing scheme in support of a specific business model actually depends on several factors, including the category of work or other subject matter concerned, the initial ownership of rights on those works or other subject matter, and the (combination of) rights necessary to allow for a workable business model. Some rights are presumed by law to be transferred to a producer upon completion of the work, while other rights may be transferred voluntarily to a CRMO for more effective commercial exploitation. Taking cinematographic works as an example, film producers are known to administer their rights individually.[10] They are therefore likely to license their right of reproduction and making available directly to intermediaries such as Netflix, who license the service to consumers via an Internet platform or a cable retransmission service. However, Netflix also needs to obtain a licence from the CRMOs representing the rights of music authors and performing artists to ensure that the musical works integrated in the cinematographic works can be properly reproduced and made available to the public. As the chain of distribution of digital content in this constellation almost always entails a licence of use for the consumer, we believe that the predominant characteristic of this form of licensing should logically be 'individual', knowing that CRMOs are not in the business of granting licences to consumers.

The conditions set by contract for the use of digital content, together with the technical protection measures (TPM) applied to the content, e.g. the 'packaging' of the digital content, may indeed have important repercussions for consumers and their ability to enjoy the content that they lawfully access or acquire.

3 The Nature of the Transaction

In the context of 'individual licensing' schemes, two inter-connected elements influence the nature of the transaction between the copyright owner and the consumer with respect to a lawfully acquired copy of a work: first, whether the work qualifies as a good or a service; and second, whether the transaction qualifies as a purchase or a licence. The concepts of 'goods' and 'services' are not harmonized at the European level, especially as they relate to the requirement of 'tangibility'. Similarly the Directive on Copyright in the Information Society[11] does not regulate the issue of end-user contracts as such. However, it does create a legal framework within the boundaries of which rights owners are able to license their rights to end-users and to enforce them.[12] This framework allows right holders to put restrictions on the access to and use of digital content. The double qualification is important, as in consumer protection law distinct legal consequences may be attached to different types of transactions.

It has been argued that the medium in which the digital content is embodied essentially determines the tangible or intangible nature of the content: a movie on a DVD would be tangible, whereas the same movie downloaded through the Internet would be intangible. While the distinction between goods and services can

[10]Europe Economics / L. Guibault / O. Salamanca / S. van Gompel (2015).

[11]Directive 2001/29/EC of the European Parliament and of the Council of 22 May 2001 on the harmonisation of certain aspects of copyright and related rights in the information society, OJ 2001 L167/10.

[12]N. Helberger / L. Guibault / M. Loos / C. Mak / L. Pessers / B. van der Sloot (2012); M. van Eechoud / P.B. Hugenholtz / S. van Gompel / L. Guibault / N. Helberger (2009).

intuitively be made between a movie distributed on a CD and one made available through the Internet, it is quite a challenge to apply this distinction to a vast array of forms of online or off-line distribution of digital content that are neither true goods nor pure service. To see how the consumer's position with respect to copyright protected works has evolved over time, along with the development of digital technology, we consider three separate instances of distribution of content to the public, going from analogue, to digital and cloud technology: physical purchase, digital download and streaming.[13]

3.1 Physical Purchase

Copyright owners enjoy under copyright law the exclusive rights of reproduction, distribution and communication to the public. The right of distribution concerns the control of the distribution of the work incorporated in a tangible article. This right is exhausted by the first sale, or other transfer of ownership, of the original of a work or copies thereof by the right holder or with his consent. In Europe, the distribution right is exhausted with respect to any sale within the territory of the European Union.[14] The copyright holder has therefore the exclusive right to distribute his work on a CD, DVD or flash drive.[15] Once the work is sold on such a tangible medium, the purchaser becomes the owner of the physical object. In other words, the consumer becomes the owner of the physical copy of the work and, in application of the exhaustion doctrine he/she may resell it, destroy it or give it away. As purchasers of tangible goods, consumers of works on CDs, DVDs or other tangible media entertain reasonable expectations in terms of workability and functionality.

Be that as it may, consumers of tangible media hardly ever obtain the transfer of rights in the digital content itself. Instead, consumers receive an implied or express license to use the content as part of the 'wrapping' of the product.[16] Express licences can be either printed on or inside the box or they can be made to appear on a screen when opening or running the digital content on a device. It is not uncommon to see that, in an effort to curb piracy, TPMs are applied together with licence terms, so as to prohibit acts of reproduction or communication to the public that would otherwise be permitted under the law. Whether a term in a licence is deemed unfair or unreasonable towards consumers of copyrighted material largely depends on the country's approach to the copyright regime and to the principle of freedom of contract.[17]

[13]R.M. Hilty (2015), 3.

[14]Information Society Directive, Article 4(1); Case C-479/04, Judgment of the Court (Grand Chamber) of 12 September 2006, (Laserdisken v/ Kultuministeriet).

[15]S. Dusollier (2010), 26.

[16]R.M. Hilty (2015), 4.

[17]L. Guibault (2002), 299.

3.2 Digital Download

Leaving the realm of the tangible objects, online platforms now offer digital files for download by members of the public. Such digital downloads can be marketed on the basis of numerous business models: pay-per-download, pay-per-use, pay-per-source (e.g. a specific title), pay-per-day, flat access fee, or subscription. Downloadable digital files are also 'packaged' along with licence terms enforced through TPMs. The question is how to qualify the digital copy once downloaded onto one's device: under which conditions could the consumer be considered to 'own' the copy of the copyright protected work? And what kind of expectations can he/she entertain with respect to the content?

When the work is not embodied in a tangible medium, the distribution right is not applicable. Rather the exclusive right involved is that of communication to the public, which includes the right to make it available to the public in such a way that members of the public may access them from a place and at a time individually chosen by them. The Directive on Copyright in Information Society specifies that the exclusive right is not exhausted by any act of communication to the public nor of making available to the public.[18] According to Recital 29 of the Directive, 'the question of exhaustion does not arise in the case of services and on-line services in particular. This also applies with regard to a material copy of a work or other subject matter made by a user of such a service with the consent of the rightholder. Therefore, the same applies to rental and lending of the original and copies of works or other subject matter, which are services by nature. Unlike CD-ROM or CD-I, where the intellectual property is incorporated in a material medium, namely an item of goods, every on-line service is in fact an act which should be subject to authorization where the copyright or related right so provides.'

In view of the seemingly unambiguous text of the Directive, national courts mostly followed a conservative approach to the issue of exhaustion in the online environment.[19] German courts ruled for example that since the exhaustion doctrine does not apply to works that are made available on the Internet, a lawful purchaser cannot offer her software or music downloads for sale to other users, irrespective of the method of transfer (e.g. on eBay or per email or otherwise).[20] This approach has been criticized on the ground that such unequal treatment between the physical and non-physical copies of works is unjustified either for technological or trade-related reasons. While the prohibition on re-sale is believed to prevent piracy, it inhibits consumers of non-physical copies of works from realizing the resale value of their

[18]Copyright Directive, Article 3(3); cf. also, Case 62/79 Judgment of the Court of 18 March 1980, ECR 1980, p. 881 (Coditel v. Ciné Vog Films et al.).

[19]See the review of jurisprudence in E. Linklater (2014).

[20]Court of Appeal Dusseldorf, Decision of 29.06.2009 I-20 U 247/08; see also German Supreme Court, (OEM case), decision of 06.07.2000 I ZR 244/97; District Court Berlin, decision of 14.07.2009, 6 O 67/08.

goods. The argument has been put forward that re-sale could be possible by using watermarking technology which allows authentication of non-physical copies.[21]

The Court of Justice of the EU opened the door to the application of the exhaustion doctrine to the re-sale of 'used' software licences in the UsedSoft case.[22] On the basis of the provisions of the Computer Programs Directive, the Court ruled that 'in the event of the resale of a user licence entailing the resale of a copy of a computer program downloaded from the copyright holder's website, the licence having originally been granted by that rightholder to the first acquirer for an unlimited period in return for payment of a fee intended to enable the rightholder to obtain a remuneration corresponding to the economic value of that copy of his work, the second acquirer of the licence, as well as any subsequent acquirer of it, will be able to rely on the exhaustion of the distribution right under Article 4(2) of that [Computer Programs] directive, and hence be regarded as lawful acquirers of a copy of a computer program within the meaning of Article 5(1) of that directive and benefit from the right of reproduction provided for in that provision.'[23]

The criterion retained by the Court is therefore whether the software was licenced 'for an unlimited period in return for payment of a fee', in which case the transaction could be assimilated to a sale. An additional factor used to assess the nature of the transaction is whether the digital download by the consumer onto his/her computer can lead to a permanently stored file. The more permanent is the storage, the closer the transaction resembles the sale of a tangible object, the use of which is subject of course, to the terms of a licence for the use of the copyrighted work.[24]

The UsedSoft decision gave rise to numerous commentaries, mostly favorable to the Court's position.[25] As the UsedSoft decision dealt exclusively with software, the question remains at this stage whether the criteria developed by the Court with respect to the exhaustion doctrine will be extended to other categories of works licensed in digital format. The Court of Justice will hopefully shed some light on the issue when it renders decision in the Vereniging Openbare Bibliotheken case.[26] The last question put to the Court in this case is whether 'Article 4(2) of Directive 2001/29 is to be construed as meaning that the initial sale or other transfer of ownership of material as referred to in that provision also means making available remotely by downloading, for use for an unlimited period, a digital copy of copyright-protected

[21]T. Kreutzer (2011), 14-15.

[22]Case C-128/11, Judgment of the Court (Grand Chamber) of 3 July 2012 (UsedSoft GmbH v. Oracle International Corp.).

[23]*Id.*, para. 88.

[24]R.M. Hilty (2015), 9.

[25]B. Batchelor / L. Montani (2015), 591; P. Mezei (2015); M. Savič (2015); S. Karapapa (2014).

[26]Case C-174/15, Request for preliminary ruling by the Court of Justice lodged on 17 April 2015 (Vereniging Openbare Bibliotheken v Stichting Leenrecht; interveners: Nederlands Uitgeversverbond and Others).

novels, collections of short stories, biographies, travelogues, children's books and youth literature?'

3.3 *Streaming*

One step further in the 'dematerialization' of content is streaming, which can be defined as the transfer of data (as audio or video material) in a continuous stream especially for immediate processing or playback.[27] This form of exploitation entails no independent purchase, but depends on authorization from an online platform.[28] Streaming in principle does not enable the download of copies of works on the computer memory or portable media for any significant length of time. As Hilty correctly observes, 'mere access [in the case of streaming] requires neither a distribution of works via tangible carriers nor a download by the user'.[29] In such circumstances, the exclusive right involved is the right to make the work available to the public, which is not exhausted by any act of making available to the public.[30] From the consumers' perspective, when no analogy can be drawn with a sale, the dematerialization of content results in qualifying the transaction as a service. In this case, the licence is the product![31] In the absence of a download by the consumer, what kind of expectations can he/she entertain with respect to the content? Are consumers entitled to have reasonable expectations in respect of services? Are those expectations only those molded by the licensing terms?

In the end, the classification of digital content pursuant to consumer contract law may need to occur on a case-by-case basis. Not all digital content can be qualified as a good, whereas not all digital content falls under the definition of service. In short, the nature of the transaction changes as technology evolves and as copyright-protected content dematerialises.

4 The Position of the Consumer

The fact that digital content is only 'licensed' rather than 'sold' to consumers poses difficulties when assessing the reasonable expectations consumers may hold with regard to that content. Right holders and traders play an important role in shaping the expectations consumers have regarding the functionality and usability of digital content, through their communications with consumers and the application of

[27]Merriam-Webster Dictionary, available at: www.merriam-webster.com/dictionary/streaming.

[28]S. Karapapa (2014).

[29]R.M. Hilty (2015), 3.

[30]A.-É Credeville / J.-P. Dardayrol / J. Martin (2012), 11.

[31]Referring to a seminal quote from R. Gomulkiewicz (1998).

licensing terms. Situations where consumers are unable to use the product in a way that corresponds to their reasonable expectations give rise to complaints about non-conformity. The consumer's reasonable expectations as to the functionality of a good and her ability as the owner of the good to benefit from that functionality determine not only the extent to which suppliers are obliged to inform the consumer about the main characteristics of that good, but also how the fairness of the contractual conditions and commercial practices related to the process of selling the good are assessed.[32] But what is the consumers' position in cases where there is no tangible good sold or licensed?

European consumer protection law hinges on the distinction between goods and services.[33] Conscious of the emerging paradox in the online environment, the Consumer Rights Directive[34] creates a special regime for digital content contracts. Digital content is defined in Article 2 under (11) as "data which are produced and supplied in digital form", whereas Recital 19 of the Directive lists examples that fall within the definition, leaving open which rules shall apply outside the areas harmonised by the Directive. More specifically, the recital further indicates that where digital content is supplied on a tangible medium (such as a CD or DVD) it should be considered as a 'good' within the meaning of the Directive. By contrast, the Directive keeps silent about the classification of digital content that is supplied online. Instead, it provides specific rules with regard to information obligations where the contract is concluded at a distance. The Directive thereby avoids the difficult question of classification, but takes away the unintended consequences of such a distinction by stating that both forms of digital content delivery (tangible or not) fall under the scope of the Directive.[35]

Consumer protection law grants consumers certain rights against suppliers of products that deviate from consumer's legitimate expectations, or who fail to take account of their lawful interests. In a highly competitive market such as the market for digital content, the sales price is rarely an issue for consumers. Were it an issue, consumer protection law would offer little help anyway since, according to the *iustum pretium* doctrine, clauses relating to price or other main characteristics of the contract are not open for judicial review.[36] Under consumer sales law, consumers can complain about unfair contract terms or about products that do not conform to the level of functionality that should normally be expected from similar products. With respect to digital content, research shows that the consumers' main concerns

[32]N. Helberger / L. Guibault (2012).

[33]See M. Schmidt-Kessel (2011).

[34]Directive 2011/83 on Consumer Rights, OJ L304/64–88 (2011).

[35]M. Loos / N. Helberger / L. Guibault / C. Mak / L. Pessers / K.J. Cseres / B. van der Sloot / R. Tigner (2011), 99-102.

[36]Council Directive 93/13/EEC of 5 April 1993 on unfair terms in consumer contracts, OJ L 95, 21.4.1993, p. 29-34, art. 4(2): "2. Assessment of the unfair nature of the terms shall relate neither to the definition of the main subject matter of the contract nor to the adequacy of the price and remuneration, on the one hand, as against the services or goods supplies in exchange, on the other, in so far as these terms are in plain intelligible language".

relate to: (1) restrictions on the making of private copies; (2) the lack of interoperability between devices; and (3) the lack of access/restrictions on use from different territories, otherwise known as geo-blocking.[37] All three concerns have their root in the way copyright is exercised through individual licensing schemes, more particularly through the combined application of restrictive licence terms and TPMs. In the following pages, we briefly discuss the role of copyright law as a support for the current licensing practice and consider how the law can provide a response to each consumer concern.

4.1 Private Copying

In absence of explicit permission from the rights holder, reproductions of copyright protected works for private purposes are only lawful if authorized by law. Article 5 (2)(b) of Directive on Copyright in the Information Society does this by allowing Member States to adopt an exception 'in respect of reproductions on any medium made by a natural person for private use and for ends that are neither directly nor indirectly commercial, on condition that the right holders receive fair compensation which takes account of the application or non-application of technological measures to the work or subject-matter concerned'. The requirement that reproductions be made 'by a natural person for private use and for ends that are neither directly nor indirectly commercial' clearly excludes any form of commercial copying, be it for legitimate business-related purposes or ordinary 'piracy'. Moreover, Article 5(2)(b) does not permit Member States to adopt exemptions allowing 'private' copying by or within business enterprises or other *legal* persons, even if such copying has no commercial purpose. Consequently, the scope of any exemption permitted by Article 5(2)(b) is fairly limited, as must be any system of private copying levies directly associated with it. It is settled case law of the Court of Justice that levies, as a form of 'fair compensation' prescribed by Article 5(2)(b), cannot serve to compensate right holders for losses incurred by acts not exempted pursuant to this provision, such as intra-company uses, or acts of piracy.[38]

The last sentence of Article 5(2)(b) refers to the application of TPMs designed to prevent or restrict acts in respect of works, which are not authorized by the right holder. TPMs can also be used to control the number of reproductions. In practice, the application of a TPM on a work pursuant to the Directive is likely to result in preventing or at least limiting the consumer from exercising the exception of private copy recognized in that same Directive. This happens, for example, each time a work is protected by means of an anti-copy mechanism. In this case, the anti-copy technique prevails over the private copying exception. Whenever rights

[37] *Id.*, 35.

[38] Case C-463/12, Judgment of the Court (Fourth Chamber) of 5 March 2015, (Copydan Båndkopi v. Nokia Danmark A/S.).

holders design their TPM in such a way that private copies are possible, then Member States are not allowed to intervene at all, on the basis of Article 6(4).[39]

Technical restrictions are often reinforced by licence terms. The Directive on Copyright in Information Society contains very few provisions pertaining to the use of contractual licences as a means to determine the conditions of use of copyright protected works. Nor does the Directive actively regulate the intersection between copyright exceptions and contracts. With respect to the limitations on copyright, Recital 45 declares that 'the exceptions and limitations referred to in Article 5(2), (3) and (4) should not, however, prevent the definition of contractual relations designed to ensure fair compensation for the rightholders insofar as permitted by national law.' What the precise meaning of Recital 45 is remains unclear. It could be referring, for example, to the conclusion of extended collective licensing agreements for acts of private copying and other uses, following the Scandinavian model. In the *Copydan* case, the Court of Justice did rule, however, that individual licensing systems have no bearing on the obligation to pay the fair compensation owed by virtue of Article 5(2)(b) of the Information Society Directive.[40] In other words, the compensation owed for private copying activities will keep being collected even if the works are also licensed as part of an individual licensing scheme. This leads in practice to double payment on the part of the consumer: first by paying a license fee for the use of TPM-controlled content, second by paying a levy on media or equipment. Or consumers may end up paying a levy on blank media for works that cannot be copied.

The 'tangible' or 'intangible' character of a copy of a work has, in principle, no bearing on the consumer's ability to make a reproduction for private purposes: a private copy is lawful only if the conditions set by Article 5(2)(b) of the Directive are met. In the specific case of cloud computing and digital private recorders, the application of Article 5(2)(b) can be problematic insofar as the provision has been repeatedly interpreted as forbidding anyone from making a copy on behalf of someone else. Since the exempted copy must be for the natural person's own private use, this excludes any system based on the storage of copies on a cloud computing's server. This leads to a rather paradoxical situation, where a TV catch-up service offering consumers the possibility to store their favorite television programs in the cloud doesn't fall under the private copying exception, whenever the storage space is under the control of the service provider instead of the

[39]See Information Society Directive, Article 6(4) para. (2): "A Member State may also take such measures in respect of a beneficiary of an exception or limitation provided for in accordance with Article 5(2)(b), unless reproduction for private use has already been made possible by rightholders to the extent necessary to benefit from the exception or limitation concerned and in accordance with the provisions of Article 5(2)(b) and (5), without preventing rightholders from adopting adequate measures regarding the number of reproductions in accordance with these provisions". Guibault (2008), p. 3; Dusollier (2005).

[40]Case C-463/12, Judgment of the Court (Fourth Chamber) of 5 March 2015, (Copydan Båndkopi v. Nokia Danmark A/S.).

consumer herself.[41] In this sense, the authors of the French report entitled '*Informatique dans les nuages*' suggest that the legal requirement of unity between the person making the copy and the one using this copy—as established in France through case law—should be reassessed in the light of cloud services. According to the authors, this standpoint is contrary to the notion of net neutrality.[42]

So, when downloading or streaming digital content, do consumers have a reasonable expectation to be able to make a reproduction of that content for private purposes? This is a question to which the law can hardly provide an answer. Arguably the consumers' expectations are primarily shaped on the basis of the law, their past experience with similar products and the communications made by content providers: if consumers have been able to make a private copy of their CDs and digital downloads for years, it could be argued that the sudden impossibility to do so renders that product unfit for purpose. Helberger and Hugenholtz (2007), p. 1082. Considering the above, it is unlikely that the same would hold true with respect to a streaming service: the absence of a possibility to make a private copy in this case may not be seen as affecting the functionality of the service. Consumer protection law in this case only requires that the provider give sufficient prior information about the functionality of the digital content service or allow consumers to withdraw from the transaction within a certain period of time. On the other hand, the problem of double payment is a point that should definitely be addressed by the legislator. Whether consumer protection law is the right vehicle to do so is doubtful, especially since the problem arises from two co-existing but conflicting rules of copyright law, e.g. allowing for the payment of fair compensation to rights owners for private copying activities while at the same time allowing the individual licensing of works protected by contracts and TPMs.

4.2 Interoperability of Devices

Besides the restrictions on the making of private copies, the issue of interoperability between playing devices was listed at a certain point in time as one of the main concerns of consumers of digital content.[43] Lack of interoperability or limited degree of compatibility between different devices and services is often caused by the use of TPMs aimed at preventing acts of piracy and by the use of different standards and formats for the distribution of online content. As a result, consumers are locked into the choices they once made with regard to the particular devices and digital content, because the investments made are lost when the consumer purchases new and incompatible hardware. More than a decade ago, French and

[41] BGH 22.4.2009 (Videorecorder); Court of Appeal of Paris, 1st ch. 14 December 2011 (Wizzgo/ Metropole Television and others).

[42] A.-É. Crédeville / J.-P. Dardayrol / J. Martin (2012), 15.

[43] Europe Economics (2011), 57.

Belgian courts ruled that the impossibility to play music CDs on different players constituted an instance of non-conformity.[44] A comparative analysis conducted in 2011 demonstrated that even though an explicit legal obligation to inform the consumer about a lack of interoperability was normally missing, in most Member States, interoperability was considered an essential characteristic of the digital content, or an element of normal functioning of the digital content.[45] Evidence also suggested, however, that the limitations imposed by licensing rules and TPMs would likely exacerbate these problems related to access to digital content. It has therefore become a reasonable consumer expectation to be able to access or use digital content on different devices.

As no technical standard has imposed itself on the market for digital content, and as providers can put forward reasonable justification in keeping using their own standard or format, interoperability between hardware, products and services may still be far off. A lack of interoperability remains problematic, in particular when the consumer is not made aware of it before the conclusion of the contract. This is relevant with regard to the purchase both of the digital content itself and of the hardware on which it is intended to be used. This is the reason why the European legislature? introduced Article 5 (1) sub- (g), (h), (s) and (t) in the Consumer Rights Directive, requiring traders to inform consumers up front about the functionality and interoperability of digital content. One might argue that by doing so, the Consumer Rights Directive took a first, albeit cautious, step in developing a more consumer-oriented perspective on copyright law in consumer protection law.

4.3 Geo-blocking

Individual as well as public interest objectives are also at stake in realizing the availability of access to services from other Member States and with regard to cross-border contracts. Consumers are consistently faced with geographical (technical) restrictions, making it impossible for users from one country to access digital content services in another European country, as well as discrimination on basis of geographical location.[46] Most often, these restrictions are the result of the way in which copyrights are licensed, e.g. on a territorial basis. This constitutes another

[44]Brussels Court of Appeal, 9 September 2005 (Test Achats v. EMI Recorded Music Belgium et al.); Cour de cassation, (1st chamber, civil section), 28 February 2006, (Studio Canal, Universal Pictures Video France and SEV / S. Perquin and UFC Que Choisir); Tribunal de Grande Instance de Nanterre, 6th chamber, Judgment of 24 June 2003, Association CLCV / EMI Muisc France; Tribunal de Grande Instance de Nanterre, 6th chamber, Judgment of 2 September 2003, Francoise M. / EMI Music France, Auchan France; Tribunal de Grand Instance de Paris, 3rd chamber, 2e section, Stéphane P., UFC Que Choisir/Société Films Alain Sarde et, Judgment of 30 April 2004.

[45]CSECL, IViR and ACLE (2011), 51.

[46]N. Helberger (2007), 472.

problem consumers frequently mention, and one that can seriously hamper the functioning of an Internal Market for digital content services.[47]

One of the basic tenets of copyright law is the territorial nature of the protection granted, which derives from the Berne Convention. The existence and scope of the copyright protection are determined by the law in force in the territory where protection is claimed. Works are, accordingly, protected in Europe by a bundle of 28 parallel (sets of) exclusive rights. Of course, in the days where digital content was sold primarily on physical carriers, the exhaustion doctrine applied and consumers were free to do as they pleased with their lawfully purchased copies. As the doctrine of exhaustion does not apply to services, however, the problem of cross-border access to and use of digital content is very tangible, at least within the European Union.

The principle of territoriality has come under strain over the last decade. Hugenholtz calls it the Achilles' heel of the European copyright acquis.[48] While decades of case law of the European Court of Justice confirmed the principle of territoriality,[49] the attitude of the Court towards territorial licensing seems to have changed. In its *Premier League* decision the Court explicitly stated that territorial exclusivity is "irreconcilable with the fundamental aim of the Treaty, which is completion of the internal market."[50] This decision came at a time when the principle of territoriality in copyright law started to come under high political pressure, because it contradicts the European single market policy and consumers' right to choice and non-discrimination.[51] Despite this new line of jurisprudence, individual licensing schemes for digital content are still offered across Europe on a territorial basis: service providers would have too much to lose if they changed this.[52]

In response to this specific consumer concern, the European Commission recently published a proposal for a Regulation of the European Parliament and of the Council on ensuring the cross-border portability of online content services in the internal market.[53] Explaining the reasons for and objectives of the proposal, the

[47]Case C-403/08 en C-429/08, decision of European Court of Justice of 4 October 2011 (Premier League).

[48]M. van Eechoud / P.B. Hugenholtz / S. van Gompel / L. Guibault / N. Helberger (2009), 309.

[49]Case 62/79, decision of European Court of Justice of 18 March 1980 (Coditel I), EC.R. 1980, 881, para. 15, 16. See also: Case C-192/04, decision of the European Court of Justice of 14 July 2005, (Lagardère Active Broadcast), E.C.R. 2005, 7199.

[50]Case C-403/08 en C-429/08, decision of European Court of Justice of 4 October 2011 (Football Association Premier League*)*, para. 115.

[51]See: European Commission, Report from the Commission to the Council, the European Parliament, the European Economic and Social Committee and the Committee of the regions, Second report on the implementation of Directive 98/84/EC of the European Parliament and of the Council of 20 November 1998 on the legal protection of services based on, or consisting of, conditional access, Brussels, 30 September 2008, COM(2008) 593 final.

[52]Wiebe (2010), p. 321.

[53]Brussels, 9 December 2015, COM(2015) 627 final.

European Commission emphasises that the Internet has become a key content distribution channel and that Europeans today expect to use online content services from wherever they are in the Union. The Commission has therefore made the issue of cross-border access to digital content one of the main points of its copyright reform endeavours for the coming years. In its current version, the gist of the proposal is contained in Article 3, which establishes the obligation for the provider to enable a subscriber to use the online content service while the subscriber is temporarily present in a Member State other than the Member State of residence. The choice of a regulation as legislative instrument to address this issue is somewhat striking, as it would have immediate application to all existing and future contracts and acquired rights relating to online content services. Only time will tell whether this new proposal in its current state will survive the adoption process.

5 Conclusion

In conclusion, the development of digital technology has had a significant impact on the position of consumers of licensed copyrighted content. Consumers were in a much better position to access and use digital content distributed in a tangible format. First, they could benefit from the application of the exhaustion doctrine, according to which they could dispose of any lawfully acquired tangible embodiment of a work as they wished. Second, they could in certain circumstances invoke the protection of consumer protection law if the products they had bought were not displaying the expected functionality. The disembodiment of the content and the practice of individual licensing have meant so far that consumers are at the mercy of the service providers: consumers' actions are limited by the terms of use and the restrictions enforced through TPMs without useful recourse to consumer protection law.

Suggesting an adequate regulatory framework for digital content requires a thorough understanding of the characteristics of digital content markets and products, the concrete concerns that consumers experience as well as the extent to which these concerns are already addressed by existing law, and the gaps in the present legal regime that may cause an imbalance to the disadvantage of digital consumers. While digital consumers share many of the general concerns and challenges that consumers in any other market experience, their situation is also special in a number of respects. Digital reality has changed the public's perception of copyright protected works for good: since digital content can be accessed and used by everyone in the comfort of her own home, it has become a consumer product. Based on their experience with analogue goods, consumers have developed specific expectations towards digital content that they want to see met.

References

Arnerstål, S. (2015), Licensing digital content in a sale of goods context, Journal of Intellectual Property Law & Practice 10 (10), 750-758

Batchelor, B. / Montani, L. (2015), Exhaustion, essential subject matter and other CJEU judicial tools to update copyright for an online economy, Journal of Intellectual Property Law & Practice 10 (8), 591-600

CSECL, IViR, and ACLE (2011), Analysis of the applicable legal frameworks and suggestions for the contours of a model system of consumer protection in relation to digital content contracts, University of Amsterdam, final report, study commissioned by the European Commission

Cooke, C. (2015), Dissecting the digital dollar – How streaming services are licensed and the challenges artists now face, Music Managers Forum

Crédeville, A.-É. / Dardayrol, J.-P. / Martin, J. (2012), Rapport de la commission spécialisée 'Informatique dans les nuages', Conseil supérieur de la propriété littéraire et artistique

Dusollier, S. (2005), Droit d'auteur et protection des oeuvres dans l'univers numérique: droits et exceptions à la lumière des dispositifs de verrouillage des oeuvres, Larcier

Dusollier, S. (2010), The Relations Between Copyright Law And Consumers' Rights From A European Perspective, European Parliament, DG for Internal Policies, Policies Department: Citizens' Rights and Constitutional Affairs

van Eechoud, M. / Hugenholtz, P.B. / van Gompel, S. / Guibault, L. / Helberger, N. (2009), Harmonizing European Copyright Law: The Challenges of Better Lawmaking, Information Law Series 19, Kluwer Law International

Europe Economics (2011), Digital Content Services for Consumers: Assessment of Problems Experienced by Consumers – LOT 1, Report 4: Final Report, prepared for the European Commission, available at: ec.europa.eu/justice/consumer-marketing/files/empirical_report_final_-_2011-06-15.pdf

Europe Economics, Guibault, L. / Salamanca, O. / van Gompel, S. (2015), Study on the remuneration of authors and performers for use of their works and fixations of their performances, report commissioned by the European Commission, DG Communications Networks, Content & Technology, Document Nr. MARKT/2013/080/D

Fried, N. (2015), We shouldn't get in the way of streaming video innovation, available at: www.mpaa.org/we-shouldnt-get-in-the-way-of-streaming-video-innovation/#.ViYIACtIlg

Gomulkiewicz, R. (1998), The License is the Product: Comments on the Promise of Article 2B for Software and Information Licensing, 13 Berkeley Technology Law Journal 891

Guibault, L. (2002), Copyright Limitations and Contracts: An Analysis of the Contractual Overridability of Limitations on Copyright, Kluwer Law International

Guibault, L. (2008), Accommodating the Needs of iConsumers: Making Sure They Get Their Money's Worth of Digital Entertainment, Journal of Consumer Policy, 2008-4, 409

Helberger, N. (2007),"Access denied": How some e-commerce businesses re-errect national borders for online consumers, and what European law has to say about this, European Journal of Consumer Law, vol. 4, 472-506

Helberger, N. / Guibault, L. (2012), Clash of cultures – integrating copyright and consumer law, Info, 2012-6, 23-33

Helberger, N. / Guibault, L. / Loos, M. / Mak, C. / Pessers, L. / van der Sloot, B. (2012), Digital Consumers and the Law – Towards a Cohesive European Framework, Kluwer Law International

Helberger, N. / Hugenholtz, P.B. (2007), No place like home for making a copy: private copying in European copyright law and consumer Law, Berkeley Technology Law Journal, vol. 22, 1061-1098

Hilty, R.M. (2015), Exhaustion in the Digital Age, Forthcoming in: I. Calboli / E. Lee (Eds.), Research Handbook on Intellectual Property Exhaustion and Parallel Imports, 2016, Max Planck Institute for Innovation & Competition Research Paper No. 15-09, Edward Elgar

Karapapa, S. (2014), Reconstructing copyright exhaustion in the online world, Intellectual Property Quarterly vol. 4, 307-325
Kreutzer, T. (2011), Verbraucherschutz im Urheberrecht, Studie im Auftrag des Verbraucherzentrale Bundesverbands
Linklater, E. (2014), UsedSoft and the Big Bang Theory: Is the e-Exhaustion Meteor about to Strike?, JIPITEC, vol. 5 no. 1
Loos, M. / Helberger, N. / Guibault, L. / Mak, C. / Pessers, L. / Cseres, K. J. / van der Sloot, B. / Tigner, R. (2011), Analysis of the applicable legal frameworks and suggestions for the contours of a model system of consumer protection in relation to digital content contracts, final report prepared for the European Commission, University of Amsterdam
Malcom, J. (2015), Consumers Deserve Protection Against the Scourge of DRM — Will the UN Help?, Electronic Frontier Foundation, 8 January 2015, available at: www.eff.org/deeplinks/2015/01/tell-un-consumers-deserve-protection-against-scourge-drm
Mazziotti, G. (2007), EU Digital Copyright Law and the End-User, 2008, Springer
Mezei, P. (2015), Digital First Sale Doctrine Ante Portas – Exhaustion in the Online Environment, JIPITEC, vol. 6 no. 1
Savič, M. (2015), The legality of resale of digital content after UsedSoft in subsequent German and CJEU case law, E.I.P.R., 37(7), 414-429
Schmidt-Kessel, M., The application of the Consumer Rights Directive of digital content (January 2011), DG Internal Policies, Policy Department A, Economic and Scientific Policy, IP/A/IMCO/NT/2010-17, PE 451.491, p. 5
Schovsbo, J. (2008), Integrating Consumer Rights into Copyright Law: From a European Perspective, Journal of Consumer Policy 2008-31, no. 4, 393-408
Wiebe, A. (2010), The economic perspective: exhaustion in the digital age, in: L. Bently / U. Suthersanen / P. Torremans (Eds.), Global Copyright Three Hundred Years Since the Statute of Anne, From 1709 to Cyberspace, 321, Edward Edgar

Individual Licensing Models and the Role of Internet Platform Providers

Kung-Chung Liu

Contents

Abstract Internet platform providers (IPPs) have the potential of reaching every online user of copyrighted works and of enhancing the licensing efficiency of copyrighted works. This chapter explores legal mechanisms to transform this potential into reality: an obligation on copyright holders to issue license to active IPPs, an obligation on passive IPPs to acquire license from collective management organizations (CMOs) and the oversight over IPPs. It then discusses the desirability of cooperation among IPPs and CMOs. It concludes by venturing to advocate an international agreement that would facilitate global licensing of copyrighted works.

Kung-Chung Liu is Director, Applied Research Center for Intellectual Assets and the Law in Asia, Singapore Management University/Professor, Renmin University.

K.-C. Liu (✉)
Singapore Management University, Singapore, Singapore

Renmin University, Beijing, People's Republic of China
e-mail: kcliu@smu.edu.sg

K.-C. Liu, R.M. Hilty (eds.), *Remuneration of Copyright Owners*, MPI Studies on Intellectual Property and Competition Law 27, DOI 10.1007/978-3-662-53809-8_13

1 Introduction

The Internet is accessed through a wide range of platform providers, which include Internet service providers (ISP) in the narrower sense (browsers and search engines such as Google), telecom service providers (fixed or mobile, such as AT&T, Deutsche Telecom, and Vodafone), aggregators of services (such as the numerous apps put onto iPhones by Apple), multi-media (including written, audio, video and audiovisual content, such as iTunes, Netflix, SIPX, and TuneCore), and social media (Facebook, YouTube, and Twitter). IPPs (or ISPs in the broader sense) can be copyright holders, CMOs (such as CELAS), and commercial licensees and therefore cooperate with or compete against copyright holders (their CMOs) and/or incumbent commercial exploiters of copyrighted works.

IPPs have the great potential of reaching every online user of copyrighted works from anywhere and of enhancing the licensing efficiency of copyrighted works and reducing transaction costs. Thus, the "question is how best to realize the full potential of the Internet both as a legitimate market place for works and as a vehicle for streamlining licensing transactions.[1]" This chapter explores legal mechanisms to transform this potential into reality. Section 2 explains why and how the Internet and mobile communication devices have become game changers in the realm of copyright licensing. Section 3 depicts the tragic phenomenon of how individuals and IPPs are being mired in legal battles brought by right holders. Section 4 discusses the legal intervention required to make IPPs work, namely two kinds of non-voluntary copyright licensing and the oversight over IPPs. Section 5 ponders over the merits of cooperation among IPPs and CMOs respectively. Section 6 concludes with a probe into a possible international agreement that would facilitate global licensing of copyrighted works.

2 Internet and Mobile Communication Devices as Game Changer

2.1 Direct and Individual Licensing Once Again Practicable

The licensing of copyright started from individually negotiated agreements. With the proliferation of copyrights and protected contents and wide-spread, cross-border exploitation of copyrighted works, the licensing of copyright became collective, feasible only through CMOs, which can help significantly reduce the transaction costs of licensing and managing of copyrighted works, if they function properly.[2] The rise of the Internet and the ubiquitous penetration of mobile

[1]S. Perlmutter (2014), 50.

[2]For more discussion see the chapter by S. Nérisson.

communication devices, especially smart phones, make direct and individual licensing to end users once again practicable. Nowadays almost everyone subscribes to one or several IPPs and pays a fee to access the Internet under their real name, as the popularity of online payment demands.

Also due to the Internet and mobile communication devices creators are regaining access to their fans. Websites of individual or aggregate creators accessible to their fans make direct sale, fair trade, license or subscription of contents possible. As an example, in Taiwan indievox.com sells independent music (non-Big-Four labels[3]) with 3000 bands joining and charging different prices.[4] In addition, social media on the Internet are also becoming platforms for content creators to get exposure, and for new trends and markets. While copyright holders may form their own IPPs, IPPs formed by non-copyright owners can acquire copyrights or licenses and sublicense them out to end users. In the US, for example, DMX contracts directly with individual music composers and their publishers to reduce the cost of business associated with blanket licenses of ASCAP (The American Society of Composers, Authors and Publishers) and BMI (Broadcast Music, Inc.) and undermines the revenue of those licenses as streaming becomes popular.[5]

As a result of direct licensing, traditional CMOs are becoming less indispensable and sometimes even redundant.

2.2 *Transparency Can Be Better Expected*

CMOs are oftentimes plagued with downsides; setting the abuse of market dominance issue aside, opaqueness in operation and underpayment of the actual creators are the two eminent ones. As the US Copyright Office reports in the 2015 "Copyright and the Music Market Place" study, "a paramount concern of songwriters and recording artists is transparency in reporting and payment. As digital licensing deals multiply and increase in complexity, it can become quite difficult to follow the money. Songwriters and artists want to ensure that they understand the royalty scheme, are able to track the use of their works, and are paid what they are owed".[6]

[3]According to Wikiwand, Universal Music Group, Sony BMG, EMI Group (now a part of Universal Music Group (recording) and Sony/ATV Music Publishing (publisher)) and Warner Music Group are collectively known as the "Big Four" labels, available at: https://www.wikiwand.com/en/Music_industry.

[4]To download a single, one needs to pay a royalty ranging between NT$ 19 and 25 (1 US$ equals 33 NT$), available at: www.indievox.com/.

[5]I.L. Pitt (2015), vii.

[6]US Copyright Office (2015), 187.

Operational opaqueness leads to corruption.[7] In addition, high administrative costs are commonly associated with CMOs,[8] alienating copyright to benefit commercial intermediaries rather than the actual creators. Ill-functioning CMOs would render the continuous expansion of copyright, especially through Free Trade Agreements in the post-TRIPS era, a senseless legal pursuit and copyright law "omnipresent, distracting, irrelevant.[9]"

In contrast, IPPs have the technical capability to keep track of subscribers' use of contents and are also actually collecting data about that usage, which if properly utilized can provide the ultimate transparency, accountability, and efficiency that were previously unthinkable. With transparent book-keeping and auditing come much faster royalty calculation, payment and distribution.[10] "The digital revolution ... offers substantial opportunities to reduce, virtually to the costs of electricity, the transaction costs... thus making it possible for revenues to be returned to creators with a degree of perfection unavailable even to the collecting societies.[11]"

3 Individuals and IPPs Mired in Legal Battles Waged by Right Holders

Unfortunately, instead of embracing Internet as a liberating and enabling instrument for fulfilling the purpose of copyright law, i.e. effective dissemination of works and fair compensation of creators, copyright holders have sued IPPs for indirect, contributory and/or joint infringement of copyright the world over. In the US, where such lawsuits are most prevalent, the Recording Industry Association of America (RIAA) has sued the following major peer-to-peer (P2P) companies one after the other beginning with the 1999 suit against Napster: Scour, Aimster, AudioGalaxy, Morpheus, Grokster, Kazaa, iMesh, and LimeWire. Although RIAA has won most of these legal battles, it is still losing the war. Right after an existent P2P was shut down, new networks quickly appeared. Alternatively, RIAA took a different strategy since 2008 and attempted to work with ISPs to persuade them to adopt a three-strikes-and-you're-out system for unauthorized file sharing: first two warnings before cutting off Internet service at the third offense, a tactic as controversial as ineffective.

---

[7]One notorious extreme is the Italian CMO, Societá Italiana degli Autoro ed Editorie (SIAE) which reported losses of US$ 53 million in 1999 even though collections were up. SIAE later again made a US$ 52.3 million loss by investing in Lehman Brothers when the latter went broke in 2008; see W. Patry (2011), 181–182.

[8]E.g. the Copyright Clearance Center in the US earns a 15 % commission and 15 % administrative fee on revenue it collects, see: en.wikipedia.org/wiki/Copyright_Clearance_Center.

[9]Borrowing from the subtitle of the book "Intellectual Property – omnipresent, distracting, irrelevant" by W. Cornish (2004).

[10]I. Pitt (2015), 162.

[11]P. Goldstein (2015), 153–154.

RIAA's legal assault was later expanded to target Internet users in the US. Although the anonymity of netizens makes the revealing of their names and addresses difficult, RIAA resorted to a special subpoena power of the 1998 Digital Millennium Copyright Act (DMCA) to force ISPs to hand over such information. Between August and September 2003,[12] RIAA issued more than 1500 subpoenas to ISPs in the US.[13] In September 2003, RIAA sued 261 American music fans for sharing songs on P2P networks. Within 5 years, RIAA has filed, settled, or threatened legal actions against at least 30,000 individuals. Most lawsuit targets settle their cases for amounts ranging between $3000 and $11,000.[14] But suing music fans has proven to be an ineffective response to P2P file-sharing which is more popular than ever. The lawsuit campaign has not resulted in any royalties to artists.[15] RIAA announced in 2008 that it would stop suing consumers directly.[16]

The failure of RIAA's lawsuits did not prevent copyright holders from targeting individual online users. The most recent example is the lawsuit filed by Dallas Buyers Club LLC (DBCL)[17] and Voltage Pictures LLC on 14 October 2014 in the Federal Court of Australia against iiNet Limited (iiNet) and 6 other ISPs, claiming that DBCL et al. had identified account holders (4726 IP addresses) who had infringed the copyright on their film by sharing the film online using BitTorrent, and seeking preliminary discovery of the identity of each of those account holders, as those account holders might either be infringing the applicants' copyright, or may be able to help the applicants in identifying the actual infringers. While granting DBCL's application, Justice Perram stayed the order and imposed conditions to address concerns about **speculative invoicing.**[18] In a parallel effort, DBCL

[12]On 19 December 2003, in RIAA v. Verizon, 351 F. 3d 1229 (D.C. Circuit 2003) the D.C. Appeals Court ruled that the DMCA subpoena provision did not authorize RIAA's "driftnet fishing" tactics, overturned the lower court ruling, and found that the DMCA subpoenas were available only where the allegedly infringing material was stored on the ISPs' own computers, not for situations involving P2P file-sharing where the material was stored on a subscriber's individual computer.

[13]Electronic Frontier Foundation (2008), 3.

[14]Electronic Frontier Foundation (2008), 5.

[15]Electronic Frontier Foundation (2008), 1.

[16]B. Slattery (2008).

[17]Dallas Buyers Club is a 2013 American biographical drama film, co-written by Craig Borten and Melisa Wallack, directed by Jean-Marc Vallée.

[18]Speculative invoicing is a practice which commonly involves sending intimidating letters of demand to alleged infringers seeking significant sums for an alleged infringement by threatening court action if the sums are not paid. To prevent speculative invoicing, DBCL was asked to submit to Justice Perram a draft of any letter it proposes to send to account holders associated with the IP addresses which have been identified. DBCL provided copies of the proposed letters, which included four demands: payment for the cost of purchasing a copy of the film (payment cost); payment of a license fee by each uploader (license fee); punitive damages depending on any other copyrighted works that person had downloaded (additional damages); and cost of DBCL's expenditure in obtaining the details of each infringer (expenditure fee). DBCL's application that the stay be lifted was dismissed because Justice Perram found that DBCL's demands beyond the payment of cost and expenditure fee (permissible heads of damage) were not acceptable. For details see Dallas Buyers Club LLC v. iiNet Limited [2015] FCA 317 (April 7, 2015) and 838 (August 14, 2015). K.A. Hayne / A. Fehrenbach (2015).

identified more than 500 Singapore Internet protocol addresses from subscribers of the three major ISPs and has obtained an order from the High Court to compel all three ISPs to release the details of subscribers linked to the IP addresses in question. In April 2015 DBCL sent out letters to Internet users in Singapore asking for a written offer of damages and costs within 3 days of receiving the letter.[19]

Obviously, speculative invoicing is hurting netizens, and especially so in countries where statutory damages are foreseen and courts have no discretion not to apply them to minor cases.[20]

4 Legal Intervention Required to Materialize IPPs' Potentials

To cope with the problems derived from online licensing of copyrighted works, a diverse range of solutions has been proposed throughout the last 15 years, starting from the establishment of a global Internet licensing agency,[21] a fair copyright system,[22] and the so-called "reverse liability rule",[23] to voluntary and compulsory license schemes. The Electronic Frontier Foundation advocates a voluntary collective licensing regime as a mechanism that would fairly compensate artists and rights holders for P2P file sharing: the music industry forms one or more collecting societies, which then offers file sharing music fans the opportunity to "get legit" in

[19]See Dallas Buyers Club case: Uphill task to sue users, say lawyers, available at: www.straitstimes.com/singapore/courts-crime/dallas-buyers-club-case-uphill-task-to-sue-users-say-lawyers.

[20]In the US, statutory damages, written into the Digital Theft Deterrence and Copyright Damages Improvement Act of 1999, are between US$ 750 and US$ 30,000 per work or US$ 750 and US$ 150,000 per work if willful. In Singapore statutory damages can go up to S$ 10,000 per title per person (Section 119 (2)(d) of the Copyright Act). In the 2016 "White Paper on Remixes, First Sale, and Statutory Damages," the US Department of Commerce's Internet Policy Task Force sets forth its conclusions on the appropriate calibration of statutory damages in the contexts of individual file sharers and secondary liability for large-scale infringement. The White Paper recommends amending the Copyright Act to incorporate a list of factors for courts and juries to consider when determining the amount of statutory damages. In addition, it advises changes to remove a bar to eligibility for the Act's "innocent infringer" provision, and to lessen the risk of excessively high statutory damages in the context of secondary liability for online service providers. See ntia.doc.gov/press-release/2016/commerce-recommends-amendments-copyright-act.

[21]J. Sterling, (2010), 295.

[22]L. Hilman (2013). Such fair trade copyright would encourage users to donate to recording artists on digital platforms and distribute the donations to artists.

[23]Kembrew McLeod and Peter DiCola advocate the idea of allowing copyright owners a choice between a compulsory license and a reverse liability rule. Under the reverse liability rule, copyright owners can block the use of their works by paying a fee to the government fund that would in return financier some other works. See K. McLeod / P. DiCola (2011), 265. The idea was also picked up by Dan Burk in the realm of patent law, according to which a patentee who wishes to enforce his patent rights disregarding FRAND terms has a right to injunction only if he pays the costs of the competitor who needs to adopt an alternative technology. See D. Burk (2013), 7.

exchange for a reasonable regular payment. So long as they pay, the fans are free to keep doing what they are going to do anyway.[24] In the literature, compulsory license model complemented by levy arrangement has also been suggested.[25] None of these initiatives has been adopted by legislators or markets.[26]

As an alternative, this chapter seeks to capitalize on the potential of IPPs, and suggests two kinds of non-voluntary copyright licensing with reasonable royalty rather than levy to make IPPs work.[27] As accepted by more and more people, copyright in its exclusive form is not up to the challenges we are now facing, and has to be reformed in a way that is working with and not against the technical and business advancement of the Internet. The Internet has becomes hugely popular because it follows the social fact that people like to borrow and share words, ideas, sounds, and images.[28] Copyright law of the online world should address these demands and eradicate barriers to market entry in the copyright industries.[29] "Copyright entails obligations. Its use shall also serve the public good."[30,31] Such obligation can take the form of compulsory license if it is perceived that negotiation between parties is nevertheless necessary; it can also be stipulated as statutory license if it is acknowledged that negotiation between parties is redundant.[32]

Non-voluntary licensing over the medium to longer term can only benefit right holders, as it expands the base for licensing exponentially and encourages innovative usage. As a result, non-voluntary licensing can generate much more than enough revenues to offset the initial losses from not being able to charge as much as right holders would have. "Substantial financial rewards can come from giving up some control, in the form of liability rules. This is a lesson the music industry might want to contemplate as it struggles to adjust to new technologies[33]". To borrow from Daniel Gervais, "Historically, copyright industries have done well,

[24]Electronic Frontier Foundation (2008), 13.

[25]L. Hilman (2013), 191, 194 et seq.

[26]According to L. Hilman (2013), 195, "Complexity might have been the main barrier for implementation. Too many participants, interests and agendas need to be settled in order to make such systems feasible."

[27]However, Goldstein is of the opinion that transaction costs are not immutable and can be reduced through institutional innovation to such a level that non-voluntary copyright licensing could not be justified, see P. Goldstein (2015), 153.

[28]K. McLeod / P. DiCola (2011), 266.

[29]For similar opinions see the chapters by R. Mittal and by M.R.F. Senftleben.

[30]This follows the spirit of Article 14(2) of the German Basic Law which provides: "Property entails obligations. Its use shall also serve the public good."

[31]For similar opinion see W. Patry (2011), 262: "Copyright owners should also support the good guys by providing reasonably priced, convenient authorized goods. If they don't, no copyright law can help them."

[32]For similar opinions and more discussion see the chapters by H. Sun, W.L. Ng-Loy and C. Geiger.

[33]K. McLeod / P. DiCola (2011), 262.

one could argue, when the primary focus was not to minimize unauthorized uses but rather to maximize authorized use.[34]"

4.1 Two Kinds of Non-voluntary Licensing Needed

4.1.1 Copyright Holders (and CMOs) Have to Grant Licenses to Active IPPs

IPPs can actively broker between copyright holders and online end users of copyrighted works by offering related services. In that capacity, IPPs will have to acquire licenses from copyright owners or their CMOs and thereby compete against them. Faced with competition, copyright owners or their CMOs are tempted to refuse to license or exercise "price squeeze" to drive IPPs out. To prevent that from happening, copyright owners that have put their copyrighted works online for use must be imposed an obligation to grant license to any willing IPPs. CMOs are to be subject to this obligation too if they are not already obliged by law to grant license.[35] Non-voluntary license is justified, as such copyrighted content cannot be reasonably duplicated and constitutes the prerequisite for market entry, and the denial of access to such content will wipe out competition in an adjacent market (e.g. online enjoyment of copyrighted work).

The proposal was inspired by the newly revised Danish Copyright Act, effective since October 29, 2014. Article 35(4) of the Danish Copyright Act allows licensing of simultaneous and unaltered online retransmission, on-demand use, store TV services and public performance, and any other possible exploitation (that is relevant to copyright and therefore needs clearance) of TV content (linear TV channels) via all platforms (CATV, IPTV, web TV/OTT, DTT, PC, tablets and smart phones etc.) from broadcasters, including even foreign European broadcasters ("Danish licenses for Europe") by distributors to their customers under specific extended collective license.[36] Furthermore, Article 35(5) of the Danish Copyright Act allows on-demand use of on-demand content from broadcasters under specific extended collective license.[37] As a result, the extended collective license of Article 35(4) and (5) may be invoked by any third-party users who have made the agreement on the exploitation of works in question with an organization

[34]D. Gervais (2010), 17.

[35]In many countries, Germany (Article 6 of the Act on the Management of Copyrights and Related Rights [Gesetz über die Wahrnehmung von Urheberrechten und verwandten Schutzrechten]) and Taiwan (Article 32 of the Copyright Collective Management Organization Act) for example, CMOs may not refuse to grant license to willing users.

[36]Section 35(4) of the Danish Copyright Act; see T. Foged (2015), 22. Specific extended collective license pursuant to Article 50(2) is different from general extended collective license pursuant to Article 50(1).

[37]Section 35(5) of the Danish Copyright Act; see T. Foged (2015), 23.

comprising a substantial number of authors (right holder organizations, which need to be approved by the Minister of Culture) of a certain type of works which are used in Denmark. However, if a right holder organization or a broadcaster unreasonably refuses to consent to retransmission or on-demand use, the Copyright License Tribunal can no longer grant such permission.[38]

It is conceivable that in the context of non-voluntary licensing, IPPs and CMOs could fail to reach consensus on the reasonable royalty. Therefore a dispute settlement mechanism such as copyright tribunal under the oversight of courts to mediate an agreement is necessary. At any rate, before the agreement is actually reached, right owners and CMOs shall be prevented from suing their patrons (the individual netizens) and brokers of their works (IPPs), so long as IPPs pay right owners or CMOs what is considered objectively fair, and deposit the difference at the dispute settlement body for the benefit of right owners or CMOs.

To preserve legal peace on the Internet, which is the precondition for its continued growth, it is further suggested that the non-voluntary licensing agreement between CMOs and IPPs should exempt all non-commercial uses and dissemination (including reproduction, public performance, distribution, and making available to the public) of copyrighted works by users of active IPPs.

4.1.2 Passive IPPs Must Acquire License from CMOs

IPPs can passively be used by online end users to enjoy copyrighted works through their platforms. Such usage directly benefits IPPs, as the heightened usage of content would trigger greater need for more paid bandwidth or ads. It's only fair for IPPs to share their increased revenues with right holders. However, as right holders are numerous and hugely dispersed, IPPs should acquire a license from CMOs, which manage online exploitation of copyrighted works, and pay them a reasonable fee. For practical reasons, CMOs can only grant such a license through their joint organization (more see *infra* Sect. 5).

When determining the reasonable share that IPPs would have to pay CMOs for their end users, one distinction must be made: There are users who are willing to pay extra to get access to copyrighted content, and users who are undiscerning, used to paying a flat-rate to IPPs, and reluctant to make extra payment for any content managed by CMOs. In the former case, users are already paying CMOs directly. Only in the latter case would IPPs have to pay for their users, most likely in a lump sum (percentage of the subscription fees). In return, IPPs can recoup the payment to CMOs either through the increased ads-sponsorship that will follow the rising lawful online use, or through charging their users higher access or subscription fees.

[38]Section 35(7) of the Danish Copyright Act; see T. Foged (2015), 19.

To preserve legal peace on the Internet, the payment to CMOs by IPPs should also exempt all non-commercial uses and dissemination (including reproduction, public performance, distribution, and making available to the public) of copyrighted works by users of passive IPPs.

4.2 *Oversight of IPPs as CMOs*

Successful IPPs could enjoy overwhelming market power, and if unchecked would amplify the shortcomings of traditional CMOs. One pressing issue would be the transparency in the equity structure of IPPs which are partially held by right owners. For instance, major labels together reportedly negotiated an 18 % stake in the super online music licensor Spotify.[39] Such equity deals and whether and how the value received by the labels will negatively impact the royalties that are to be paid to artists and songwriters and therefore must be reported to artists and songwriters.

The prerequisite for overseeing the operation of IPPs would be to have access to their collected data about the usage of copyrighted works, whether through downloads or streaming.[40] Irrespective of who owns these valuable data, be it the generators of the data,[41] IPPs, or an objective third party, a basic legal principle should be that these data must be made available to legitimate stakeholders.

In addition, the deficiency of right holders going "unpaid because there are no industry-wide, certified accounting and auditing requirements" must be remedied to ensure that "intermediaries are all acting in good faith".[42] Therefore, legal intervention is warranted in requiring that IPPs establish standards for usage registration, accounting, and auditing and develop compatible systems that ensure the exchangeability of data among and between IPPs and CMOs.[43]

[39]Record labels part owner of Spotify, available at: www.swedishwire.com/jobs/680-record-labels-part-owner-of-spotify. Before the Swedish Spotify was launched a number of record companies bought 18 % of the company's stocks: Sony BMG (5.8 %), Universal Music (4.8 %), Warner Music (3.8 %) and EMI (1.9 %).

[40]I. Pitt asks similar question in the context of music works. See I. Pitt (2015), 263.

[41]According to the theory of the so-called "Skripturakt" adopted by the German Court of Appeal of Nuremberg, the person who generates the data gets the right to the data. See T. Hoeren (2014), 753. However, such a rule of thumb does not seem to fit the scenario of IPPs and CMOs.

[42]I. Pitt (2015), viii.

[43]D. Gervais (2010), 20. Noteworthy is the Linked Content Coalition (LCC, www.linkedcontentcoalition.org): a not-for-profit global consortium of standards bodies and registries. LCC members are organizations who create and manage data standards associated with content of one or more types, particularly for identifiers, metadata and messaging. The purpose of the LCC is to facilitate and expand the legitimate use of content in the digital network through the effective use of interoperable identifiers and metadata.

4.3 Intervention Instrument

If we agree to introduce the two kinds of non-voluntary copyright licensing and the oversight of IPPs mentioned in the above, then the next question would be which instrument to take? It seems that a hybrid of the application of general competition law and copyright legislation is the right way to go. General competition law is ideal for ex post oversight of IPPs, whereas copyright law is better suited for ex ante, continuing and detailed regulation and oversight. In particular, procedural copyright law, which mainly deals with the efficient exercise and management of rights (such as the German Act on the Management of Copyrights and Related Rights and the like) as opposed to substantive copyright law that deals with the rights issues (coverage, terms etc.) remains the ideal intervention instrument.

5 Cooperation Among IPPs and CMOs Desirable

It would further cut the transaction costs for users, copyright holders, IPPs and CMOs alike if a consortium of national IPPs (CIPP) or even a consortium of global IPPs (GCIPP) can be formed. CIPP and GCIPP are warranted to counter the market power of CMOs and/or their alliances, as CMOs usually possess market power which is often further strengthened by cross-border agreements among CMOs.[44] As a matter of fact, IPPs are to some extent already internationally organized as evidenced by international organizations such as the Global System for Mobile Communications Association (GSMA[45]) and the Internet Corporation for Assigned Names and Numbers (ICANN).

Cooperation is equally welcome on the side of CMOs. On a national level, there is already the necessity to drastically shrink the number of CMOs to no more than one per type of work.[46] Existent CMOs could be induced to form a consortium

[44]One such example is the so-called Santiago Agreement by five big CMOs, namely BMI (the US), BUMA (the Netherlands), GEMA (Germany), PRS (the UK) and SACEM (France) which was later joined by all other CMOs within the European Economic Area—except for the Portuguese SPA and Swiss SUISA—and legitimized by the General Court of the EU (GCEU). According to this Agreement, each participating CMO could be the only one entitled to grant a non-exclusive license to users established in its territory, which would be valid for all EU territories and would cover the whole music repertoires of all participating CMOs. The EU Commission ruled that the Agreement was a concerted practice contrary to EU competition rules, which was rejected by the GCEU on appeal. GCEU concluded that it had not been proved that CMOs were engaging in an anticompetitive behavior, for more see T. Woods (2010), 115–117 and the chapter by R. Xalabarder.

[45]According to: www.gsma.com/aboutus, the GSMA represents the interests of mobile operators worldwide, uniting nearly 800 operators with more than 250 companies in the broader mobile ecosystem, including handset and device makers, software companies, equipment providers and internet companies, as well as organizations in adjacent industry sectors.

[46]W. Patry (2011), 182.

among themselves (CCMO) to further minimize transaction costs by issuing joint licenses. A global CCMO (GCCMO) could be a reply to the interconnected Internet, which knows no national boundaries. In fact, in addition to international agreements (the Santiago Agreement for example) CMOs also have their associations, such as the International Confederation of Societies of Authors and Composers (CISAC), International Federation of Reproduction Rights Organization (IFPRO), the International Federation of the Phonographic Industry (IFPI), and the International Federation of Musicians (FIM), which are the basic constituents of the proposed CCMO and GCCMO.

Each consortium could act as the umbrella organization and the centralized registry of works, copyright owners, rights, and usage for all IPPs and COMs respectively.

6 Looking Forward: An International Agreement Needed

In the interconnected world, global licensing of copyrighted works is indispensable. Any national legislation that regulates activities taking place on the Internet would not succeed without international cooperation. Practically speaking, "Global licensing can only be accomplished by legislative and treaty action.[47]" The domestic legal intervention through the two above-mentioned non-voluntary copyright licensing mechanisms will only be successful if an international agreement on adopting these mechanisms is reached. The TRIPS Agreement could be the ideal vehicle to mandate that members of the TWO introduce such a mechanism and work cooperatively to see its cross-border implementation.

Such an international agreement would have to factor in developmental differences among countries[48] and foresee, in case national IPPs and CMOs failed to reach consensus, a body in charge of the establishment of standards for recording usage, registration (of rights, rights owners and their CMOs/agents), accounting and auditing, data (aggregation, exchange and public access), and for determining differentiated reasonable royalties that national IPPs have to pay foreign CMOs.

Through such an international agreement, every online user of copyrighted works, rich or poor, can make his/her contribution, great or humble, directly or indirectly, to the payment of right holders and eventually the sustainability of the copyright ecology; every new market entry, innovative or imitative, will get to try its potential; and every creator will get paid for the use of his/her digital works.

To many, such an international agreement may seem unrealistic. However, absent such an agreement national copyright legislatures will be forced to legislate beyond their national borders (such as the Danish licenses for Europe) in a disarrayed and even contradictory manner, online users will be overshadowed by

[47]W. Patry (2011), 188.

[48]W. Patry (2011), 252.

whimsical lawsuits (e.g. speculative invoicing), new market entries will be slowed down and the distribution of copyright-generated revenues will tilt toward right owners in countries which have functional CMOs. At the end of the day, the core of the matter is really just about whether we can afford to think about copyright in a global marketplace. Can we?[49]

References

Bowrey, K. (2005), Can We Afford to Think About Copyright in a Global Marketplace?, in: F. Macmillan (Ed.), New Directions in Copyright Law, Volume I, 54–72, Edward Elgar

Burk, D. (2013), Intellectual Property in the Cathedral in: D. Beldiman (Ed.), Access to Information and Knowledge – 21st Century Challenges in Intellectual Property and Knowledge Governance, Edward Elgar; UC Irvine School of Law Research Paper, 2012-77, available at: ssrn.com/abstract=2170093

Electronic Frontier Foundation, RIAA v. The People: Five Years Later (2008)

Foged, T. (2015), Danish Licenses for Europe, E.I.P.R., 15–24

Gervais, D. (2010), Collective Management of Copyright: Theory and Practice in the Digital Age, in: D. Gervais (Ed.), Collective Management of Copyright and Related Rights, 2nd ed., 1–28, Kluwer Law International

Goldstein, P. (2015), Future Platforms for Copyright Licensing, 46 IIC, 153–154

Hayne, K.A. / Fehrenbach, A. (2015), Speculative invoicing – not the Australian way, Lexology of 14 September 2015, available at: www.lexology.com/library/detail.aspx?g=10b5f236-357c-4104-b568-94ac6d43276b

Hilman, L. (2013), Fair Trade Copyright, 36 Columbia Journal of Law & the Arts, No. 157, available at: ssrn.com/abstract=2698069

Hoeren, T. (2014), Big Data and the Ownership in Data: Recent Developments in Europe, E.I.P.R., 751–754

McLeod, K. / DiCola, P. (2011), Creative License: The Law and Culture of Digital Sampling, Duke University Press

Patry, W. (2011), How to Fix Copyright, Oxford University Press

Perlmutter, S. (2014), Making Copyright Work for a Global Market: Policy Revision on the Both Sides of the Atlantic, 38 Columbia Journal of Law and the Arts, 1, 49–68

Pitt, I.L. (2015), Direct Licensing and the Music Industry – How Technology, Innovation and Competition Reshaped Copyright Licensing, Springer

Slattery, B. (2008), RIAA Stops Suing Individuals: Are We Home Free?, PCWorld of 19 December 2008, available at: www.techhive.com/article/155769/riaa_p2p_lawsuits.html

Sterling, J.A.L. (2010), Online Exploitation and Licensing, in: L. Bently / U. Suthersanen / P. Torremanns (Eds.), Global Copyright, 291–296, Edward Elgar

US Copyright Office (2015), Copyright and the Music Market Place, available at: http://copyright.gov/policy/musiclicensingstudy/copyright-and-the-music-marketplace.pdf

Woods, T. (2010), Multi-territorial Licensing and the Evolving Role of Collective Management Organizations, in: D. Gervais (Ed.), Collective Management of Copyright and Related Rights, 2nd ed., 105–133 Kluwer Law International

[49]Borrowing from the chapter title from Kathy Bowrey, see K. Bowrey (2005), 54.

The Copyright Holdout Problem and New Internet-Based Services

John T. Cross and Peter K. Yu

Contents

Abstract This chapter examines the holdout problem involving a copyright holder's refusal to license digital content to internet users or third-party intermediaries despite the possibilities of socially valuable uses. It begins with two case studies illustrating the classic holdout problem, which often arises when transaction costs are high or when parties have drastically different expectations. The first case study focuses on the developments concerning Google Books. The second case study examines YouTube and the emergent development of user-generated content. The chapter concludes with three sets of preemptive legal responses that can help address the internet-related copyright holdout problem: limitations and exceptions

John T. Cross is Grosscurth Professor of Intellectual Property Law and Technology Transfer at Louis D. Brandeis School of Law, University of Louisville.
Peter K. Yu is Professor of Law and Co-Director of the Center for Law and Intellectual Property at Texas A&M University School of Law.

J.T. Cross (✉)
Louis D. Brandeis School of Law, University of Louisville, Louisville, KY, USA
e-mail: john.cross@louisville.edu

P.K. Yu
School of Law, Texas A&M University, Fort Worth, TX, USA
e-mail: peter_yu@msn.com

K.-C. Liu, R.M. Hilty (eds.), *Remuneration of Copyright Owners*, MPI Studies on Intellectual Property and Competition Law 27, DOI 10.1007/978-3-662-53809-8_14

in copyright law, compulsory or statutory licensing arrangements, and exogenous constraints imposed by competition law.

1 Introduction

The mass popularization of the internet and the rapid proliferation of new communication technologies have provided new ways to put copyright works to creative or innovative use. Although many of these new uses are both socially valuable and backed by market demand, copyright holders remain reluctant to work with internet users and third-party intermediaries to facilitate such uses.

Even worse, the copyright holders' differing expectations of remuneration have precipitated a classic holdout problem that makes negotiation exceedingly costly and highly difficult, if not impossible. Failing to reach an agreement with the relevant rights holders, many new internet-based services cannot take advantage of the new uses of copyright works. Those who manage to do so also face high risks of litigation from copyright holders.

This chapter examines the holdout problem involving a copyright holder's refusal to license digital content to internet users or third-party intermediaries despite the possibilities of socially valuable uses. It begins with two case studies illustrating the classic holdout problem, which often arises when transaction costs are high or when parties have drastically different expectations. The first case study focuses on the developments concerning Google Books. The second case study examines YouTube and the emergent development of user-generated content (UGC)—content that internet users have produced without the copyright holder's authorization. The chapter concludes with three sets of preemptive legal responses that can help address the internet-related copyright holdout problem: limitations and exceptions in copyright law, compulsory or statutory licensing arrangements, and exogenous constraints imposed by competition law.

2 New Internet-Based Services

2.1 Google Books

When Google Books was launched in 2004—as a combination of the Partner Program (formerly Google Print) and the Library Project—Google set out to digitize millions of printed books.[1] In just over 10 years, this tech giant has digitized more than 20 million books. Google obtained these books from major research libraries and scanned them into its database. Participating libraries included the

[1]All of the factual information in this section is taken from opinions of the trial and appellate courts.

Library of Congress, the New York Public Library and a number of university libraries, such as those at Harvard, Michigan, Oxford and Stanford.

Once a book enters the database, a user can find it through an ordinary Google search. If the book is no longer protected by copyright, the user can obtain the entire book. If the book remains protected, however, a Google search will provide basic information about the work, as well as up to three "snippets" of pages containing the search terms. Each snippet, with the highlighted terms, is roughly one-eighth of a page. While Google derives no revenue directly from Google Books, it gains the indirect benefit of enhanced strength in the overall internet search market.

In 2005, the Authors Guild and several individual authors sued Google in the United States for copyright infringement. Plaintiffs sought the certification of the case as a class action on behalf of all similarly situated authors who still owned copyrights in their works. After years of negotiations, the parties reached a settlement that would bind not only the named plaintiffs but also the entire class. This settlement called for fixed payments to all authors whose copyright works were included in Google's database. It further proposed to establish a fund to compensate authors who were unknown or could not be found.

In March 2011, a trial judge rejected the settlement proposal, finding it unfair to many class members. The case then proceeded on both the class certification and copyright infringement issues.[2] Two years later, the judge held that Google's search and snippet view functions qualified as fair use under U.S. copyright law.[3] This ruling was affirmed by the U.S. Court of Appeals for the Second Circuit in an extensive opinion in October 2015.[4] Because fair use is a complete defense to liability and the U.S. Supreme Court has elected not to review the ruling, any settlement agreement providing compensation for the copyright holders is now moot.

Of particular importance to the courts' fair use rulings is the fact that over 90 % of the books scanned into Google's database are non-fiction works. More importantly, the vast majority of these works are no longer in print. These crucial factors not only affected the courts' fair use analyses, but also highlighted several socially valuable functions of Google Books.

First, the availability of online searches makes it far easier for individuals to access works that are relevant to research and knowledge. Prior to digitization, users had to search multiple collections in research libraries. Even then, they had access to only general information such as title, author and classification. Searches by keywords, by contrast, are far more useful.

Second, Google Books allows users to conduct text and data mining, thereby determining the frequency at which certain terms and usages appear over time in all

[2] Authors Guild v. Google, Inc., 770 F. Supp. 2d 666 (S.D.N.Y. 2011).
[3] Authors Guild v. Google, Inc., 954 F. Supp. 2d 282 (S.D.N.Y. 2013).
[4] Authors Guild v. Google, Inc., 804 F.3d 202 (2d Cir. 2015).

the digitized works. Such activities would have been impracticable if the books were unavailable in digital form.

The proposed Google Books settlement would have added a third, and arguably even more valuable, benefit. Many of the works scanned into Google's database are "orphan" works, works whose authors are unknown or uncontactable. Because the settlement would have given users full access to these works, it would have allowed the knowledge contained in these works to be widely disseminated among members of society—a result that would not have been practicable under traditional distribution schemes.

While the orphan works in question are all available in libraries, in particular those supplying the scanned books to Google, the search and travel costs of using these works would often prove prohibitive. Thus, the Google Books settlement would have provided a basic framework for utilizing orphan works without overwhelming transaction costs—even though the amount of the fees to be paid to authors were probably much lower than the copyright owners would have agreed to in face-to-face negotiations.

2.2 *YouTube and UGC*

YouTube is another highly popular service provided by Google. Since its launch in February 2005, the service has posted an ever-growing number of videos, the vast majority of which were created by internet users themselves. As of this writing, "YouTube delivers 4 billion videos every day to 1 billion users who watch a total of 6 billion hours of video each month, bringing in $3.6 billion in net revenue. Over 100 hours of video are uploaded to YouTube every minute."[5]

Although YouTube was originally created as an independent start-up, Google quickly acquired it for $1.65 billion in a stock-for-stock transaction in October 2006.[6] At its launch, the service featured mostly amateur videos shot from home using webcams. Commentators generally describe this type of content as UGC.

The development of UGC is socially valuable, for a number of reasons. To begin with, YouTube provides an exciting environment in which internet users mix content with preexisting works, copyrighted or otherwise. It therefore "open[s] the door for the public to actively participate in cultural production."[7] It also ensures that

> everyone – not just political, economic, or cultural elites – has a fair chance to participate in the production of culture, and in the development of the ideas and meanings that constitute them and the communities and subcommunities to which they belong.[8]

[5]M. Strangelove (2015), 162.

[6]A.R. Sorkin (2006).

[7]P.K. Yu (2011), 895.

[8]J.M. Balkin (2004), 4.

In addition, YouTube—with the tagline "Broadcast Yourself"—serves as a repository for alternative content, often with surprise elements absent from mass-market entertainment products. As J.D. Lasica aptly observes, "Where big media will continue to offer polished, mass market shows with linear narrative, high production values, and orchestrated story lines, the video of participatory culture will be marked by the quirky, personal, edgy, raw, unpolished, unscripted, unconventional, hyper-realistic, and genuinely surprising."[9] Similar to Facebook, Twitter and Tumblr, YouTube brings an important social element that is often missing from passive media, such as movies, television programs, music and books.[10]

Moreover, YouTube can provide important benefits to copyright holders. While "people use YouTube as a stepping-stone to mainstream media, . . . the mainstream media [also] use YouTube to promote their programs, especially in 'webisode' format."[11] YouTube can also enable content providers to reach out directly to fans. As Mark Lemley observed:

> People don't go see movies – at least good movies – and then stop thinking about them. People want to be engaged with their content. They want to have connections with the musicians they like. They want to go to concerts and experience music live. They want to engage in an ongoing relationship, and there's revenue there to be had by meeting that demand – providing that collaborative experience can be lucrative.[12]

Notwithstanding these many social benefits, YouTube quickly attracted infringing content, to the dismay of copyright holders. A widely discussed early example was the unauthorized posting of the "Lazy Sunday" clip from NBC's *Saturday Night Live*.[13] Frustrated by the growing copyright infringement on YouTube, Viacom filed a $1 billion copyright lawsuit against Google in March 2007.[14] Later that year, a group of music publishers and the English Football Premier League also filed a class action lawsuit alleging copyright infringement.[15]

In June 2010, the trial court found that YouTube was protected by the internet service providers' safe harbor provided by the Digital Millennium Copyright Act (DMCA).[16] Although the appellate court found that a reasonable jury could have concluded that YouTube might have known enough of the infringements at issue to be disqualified from such protection,[17] the trial court, on remand, found YouTube to

[9]J.D. Lasica (2005), 95.

[10]P.K. Yu (2011), 898.

[11]J. Kim (2012), 54–55.

[12]M.A. Lemley (2011), 134.

[13]E. Lee (2008), 1487.

[14]M. Helft / G. Fabrikantmarch (2007).

[15]Associated Press (2007); M. Helft (2007).

[16]Viacom International, Inc. v. YouTube, Inc., 718 F. Supp. 2d 514 (S.D.N.Y. 2010).

[17]Viacom International, Inc. v. YouTube, Inc., 676 F.3d 19 (2d Cir. 2012).

have fallen within the safe harbor.[18] By November 2013, both cases have been settled.[19]

While the lawsuits were underway, Google introduced a copyright management system, starting with Video ID and eventually expanding to cover both audio and video materials in the form of Content ID.[20] Under this system, copyright holders whose works have been used without authorization can decide whether they want to monetize their works, utilize the data of those users who accessed the works without authorization or simply block the unauthorized access. As Google explained in comments submitted to the U.S. Department of Commerce:

> Rightsholders deliver to YouTube reference files (these can be audio-only or video) of content they own, metadata describing that content, and policies describing what they want YouTube to do when it finds a match. Rightsholders can choose between three policies when an upload matches their content: 1) make money from them (for monetized videos the majority of the revenue goes to rightsholders); 2) leave them up and track viewing statistics; or 3) block them from YouTube altogether. Content ID compares videos uploaded to the site against those reference files, automatically identifies the content, and applies the rightsholder's preferred policy. The Content ID system is made available to rightsholders at no cost – in fact, if the rightsholder opts to monetize matches, Google effectively pays them to use it![21]

Thus far, YouTube's Content ID is only available to those copyright holders who "own exclusive rights to a substantial body of original material that is frequently uploaded by the YouTube user community."[22] Nevertheless, other copyright holders can still rely on the "notice and takedown" mechanism provided by the DMCA or other similar statutes.[23] Even better, all copyright holders will have the opportunity to determine whether they should tolerate the unauthorized uses or initiate takedown requests.[24]

Today, YouTube offers a wide variety of content, ranging from noncommercial videos to professionally produced premium content and from experimental media projects to pay-per-view movies. In addition, the service now features advertisements, product placements and other licensing and collaborative arrangements. According to Morgan Stanley, Google could bring in revenue of about $20 billion by 2020, with operating income reaching as high as $5 billion.[25]

---

[18]Viacom International, Inc. v. YouTube, Inc., 940 F. Supp. 2d 110 (S.D.N.Y. 2013).

[19]O. Gibson (2013); L. Kaufman (2014).

[20]J. Kim (2012), 55.

[21]Google, Inc. (2013), 3.

[22]Google, Inc. (2016).

[23]R. Tushnet (2014), 1464-1465.

[24]E. Lee (2008), 1486-1488; T. Wu (2008), 619.

[25]C. Thompson (2013).

3 Preemptive Legal Responses

In both case studies, copyright holders resorted to lawsuits after they failed to reach agreements with Google over content licensing. Although both the Google Books and UGC situations involved socially valuable uses of copyright works, the relevant copyright holders were reluctant to license content due to the low price they would have obtained from Google. Yet, because the pricing arrangements the rights holders expected were based on arguably outdated business models and consumer habits, the arrangements were both unworkable and unacceptable.

A major part of the challenge to developing workable arrangements in these contexts is transaction costs. Both the Google Books and UGC situations involve a tremendous number of rights holders and internet users. The costs of simply finding these rights holders are significant. Even after they have been found, users would still need to incur additional transaction costs in negotiating licenses agreeable to both sides. Given the relatively small-scale uses involved, these transaction costs are prohibitive, making it extremely unlikely for the parties involved to reach consensual arrangements.

Indeed, the disagreement between Google and copyright holders in both situations illustrates the classic copyright holdout problem. In both cases, the parties involved fail to reach an agreement owing to the high transaction costs as well as their drastically different expectations. As a result, the law had to intervene to force a deal on the parties. In the Google Books situation, courts found the project's search and snippet view functions as fair use. In the cases involving YouTube and UGC, by contrast, negotiations were conducted in the shadow of litigation or the threats thereof.

To help address, and perhaps preempt, the internet-related copyright holdout problem, this section focuses on three different sets of preemptive legal responses.

3.1 Limitations and Exceptions

The first set of preemptive legal responses concerns limitations and exceptions to copyright. Copyright law grants to the copyright holder a bundle of rights, including the rights of reproduction, distribution, adaptation and communication to the public. Yet, as expansive as they may be, these rights are qualified by limitations and exceptions.

A case in point is the EU InfoSoc Directive, which allows member states to introduce exceptions for a large number of activities, including teaching or scientific research, criticism or review; promotion of public security; and caricature, parody or pastiche.[26] Although this directive was created with the internet in mind and was adopted in large part to implement the WIPO Internet Treaties, it has been

[26]Directive 2001/29 art. 5.

repeatedly criticized for its failure to adequately address the rapidly emerging needs of the digital environment.

From December 2013 to March 2014, the European Commission held a consultation on modernization of the EU copyright regime. Among the questions explored in this exercise was whether and how to update the directive's exhaustive list of limitations and exceptions.[27] Although the Commission announced its plan to introduce a new mandatory, harmonized disability exception to implement the Marrakesh Treaty to Facilitate Access to Published Works for Persons Who Are Blind, Visually Impaired or Otherwise Print Disabled, it has yet to provide concrete information concerning whether it will introduce any new limitation or exception.[28] It also does not indicate whether or how it will adapt existing limitations and exceptions to the digital and cross-border environments.

Like the European Union, other nations and jurisdictions have explored the introduction of new limitations and exceptions to help facilitate the development of new internet-based services. For instance, Canada took the lead by introducing an exception for the development of non-commercial UGC. Adopted in June 2012, section 29.21 of the Canadian Copyright Modernization Act states:

> It is not an infringement of copyright for an individual to use an existing work or other subject-matter or copy of one, which has been published or otherwise made available to the public, in the creation of a new work or other subject-matter in which copyright subsists and for the individual – or, with the individual's authorization, a member of their household – to use the new work or other subject-matter or to authorize an intermediary to disseminate it, if [the use satisfies four qualifying conditions – namely, the use's non-commercial nature, the source's identification, the legality of the work used and the absence of a substantial adverse effect on market exploitation].

In Hong Kong, a similar exception for the development of predominantly non-commercial UGC was also proposed as an amendment to the Copyright (Amendment) Bill 2014.[29]

In addition, the Irish Copyright Review Committee called for the creation of a new copyright exception for innovation, thereby allowing for the greater transformative or innovative use of copyright works in Ireland.[30] As of this writing, Australia is also debating whether to replace its existing close-ended, purpose-based fair dealing regime with an open-ended, flexible fair use regime, which the Australian Law Reform Commission argued would be better suited to the digital environment.[31]

---

[27]Commission of the European Communities (2013), 16-30.

[28]Commission of the European Communities (2015).

[29]P.K. Yu (2014, 2016).

[30]Irish Copyright Review Committee (2013), 72-75.

[31]Australian Law Reform Commission (2013), 123.

3.2 Mandatory Licenses

The second set of preemptive legal responses concerns the implementation of a mandatory licensing regime, under which a user or an intermediary could use a copyright work for specified purposes by paying a specified sum. Although this book has two chapters on compulsory licenses (the chapters by H. Sun and W.L. Ng-Loy) and one on statutory licenses (the chapter by C. Geiger), this section does not differentiate between these two types of licenses. Instead, it lumps them together as mandatory licenses based on their involuntary nature.

Courts and commentators often use compulsory or statutory licensing to refer to a regime that requires users or intermediaries to pay a specified sum before using the copyright works. However, the term "compulsory license" is also widely used in two other ways. First, many use it to refer to a particular *remedy* used in monopoly law cases, a broader subject discussed in the next section. Second, others use the term to refer to a particular species of mandatory license under which the payment is subject to negotiation, rather than established *a priori*. To avoid semantic confusion and in view of this section's focus on preemptive legal responses, this discussion will refer to as mandatory licenses all licenses imposed upfront by statutes or authorities regardless of how the license rates are set.

Mandatory licenses have been widely used in the copyright system. In Europe, they exist for mechanical reproduction of musical works, recording for educational purposes, modification of works for the visually impaired, and private copying and recording (where a levy is imposed). A properly constructed mandatory licensing regime is beneficial because it can enable the distribution of copyright works with relatively low transaction costs. It also spares users or intermediaries the trouble of having to rely on defenses such as fair use or fair dealing, which are often highly fact-specific and therefore unpredictable.

In theory, mandatory licensing could provide a workable solution to the problems in both the Google Books and UGC situations. The devil is in the details, however. A licensing regime would need to carefully define the conditions under which mandatory licenses are available, not only as a matter of copyright policy, but also by reference to the constraints on limitations and exceptions imposed by the Berne Convention for the Protection of Literary and Artistic Works and the Agreement on Trade-Related Aspects of Intellectual Property Rights of the World Trade Organization.

In the Google Books situation, exactly how does a legislature define an orphan work, especially in a system that does not require such formalities as registration and copyright notice? A mandatory licensing regime would need to place some obligation on the user or the intermediary to conduct a good-faith search for the copyright holder. Similarly, while mandatory licensing may be justified in the case of reference works, will such licensing be equally appropriate for fictional works? What about unpublished *drafts*? Does it matter whether the author, for whatever reason, wants them undisclosed?

Similar challenges would arise when implementing a mandatory licensing regime for UGC. The primary argument in favor of allowing such uses is that they involve the uses of the copyright works for either non-commercial purposes (such as social commentary) or commercial purposes in yet-to-exploit markets. That fact, however, creates a serious practical problem—namely, how to determine the rate the user should pay?

Many of the works that users want to use or adapt are well-known works of significant value to the copyright holders. These rights holders, rightly or wrongly, fear that the adaptation of such works for political or other purposes may harm the value of their works. As a result, they ask for high royalty rates in a mandatory licensing regime. By contrast, users and intermediaries derive limited value from their works. Accordingly, they would avail themselves of the license only if the rates are quite low.

There is also a significant conflict between mandatory licenses and copyright policy, a problem that presents itself acutely in the UGC context. It is very difficult to draw the line between where copyright interests end and allowable uses begin. Copyright gives the right holder benefits in not only the market for copies of the work, but also some derivative and related markets.

For example, the adaptation right grants the copyright holder the exclusive right to alter the work in ways that appeal to different audiences. Similarly, the moral right of integrity gives the author some ability to prevent changes in the work that may affect his or her reputation. Contrary to the intended goals of these rights, however, many UGC works use the work for the express purpose of criticizing the author.

If these serious problems can be overcome, a mandatory licensing regime would prove useful to facilitating the socially valuable uses in both the Google Books and UGC situations. Voluntary negotiations are not an option in either case. Such negotiations, especially those involving orphan works, would incur overwhelming transaction costs. For the reasons noted above, copyright holders would also be extremely reluctant to grant licenses for the creation of many UGC works.

From the standpoint of copyright holders, a clear and predictable mandatory licensing regime could also be preferable to relying on limitations and exceptions. Rather than simply allowing the use, a mandatory license would provide at least some payment to offset the economic harm suffered by the copyright holder.

3.3 Competition Law

The final set of preemptive legal responses utilizes competition law to force copyright holders to make their works available to users and intermediaries. At the risk of oversimplification, "competition law" comprises two distinct branches. The first, commonly referred to as unfair competition or unfair trade practices law, focuses on how the actions taken by particular firms in the process of competition affect either individual competitors or consumers.

The second, monopoly law (or antitrust law in the United States), focuses on how the actions of one or more market players affect markets themselves. While unfair competition law may provide an interesting remedy in particular cases, it is too fact-specific to provide a general solution to either the Google Books or UGC situation. Monopoly law, by contrast, can provide a scalable solution.

Although Martin Senftleben's chapter in this book explores in great depth the application of monopoly law, it may be useful at this juncture to make a few general observations about how monopoly law may apply to the problems at hand. At the outset, the effectiveness of monopoly law as a tool to deal with recalcitrant copyright holders will likely differ among nations. In Europe, the competition authorities have been willing to look to monopoly law to limit the exercise of intellectual property rights. For instance, the European Commission has investigated several large technology companies—including Microsoft, IBM and Google—for the way they use intellectual property rights. The Commission has also proven quick to investigate the use of these rights in standard-setting.

By contrast, courts and competition authorities in both Canada and the United States are typically more reluctant to use monopoly law to police intellectual property rights. While these rights are not immune from monopoly law, there is almost a presumption that any additional market power vested in an intellectual property holder is an intended consequence of intellectual property law. Moreover, the standard for proving that a company enjoys a "dominant position" is significantly higher in these nations than it is in Europe. Rather than looking to monopoly law, courts and competition authorities in Canada and the United States expect these market considerations to appear either directly in intellectual property law or indirectly through the incorporation of monopoly-type considerations into such law (as in the case of the "abuse" doctrine employed by U.S. courts).

Monopoly law focuses on markets. In analyzing the Google Books and UGC situations under monopoly law, however, it is important to distinguish between two different "markets." The first is the primary market in which the copyright work is sold. The second is an ancillary market in which the copyright work is an asset that gives a competitor an advantage. Consider, for example, a well-known sound recording. The copyright holder will be competing in the primary market by selling the recording. Someone wanting to modify this recording to make social commentary will compete in an ancillary market. Distinguishing between these two markets is important, in large part because different monopoly law doctrines come into play.

3.3.1 Competition in the Primary Market

In theory, a user or an intermediary could invoke three monopoly law doctrines to force a copyright holder to license its work. The first, sometimes called "abuse of a dominant position," focuses on the actions of a single party who uses its existing market power to limit competition in the primary market. The second, called the "essential facilities" or "bottleneck" doctrine, is a variation on the first and considers whether something controlled by one competitor is an essential asset or input for competition. The third doctrine involves the special rules that apply when two or more parties enter into an agreement that unduly restricts competition. Such rules would apply when the copyright holder licenses the work to some but not others. This section will briefly address each doctrine in turn.

3.3.1.1 Abuse of Dominant Position

Monopoly law attempts to reduce the damage caused by firms that hold too much market power. However, other than in the case of mergers, monopoly law is not an absolute bar against a firm holding or gaining control of a market. Instead, monopoly law ordinarily kicks in only when a firm engages in some "bad act" designed to increase or preserve its market power. A copyright holder's refusal to license to someone else who wants to compete in the same market is simply not a "bad act." Instead, it is an act designed to ensure that competitors engage in real competition by selling their own goods or services.

Monopoly law places no obligation on a party to help its competitors out by allowing them to sell the same product the party itself sells. The 1997 decision of the Canadian Competition Bureau in Director of Investigation and Research v. Warner Music Canada Ltd. illustrates this principle well.[32] In this case, Warner operated a mail order sound recording business. Warner owned the copyrights in a number of high-demand works. Warner's competitors brought a complaint before the Competition Bureau, arguing that they needed to sell the same recordings to compete effectively in the market. The Bureau rejected this claim, finding it not only insufficient as a matter of monopoly law, but also at odds with the purposes of copyright.

The Google Books situation presents a variation on this theme. What if the copyright holder refuses to participate at all in the market by ceasing the distribution of its work? Although these two variations may be different as a matter of copyright policy, they are treated the same as a matter of monopoly law. Nothing requires a party to compete in a market. Nor is a party refusing to compete obliged to make valuable assets available to those who would like to compete. In the parlance of monopoly law, there is an absolute right to unilaterally refuse to deal.

3.3.1.2 Essential Facilities

The essential facilities doctrine is in many ways a subcategory of abuse. It comes into play when a party who controls a particular asset refuses to make that asset available to other competitors. In most essential facilities cases, the party also competes in the affected market, although it is unclear whether this is a *sine qua non*.

[32][1997] 78 C.P.R.3d 321 (Competition Tribunal).

The core problem raised by both the Google Books and UGC situations is that the copyright holder can prevent what is arguably a socially valuable use of the work. In the parlance of monopoly law, the copyright restricts the ability of others to participate in a particular "market" by denying others the ability to compete using the particular work. At first glance, it would seem natural to treat this situation using the essential facilities doctrine.

However, there are many problems with applying essential facilities reasoning to the Google Books and UGC types of situations. Most importantly, the argument works only if one defines the market in an extremely narrow, and in most cases unrealistic, way. Take, for instance, a situation where the party who owns the copyright in a popular movie character refuses to allow others to produce films incorporating that character. That refusal may benefit the right holder, as it faces no price competition for the sales of that character. But the market is not one for the single character. Rather, the market includes all characters (and possibly other works) that compete for the same audience. Because no particular work is an essential input to competition in the market, an essential facilities challenge fails on the threshold issue.

3.3.1.3 Differential Licensing

Another variation occurs when a party enters into agreements with some parties, but refuses to enter into agreements with others. This variation could arise in the UGC context, if a copyright holder allows some to use or alter the work, but not those others who want to use or alter the work in a way the right holder disapproves. If the licensed and unlicensed users compete in the same market, that decision could affect competition in the market. Similarly, an author may want the work to be sold only in physical bookstores, but not online.

Monopoly law treats agreements that restrict competition more harshly than unilateral actions, but even in this situation, monopoly law is unlikely to provide any relief. As a general matter, a party has considerable freedom to set up exclusive distribution agreements, even though such an agreement limits competition in the relevant market. A decision to limit licensing is even more rational in the UGC situation. Again, in these situations, the copyright holder fears that the disapproved use will cause harm to the reputation of either the work or the right holder. Preventing harm to a party's competitive position would likely not be deemed anticompetitive. In the United States, for example, such prevention would certainly qualify as a procompetitive effect under the "rule of reason" analysis, which balances the anticompetitive effects of the challenged practice against the practice's procompetitive effects and economic justifications.

3.3.2 Competition in Ancillary Markets

In some situations, a copyright work not only can compete in its own market, but also can affect competition in other markets. Using the same movie character as an instance, suppose the copyright holder also refuses to license that character to those who want to use it in works of political or social commentary. The entertainment and commentary "markets" are probably sufficiently distinct to qualify as separate for purposes of monopoly law. Even if the copyright holder does not compete in this downstream market, its work would be a valuable asset to those who want to compete—the starting point in an essential facilities analysis.

But again, the argument only works if the definition of the market is extremely narrow. The relevant market is not only the market for commentaries that happen to employ the copyright work, but one for commentaries on a particular topic. Even if the use of the work may make for a compelling commentary, it is still easily possible to compete in the market without using the work. Again, in only extremely rare cases will the copyright work be an essential facility in the market.

On the other hand, there is a middle ground. In some cases involving downstream markets, the use of the copyright work could be deemed crucial. These cases are where the downstream market involves criticism or commentary *of the copyright work itself*. The argument here mirrors the one used in parody cases. A parody of a work is only effective if viewers recognize the parodied work, which tends to require the use of much of the original. Similarly, a criticism or commentary on a work is most effective if it provides examples taken from the work itself.

Moreover, consumers interested in a criticism of a work will probably not view a criticism of some other work as an adequate substitute. As a result, there is a discrete submarket for criticisms of the work itself. By this logic, at least some of the *original* work is "essential" to compete in that submarket.

Even in this situation, however, there remain serious problems with the use of monopoly law. First, the scope of the essential facilities doctrine is unclear on both sides of the Atlantic. The U.S. Supreme Court has questioned whether the doctrine even exists,[33] and aside from the *Magill* case decided by the Court of Justice,[34] there are few recent EU decisions finding liability under the doctrine.

Second, even if an essential facilities doctrine exists, it probably does not apply to the situation of criticism and commentary. In most essential facilities cases, a crucial factor is that the defendant *also competes in the same market*. Most copyright holders, by contrast, do not compete in the market for criticisms of their own works. Instead, the right holders use their rights to make it more difficult for *anyone* to compete in the submarket. While that choice is arguably anticompetitive, competition is still possible.

[33]Verizon Communications, Inc. v. Law Offices of Curtis V. Trinko, LLP, 540 U.S. 398, 411 (2004); Aspen Skiing Co. v. Aspen Highlands Skiing, Corp., 472 U.S. 585, 611 n. 44 (1985).
[34]Joined Cases C-241 & C-242/91 P, Radio Telefis Eireann v. Commission, E.C.R. I-743 (1995).

Third, the liberal application of abuse and essential facilities reasoning in copyright cases runs afoul of the basic tenets of the copyright regime. Copyright involves exclusive rights to market the author's message, but it also gives the author considerable rights to control how that message is conveyed. Even putting moral rights aside for a moment, the copyright holder retains considerable control over the means in which its work is displayed and distributed to the public, or indeed whether it is distributed at all. Using monopoly law to force the copyright holder to make the works available in a market would considerably diminish its control over the message.

In short, then, monopoly law is a clumsy took for addressing the Google Books and UGC situations. Its myopic focus on markets does not really take into account the many arguments justifying some requirement for copyright holders to make their works available. Copyright law, by contrast, often considers these sorts of issues. Accordingly, such law is far better suited to addressing situations involving orphan works or UGC, whether by limiting the rights of the copyright holder or through a mandatory licensing regime.

4 Conclusion

The use of copyright works has become increasingly intertwined with internet users' daily activities. Whether it is to conduct research online or to express feelings through a home-made video, the internet has brought users in close contact with copyright law. Unfortunately, neither the current law nor existing licensing arrangements were designed with user-based activities in mind. As a result, users and intermediaries often have great difficulty obtaining the licenses needed to facilitate the new uses of copyright works.

This chapter focuses on the copyright holdout problem relating to new internet-based services. Although copyright infringement lawsuits are inevitable when boundaries are unclear and when user activities fall within the gray areas, the chapter recognizes the benefits of preemptive legal responses. After all, online searches via Google Books and the development of UGC on YouTube represent only some of the gray areas precipitated by the internet and new communication technologies. If the full potential of these technologies are to be realized and if internet users are to actively participate in cultural production, we will need to develop more innovative ways to address the internet-related copyright holdout problem.

References

Associated Press (2007), Music Publishers to Join YouTube Suit, New York Times of 7 August 2007, C8

Australian Law Reform Commission (2013), Copyright and the Digital Economy: Final Report

Balkin, J.M. (2004), Digital Speech and Democratic Culture: A Theory of Freedom of Expression for the Information Society, New York University Law Review, 79, 1–58
Commission of the European Communities (2013), Public Consultation on the Review of the EU Copyright Rules, available at: ec.europa.eu/internal_market/consultations/2013/copyright-rules/docs/consultation-document_en.pdf
Commission of the European Communities (2015), Making EU Copyright Rules Fit for the Digital Age – Questions & Answers, available at: europa.eu/rapid/press-release_MEMO-15-6262_en.htm
Gibson, O. (2013), Premier League Drops Copyright Infringement Case against YouTube, The Guardian of 11 November 2013, available at: www.theguardian.com/football/2013/nov/11/premier-league-copyright-case-youtube
Google, Inc. (2013), Comments: Department of Commerce Green Paper, Copyright Policy, Creativity, and Innovation in the Digital Economy, available at: www.ntia.doc.gov/files/ntia/google_comments.pdf
Google, Inc. (2016), How Content ID Works, available at: support.google.com/youtube/answer/2797370?hl=en-GB
Helft, M. (2007), Contributors on YouTube May Share Advertising Revenue, New York Times of 5 May 2007, C3
Helft, M. / Fabrikantmarch, G. (2007), Viacom Sues Google over Video Clips on Its Sharing Web Site, New York Times of 14 March 2007, C1
Irish Copyright Review Committee (2013), Modernising Copyright
Kaufman, L. (2014), Viacom and YouTube Settle Suit over Copyright Violations, New York Times of 19 March 2014, B4
Kim, J. (2012), The Institutionalization of YouTube: From User-Generated Content to Professionally Generated Content, Media, Culture & Society, 34, 53-67
Lasica, J.D. (2005), Darknet: Hollywood's War against the Digital Generation, Wiley
Lee, E. (2008), Warming up to User-Generated Content, University of Illinois Law Review, 1459–1548
Lemley, M.A. (2011), Is the Sky Falling on the Content Industries?, J. on Telecommunications & High Technology Law, 9, 125-135
Sorkin, A.R. (2006), Dot-Com Boom Echoed in Deal to Buy YouTube, New York Times of 10 October 2006, A1
Strangelove, M. (2015), Post-TV: Piracy, Cord-Cutting, and the Future of Television, University of Toronto Press
Thompson, C. (2013), YouTube May Be Worth $20 Billion by 2020: Morgan Stanley, CNBC of 16 May 2013, available at: www.cnbc.com/id/100743171
Tushnet, R. (2014), All of This Has Happened Before and All of This Will Happen Again: Innovation in Copyright Licensing, Berkeley Technology Law J., 29, 1447-1487
Wu, T. (2008), Tolerated Use, Columbia J. Law and Arts, 31, 617-635
Yu, P.K. (2011), Digital Copyright and Confuzzling Rhetoric, Vanderbilt J. Entertainment and Technology Law, 13, 881-939
Yu, P.K. (2014), Can the Canadian UGC Exception Be Transplanted Abroad?, Intellectual Property J., 26, 175-203
Yu, P.K. (2016), The Quest for a User-Friendly Copyright Regime in Hong Kong, American University International Law Review 2016, 31 (forthcoming)

Impacts of Competition Law: Monolithic Copyright, Market Power and Market Definition

Martin R.F. Senftleben

Contents

Abstract A monolith can be described as a geological feature "consisting of a single massive stone or rock, such as some mountains." In architecture, it may refer to "a single large piece of rock placed as, or within, a monument or building." (Available at: en.wikipedia.org/wiki/Monolith) A literary or artistic work may constitute a monolith in its own right. As a single large piece of information, it may stand out from works of the same category. Similarly, collections of works may become so dense that they resemble a single massive information monolith. In both cases, the market power resulting from copyright ownership may be considerable. Hence, the question arises whether competition law can serve as a vehicle to ensure reasonable access conditions and prevent an artificial supply shortfall.

Martin R.F. Senftleben is Professor of Intellectual Property and Director of the Kooijmans Institute for Law and Governance at the Vrije Universiteit Amsterdam and Of Counsel at Bird & Bird.

M.R.F. Senftleben (✉)
Faculty of Law, Vrije Universiteit Amsterdam, Amsterdam, The Netherlands
e-mail: m.r.f.senftleben@vu.nl

K.-C. Liu, R.M. Hilty (eds.), *Remuneration of Copyright Owners*, MPI Studies on Intellectual Property and Competition Law 27, DOI 10.1007/978-3-662-53809-8_15

1 Introduction

The scope of the exclusive rights of copyright owners can be recalibrated in different ways. Inside the copyright system, the adoption of limitations can lead to an appropriate balance between the exclusive rights of copyright owners on the one hand, and competing economic, social and cultural interests on the other.[1] Additional balancing tools are available outside the copyright system.[2] If the delicate balance between rights and freedoms is lost, human rights may be invoked as an external balancing tool.[3]

In the EU, the impact of fundamental freedoms on the configuration of copyright's balance has been enhanced in recent years. In *Painer*, the Court of Justice of the European Union (hereinafter: "Court of Justice") underlined the need for an interpretation of the right of quotation in Article 5(3)(d) of the Information Society Directive[4] that enables the effectiveness of the provision and safeguards its purpose.[5] More specifically, the Court clarified that Article 5(3)(d) was

> intended to strike a fair balance between the right of freedom of expression of users of a work or other protected subject-matter and the reproduction right conferred on authors.[6]

In its further decision in *Deckmyn*, the Court followed the same path with regard to parody. It underlined the need to ensure the effectiveness of the parody exemption in Article 5(3)(k) of the Information Society Directive[7] as a means to balance copyright protection against freedom of expression.[8] In practice, courts may thus give copyright limitations a relatively broad scope even though the underlying copyright statute, such as the Information Society Directive in the EU, does not qualify these limitations as rights but includes them in the catalogue of exceptions to exclusive rights instead.

A relatively broad scope may be given at least to limitations supporting the creation of a new work, such as the quotation right and the exemption of parody.[9] As the examples taken from the jurisprudence of the Court of Justice demonstrate, the fundamental guarantee of freedom of expression plays a crucial role in this

---

[1]As to the room available for the introduction of exceptions and limitations, see C. Geiger / D. Gervais / M.R.F. Senftleben (2014), 581; D. Gervais (2009–2010), 510–511; A. Kur (2009), 307–308; C. Geiger / J. Griffiths / R.M. Hilty (2008), 707; M.R.F. Senftleben (2004), 243–244.

[2]C. Geiger (2004), 391–412; T. Dreier (2001a), 295–316.

[3]C. Geiger (2006), 371; A. Strowel / F. Tulkens / D. Voorhoof (2006); P.B. Hugenholtz (2002), 239; S. Macciacchini (2000); Y. Benkler (1999), 355; N.W. Netanel (1996), 283.

[4]Directive 2001/29/EC of the European Parliament and of the Council of 22 May 2001, on the harmonisation of certain aspects of copyright and related rights in the information society (OJ 2001 L 167, 10).

[5]Court of Justice, 1 December 2011, Painer, C-145/10, ECLI:EU:C:2011:798, para. 132–133.

[6]Court of Justice, *id.*, para. 134.

[7]Court of Justice, 3 September 2014, Deckmyn, C-201/13, ECLI:EU:C:2014:2132, para. 22–23.

[8]Court of Justice, *id.*, para. 25–27.

[9]M.R.F. Senftleben (2012), 395–398.

context. Relying on Article 11 of the EU Charter of Fundamental Rights and Article 10 of the European Convention on Human Rights, the Court of Justice could interpret the quotation right and the parody exemption less strictly than limitations without a comparably strong freedom of speech underpinning. In both the *Painer* and the *Deckmyn* decisions, the Court emphasized the need to achieve a "fair balance" between, in particular, "the rights and interests of authors on the one hand, and the rights of users of protected subject-matter on the other."[10] The Court thus referred to quotations and parodies as user "rights" rather than mere user "interests".

External balancing tools, such as the fundamental guarantee of freedom of expression, can thus have a deep impact. In particular, the guarantee of freedom of expression can broaden areas of freedom that are relevant to the creative process leading to a new literary or artistic work. The question whether a quotation or parody requires the authorization of the copyright owner will often arise during the process of making a new work. It may be said that the quotation right and the parody exemption concern the possibility of control over creative use: they limit the copyright owner's power to exert control over the creation and dissemination of transformative, derivative works.[11]

With regard to the supply market—understood as the market for the dissemination of protected works without transformative modifications—a recourse to the fundamental guarantee of freedom of expression and information is less common. In *Technische Universität Darmstadt*, the Court of Justice recognized that the copyright limitation for offering reading terminals in publicly accessible libraries laid down in Article 5(3)(n) of the Information Society Directive

> would risk being rendered largely meaningless, or indeed ineffective, if those establishments did not have an ancillary right to digitise the works in question.[12]

As in *Painer* and *Deckmyn*, the Court thus sought to enable the effectiveness of the copyright limitation and safeguard its purpose. However, it refrained from directly referring to fundamental rights and freedoms in this context. Nonetheless, content repositories, such as libraries, and content aggregators, such as (dedicated) search engines, are central to offering an information infrastructure that is conducive to the making of new literary and artistic works. In contrast to the quotation right and the parody exemption, the contribution of content repositories and aggregators does not concern the final process of creation but the preliminary stage of finding and studying potential sources of inspiration. In this context, the term "aggregator" can be understood to refer to a party which provides an overview of available literary and artistic works together with a short indication of contents

---

[10] Court of Justice, 1 December 2011, Painer, C-145/10, ECLI:EU:C:2011:798, para. 132; 3 September 2014, Deckmyn, C-201/13, ECLI:EU:C:2014:2132, para. 26.

[11] R.M. Hilty / M.R.F. Senftleben (2015), 326–330; C. Geiger (2010), 532–533.

[12] Court of Justice, 11 September 2014, Technische Universität Darmstadt, C-117/13, ECLI:EU:C:2014:2196, para. 43.

and a link to the primary source. A "repository", by contrast, holds literary and artistic works and makes them available from its own server.

The particular importance of access to information offered by content repositories and aggregators clearly comes to the fore, for instance, in Pierre Bourdieu's sociological analysis of the process of creation.[13] According to Bourdieu, each new generation of authors must first learn of the aesthetic positions that have already been taken by previous creators in order to be capable of creating new works on the basis of pre-existing material. Unless newcomers master the history of their particular art and know the heritage of former generations, they are inhibited from detecting structural gaps that allow them to take a legitimate and plausible next step in the evolution of literary and artistic works.[14] Therefore, the guarantee of freedom to use pre-existing material for new creations, as in the case of the right of quotation and the exemption of parody, is only one way of encouraging the incessant renewal of the cultural landscape. In addition, support can be offered by encouraging the use of existing works for the purpose of establishing content repositories and (dedicated) search engines—measures that allow new generations of authors to explore pre-existing creations and find starting points for the formulation of new aesthetic positions and the making of new literary and artistic works.[15]

In this latter regard—the provision of a rich and diverse information infrastructure—competition law may have a crucial role to play. If freedom of expression is invoked to offer sufficient room for the final creative process as such, it may be the task of competition law to serve as an external balancing tool with regard to a copyright owner's control over supply in the form of content repositories and aggregators. This does not mean that competition law should erode the exclusive right to copy and disseminate works altogether. However, a competition law investigation may be appropriate when a copyright owner systematically refuses to contribute to content repositories and aggregation systems that offer enhanced access to the cultural landscape and support the creation of new works in this way. Hence, it is worthwhile to explore the potential impact of competition law on the power of copyright owners on supply markets.

Against this background, the following examination focuses on the *potential* impact which competition law could have in a copyright context. It is a thought experiment raising the question of whether the control mechanisms of competition law could be aligned with the objectives of copyright law to such an extent that competition law would finally become a tool to influence the licensing practices of copyright owners in a way that can be deemed desirable from a copyright perspective. On its merits, the following analysis thus views competition law through the

[13]M.R.F. Senftleben / L. Anemaet (2015), 6.

[14]P. Bourdieu (1992/1999), 385.

[15]In this sense also J.E. Cohen (2006), 154–155.

lens of copyright law. It seeks to recalibrate competition law in line with the objectives of copyright law. For this purpose, the analysis rejects the traditional market definition used in competition law and traces the conceptual contours of an alternative approach (following Sect. 2) before embarking on an examination of the potential impact of competition law on licensing practices in the area of content repositories and aggregation systems (Sect. 3). Drawing conclusions, it will be shown (Sect. 4) that competition law, indeed, could constitute an important external balancing tool that complements the corrective function which human rights fulfil already in the case of an overly restrictive exercise of copyright.[16]

2 Market Definition

A substantial hurdle to be surmounted when seeking to apply competition law more broadly in a copyright context is the basic requirement of market power allowing the erosion of competitive market structures. In EU legislation, Article 102 of the Treaty on the Functioning of the European Union (TFEU) reflects this requirement by referring to an abuse of a dominant position:

> Any abuse by one or more undertakings of a dominant position within the internal market or in a substantial part of it shall be prohibited as incompatible with the internal market in so far as it may affect trade between Member States.

In this context, market dominance is understood to refer to a position of economic strength which enables an undertaking

> to prevent effective competition being maintained on the relevant market by affording it the power to behave to an appreciable extent independently of its competitors, its customers and ultimately of the consumers.[17]

Evidently, the crux of this definition lies in determining the correct reference point for the assessment: the "relevant market". A broad reference point, such as a whole segment of literary or artistic creativity, may allow even powerful market participants to escape more thorough scrutiny in the light of competition law. A narrow reference point, which brings the market for an individual work into focus, will pave the way for relatively strict control under competition law standards. Traditionally, it has been difficult to arrive at this focus on the market for an individual work in copyright cases because literary and artistic productions will often be deemed substitutable from the perspective of consumers.

[16]As to a potential combination of human rights and competition considerations, see T. Mylly (2013), 115–117.

[17]Court of Justice, 13 February 1979, Hoffmann-La Roche, C-85/76, 1979 ECR 461, para. 38.

2.1 *Traditional Focus on Consumptive Use*

According to the traditional definition used in competition law cases, the relevant product market underlying the investigation comprises "all those products and/or services which are regarded as interchangeable or substitutable by the consumer, by reason of the products' characteristics, their prices and their intended use."[18] In the identification of the relevant market, the question of substitutability thus plays a central role. As the European Commission explains,

> for the definition of the relevant market, demand substitution constitutes the most immediate and effective disciplinary force on the suppliers of a given product, in particular in relation to their pricing decisions. A firm or a group of firms cannot have a significant impact on the prevailing conditions of sale, such as prices, if its customers are in a position to switch easily to available substitute products or to suppliers located elsewhere.[19]

In addition to demand-side substitutability, supply-side factors may be taken into account.[20] In the field of literary and artistic productions, this may include the particular expertise of a record label, book publisher or film producer in a given area, an established reputation, long-standing relations with authors, knowledge of the customer base, and access to sales channels and customers directly.[21] A confinement of the analysis to supply-side substitutability, however, implies a departure from the basic consideration that, because of their elasticity, supply-side factors should only be considered if their effects are "equivalent to those of demand substitution in terms of effectiveness and immediacy."[22] Moreover, a focus on supply-side factors may soften the standard of review to such an extent that a dominant position will hardly ever be found.[23] Therefore, demand-side factors offer a more solid basis for the development of an alternative approach seeking to employ competition law as an external instrument to encourage the inclusion of protected works in content repositories and aggregation systems.

Hence, it is of crucial importance to identify the particular problems arising from a demand-based analysis. Josef Drexl describes the dilemma of demand-side substitutability in copyright cases as follows:

> Based on the copyright concept of originality, works are certainly different. But this does not mean that they are not substitutable in terms of competition law. [...] To be substitutes, products do not have to be fully identical. The question rather is whether certain factors become so important that from a consumer's perspective works cannot be considered substitutable. The problem in the entertainment industry is that consumer perceptions are

[18]European Commission (1997), para. 7.

[19]European Commission (1997), para. 13.

[20]European Commission (1997), para. 20.

[21]European Commission, 29 July 2003, COMP/M.3197, Candover/Cinven/Bertelsmann-Springer, para. 14–15; European Commission, 15 February 1999, IV/M.1377, Bertelsmann/Wissenschaftsverlag Springer, para. 9–12.

[22]European Commission (1997), para. 20.

[23]R.M. Hilty (2009), 639.

> not defined by objective needs – as, for instance, in the case of patented pharmaceuticals – but by highly individual tastes and preferences. For some movie fans, a science fiction film may be a substitute to a love story; for others it is not. This seems to make the application of the concept of demand-side substitutability very speculative and unreliable.[24]

The central problem, therefore, is the absence of objective needs. Consumer tastes may vary considerably. For some consumers, almost every work in a certain category may be substitutable—even bestsellers, literary milestones and unique works of art—while for others hardly any work may be substitutable because of a refined taste. Depending on the degree of sophistication of the consumer group chosen as a reference point, a considerable degree of substitutability and a very limited degree of substitutability are both plausible outcomes of a demand-based inquiry.

Traditionally, however, the competition law analysis does not focus on connoisseurs of a particular work or repertoire. By contrast, importance is attached to consumer surveys on usage patterns and attitudes, data from consumer's purchasing patterns, the views expressed by retailers and more generally, market research studies submitted by the parties and their competitors to establish whether "an economically significant proportion of consumers consider two products as substitutable, also taking into account the importance of brands for the products in question."[25] Hence, the traditional analysis brings a broader consumer group into focus. In many cases, this broader, "economically significant" group of consumers will be more willing to consider copyrighted works substitutable than an individual aficionado of a given work or repertoire. The room for exerting competition law control is thus likely to be curtailed in comparison with an analysis based on the refined taste of a connoisseur.

2.2 *Alternative Focus on Productive Use*

To broaden the field of application of competition law in copyright cases, it is thus necessary to change the perspective. Instead of considering an "economically significant proportion of consumers" interested in consumptive use of literary and artistic works, it is preferable—in line with the introductory remarks made above (Sect. 1)—to focus on end-users who seek access to protected material for the purpose of finding inspiration for the creation of new literary and artistic works. As a result, an emphasis can be put on the productive study, remix and reuse of pre-existing material for the purpose of cultural follow-on innovation.

This alternative focus on productive reuse corresponds with the societal goals underlying copyright protection. For an adequate understanding of the copyright system, it is important to bear in mind that copyright law, on its merits, is a cyclic

---

[24]J. Drexl (2013), 75.

[25]European Commission (1997), para. 41.

inspiration system. It is the core function of copyright law to further the incessant process of the creation of fresh, original human expression on the basis of pre-existing sources of inspiration. The author's essential trait is her ability to find new ways of individual expression in a given cultural environment. Building blocks for a new cultural creation are extracted from existing expressions, forms and traditions.[26]

On the one hand, copyright protection generates the economic incentives necessary to achieve the desired production and dissemination of literary and artistic works. At the core of this incentive rationale lies the economic insight that literary and artistic works constitute "public goods". Because of non-rivalry in consumption[27] and non-excludability in use,[28] they are unlikely to be created in sufficient quantities in the absence of appropriate incentives.[29]

On the other hand, however, the grant of exclusive rights as part of a strategy to ensure the required incentives involves considerable costs in terms of access to information and cultural follow-on innovation. Once copyright holders obtain exclusive rights, consumers may be inhibited from access to copyrighted works, and future creators may be inhibited from basing new creations on pre-existing ones. The incentive scheme intended to spur the creation and dissemination of works inevitably becomes a burden on the creation and dissemination of secondary works.[30]

To achieve optimal results for society as a whole, copyright law thus requires a constant effort to strike a proper balance between costs and benefits. As summarized by Guy Pessach, the conceptual contours of protection are to be drawn

> in a manner that concurrently maximizes the incentive for investing resources in the production and dissemination of diversified, socially valued creative works; and to minimize the costs and burdens that copyright imposes on the public and on other creators.[31]

Hence it follows that, on the one hand, it is necessary to consider the beneficial effect of copyright which consists, at least theoretically, of the incentive to create for authors. On the other hand, the detriment to the users of literary and artistic works must be factored into the equation: they have to seek the authorization of the copyright holder if they want to enjoy or modify a copyrighted work.[32]

---

[26]See the analysis of research on the social psychology of creativity by J.E. Cohen (2006), 154–155.

[27]Use by one actor does not restrict the ability of another actor to benefit as well.

[28]Unauthorized parties ("free riders") cannot be prevented from use.

[29]W.W. Fisher (1988), 1700; W.M. Landes / R.A. Posner (1989), 326; N.W. Netanel (2008), 84–85. The grant of property rights is only one strategy for providing these incentives. A system of public subsidies could solve the problem as well. Cf. R.A. Posner (2005), 58–59; S.P. Calandrillo (1998), 301.

[30]R.A. Posner (2005), 57; G. Pessach (2003), 1077; Y. Benkler (1999), 392–393.

[31]G. Pessach (2003), 1077.

[32]L.L. Weinreb (1998), 1231; S.P. Calandrillo (1998), 304. See in respect of the 'deadweight loss' that results from the grant of exclusive rights W.W. Fisher (1988), 1700–1702.

Against this background, it makes sense to broaden the perspective when it comes to competition law cases involving copyrighted material. The full potential of competition law to serve as a safeguard against the abuse of exclusive rights relating to literary and artistic works will only come to light when productive use is taken into consideration. The traditional focus on an "economically significant proportion of consumers" is thus doubtful in copyright cases. Instead, the substitutability of a work or repertoire should be assessed from the perspective of a productive user who seeks access to an existing work because it may be an important source of inspiration for the creation of a new work. In this way, the overarching objective of copyright law—the incessant renewal of the cultural landscape—can be integrated in the competition law analysis, and competition law can be aligned with the rationales of copyright protection. As a result, it becomes an important additional instrument to support the incessant renewal of the cultural landscape.

Interestingly, this shift to a productive use perspective leads to a much less "speculative and unreliable"[33] outcome of the inquiry into substitutability. As explained, an argument based on substitutes for the consumption of a particular literary and artistic work misses the point because it does not focus on the needs of authors seeking to use pre-existing material for the purpose of creating new works. It is not the vulnerability of the process of consumption but the vulnerability of the process of production that must be considered when assessing the potential corrosive effect of the abuse of a dominant position in the field of copyrighted material.

With regard to this production perspective, Pierre Bourdieu's sociological analysis of the field of literary and artistic production again offers important insights. According to Bourdieu, it would be wrong to assume substitutability of literary and artistic works in the context of the production of new works. His analysis shows that the room for the evolution of new directions in the creation of literature and art depends on the range of options that is available in the light of positions that have already been taken by previous creators.[34] For a new generation of authors to challenge the leading avant-garde, it must detect the structural gaps within the texture of already known literary and artistic positions. It must formulate an alternative position against the background of the weaknesses and contradictions of the present state of the art.[35] The positions that have already been taken in the literary and artistic field thus determine the room for new positions and new impulses for the creation of literary and artistic works. In other words, all taken positions predetermine the room available for cultural follow-on innovation.[36]

For an author seeking to formulate a new literary or artistic position in the light of a position reflected in a particular pre-existing work, this has far-reaching consequences. If the work is not available for this purpose, the envisaged cultural

---

[33] J. Drexl (2013), 75.

[34] P. Bourdieu (1992/1999), 370.

[35] P. Bourdieu (1992/1999), 372 and 379–380.

[36] For examples in the field of literature and music, see P. Bourdieu (1992/1999), 379–384.

innovation step will simply not take place. Hence, *every* pre-existing literary or artistic position that is not available for cultural follow-on innovation reduces the range of options which later generations of authors have at their disposal to find and formulate new positions. It can thus be said that every literary and artistic work that is unavailable because of the abuse of a dominant position on the market for literary and artistic works reduces the resources available for cultural follow-on innovation and, potentially, thwarts the evolution of a new work.

2.3 Resulting Concept of Relevant Market

Practically speaking, this insight need not lead to the conclusion that, by definition, every literary or artistic work is non-substitutable and constitutes a relevant market of its own when it comes to the assessment of market dominance. By contrast, an individual work can only be deemed a separate market if it is clear, from the outset, that the work will be indispensable for the creation of a particular new work.[37] Considering the creative process leading to a new work, however, this focus on a particular pre-existing work is likely to arise only at the final stage of making the new work. As long as an author is in the preparatory phase of exploring sources of inspiration to identify a potential catalyst that could serve as a basis for the creation of a new work, it is crucial to have access to a broad repertoire of works that may potentially offer the required creative stimulus.

Hence, the creative process remains "speculative and unreliable" at least to some extent. Nonetheless, the outlined production perspective allows a more concrete delineation of the relevant market. Taking the needs of a secondary creator as a starting point instead of aligning the inquiry with the consumption patterns and preferences of the end consumer, the relevant market can be described as the pool of works that might function as a source of inspiration for the particular type of literature or art of the secondary author concerned: jazz music in the case of a jazz composer, scientific publications in the case of an academic writer, comic books in the case of a comic-strip artist, or horror movies in the case of a director in this film genre. This is not to say that artists only look for inspiration in their own field of creativity. By contrast, they may have a particular interest in other disciplines. The potential contribution of sources of inspiration outside their own discipline, however, does not seem concrete and foreseeable enough to justify their inclusion in the determination of the relevant market. This is different in the case of pre-existing works in the same field of literary or artistic production. A contribution to the creation of a new work belonging to the same discipline seems much more likely. Apart from mere inspiration, this contribution may consist of an example of a particular technique or style. Within the relevant field of creativity, each individual repertoire of works can then be deemed non-substitutable because it

[37]Reference to "single source" situation, as described by Hilty.

is not foreseeable which collection of pre-existing works contains the required creative input for the creation of a new work.

Non-substitutability is thus to be assumed with regard to all repertoires of creative sources that could potentially become important for the creative activities of an individual author in a particular field of literature or art. Apart from the exceptional case where an individual work appears non-substitutable from the outset, each collection of potential sources of inspiration thus forms an individual relevant market. Each collection can be deemed non-substitutable from the perspective of the secondary author.

This approach to the identification of the market relevant to the dominance analysis is not entirely new. In *Candover / Cinven / Bertelsmann-Springer*, the European Commission came close to the outlined approach by explaining:

> From a demand-side point of view, it is rare that two different publications be viewed as perfect substitutes. There usually are differences in the coverage, comprehensiveness and content provided by two different publications. From the point of view of functional interchangeability, two different publications could hardly be regarded as substitutable by the end-users, the readers. This applies to publications pertaining to different areas of professional publishing and addressed to different customer groups as well as within professional categories. Therefore, Consumers will rarely substitute one publication for another in reaction to their relative prices. In this case, a strict demand approach would lead to the definition of a multitude of relevant markets of imprecise boundaries and small dimensions. This would not allow to properly assess the competitive relations between the different publishers and the impact of the notified merger on competition.[38]

This statement points in the direction of distinguishing between various, relatively small markets—potentially even distinguishing between markets for individual works. Given this fragmentation of the reference point for the assessment of market dominance, the Commission rejected this approach in *Candover / Cinven / Bertelsmann-Springer*. It feared that, at least in the context of merger control, the "multitude of relevant markets" would not allow an appropriate appreciation of market power. Preference was therefore given to an analysis based on supply-side considerations.[39]

3 Refusal to License

In *Candover / Cinven / Bertelsmann-Springer*, this rejection of the demand-side approach seemed understandable. In fact, supply-side factors, such as the aforementioned criteria of a particular expertise, an established reputation, long-standing relations with authors, knowledge of the customer base, and access to sales

[38] European Commission, 29 July 2003, COMP/M.3197, Candover/Cinven/Bertelsmann-Springer, para. 13.

[39] European Commission, 29 July 2003, COMP/M.3197, Candover/Cinven/Bertelsmann-Springer, para. 14.

channels and customers directly, may allow a better assessment of the potential corrosive effect of a merger.[40] However, the same caution seems unnecessary in other cases, such as a refusal to license. When it comes to the question whether a refusal to license amounts to an abuse of a dominant position in the marketplace, the focus on each individual repertoire in a given area of literary and artistic creativity can pave the way for an improvement of the overall information infrastructure that is available for secondary authors and cultural follow-on innovation.

3.1 Special Responsibility as a Starting Point

To achieve this result, the special responsibility of the right holder vis-à-vis the dominated market can serve as a useful starting point. Matthias Lamping described this responsibility as follows:

> The mere fact that there are no or at least no substantial competitors does not oblige the monopolist to create competition at the expense of its well-acquired market position. However, despite the lack of actual competition, the dominant company will be expected to behave as if it were operating in a perfectly competitive market environment. This includes not only its general responsibility towards satisfying market needs but also its pricing and innovation behaviour. If not only competition by imitation but also competition by substitution is eliminated, as is the case where an intellectual property right constitutes an indispensable facility, it follows that the right holder must either himself exploit the market opportunities protected by the intellectual property right or enable others to do so. If he fails on both ends, competition law must intervene.[41]

When each individual repertoire of literary and artistic works is seen as a non-substitutable, indispensable facility, this special responsibility thus imposes the obligation on the right holder to offer sufficient access to the repertoire for the purpose of productive re-use: the right holder must either himself exploit the market opportunity to offer an information infrastructure that allows secondary authors to study the pre-existing repertoire and find sources of inspiration for the creation of a new work, or enable others to do so and develop appropriate information portals.

To escape the verdict of an abuse of dominant position, the right holder is thus bound to refrain from behaviour that blocks access to the non-substitutable repertoire at issue. As a sword of Damocles, the assumption of special responsibility following from the copyright holder's dominant position can have the effect of spurring investment in modern access and supply tools. In case of reluctance to support the development of a modern information infrastructure, the right holder would have to fear that competition law will intervene and pave the way for a broader dissemination of the repertoire.

---

[40]European Commission, 29 July 2003, COMP/M.3197, Candover/Cinven/Bertelsmann-Springer, para. 14–15; European Commission, 15 February 1999, IV/M.1377, Bertelsmann/Wissenschaftsverlag Springer, para. 9–12.

[41]M. Lamping (2015), 133; B. Conde Gallego (2006), 27–28; J. Drexl (2004), 806–807.

3.2 *Support of Content Aggregation Services*

More concretely, the special responsibility following from the identification of individual collections of works as relevant markets for the assessment of market dominance implies an obligation to play an active role in the development of content repositories and aggregation services. This particular aspect of a collection of works constituting an indispensable facility is often underlined with regard to scientific publications. Josef Drexl, for example, refers to library services in this context:

> Yet there are cultural and creative products where one can seriously consider whether a certain product constitutes a proper market. One example of this may be scientific journals, access to which is indispensable both for the author of an article who depends on access to the journal for his academic career and scientific academic libraries and institutes for which the subscription of such "must-have" journals is mandatory.[42]

The above-described dominance analysis based on the needs of secondary authors allows the generalization of this statement: not only in the area of scientific journals but also in other areas of literary and artistic production, it can be assumed that a given repertoire of works that may offer impulses for cultural follow-on innovation is indispensable both for secondary authors and for content repositories and aggregators in the literary and artistic sector concerned.

This broadened obligation to support the activities of content repositories and aggregators can also be placed in the context of the refusal-to-license criteria developed by the Court of Justice. In *IMS Health*, the Court explained that the refusal to grant a licence, even if it was the act of an undertaking holding a dominant position, could not in itself constitute abuse of a dominant position. Only in exceptional circumstances, the exercise of copyright amounted to abusive conduct.[43] Such exceptional circumstances came to the fore where the refusal to grant a licence prevented the emergence of a new product for which there was potential consumer demand, the refusal was not justified by objective considerations, and it was likely to exclude all competition in the secondary market.[44]

3.2.1 New Product Requirement

In general, content repositories and aggregators in the field of literary and artistic works may be described as providers of information platforms that offer an overview of works in a particular area of creativity. They add value by combining as many available repertoires as possible. As a result, they support the activities of secondary authors embarking on the creation of a new work. They offer

[42] J. Drexl (2013), 42; R.M. Hilty (2009), 639.

[43] Court of Justice, 29 April 2004, IMS Health, C-418/01, [2004] ECR I-05039, para. 34–35.

[44] Court of Justice, 29 April 2004, IMS Health, C-418/01, [2004] ECR I-05039, para. 38 and operative part.

unprecedented—and thus "new"—possibilities of browsing and identifying pre-existing works that may contain the required creative input for the envisaged new work. Within this broad understanding of relevant activities, the products of content repositories and the services of content aggregators may range from the provision of direct access to a wide variety of works stemming from different copyright owners, as in the case of libraries, to mere listings and short indications of the contents of works from diverse sources, as in the case of (dedicated) search engines.

Quite clearly, these new products—information repositories and aggregation systems—can function as catalysts for creative processes by bringing pre-existing works to the attention of secondary authors—works that may otherwise have been overlooked. It thus seems safe to assume that there is "potential consumer demand" in the sense of the first condition developed by the Court of Justice in *IMS Health*—at least when "consumer demand" is understood as "secondary author demand" in line with the focus on cultural follow-on innovation underlying the present inquiry. It also seems clear that the emergence of new information repositories and information search engines will often depend on licenses. A library can hardly offer direct access to a wide variety of works stemming from different copyright owners if it cannot obtain the necessary licences. Similarly, a search engine may have difficulty justifying the display of content snippets in the case of literary works, or entire works in the case of artworks, on the basis of copyright limitations, an implied licence or a safe harbour provision. Decisions on image search services illustrate the complexity of the legal framework in which content aggregators may have to operate.[45]

To a certain extent, the situation is comparable with the facts underlying the *Magill* decision of the Court of Justice. At the time of the *Magill* judgment, no comprehensive weekly television guide was available on the market in Ireland or in Northern Ireland. Each television station published a television guide covering exclusively its own programmes and claimed copyright protection for its own weekly programme listings to prevent their reproduction by third parties.[46] Against this background, the Court of Justice confirmed that the application of competition law was legitimate to allow the emergence of a comprehensive weekly television guide which Magill sought to publish.[47]

In this vein, it can be argued that it should be possible to invoke competition law to ensure that copyright owners do not prevent the emergence of rich and diverse information repositories and aggregation systems capable of satisfying the information needs of secondary authors in a given area of literary or artistic creativity. Even if each copyright owner offers a repository or search function in respect of its own repertoire of pre-existing works, secondary authors seeking to find creative

---

[45]M.R.F. Senftleben (2013), 85–91.

[46]Court of Justice, 6 April 1995, "Magill", C-241/91 P and C-242/91 P, [1995] ECR I-743, para. 7.

[47]Court of Justice, 6 April 1995, "Magill", C-241/91 P and C-242/91 P, [1995] ECR I-743, para. 91.

source material for a new work would still be deprived of an information platform providing an overview of a wide variety of pre-existing repertoires stemming from different copyright owners.

To further the evolution of content repositories and aggregators, it thus makes sense to expose copyright holders to the risk of competition law imposing an obligation to grant a licence. It is to be considered in this context that the underlying concept of "refusal to license" includes not only an outright refusal—general unwillingness to grant a licence—but also the constructive refusal where contractual terms and conditions offered by the right holder are too burdensome to be acceptable. The Damocles sword of a competition law intervention is thus likely to have a desirable, disciplining effect on the licensing practices of copyright owners.

3.2.2 No Objective Justification

The second condition in the test following from *IMS Health* is the absence of an objective justification for the refusal of a licence.[48] Despite the dominant position which a right holder has in respect of a collection of pre-existing literary or artistic works, a refusal to license may be admissible if it serves a legitimate objective that is in the public interest, such as a public health objective or the protection of consumers. A refusal to license is also admissible when it constitutes legitimate business behaviour.[49] This can be understood to prevent an overbroad application of competition law constraints. While the copyright owner may be under an obligation to grant a licence, this does not imply that he must accept whatever terms and conditions the prospective licensee considers appropriate. With regard to search engine services, the case *Innoweb / Wegener*, for instance, sheds light on the outer limits of inroads into exclusive rights which the right holder would have to accept. The case concerned a so-called "meta search engine" bundling offers of second hand cars that could be found on several online sales platforms. Offering this overview of available second hand cars, Innoweb reduced the need to visit the individual source websites, such as Wegener's online database of second hand cars. Nonetheless, Innoweb was reluctant to pay for the use of source data stemming from Wegener's platform.[50] Against this background, the Court of Justice underlined the legitimate interest of the right holder to recoup investment:

> That activity on the part of the operator of a dedicated meta search engine such as that at issue in the main proceedings creates a risk that the database maker will lose income, in particular the income from advertising on his website, thereby depriving that maker of revenue which should have enabled him to redeem the cost of the investment in setting up and operating the database.[51]

[48] Court of Justice, 29 April 2004, IMS Health, C-418/01, [2004] ECR I-05039, para. 38.

[49] M. Lamping (2015), 139.

[50] Court of Justice, 19 December 2013, C-202/12, ECLI:EU:C:2013:850, para. 8–14.

[51] Court of Justice, 19 December 2013, C-202/12, ECLI:EU:C:2013:850, para. 41.

If this rule is applied to copyright cases by analogy, the copyright owner thus has a legitimate interest in redeeming the investment made in his repertoire of pre-existing literary and artistic works. The obligation to grant a licence which may result from the application of competition law must not frustrate the business activities of the copyright owner altogether. Hence, there is no obligation to accept a licence not offering a fair remuneration for the investment made by the copyright owner. In a case trespassing this threshold of fair remuneration, the right holder would have an "objective justification" to deny the conclusion of a licensing agreement in spite of his dominant position with regard to a non-substitutable repertoire of works.

3.2.3 Market Leveraging

The final condition in the test following from *IMS Health* raises the question of market leveraging. Asking whether the refusal to license would exclude "all competition in a secondary market",[52] the Court of Justice, on its merits, requires an inquiry into whether the right holder obtains an unjustified competitive advantage because the refusal to license allows him to extend his dominant position to a downstream market that is economically self-contained. The crucial question, then, is whether the market opportunities in the secondary market can still be seen as part of the specific subject matter of the intellectual property at issue, or rather as an incidental by-product of the exclusive rights of the right holder.[53]

At least with regard to content repositories, this is a delicate question. On the one hand, the control over the reproduction and dissemination of literary and artistic material clearly constitutes the very substance of copyright. Insofar as content repositories offer direct access to pre-existing works (as in the case of libraries), the refusal to license, therefore, does not appear as an attempt to exclude competition on a downstream market. The copyright owner does not seek to expand its dominant position to a further, dependent market. By contrast, the refusal to license reflects the aim to keep control over the primary market for the repertoire of works at issue. The copyright owner seeks to prevent a content repository from providing a substitute for his own offer of literary and artistic works.

On the other hand, the development of an information platform offering a rich and diverse overview of available resources for cultural follow-on innovation, such as a content repository or (dedicated) search engine, can be qualified as a downstream product with added value. The copyright owner can hardly claim that this additional product still belongs to the specific subject-matter of his copyright. Copyright relates to a literary or artistic work as such. It offers an exclusive right to exert control over the use of this specific cultural creation. This does not imply

---

[52]Court of Justice, 29 April 2004, IMS Health, C-418/01, [2004] ECR I-05039, para. 38 and operative part.

[53]M. Lamping (2015), 133–134; K.-N. Peifer (2006), 7; T. Dreier (2001b), 53, 60, 70–71.

control over related information platforms which integrate repertoires from diverse sources and offer browsing and search functions with regard to individual works enjoying copyright protection. Viewed from this perspective, the possibility to integrate a wide variety of works in an information repository or search system can be regarded as a by-product of literary and artistic works. It is not the very substance of the intellectual property concerned. The literary and artistic works included in a content repository or aggregation system are pre-products and building blocks. The more complex repository or aggregation system, however, has individual characteristics and distinct functions which constitute a separate market.[54]

With regard to this secondary market for information platforms, the additional question arises as to whether the copyright owner is capable of excluding "all competition". The answer to this question depends on the degree of content density that is taken as a reference point. If it is deemed sufficient to enable competition between information platforms merely reflecting the works available in some selected repertoires of different right holders, it may be said that the refusal to grant a licence by only one right holder would not exclude competition in the market for content aggregators altogether. It remains possible to compete with regard to repertoires of other right holders who are willing to enter into a licensing agreement. As a result, the control of licensing practices on the basis of competition law would become a toothless tiger: each owner of a repertoire of literary and artistic works could escape more thorough scrutiny in the light of competition law standards by arguing that, despite his refusal to license, competition remains possible with regard to repertoires of other right holders who may be willing to make their content available.

Hence, it is more convincing to take as a reference point the aim to establish information platforms which provide an overview of all available repertoires of literary and artistic works that may be relevant to follow-on innovation in a particular area of cultural creativity. Competition between providers of these platforms would then be possible at the level of the individual user experience, depending on the classification and arrangement of literary and artistic works, the ease of operation, the availability of support tools, the efficiency of the search algorithm etc. A competitive advantage could only be obtained by offering a particularly user-friendly system that further enhances the added value for users.

3.3 Contribution to Follow-On Innovation

In the light of the criteria set forth by the Court of Justice in *IMS Health*, it is thus possible to arrive at the application of competition law to prevent a copyright owner from refusing to grant a licence for the inclusion of his repertoire of literary and artistic works in a content repository or aggregation system. The application of the

[54] B. Conde Gallego (2006), 20; T. Höppner (2005), 462–463.

IMS Health criteria, however, raises difficult questions. In particular, the criterion of market leveraging may cast doubt upon the applicability of competition law. If a content aggregator offers direct access to literary and artistic works, the conclusion seems inescapable that the primary, upstream market for literary and artistic works is affected even though the content aggregator adds features, such as search and browsing functions, that constitute a secondary, downstream element.

Nonetheless, this amalgam of upstream and downstream features need not pose an insurmountable hurdle. The discussed tests developed by the Court of Justice—new product, market leveraging, absence of objective justification—are only one set of criteria that evolved in jurisprudence. In fact, the Court's assumption that these tests must be applied cumulatively has been criticized heavily in literature.[55] Against this background, the *Microsoft* decision of the General Court is often regarded as a departure from the dogma of cumulative application in the EU.[56] Following a relaxed standard of independent application of the new product and market leveraging criteria, market leveraging only constitutes one factor in the analysis. If this factor does not weigh clearly in favour of exercising competition law control, an exceptional circumstance justifying the invocation of competition law may still be based on the fact that the refusal to license frustrates the evolution of a new product for which there is potential demand.[57]

Apart from this option to apply the *IMS Health* tests as independent factors, it is also possible to embark on a re-conceptualization of the relationship between copyright protection and competition law control. The starting point for this is the above-described, overarching function of the copyright system to ensure the incessant renewal of the cultural landscape. As already explained above, copyright law can be seen as an inspiration system. It is the core function of copyright law to further the continuous process of the creation of fresh, original human expression on the basis of pre-existing sources of inspiration.

Following this functional approach to copyright protection, it is consistent to allow the application of competition law in cases where the exercise of copyright would block the evolution of a market for products that have a conducive effect on cultural follow-on innovation. As Beatriz Conde Gallego argued, an intervention by virtue of competition law need not always be confined to a refusal to license that concerns a downstream market. In the absence of competition by substitution, it can also be legitimate to employ competition law as a means of enabling certain forms of competition by imitation.[58] In particular, such an extension of competition control seems appropriate when the copyright owner's refusal to license is contrary to the overarching goal of copyright law to stimulate cultural follow-on innovation.[59]

[55] A. Heinemann (2006), 713; B. Conde Gallego (2006), 25–26.

[56] M. Lamping (2015), 135–136; J. Drexl (2013), 122.

[57] M. Lamping (2015), 135–136; T. Höppner (2005), 463–464.

[58] B. Conde Gallego (2006), 27.

[59] B. Conde Gallego (2006), 28.

Even if a content repository offers direct access to copyrighted material and thus develops activities on the primary market for literary and artistic work, it may thus still be possible to assert competition law against the copyright owner's refusal to license. This is plausible at least when the overarching function of copyright to stimulate cultural follow-on innovation is better served by obliging the right holder to grant a licence. If the compulsory licensing paves the way for the development of new, value-added products[60] that can have a positive effect on the creation of new works, the competition law intervention appears as a justified correction of copyright exclusivity.

4 Conclusion

In sum, it is thus conceivable to enhance the mitigating effect of competition law on restrictive licensing practices of copyright owners. Competition law could become an external balancing tool that limits the market power of copyright owners with regard to content repositories, such as libraries, and aggregation systems, such as (dedicated) search engines. To attain this goal, the identification of the relevant market underlying the analysis would have to be aligned with the needs of productive users looking for sources of inspiration instead of taking mere consumptive use as a reference point. Considering the information needs of secondary authors, each individual repertoire of works in a given sector of creativity can be seen as an indispensable facility.

An obligation to grant a licence for the integration of a non-substitutable repertoire of works in a content repository or aggregation system can be inferred from the consideration that, otherwise, the copyright owner could thwart the emergence of a new, more advanced information product for which there is potential demand. The added value of content repositories and aggregation systems for secondary authors would be lost. The denial of a licence would also be in conflict with the overarching objective of copyright law to further cultural follow-on innovation. It may be added that search and browsing functions of content repositories and aggregators form a downstream market to which the copyright owner could expand his market dominance if control on the basis of competition law were unavailable.

The application of competition law as a safeguard against overly restrictive licensing practices in the area of content repositories and aggregation systems would also lead to a more robust arsenal of external balancing tools that can be used to prevent dysfunctional effects of copyright protection. Human rights and competition law would become complementary instruments to ensure a well-functioning information infrastructure: while the fundamental guarantee of freedom

[60]With regard to this particular form of compulsory licensing, see R.M. Hilty / M.R.F. Senftleben (2015), 330–337.

of expression can be invoked to exempt the use of protected material as building blocks for a new literary or artistic work, the scrutiny based on competition law prevents copyright owners from developing licensing practices that impede the development of rich and diverse information portals. Hence, competition law ensures the availability of appropriate information resources in the preliminary phase of studying pre-existing works and identifying potential sources of inspiration that may ultimately lead to a new literary or artistic production.[61]

However, it is to be pointed out that the present inquiry focussed on the possibility to enhance the impact of competition law on licensing practices of copyright owners. If the application of competition law is aligned with copyright objectives, it becomes possible to create additional room for compulsory licensing in favour of content repositories and aggregators. This does not mean, however, that content repositories and aggregators should not be subject to the same scrutiny in the light of competition law once they have acquired a dominant position on the market for information portals offering an overview of a wide variety of work repertoires from different copyright owners.

References

Benkler, Y. (1999), Free as the Air to Common Use: First Amendment Constraints on Enclosure of the Public Domain, New York University Law Review 74, 355-446

Bourdieu, P. (1992/1999), Die Regeln der Kunst. Genese und Struktur des literarischen Feldes, Suhrkamp 1999 (French original: Bourdieu, P., Les règles de l'art. Genèse et structure du champ littéraire, Éditions du Seuil 1992)

Calandrillo, S.P. (1998), An Economic Analysis of Property Rights in Information: Justifications and Problems of Exclusive Rights, Incentives to Generate Information, and the Alternative of a Government-Run Reward System, Fordham Intellectual Property Media & Entertainment Law Journal 9, 301-359

Cohen, J.E. (2006), Copyright, Commodification, and Culture: Locating the Public Domain, in: L. Guibault / P.B. Hugenholtz (Eds.), The Future of the Public Domain – Identifying the Commons in Information Law, 121-166, Kluwer Law International

Conde Gallego, B. (2006), Die Anwendung des kartellrechtlichen Missbrauchsverbots auf „unerlässliche"Immaterialgüterrechte im Lichte der IMS Health- und Standard-Spundfass-Urteile, GRUR Int., 16-28

Dreier, T. (2001a), Balancing Proprietary and Public Domain Interests: Inside or Outside of Proprietary Rights?, in: R. Dreyfuss / D. Leenheer-Zimmerman / H. First (Eds.), Expanding the Boundaries of Intellectual Property – Innovation Policy for the Knowledge Economy, 295-316, Oxford University Press

Dreier, T. (2001b), Primär- und Folgemärkte, in: G. Schricker / T. Dreier / A. Kur (Eds.), Geistiges Eigentum im Dienste der Innovation, 51-81, Nomos

Drexl, J. (2004), Intellectual Property and Antitrust Law: IMS Health and Trinko – Antitrust Placebo for Consumers Instead of Sound Economics in Refusal-To-Deal Cases, IIC 35, 788-808

[61] For an in-depth analysis of a potential interplay of human rights and competition law, see T. Mylly (2009).

Drexl, J. (2013), Copyright, Competition and Development, Report by the Max Planck Institute for Intellectual Property and Competition Law, Munich, December 2013, available at: http://www.wipo.int/ip-competition/en/
European Commission (1997), Commission Notice on the definition of the relevant market for the purposes of Community competition law, Official Journal No. C 372, p. 5-13, available at: http://eur-lex.europa.eu/legal-content/EN/TXT/?uri=uriserv:OJ.C_.1997.372.01.0005.01.ENG
Fisher, W.W. (1988), Reconstructing the Fair Use Doctrine, Harvard Law Review 101, 1659-1795
Geiger, C. (2004), Droit d'auteur et droit de public à l'information, Litec
Geiger, C. (2006), "Constitutionalising" Intellectual Property Law? The Influence of Fundamental Rights on Intellectual Property in the European Union, IIC 37, 371-406
Geiger, C. (2010), Promoting Creativity through Copyright Limitations: Reflections on the Concept of Exclusivity in Copyright Law, Vanderbilt Journal of Entertainment and Technology Law 12, 515-548
Geiger, C. / Gervais, D. / Senftleben, M.R.F. (2014), The Three-Step Test Revisited: How to Use the Test's Flexibility in National Copyright Law, American University International Law Review 29, 581-626
Geiger, C. / Griffiths, J. / Hilty, R.M. (2008), Declaration on a Balanced Interpretation of the "Three-Step Test" in Copyright Law, IIC 39, 707-713
Gervais, D. (2009-2010), Fair Use, Fair Dealing, Fair Principles: Efforts to Conceptualize Exceptions and Limitations to Copyright, Journal of the Copyright Society of the U.S.A. 57, 499-520
Heinemann, A. (2006), Gefährdung von Rechten des geistigen Eigentums durch Kartellrecht? Der Fall "Microsoft" und die Rechtsprechung des EuGH, GRUR, 705-713
Hilty, R.M. (2009), Renaissance der Zwangslizenzen im Urheberrecht? – Gedanken zu Ungereimtheiten auf der urheberrechtlichen Wertschöpfungskette, GRUR, 633-644
Hilty, R.M. / Senftleben, M.R.F. (2015), Rückschnitt durch Differenzierung? Wege zur Reduktion dysfunktionaler Effekte des Urheberrechts auf Kreativ- und Angebotsmärkte, in: T. Dreier / R.M. Hilty (Eds.), Vom Magnettonband zu Social Media – Festschrift 50 Jahre Urheberrechtsgesetz, 317-338, C.H. Beck
Höppner, T. (2005), Missbräuchliche Verhinderung "neuer" Produkte durch Immaterialgüterrechte – Zur Anwendung von Art. 82 EG auf Lizenzverweigerungen, GRUR Int., 457-464
Hugenholtz, P.B. (2002), Copyright and Freedom of Expression in Europe, in: N. Elkin-Koren / N.W. Netanel (Eds.), The Commodification of Information, 239-263, Kluwer Law International
Kur, A. (2009), Of Oceans, Islands, and Inland Water – How Much Room for Exceptions and Limitations Under the Three-Step Test?, Richmond Journal of Global Law and Business 8, 287-350
Lamping, M. (2015), Refusal to Licence as an Abuse of Market Dominance – From Commercial Solvents to Microsoft, in: R.M. Hilty / K.-C. Liu (Eds.), Compulsory Licensing – Practical Experiences and Ways Forward, 121-145, Springer
Landes, W.M. / Posner, R.A. (1989), An Economic Analysis of Copyright Law, Journal of Legal Studies 18, 325-363
Macciacchini, S. (2000), Urheberrecht und Meinungsfreiheit, Stämpfli
Mylly, T. (2009), Intellectual Property and European Economic Constitutional Law – The Trouble with Private Informational Power, IPR University Centre
Mylly, T. (2013), Intellectual Property and Competition Law in the Information Society, in: C. Geiger (Ed.), Constructing European Intellectual Property – Achievements and New Perspectives, 94-122, Edward Elgar
Netanel, N.W. (1996), Copyright and a Democratic Civil Society, Yale Law Journal 106, 283-387
Netanel, N.W. (2008), Copyright's Paradox, Oxford University Press
Peifer, K.-N. (2006), Das Territorialitätsprinzip im Europäischen Gemeinschaftsrecht vor dem Hintergrund der technischen Entwicklungen, ZUM, 1-8

Pessach, G. (2003), Copyright Law as a Silencing Restriction on Noninfringing Materials: Unveiling the Scope of Copyright's Diversity Externalities, Southern California Law Review 76, 1067-1104

Posner, R.A. (2005), Intellectual Property: The Law and Economics Approach, Journal of Economic Perspectives 19, 57-73

Senftleben, M.R.F. (2004), Copyright, Limitations and the Three-Step Test – An Analysis of the Three-Step Test in International and EC Copyright Law, Kluwer Law International

Senftleben, M.R.F. (2012), Quotations, Parody and Fair Use, in: P.B. Hugenholtz / A.A. Quaedvlieg / D.J.G. Visser (Eds.), A Century of Dutch Copyright Law – Auteurswet 1912-2012, 359-398, deLex

Senftleben, M.R.F. (2013), Internet Search Results – A Permissible Quotation?, Revue Internationale du Droit d'Auteur (RIDA) 235, 3-111

Senftleben, M.R.F. / Anemaet, L. (2015), Het verleidelijke gezang van een Griekse Sirene – Auteursrecht in het licht van Bourdieus sociologische analyse van het literaire en artistieke veld, Tijdschrift voor auteurs-, media- en informatierecht 2015, 1-8, deLex

Strowel, A. / Tulkens, F. / Voorhoof, D. (2006) (Eds.), Droit d'auteur et liberté d'expression, Editions Larcier

Weinreb, L.L. (1998), Copyright for Functional Expression, Harvard Law Review 111, 1150-1254

Entertainment Utopia Through Compulsory Licensing and Network Neutrality

Haochen Sun

Contents

Abstract This chapter explores sensible ways of addressing the conflict between the public interest in enjoying copyrighted contents and the private interest in protecting the right to receive copyright royalties. It utilizes the recent landmark litigations over online television streaming technologies, such as Aereo and TVCatchup, to analyze the nature of this type of conflict of interest. The chapter further considers the roles of compulsory licensing and network neutrality in promoting the public interest in the provision of online streaming services and in guarding the private interest in the protection of copyrights.

Haochen Sun is Associate Professor of Law and Director of the Law and Technology Center at the University of Hong Kong Faculty of Law.

H. Sun (✉)
Faculty of Law, University of Hong Kong, Hong Kong, People's Republic of China
e-mail: haochen.sun@hku.hk

K.-C. Liu, R.M. Hilty (eds.), *Remuneration of Copyright Owners*, MPI Studies on Intellectual Property and Competition Law 27, DOI 10.1007/978-3-662-53809-8_16

1 Introduction

Thanks to rapid technological advances, we now live in an age in which copyrighted contents can be accessed and enjoyed with unprecedented convenience. Just subscribe to the iTune streaming service. The subscriber can instantly listen to anything available at this largest digital music store in the world. Just open the Google Books website. This digital library enables users to search the full text of 25-million scanned books wherever and whenever Internet access is available.[1] Indeed, the multitude of developments in digital technology has truly laid the technological foundation for shaping copyright law as an engine for the encouragement of learning as stated by the Statute of Anne, the first copyright statute in human history.[2]

Copyright owners, however, face mounting challenges to receive royalties for access to and use of their works. Although they have withstood the challenges posed by the peer-to-peer file sharing technology well, they are now confronted with the mushrooming of online streaming technologies that provide live and time-shifted streaming of copyrighted television programs.

Against these backdrops, this chapter explores sensible ways of addressing the conflict between the public interest in enjoying copyrighted contents and the private interest in protecting the right to receive copyright royalties. It utilizes the recent landmark litigations over online television streaming technologies, such as Aereo and TVCatchup, to analyze the nature of this type of conflict of interest. The chapter further considers the roles of compulsory licensing and network neutrality in promoting the public interest in the provision of online streaming services and in guarding the private interest in the protection of copyrights.

2 The Litigations over Online Television Streaming Services Providers

Aereo offered an online streaming service that allows its subscribers to watch and record live broadcast television programs on Internet-enabled devices such as tablets and smartphones. By operating this service, Aereo utilized a system designed to convert broadcast television signals into video data suitable for streaming over the Internet. The system consisted of the following three major parts: (1) a multitude of antennas capable of receiving broadcast television signals; (2) software

[1]Google Books, available at: en.wikipedia.org/wiki/Google_Books ("As of October 2015, the number of scanned book titles was over 25 million.").

[2]The Statute of Anne, the first copyright statute, was designed as "An Act for the Encouragement of Learning, by vesting the Copies of Printed Books in the Authors or purchasers of such Copies..." Statute of Anne, London (1710), available at: www.copyrighthistory.org/cgi-bin/kleioc/0010/exec/ausgabe/"uk_1710".

capable of converting signals received by the antennas into signals for Internet streaming to Aereo subscribers; and (3) a user interface that helps Aereo subscribers' Internet-enabled devices to receive the streamed signals and then display television programs on the devices.

Aereo, however, did not obtain permissions to rebroadcast copyrighted television programs. In 2012, a group of television content providers sued Aereo for infringing their copyrights. In 2014, the U.S. Supreme Court ruled that Aereo's service was copyright infringing. Core to this case was whether Aereo infringed the right of public performance. Under the U.S. Copyright Act, a copyright owner has the exclusive right to "perform the copyrighted work publicly".[3] The right of public performance was expanded by the "Transmit Clause" added to the Copyright Act. The Transmit Clause provides that "perform" includes the right "to transmit . . . a performance . . . of the work . . . to the public".[4]

It was not disputed whether Aereo had performed works. The Transmit Clause makes it clear that copyright owners' right of public performance covers the act of publicly transmitting performances of works. Ostensibly, Aereo transmitted the copyrighted contents originally performed by broadcasters concerned. What was very controversial in this case pertained to whether Aereo had performed works *publicly*. The Supreme Court decided that Aereo had performed works *publicly* on the following grounds.

First, the Court defined the nature of Aereo's system, holding that it was not distinguishable from other cable systems that make public performances of works. The Court found that Aereo's commercial objective was the same as that of a cable company.[5] Both intend to charge subscribers fees for viewing televised programs. Moreover, the user's viewing experience in Aereo's system was not significantly altered.[6] By holding that Aereo was identical with cable systems, the Court implied that unauthorized performances of works for commercial purposes are very likely to be carried out publicly. It pointed out that "Congress would as much have intended to protect a copyright owner from the unlicensed activities of Aereo as from those of cable companies."[7]

Second, the Court ruled that performances are aggregatable, and aggregation would lead to public performance. That is, the Supreme Court argued that an entity may communicate a performance of a work through "multiple, discrete transmissions."[8] The Court further provided examples to demonstrate this point. For instance, a politician can communicate ideas and speeches to constituents in a multitude of ways, whether she communicates each idea in individual phone calls or to each constituent in a public square. A person can sing a song to his family

[3] 17 USC §106 (4).

[4] 17 USC §101.

[5] American Broadcasting Companies v. Aereo, 573 U.S. (2014) (hereinafter Aereo).

[6] *Id.*

[7] *Id.*

[8] *Id.*

whether he sings it to one person at a time or all at the same time. In the same vein then, Aereo may transmit the same performance of a work through one or multiple transmissions of the work.[9]

Third, the Supreme Court held that "the public" consists of a large group of people with no connection with one another. While the U.S. Copyright Act does not provide a definition for "the public", it does state that an entity performs a work publicly when it performs at "any place where a substantial number of persons outside of a normal circle of a family and its social acquaintances is gathered."[10] This provision is highly relevant to the *Aereo* case because "what…constitute [s] 'the public' often depends upon [people's] relationship to the underlying work."[11] Aereo was precisely in the business of transmitting the same performance of a work to a large number of viewers who have no connection with one another.

The UK equivalent of Aereo is TVCatchup, another Internet television service for viewing online streaming of UK television channels. It works only within the UK, but enables users within that country to access the service via Internet-enabled devices. TVCatchup's method of function is basically identical to Aereo: aerials pick up signals transmitted by television broadcasters, and a series of servers convert the signals so that the broadcast can be streamed to the subscribers' devices almost instantaneously. TVCatchup's servers only create a stream upon a user's request, and that stream is for that individual subscriber only.

TVCatchup was sued for infringing the right of communication to the public under the Copyright Directive in the European Union.[12] Article 3 of the Copyright Directive (Directive 2001/29) prescribes that "authors [have] the exclusive right to authorise or prohibit any communication to the public of their works, by wire or wireless means, including the making available to the public of their works in such a way that members of the public may access them from a place and at a time individually chosen by them." Accordingly, the Court of Justice of the European Union (CJEU)[13] analyzed the meaning of the term "public" under Article 3 by applying a so-called "teleological approach".[14] Pursuant to this longstanding interpretive method, in determining the meaning and scope of a given provision of Community law, the Court must give due regard to the larger aims of the Directive

---

[9]*Id.*

[10]17 USC §101.

[11]Aereo.

[12]Directive 2001/29/EC of the European Parliament and of the Council of 22 May 2001 on the harmonisation of certain aspects of copyright and related rights in the information society.

[13]ITV Broadcasting Ltd and others v. TVCatchup Ltd, C-607/11, 3 CMLR 1 (CJEU) (2013) (hereinafter TV Catchup).

[14]See N. Fennelly (1996); K. Lenaerts / J.A. Gutiérrez-Fons, (2014).

of which it forms part.[15] In *TV Catchup*, the Court noted, "the principal objective of Directive 2001/29 is to establish a high level of protection of authors, allowing them to obtain an appropriate reward for the use of their works, including on the occasion of communication to the public."[16] It also acknowledged that the language of the Directive's preamble stated in express terms that "this right should be understood in a broad sense."[17] For these reasons, then, the Court defined the meaning of "public" in a broad manner.

In this vein, the Court took pains to restate the expansive character of the term "public." Drawing on its own case law, the Court observed that the term "public" describes "an indeterminate number of potential recipients" and thereby implies "a fairly large number of persons."[18] In assessing whether a work is communicated to a large number of persons, a court may have regard to "the number of persons who have access to the work at the same time and successively."[19] In this respect, even if a given work is communicated to recipients on a one-to-one basis, it may be still communicated to "a large number of persons" given that this method does not prevent simultaneous access en masse to the said work.[20] In a simple application of the law, the Court in *TV Catchup* found that the defendant company communicated the television broadcasts to a public by virtue of the retransmission thereof over the Internet. The Court found that the said retransmission was aimed at all British residents who claimed to hold a valid television licence, all of whom could simultaneously access the broadcasts over the Internet.[21] On this account, the retransmission targeted "an indeterminate number of potential recipients" and thereby "a large number of persons."[22]

3 Conflict of the Public Interest and the Private Interest

In fact, Aereo-type technologies can promote not only consumer well-being but also positive societal developments. Such technologies were developed to provide consumers with reasonably priced means of viewing television programs.[23] By

[15]See e.g. ECJ Sociedad General de Autores y Editores de España (SGAE) v. Rafael Hoteles SA C-306/05, ECR I-11543 (2006), para. 34.

[16]TV Catchup, para. 20.

[17]*Id.*

[18]*Id.*, para. 32.

[19]*Id.*, para. 33.

[20]*Id.*, para. 34.

[21]*Id.*, para. 35.

[22]*Id.*, para. 36.

[23]Brief of Amici Curiae – The Consumer Federation of America and the Consumers Union in support of the Respondent, 11, available at: www.americanbar.org/content/dam/aba/publications/supreme_court_preview/briefs-v3/13-461_resp_amcu_cfa-cu.authcheckdam.pdf.

enabling private recording and reception in the digital age, Aereo-type technologies helped small and independent broadcasters disseminate their diverse content more broadly, which could benefit the public, especially minority audiences.[24] Moreover, Aereo-type technologies promote healthy competition in the broadcasting industry, which will ultimately benefit consumers in general.[25]

As discussed in the previous part, courts in the U.S. and E.U. focused on analyzing whether the operation of online television streaming technologies had caused harm to the relevant copyright owners. The determination of whether copyrighted contents had been communicated to *the public* was an essential step to the judicial finding of copyright infringements. Both the *Aereo* and *TV Catchup* rulings have been said to ascribe a newfound importance to the right of public performance or the right to communicate to the public as a means of combatting unlicensed retransmissions of works over the Internet. According to Keane, both rulings serve as "a much-needed riposte to the culture of free-riding that has spread insidiously with the rise of media."[26] Therefore, both rulings have made clear that creators of online television streaming technologies will require a licence for the retransmission of a given work from its rights-holder.[27]

However, the U.S. Supreme Court and the CJEU did not consider meticulously the extent to which the online television streaming technologies had enhanced the public interest in accessing and using television contents. For example, in the *Aereo* case, the U.S. Supreme Court merely mentioned that "the doctrine of 'fair use' can help to prevent inappropriate or inequitable applications of the [public performance right]."[28] Nevertheless, it did not consider that the fair use doctrine, a doctrine designed to protect the public interest, could have exempted Aereo from copyright infringement liability. Instead, the Court implied that the fair use doctrine could not shield Aereo by asserting that "Congress would ... have intended to protect a copyright owner from the unlicensed activities of Aereo ...".[29]

In a similar case, *WPIX, Inc. v. IVI, Inc.*,[30] the United States Court of Appeals for the Second Circuit considered the public interests involved as follows:

[24]Brief of Amici Curiae – Small and Independent Broadcasters in Support of Respondent, 9, available at: sblog.s3.amazonaws.com/wp-content/uploads/2014/04/13-461_resp_amcu_sib.authcheckdam.pdf.

[25]Brief of Amici Curiae – Competition Law Professors in support of the Respondent, 19, available at: sblog.s3.amazonaws.com/wp-content/uploads/2014/04/13-461-bsac-Competition-Law-Professors-1.pdf.

[26]B. Keane (2013), 171.

[27]B. Keane summarises the practical significance of TV Catchup as follows: "any interference with an original broadcast or communication of a work on the internet requires the author's authorisation and fair remuneration." B. Keane (2013), 170.

[28]Aereo.

[29]*Id.*

[30]No. 11-788 (2d Cir. 2012).

> Here, streaming television programming live and over the Internet would allow the public — or some portions of the public — to more conveniently access television programming.
>
> On the other hand, the public has a compelling interest in protecting copyright owners' marketable rights to their work and the economic incentive to continue creating television programming. Inadequate protections for copyright owners can threaten the very store of knowledge to be accessed; encouraging the production of creative work thus ultimately serves the public's interest in promoting the accessibility of such works.
>
> Plaintiffs are copyright owners of some of the world's most recognized and valuable television programming. Plaintiffs' television programming provides a valuable service to the public, including, *inter alia*, educational, historic, and cultural programming, entertainment, an important source of local news critical for an informed electorate, and exposure to the arts. Plaintiffs' desire to create original television programming surely would be dampened if their creative works could be copied and streamed over the Internet in derogation of their exclusive property rights.[31]

Although the Second Circuit considered the public interest, there are major problems with its public interest analysis. First, the Second Circuit only briefly touched upon the public interest in using online streaming services. According to it, the convenience in accessing television programs is the only public benefit that online streaming services afford. The Second Circuit over-simplified the complexity of public interests that are served by online streaming services. As Sect. 3 will show, there are other important dimensions of the public interest with respect to online streaming services.

Second, while the Second Circuit was correct in pointing out that the dissemination of copyrighted works benefits the public, it eschewed the reality that copyright owners' dissemination of their works is preconditioned upon receiving financial benefits as a means to the end of protecting their own private interests. In fact, the *Aereo* case shows that many copyright owners, under most circumstances, are actually not concerned about whether the availability of their works is beneficial to the public or not. Instead, they focus on how to recoup financial returns for the creation and dissemination of their works. To protect their private interests, many copyright owners, therefore, endeavor to rely on copyright law to guard against the operation of technologies such as Aereo. For instance, it has been pointed out that "[i]f Aereo was found to be legal, broadcasters feared that consumers might cut the cord to their pay-TV service, which would mean they would get less money for their signals. Another concern was that cable and satellite operators, increasingly vocal about the rising costs of carrying broadcast signals, would use Aereo or a similar technology to get around those so-called retransmission fees."[32]

---

[31] *Id.*

[32] J. Flint / D.G. Savage (2014).

4 The Roles of Compulsory Licensing and Network Neutrality

As discussed in the preceding part, while the operation of Aereo-type technologies implicated a range of public interests, courts did not seriously consider how the public interest should be promoted when dealing with copyright infringement analysis. Instead, they applied the textualist approach to interpret the scope of the right of communication to the public or the right of public performance, both of which are core rights enjoyed by copyright owners.

In this context, legislators and policy-makers should take the responsibility to protect the public interests in enjoying increased availability of online television streaming services. In this part, I will suggest that legislators and policy-makers may consider compulsory licensing and network neutrality as legal tools to protect the public interest. Meanwhile, I will also discuss how compulsory licensing and network neutrality should be designed to benefit copyright owners as well.

4.1 Compulsory Licensing

4.1.1 Enhanced Promotion of a Myriad of Public Interests

Compulsory licensing allows the public to use copyrighted works without authorization from their copyright owners but requires the public to pay copyright owners equitable remuneration. This scheme can be applied to address the above conundrum. It would enable Aereo-type service providers to retransmit television programs online without authorization from copyright owners. Meanwhile, it would require service providers to pay equitable remuneration to the relevant copyright owners.

Compulsory licensing affirms that the right of public performance or right of communicating to the public entitles copyright owners to receive equitable remuneration by copyright owners. One should note that compulsory licensing differs from fair use. Fair use does not entitle copyright owners to charge remunerations on users. By contrast, one of the key functions of compulsory licensing is to safeguard the interests of copyright owners, making sure that they will be appropriately remunerated when their works are used by others without their authorization.

On the other hand, compulsory licensing functions to promote the protection of the public interest. It enables the public to retransmit copyrighted television programs without authorization from copyright owners. This authorization-free form of using copyrighted works by retransmitting parties would make it legal to operate Aereo-type services. It would further result in enhanced promotion of a myriad of public interests in the following steps.

First, through addressing the problem with copyright owners' refusal to grant licenses to retransmit their television programs on the Internet, compulsory licensing would legally allow the public interest-enhancing technologies like Aereo to continue their operation. For sure, Aereo-type service providers would compete with incumbent broadcasters. However, it is the consortium of major broadcasters that lodged complaints against Aereo. Each broadcaster's parent company owns a large amount of highly valuable copyrighted contents. As long as they treat Aereo-type service providers as competitors, they would anticipatorily rely on their ownership of copyrighted contents and refuse to grant licenses to retransmit.

Second, by lowering the operational costs of Aereo-type technology, compulsory licensing would make television programs a lot more affordable for the public. Under the compulsory licensing scheme, Aereo-type technology operators would be required to pay copyright owners equitable remunerations, at rates lower than regular market-rate royalties charged by copyright owners in normal circumstances. Equitable remunerations would financially enable Aereo-type technology operators to provide television programs to their subscribers at prices much lower than cable companies. They could even provide their services free of charge by relying on advertisement incomes. Therefore, the public could rely on the broadband Internet or free WiFi networks to view programs rebroadcast by Aereo-type operators, who will charge relatively low or zero premiums.

Third, compulsory licensing would enable the public to enjoy more liberty to choose television programs they wish to view, promoting the personal well-being of their individual members. With the intervention of compulsory licensing, it is anticipated that Aereo-type operators would start online streaming businesses. Therefore, consumers could choose to subscribe to a streaming service provider that best fits their needs, or find more service providers at relatively low costs. In this scenario, consumers could make decisions tailor-made to their needs and alter their decisions afterwards. This would allow them to enjoy as many television programs as possible or just the right programs that they wish to view without paying the high bundle fees that incumbent broadcasters charge. Moreover, in addition to viewing television programs live, consumers could view programs in a time-shifted manner. This function would allow subscribers to view television programs at a time and/or a place they wish, giving them enhanced freedom to enjoy programs.

4.1.2 Restrictions Needed

While compulsory licensing would greatly promote the public interest, this scheme must be operated with certain restrictions so that copyright owners' interests are adequately protected. First, only streaming service providers that have registered with national copyright offices would be legally allowed to rely on compulsory licensing to retransmit television programs online. The registration procedure would aim to make sure that copyrighted works subject to compulsory licensing are used for the provision of online streaming services rather than for other purposes. Moreover, it would make it easier for copyright owners or copyright office to ascertain who is obliged to pay compulsory licensing fees. Therefore, it serves as a gateway for copyright owners to secure payments of compulsory licensing fees.

The second restriction is concerned with the scope of television programs that would be subject to compulsory licensing. To protect the interests of the entities that create or purchase copyrighted works for televising purposes, the government should set up a time-lapse mechanism that does not allow online stream service providers to retransmit certain televised programs simultaneously when they are being broadcast for the first time. More specifically, this mechanism would allow entities that first broadcast programs to decide whether they allow others to simultaneously retransmit the programs they are broadcasting. If the entities that first broadcast programs do not allow simultaneous retransmission, others can do so only after a certain lapse of time, say one month later. This mechanism would allow those entities to secure adequate financial returns from broadcasting the most economically valuable programs.

The third restriction pertains to the amount of compulsory licensing remunerations that would be paid to the relevant copyright owners. The government should encourage stakeholders to negotiate the most reasonable amount of remunerations. This would allow the stakeholders to strike deals that meet their needs as much as possible. Meanwhile, national copyright offices should set up a tribunal to decide on the amount of compulsory licensing remunerations if negotiations fail.

If a compulsory licensing scheme for online streaming succeeds in one country, other countries may consider implementing it. However, the Internet transcends national boundaries. Countries must be proactive in cooperating together to facilitate the implementation of such a compulsory licensing scheme. For example, government leaders may work together to set up a super-national tribunal for deciding compulsory licensing remunerations.

4.2 Network Neutrality

As discussed in Sect. 4.1, compulsory licensing is of great importance for coping with the conflict of the interests of copyright owners and the public with regards to online television streaming. This section will show that network neutrality is another important vehicle for dealing with the conflict of interests in the online streaming sector.

The principle of network neutrality stands for the idea of "Open Internet", which enables consumers to use the Internet whenever and wherever possible, without restraint. This principle governs how technology should be used in the public interest.[33] It requires Internet service providers (ISPs) to treat all data on the Internet equally. Therefore, an ISP should provide the same level of Internet data access and speed to each of its users. It is not allowed to block or degrade the flow of data to any particular website and application.[34] From this perspective, network

[33]T. Wu (2003), 145–146.

[34]C. S. Yoo (2004), 38.

neutrality serves as an important principle for protecting freedom of expression and promoting healthy competition in the marketplace.[35]

Network neutrality is of crucial importance to the smooth operation of Aereo-type service providers on the Internet, whether a compulsory licensing scheme as discussed in Sect. 4.1 is adopted or not. If the compulsory licensing scheme is to be adopted, Aereo-type service providers can rely on it to retransmit contents. In countries where the compulsory licensing scheme is not to be adopted, they may still negotiate with copyright owners of the relevant contents for retransmission by paying them royalties. Even though service providers could figure out means of retransmitting contents legally by relying on compulsory licensing or obtaining permissions from copyright owners, they would still face the challenges that their retransmissions may be adversely affected by certain ISPs that provide communication networks for retransmissions. In fact, ISPs' deviations from network neutrality have increased exponentially, as evidenced by the fact that an alarming number of complaints on violation of network neutrality has been filed. It is reported that the U.S. Federal Communications Commission (FCC) received about 2000 network neutrality complaints from consumers over just a one-month period in 2015. Consumers expressed their outrage at ISPs' practices that had caused slow speeds, high prices, and data caps.[36]

Against this backdrop, certain ISPs may take measures that favor particular private networks for retransmitting televised programs over the Internet. For example, in November 2015, T-Mobile launched Binge On, a new service that offers its users unlimited video streaming on their favorite services like YouTube, Netflix, HBO NOW without using their high-speed data. It has been pointed out that Binge On, as it stands now, is likely to violate the network neutrality principle because it favors services selected by T-Mobile.[37]

Moreover, certain ISPs may carry out peering discrimination. For example, Netflix video streaming through Comcast slowed down quickly over the course of 2013. Netflix then reached an arrangement with Comcast in January 2014, agreeing to pay Comcast an undisclosed fee for improving the streaming speed for Netflix customers. Because of this financial arrangement, Comcast raised the average speed for the streaming of Netflix video programs by 65 % in the U.S., from 1.15 Mbps in January 2014 to 2.5 Mbps in March 2014. Meanwhile, the average streaming speed

---

[35]T. Wu (2003), 145–146.

[36]B. Sasso (2015), Thousands Beg FCC for Net Neutrality Crackdown, available at: www.theatlantic.com/politics/archive/2015/07/thousands-beg-fcc-for-net-neutrality-crackdown/457371/.

[37]See B. van Schewick (2016).

of Netflix video programs through the Verizon networks slowed to 1 Mbps in early 2014.[38]

This caused a dispute between Netflix and Verizon. Netflix CEO Reed Hastings accused Verizon of deliberately slowing down the streaming speed, and appealed for the application of the network neutrality principle to the dispute:

> The motivation could be to get Netflix to pay fees to stop this degradation. Were this draconian scenario to unfold with some ISP, we would vigorously protest and encourage our members to demand the open Internet they are paying their ISP to deliver.[39]

No matter whether compulsory licensing is to be adopted, network neutrality is of pivotal importance for the smooth operation of online streaming services. Even though Aereo was ruled by the U.S. Supreme Court to be a copyright-infringing service, more online streaming service providers are determined to expand their services on the basis of the permissions they obtained to retransmit copyrighted contents. Netflix, the world's largest online streaming provider, has expanded its service from the United States to Asia.[40] LeTV, the largest online streaming service provider in China, has also restructured to set foot in the cities outside China, such as Hong Kong.[41] In this context, network neutrality has become increasingly crucial for these companies to achieve business success globally.

5 Conclusion

It is evident that the development of new technologies and platforms that allow Internet users to social media—in the form of tablets, smartphones, and wireless networks, alongside a proliferation of streaming platforms that hover between the boundaries of legal and illegal broadcasting—pose a threat to the commercial interests of copyright owners. Given the globalization of media and cultural consumption, this challenge is not merely a local issue affecting certain countries, but a global issue faced by many copyright owners.

However, as this chapter has discussed, the public interest is of paramount importance in the national and global expansion of online streaming services. The copyright infringement decisions rendered by the highest courts in the U.S. and

[38] R. Waniata (2014), Comcast Jumps up in Netflix Speed Rankings after Payola-style Agreement, available at: http://www.digitaltrends.com/home-theater/comcast-jumps-netflix-speed-rankings-payola-style-agreement/.

[39] B. Thompson (2014), Netflix and Net Neturality, available at: stratechery.com/2014/netflix-net-neutrality/.

[40] D. Groves (2016), Will Netflix Succeed In Conquering Asia?, available at: www.forbes.com/sites/dongroves/2016/01/08/plenty-of-upside-but-challenges-ahead-for-netflix-in-asia/#1ed559641019.

[41] J. Liu, Hong Kong's LeTV announces price for English Premier League package, available at: www.scmp.com/news/hong-kong/education-community/article/1888806/hong-kongs-letv-announces-price-english-premier.

E.U. dealt a fatal blow to the business operation of Aereo and TVCatchup. But new technologies and new business methods still keep thriving and flourishing as long as human ingenuity sustains. Therefore, it is highly necessary to continue considering means of addressing the conflict of interests with respect to online streaming services. This chapter showed that within the ambit of copyright law, compulsory licensing is an effective scheme that has the potential to address the conflict of interests. Equally crucial is network neutrality, an increasingly important principle that governs the dissemination of copyrighted works over the boundless Internet.

References

Fennelly, N. (1996), Legal Interpretation at the European Court of Justice, Fordham International Law Journal 20 (3), 656

Flint, J. / Savage, D.G. (2014), Broadcasters Cheer as Aereo Loses Supreme Court Fight, available at: www.latimes.com/entertainment/envelope/cotown/la-et-ct-court-copyright-aereo-20140626-story.html

Keane, B. (2013), Ill Communication? The Concept of Communication to the Public under EU Copyright Law, Entertainment Law Review 24 (5), 165

Lenaerts, K. / Gutiérrez-Fons, J. A. (2014), To Say What the Law of the EU Is: Methods of Interpretation and the European Court of Justice, Columbia Journal of European Law 20, 3

van Schewick, B. (2016), T-Mobile's Binge on Violates Key Net Neutrality Principles, working paper, Stanford

Wu, T. (2003), Network Neutrality, Broadband Discrimination, Journal of Telecommunications and High Technology Law 2, 141

Yoo, C. S. (2004), Would Mandating Broadband Network Neutrality Help or Hurt Competition? A Comment on the End-To-End Debate, Journal of Telecommunications and High Technology Law 3

Compulsory Licences as an Enabler of New Business Models

Wee Loon Ng-Loy

Contents

Abstract Technology continuously throws up new modes of distribution of copyrighted works. The history of copyright is very much about keeping up with these technological advancements, making sure, on the one hand, that copyright owners' control over the use of their works is not rendered meaningless by the new mode of distribution and, on the other hand, that the public gets to enjoy the works in a different manner. In this balancing act, one option is the use of compulsory licensing. Yet national policy-makers have been slow to deploy compulsory licensing as an enabler of new business models that are built on new modes of distributing copyrighted works. Why is so? Perhaps it is due to the concern that international law does not permit use of compulsory licensing. Another reason could be the concern that compulsory licensing will not achieve the right balance. These concerns are explored in this chapter.

Wee Loon Ng-Loy is Professor at the Faculty of Law at National University of Singapore (NUS).

W.L. Ng-Loy (✉)
Faculty of Law, National University of Singapore, Singapore, Singapore
e-mail: loy.weeloon@nus.edu.sg

K.-C. Liu, R.M. Hilty (eds.), *Remuneration of Copyright Owners*, MPI Studies on Intellectual Property and Competition Law 27, DOI 10.1007/978-3-662-53809-8_17

1 Introduction

The concept of non-voluntary licensing is familiar to copyright lawyers. Essentially this is where the exclusive right granted to the copyright owner takes the form of a right to equitable remuneration, rather than an exclusive right to authorise. When the amount of equitable remuneration is determined through negotiations between the parties or, when the parties cannot reach any agreement, by a competent authority, the scheme is sometimes referred to as 'compulsory licensing'. When the amount of equitable remuneration is fixed by the law and private negotiations are dispensed with, the scheme is sometimes referred to as 'statutory licensing'.[1] For the purposes of this chapter, this distinction shall be observed.

The structure of this chapter is as follows. Section 2 will provide an overview of how non-voluntary licensing of copyright is viewed in international law. Any non-voluntary licensing, whether it is compulsory or statutory in nature, is a limitation of the exclusive rights guaranteed by international agreements. Thus, when considering if non-voluntary licensing can be deployed to facilitate the development of new business models for better exploitation of copyright works, it is important to consider if there are any boundaries imposed by these international agreements on the use of non-voluntary licensing. Would a WTO Member be in breach of any obligations under the TRIPS Agreement if it enacts compulsory licensing provisions to allow, for example, online distribution of music? Section 2 will also provide a flavour of the non-voluntary provisions existing in WTO countries.

Quite apart from considerations of legality under international law, there is also the question whether non-voluntary licensing can in fact be an enabler of new business models. What evidence is there to suggest that if compulsory licensing had been used at the turn of the twentieth century to allow online distribution of music, it would have spawned legitimate versions of Napster and Kazaa or other innovative modes of distributing music and in so doing revolutionized the way music is consumed? Section 3 will look at what may be considered a success story for our purposes. This is the statutory licensing scheme in American copyright law that governs cable retransmissions of broadcasts.

Section 4 will consider the role of compulsory licensing in the Internet TV sector. Three cases of copyright litigation between broadcasters and technology service providers will be mentioned: *ABC Inc v Aereo Inc*[2] in the US, *ITV*

[1]It should be noted, however, that this distinction between 'compulsory licensing' and 'statutory licensing' is not always maintained. For example, section 52 of the Singapore Copyright Act 1987 speaks of a 'statutory licence' for multiple copying of copyright works by educational institutions when the provision stipulates that the amount of equitable remuneration is that agreed upon between the copyright owner and the educational institution, or in default of agreement, determined by the Copyright Tribunal. On the other hand, Article 67 of the Japanese Copyright Act 1970 speaks of a 'compulsory licence' for use of orphans works when the royalty rate is fixed by a Cabinet Order.

[2]134 S Ct 2498 (2014).

Broadcasting Ltd v TVCatchup Ltd[3] in the UK, and *RecordTV Pte Ltd v MediaCorp TV Singapore Pte Ltd*[4] in Singapore. In *Aereo* and *TVCatchup*, the court held that online retransmission of broadcasts was infringing activity. In *RecordTV*, the court held that the online transmission of a recorded broadcast for time-shifting purposes was non-infringing activity. This "all or nothing" environment is not likely to be the most conducive for negotiating voluntary licences to allow use of copyrighted works in the Internet TV sector.

2 Compulsory Licensing and International Law

A preliminary observation is in order here. It was stated in the Introduction that non-voluntary licensing is a limitation of the exclusive rights granted to copyright owners. Inherent in this statement is the acceptance that the nature of copyright is an exclusive right to authorise the doing of particular acts (e.g. reproduction, public performance) in relation to the copyrighted work. Any suggestion that copyright is only a right to equitable remuneration would be treated as heresy. Yet, it should be recalled that when the Statute of Anne 1709, the world's first copyright legislation, birthed the concept of copyright for books, it also at the same time subjected the exercise of this right to the oversight of a group of distinguished men (e.g. the Lord Archbishop of Canterbury, the Lord Chancellor, the Lord Chief Justice, the Vice-Chancellors of the Two universities) who were empowered to adjudicate complaints of high and unreasonable prices charged for books. If a complaint was found to be valid, these men had the authority to limit and settle the price of the book "according to the best of their Judgements, and as to them shall seem Just and Reasonable". This proviso was not a compulsory licensing mechanism; rather, it was competition law at play within a copyright statute.[5] Nevertheless, the power that Statute of Anne conferred on an independent body to determine the price of books is akin to the empowerment of a competent authority to determine the licence fee in the non-voluntary licensing schemes of modern day copyright regimes. One might even say that, in truth, copyright was conceived as a right to equitable remuneration, rather than as an exclusive right to authorise.

The concept of copyright has of course changed dramatically since the Statute of Anne 1709. As far as international instruments are concerned, copyright is an exclusive right to authorise, and the 'downgrading' of this exclusivity to a right to equitable remuneration are the exceptions to this general rule. In the Berne Convention, there are three specific circumstances where this 'downgrade' is explicitly provided for:

[3]FSR 36 (2013).

[4]1 SLR 830 (Court of Appeal) (2011).

[5]Was this proviso ever utilised? No, according to Professor Cornish. His research also revealed that this proviso was formally abandoned in 1739. See W. Cornish (2010), 24.

- Article 11bis(2) provides for compulsory licensing in relation to the rights conferred in Article 11bis(1)(i)–(iii), one of which is the right to communicate a broadcast of the work to the public by wire.[6] For example, Australia[7] uses a compulsory licensing scheme to govern cable retransmission of broadcasts whereas the USA[8] uses statutory licensing. As a matter of interest, Singapore has a complete defence (that is, free use) for cable retransmission of broadcasts.[9]
- Article 13 provides for compulsory licensing in relation to the sound recordings of published musical works. For example, Japan[10] uses a compulsory licensing scheme in this area whereas Singapore[11] uses statutory licensing.
- Article 21 and the Appendix provides for non-voluntary licensing in relation to translations and reproductions in developing countries. For example, Thailand[12] and India[13] use a statutory licensing scheme in this area.

There is also the 'three-step test' in Article 9(2) of the Berne Convention, which applies to exceptions and limitations to the reproduction right. Professor Senftleben's research into the background of the so-called 'three-step' test shows this test envisages the use of non-voluntary licences in appropriate circumstances.[14]

As far as the TRIPS Agreement is concerned, it incorporates the specific provisions of the Berne Convention (Articles 11*bis*(2), 13 and the Appendix) on non-voluntary licences.[15] What interests us more is Article 13 of the TRIPS Agreement setting out the three-step test that demarcates the boundaries of legitimate exceptions and limitations to the rights of copyright owners. Much has been written of the scope of the three-step test and its interpretation by the WTO Dispute Resolution Panel in DS160 (*United States – section 110(5) of US Copyright Act).* For our purposes, two views about the scope of this test will be highlighted. First, the Panel in DS160 accepted that a compulsory licensing scheme is relevant when assessing if the third step of the test is infringed (that is, whether the exception or limitation unreasonably prejudices the legitimate interests of the right holder). A

[6]Article 11*bis* applies to rights in literary and artistic works. See also Article 14*bis*(1) for cinematographic works.

[7]Part VC (Retransmission of free-to-air broadcasts) of the Australian Copyright Act 1968, in particular section 135ZZK.

[8]Section 111(c) of the US Copyright Act 1976.

[9]Section 199 (3) of the Singapore Copyright Act 1987. Singapore is a signatory of the Berne Convention. Query: does this exception contravene Article 11*bis*(2)? Could this exception be justified under the 'minor exceptions' doctrine that applies to the rights provided under *inter alia* Article 11*bis*(1)? See the discussion of this doctrine in the WTO (2002), para. 6.47-6.59.

[10]Article 69 of the Japanese Copyright Act 1970.

[11]Section 56 of the Singapore Copyright Act 1987.

[12]Sections 54–55 of the Thai Copyright Act 1994.

[13]Section 32 of the Indian Copyright Act 1987.

[14]M.R.F. Senftleben (2004), 80.

[15]This incorporation is done through Article 9(1) of the TRIPS Agreement. See also, generally, the discussion in the WTO (2002), para. 6.83-6.89 which is premised on Art 11*bis*(2) of the Berne Convention being part of the TRIPS Agreement.

non-voluntary licensing scheme, which entitles the copyright owner to an equitable remuneration may change what would otherwise be considered unreasonable prejudice (unreasonable loss of income to the copyright owner) to a level which is reasonable in the circumstances.[16] Second, there is strong support amongst the academic community, shown via the *Declaration on a Balanced Interpretation of the "Three-Step Test" in Copyright Law*, that a non-voluntary licensing scheme is also relevant for the purposes of the second step of the test (that is, whether the exception or limitation conflicts with a normal exploitation of the copyright work).[17]

To be clear, this author is not suggesting that a non-voluntary licensing scheme is a 'cure all' to objections and complaints raised under Article 13 of the TRIPS Agreement. Indeed, national legislators should heed the caution issued by Professors Ricketson and Ginsburg not to fall into the trap of assuming that any limitation to the exclusive rights "can always be assuaged through the imposition of a compulsory licence".[18]

The following are examples of the circumstances in which national legislators have seen it fit to use non-voluntary licensing (outside of the scope of Articles 11*bis*, 13 and the Appendix of the Berne Convention):

- Multiple copying of literary works by educational institutions for the use of their students: Australia[19] and Singapore[20] have compulsory licensing in this area, whilst Taiwan[21] uses a statutory licence.
- Use of copyrighted works for the services of the government: Australia[22] and Singapore[23] use a compulsory licensing for this use.
- Republication etc. of a published work which, by reason of the copyright owner's refusal to republish or allow republication, has been withheld from the public: India[24] uses a compulsory licence here. Myanmar also has a similar scheme but it only applies after the death of the author.[25] The origins of this compulsory licensing scheme can be traced to the Imperial Copyright Act 1911.

---

[16]WTO (2002), para. 6.229 and footnote 205.

[17]Article 4 of the Declaration, which is published in [2008] IIC 707. See also K.C. Liu (2012), 680, (arguing that the TRIPS Agreement, when interpreted in the light of Article 7 therein, views compulsory licensing favourably).

[18]S. Ricketson / J. Ginsburg, (2006), para. 13.27.

[19]See, for example, sections 135ZJ (printed periodical articles) and 135ZMC (periodical articles in electronic form) in the Australian Copyright Act 1968.

[20]Section 52 of the Singapore Copyright Act 1987.

[21]Article 47 of Taiwanese Copyright Act 2014.

[22]Section 183 (5) of the Australian Copyright Act 1968.

[23]Section 198 (5) of the Singapore Copyright Act 1987.

[24]Section 31 (1) of the Indian Copyright Act 1957, as amended by the Copyright Amendment Act 2012. Prior to the 2012 amendment, section 31(1) applied only to Indian works.

[25]Section 4 of the Myanmar Copyright Act 1914.

3 The Role of the Cable Compulsory Licence in Delivering Television Programming via Cable to the Public in the USA

In this section, we are concerned with the question whether non-voluntary licensing can in fact be an enabler of new business models. It is an attempt to address the question that opponents of non-voluntary licensing will pose: where is the concrete evidence that non-voluntary licensing can spawn new business models to deliver copyrighted works to the public? These opponents may also warn that, instead of this positive outcome, non-voluntary licensing could destabilise the incentive structure that lies at the core of the copyright regime.

There appears to be a success story emanating from the USA. This is their use of statutory licensing to govern cable retransmissions of broadcasts of works. As mentioned above in Sect. 2, Article 11*bis*(2) of the Berne Convention specifically allows the imposition of a compulsory licensing scheme to curtail the cable retransmission right of copyright owners.[26] In the case of the USA, they have in place what is sometimes referred to as the 'cable compulsory licence' provided by section 111(c) of their Copyright Act 1976.[27] The scheme, in actual fact, is a statutory licence.

The role and operation of the cable compulsory licence was reviewed by the US Copyright Office in, *inter alia*, two reports of June 2008 and August 2011.[28] The report of June 2008 recommended the phasing out of the cable compulsory licence.[29] This report noted that the royalties fixed in the cable compulsory licence were below-market rates, and that whilst this was justifiable when the cable was a nascent industry, it had outlived its purpose now that the cable industry had grown significantly since 1976 to possess the market power to negotiate voluntary licences on equal footing with copyright owners.[30] Subsequently the report of August 2011

[26]Article 11bis applies to rights in literary and artistic works. See also Article 14bis(1) for cinematographic works and the accompanying main text.

[27]Under the US Copyright Act 1909, the predecessor of the 1976 Act, cable retransmissions of TV broadcasts did not infringe any copyright (specifically, the public performance right): see the Supreme Court decisions in Fortnightly Corp v. United Artists Television Inc 392 US 390 (1968) and Teleprompter Corp v. Columbia Broadcasting System Inc 415 US 394 (1974). This was changed in the 1976 Copyright Act, which recognised that cable retransmissions of broadcasts falls within the public performance right, but subjected these retransmissions to statutory licensing under section 111(c). For the background to s 111(c), see the US Copyright Office (1992).

[28]See also the US Copyright Office (1992), and the US Copyright Office (1997).

[29]The US Copyright Office (1998). This report reviewed the operations of the statutory licensing schemes in sections 111, 119 and 122 of the Copyright Act 1976. Sections 119 and 122 set out statutory licensing schemes for satellite carriers.

[30]See also H. Cate (1990), 191, already calling for an abolition of the cable compulsory licence because the intention of this scheme was to provide a 'subsidy' for the cable television industry in the form of below-market royalty rates, but this industry had developed to a point that it no longer warranted this 'subsidy'.

was issued to make recommendations on how the phasing out of the cable compulsory licensing scheme should be implemented.[31] Like the June 2008 report, the August 2011 report also noted that the cable network industry had achieved a significant degree of maturity and that the time has come to phase out the compulsory licensing schemes. Some statistics were provided: the cable penetration rate in the USA in 1976 was 15.5 % and by 2010, it had increased to 85 %[32]; and the number of cable networks in the USA in 1972 was a grand total of one (namely, HBO) whereas this number had increased to 565 by 2006.[33] There was also the acknowledgement that the cable compulsory licence had "ensured the efficient and cost-effective delivery of television programming in the United States" over the 35-year period from 1976 to 2010.[34]

Two observations about this cable compulsory licence example are in order. First, the fact that the royalties are fixed below-market rates is not a reason for dismissing the reported positive impact of this scheme. Inherent within non-voluntary licences is the right to receive 'equitable remuneration', but 'equitable remuneration' does not necessarily mean market rate (that is, the value that the copyright owner would receive if he had been free to authorise the use of his work). Professors Ricketson and Ginsburg have made this point, further suggesting that an acceptable interpretation of 'equitable remuneration' is an amount which provides a reasonable compensation to the copyright owner and yet enables the licensee to operate his business.[35] Other academics, via the *Declaration on a Balanced Interpretation of the "Three-Step Test" in Copyright Law*, also advocate that the three-step test should not preclude payment of compensation below market rate, and that the amount is "inherently adequate as long as there are sufficient incentives for continued creation and dissemination of works".[36] In the case of the cable compulsory licence, the royalty rates may be set at below market-rates but, given the healthy state of the copyright sectors involved in television programming, this has not adversely affected the continued creation of works.

Second, the cable compulsory licence is on its way out. It has served its purpose, and it needs to be phased out. This drives home the point that non-voluntary licensing can be used as an interim or stop-gap measure. Once the desired outcome is achieved, the scheme can be (and should be) dismantled.

---

[31]The US Copyright Office (2011). Like the June 2008 report, the August 2011 report concerned the statutory licensing schemes in sections 111, 119 and 122.

[32]*Id.*, 31.

[33]*Id.*, 32.

[34]*Id.*, at p iii.

[35]S. Ricketson / J. Ginsburg, (2006), 816–817 (in the context of the phrase 'equitable remuneration' appearing in Article 13(1) of the Berne Convention).

[36]K.-C. Liu, (2012), 680.

4 A Role for Compulsory Licensing to Deliver Television Programming via the Internet?

Given that the cable compulsory licence has played a part in an efficient and cost-effective delivery of television programming to the public in the USA, might not similar positive results have ensued from the use of non-voluntary licensing for, for example, online distribution of music?[37] Another example—one that is currently staring at us in our face—is the distribution of television programming via the Internet.[38]

Internet television was considered in the August 2011 report issued by the US Copyright Office. The report, noting that the Internet will replace cable and satellite as the preferred way to consume broadcasts, adopted a very optimistic view that "ten years hence there may be such an abundance of licensed broadcast content available on the Internet that the demand of distant broadcast signals over cable and satellite may be non-existent".[39] The US Copyright Office was not in favour of subjecting Internet retransmission of broadcasts to any non-voluntary licensing scheme, citing as a reason no market failure in the Internet television programming sector.[40]

However, the recent litigation in the US and the UK between broadcasters and Internet companies may not augur well for the US Copyright Office's prediction that there might be "an abundance of licensed content available on the Internet" by 2021. In the US, the case is *ABC Inc v Aereo Inc*.[41] Aereo sold a service which allowed its fee-paying subscribers to watch television shows over the Internet (on, for example, their laptop or cell phone) almost simultaneously as the shows were broadcast over the air. When the subscriber selected the show he wanted to watch from a menu on Aereo's website, an antenna which was assigned specifically (and only) to this subscriber would receive the broadcast signals carrying this show, and after translation by a transcoder, these signals would be streamed to the subscriber's screen. The majority of the Supreme Court held that Aereo had infringed the copyright owners' right of public performance.[42] It should be noted that a strong dissent was written by Justices Scalia, Thomas and Alito. In the UK, the case is *ITV*

[37] An advocate of non-voluntary licensing in this area is Professor Lessig: see L. Lessig (2001), 255. Cf. M. Botein / E. Samuels (2005), 69.

[38] Advocates of non-voluntary licensing in this area include the following: A. Asaro (2014), 1107; S. Balganesh, (2007), 1303.

[39] The US Copyright Office (1998), 33.

[40] The US Copyright Office (1998), 48–49. Two other reasons were given: concerns about piracy and the prohibition in agreements that the US has signed with its trading partners. One example of this prohibition is Article 16.4.2(b) of the US-Singapore Free Trade Agreement which provides that "[n]either party shall permit the retransmission of television signals (whether terrestrial, cable, or satellite) on the Internet without the authorisation of the right holder in the subject matter of the signal".

[41] 134 S Ct 2498 (2014).

[42] There are reports that Aereo intended to fit itself within the cable compulsory licence provided in section 111(c) of the US Copyright Act 1976. However, it has been settled in *WPIX Inc v. IVI Inc* 691 F 3d 275 (2nd Cir, 2012) that Internet retransmissions of broadcasts did not come within the cable compulsory licence.

Broadcasting Ltd v TVCatchup Ltd.[43] TVCatchup offered a non-fee paying Internet service to its subscribers to watch live television shows on their computer and other devices. When a subscriber selected one of the over 50 channels on TVCatchup's website, the show would be streamed to him a few seconds later than the actual time of broadcast. This delay is due to the appearance of advertisements inserted by TVCatchup. The UK court referred to the Court of Justice of the Union (CJEU) various questions relating to the ambit of the right of communication to the public. The effect of the CJEU's answers to these questions was that TVCatchup's service infringed the copyright owners' right of communication to the public.

By way of contrast, Singapore has taken a more restrictive interpretation of the right of communication to the public. In *RecordTV Pte Ltd v MediaCorp TV Singapore Pte Ltd*,[44] RecordTV offered an Internet-based digital video recorder ('iDVR') that allowed its non-fee paying subscribers to record television shows remotely from home or elsewhere via a web browser, for the purpose of watching the recorded shows at a later time. The recording was done by the registered user himself, and not by RecordTV.[45] In essence, RecordTV's technology was an online version of the video-cassette recorder and digital-video recorders which can be used by the registered user to record broadcasts for the purposes of 'time-shifting'. Such activity is permitted by a provision in the Singapore Copyright Act 1987.[46] In other words, the registered user in using RecordTV's technology to record the broadcast was not liable for copyright infringement. The copy of the recorded show was a legitimate copy. The claim of the broadcaster, MediaCorp, against RecordTV was in respect of the transmission of the copy of the recorded show to the subscriber when the latter wanted to watch the show. MediaCorp claimed that this transmission infringed its right of communication to the public.

The Court of Appeal held that RecordTV's service was not infringing activity. There were two reasons for this conclusion. First, there was no communication 'to the public' in this case. Secondly, the communicator was the registered user and not RecordTV. These reasons are not easy to justify.[47] It is submitted that the decision was driven by public policy considerations. This is evident from this passage of the judgment:

> Bearing in mind that the law strives to encourage both creativity and innovation for the common good, in a case such as the present, how should the courts strike a just and fair balance between all the interests of all affected stakeholders, *viz*, consumers, content providers as well as technology and service venders? If the law is not clear as to whether the use of improved technology which is beneficial to society constitutes a breach of

[43]FSR 36 (2013).

[44]1 SLR 830, Court of Appeal (2011).

[45]This was a finding made by the High Court, and affirmed by the Court of Appeal.

[46]See section 114 of the Copyright Act 1987. This provision permits the making of a cinematographic film that is included in a broadcast 'for the private and domestic use of the person' making the cinematographic film.

[47]For a criticism of these two grounds of the decision, W.L. Ng-Loy (2011), 373.

copyright, should the courts interpret legislative provisions in favour of the private rights of the copyright owner or the public's wider interests?

In the mind of the appellate court, the 'just and fair balance' must come down in favour of the public because of two factors. First, time-shifting is legitimate activity in Singapore. RecordTV's iDVR technology allowed members of the public to do what they could legitimately do by using other recording devices such as video-cassette recorders and digital-video recorders, and to this extent, RecordTV's technology has not caused any loss to MediaCorp. Secondly, copyright law should not be applied in a way that hinders innovation and technological advancements. What RecordTV had given to the public was superior to the existing recording technology (video-cassette recorders and digital-video recorders). For example: the registered user does not need to be at home to watch the recorded broadcast since he can access it from any place where he has access to the Internet; the registered user does not need to know the start and end times of each MediaCorp broadcast and the channel that broadcast would be aired because RecordTV's iDVR has already been pre-programmed with the relevant information. In the words of the Court of Appeal, RecordTV's service was 'a significant technological improvement over existing recording methods' and 'novel technology'.

Aereo and *TVCatchup* concerned online retransmissions of broadcasts. *RecordTV*, on the other hand, concerned online transmission of broadcast for time shifting purposes. However, given the policy-driven reasoning of the Court of Appeal, it is very likely it would also have found no infringement by RecordTV if its service was the same as that of Aereo and TVCatchup. The purpose of looking at these three cases is to highlight that the current copyright regime forces the judiciary to resolve the disputes in an "all or nothing" approach. This "all or nothing" approach is not likely to be the most conducive for negotiating voluntary licences to allow use of copyrighted works in the Internet TV sector.

5 Conclusion

Technology continuously throws up new modes of distribution of copyrighted works. The history of copyright is very much about keeping up with these technological advancements, making sure, on the one hand, that copyright owners' control over the use of their works is not rendered meaningless by the new mode of distribution and, on the other hand, that the public gets to enjoy the works in a different manner. In this balancing act, one option is the use of compulsory licensing. If there is a concern that international law only permits use of compulsory licensing in very limited circumstances, this concern is overly stated. If there is a concern that compulsory licensing will not achieve the right balance, the cable compulsory licensing scheme in the USA suggests otherwise: it has been credited with the growth of the domestic cable network industry in the country and the efficient delivery of TV programming to the American people, and we should also not forget the explosion of the film industry since 1976.

Many have lamented about the lost opportunities because of the obstinacy of the music industry in refusing to be more open to new models of businesses based on online platforms. In time to come, will similar lament be expressed in connection with the Internet television sector, or the e-books sector, or whatever new sector made possible by technological innovations?

References

Asaro, A. (2014), Stayed Tuned: Whether Cloud-based Service Providers can have their Cake and Eat it, Fordham Law Rev., 83, 1107-1142

Balganesh, S. (2007), The Social Costs of Property Rights in Broadcast (and Cable) Signals, Berkeley Technology Law J., 22, 1303-1387

Botein, M. / Samuels, E. (2005), Compulsory Licences in Peer-to-Peer File Sharing: a Workable Solution?, Southern Illinois University Law J. 30, 69-86

Cornish, W. (2010), The Statute of Anne 1709-1710: its historical setting, in: L. Bently / U. Suthersanen / P. Torremans (Eds.), Global Copyright: Three Hundred Years Since the Statute of Anne, 14-25, Edward Elgar

Liu, K.-C. (2012), The Need and Justification for a General Competition-Oriented Compulsory Licensing Regime, IIC 43(6), 679-699

Lessig, L. (2001), The Future of Ideas: the Fate of the Commons in a Connected World, Random House

Ng-Loy, W.L. (2011), The 'Whom's' in Online Dissemination of Copyright Works: To Whom and By Whom is the Communication Made?, Singapore J. of Legal Studies 2011, 373-393

Ricketson, S. / Ginsburg, J. (2006), International Copyright and Neighbouring Rights: the Berne Convention and Beyond, 2nd ed., Oxford University Press

The US Copyright Office (1992), The Cable and Satellite Carrier Compulsory Licenses: An Overview and Analysis

The US Copyright Office (1997), A Review of Copyright Licensing Regimes Covering Retransmission of Broadcast Signals

The US Copyright Office (1998), The Satellite Home Viewer Extension and Reauthorisation Act Section 109 Report

The US Copyright Office (2011), The Satellite Television Extension and Localism Act Section 302 Report

WTO (2002), Dispute Resolution Panel Report DS160 (United States – section 110(5) of US Copyright Act) of 7 January 2002, available at: www.wto.org/english/tratop_e/dispu_e/cases_e/ds160_e.htm

Statutory Licenses as Enabler of Creative Uses

Christophe Geiger

Contents

Abstract In order to enable future creativity, some uses are traditionally kept outside the control of the right owner through limitations to the exclusive right. Uses covered by a limitation can lead to an obligation to pay a fair remuneration to the creator. In these cases, these "limitation-based remuneration rights" are often called "statutory licenses". As these remunerations can provide significant revenues

---

Christophe Geiger is Professor of Law, Director General and Director of the Research Department of the Centre for International Intellectual Property Studies (CEIPI), University of Strasbourg; Affiliated Senior Researcher, Max Planck Institute for Innovation and Competition, Munich. This chapter draws for some parts on previous research of the author on limitations to copyright and more generally on how to secure creativity and access to creative works within the copyright system.

C. Geiger (✉)
Center for International Intellectual Property Studies (CEIPI), University of Strasbourg, Strasbourg, France
e-mail: christophe.geiger@ceipi.edu

K.-C. Liu, R.M. Hilty (eds.), *Remuneration of Copyright Owners*, MPI Studies on Intellectual Property and Competition Law 27, DOI 10.1007/978-3-662-53809-8_18

for creators, they constitute interesting tools for legislators in order to avoid the blocking effect of exclusivity, while at the same time ensuring that the creator can participate fairly in the creative reuse of their works. However, this option has so far been given relatively little consideration in the context of derivative works. This chapter is intended to fill that gap, exploring whether statutory licenses can offer a satisfying mechanism to enable and incentivize creative uses of copyrighted works.

1 Introduction

It is well known that copyright law has been originally conceived as a tool to provide incentives for authors to create for the benefit of society, by securing them a fair remuneration for the use of their works. In order to enable future creativity, some uses are however kept outside the control of the right owner through limitations to the exclusive right. These limitations have therefore, alongside the exclusive right, an essential role to play in providing a good and vital creative environment.[1] Uses covered by a limitation can lead to an obligation to pay a fair remuneration to the creator. In these cases, these "limitation-based remuneration rights" are often called "statutory licenses", but this terminology is not always uniformly applied.[2] As these remunerations can provide significant revenues for creators, they constitute interesting tools for legislators in order to avoid the blocking effect of exclusivity,[3] while at the same time ensuring that the creator can participate fairly in the creative reuse of their works. However, this option—long-established in many European countries for certain limitations for private use (the most frequent being the so-called "private copy exception") or for reproductions for education and research purposes[4]—has been given relatively little consideration in the context of creative reuses, especially in the context of derivative works. So far, the discussions in Europe have been concentrated rather on how to "flexibilize" existing limitations such as parody or quotation or to establish an open clause such as fair use,[5] or even to implement a specific limitation for "user-

[1]See further C. Geiger (2010a), 515; C. Geiger / F. Schönherr (2014), 110; R.M. Hilty (2014), 207; R. Okediji (2017).

[2]On the issue of terminology, see more detailed *infra* at Sect. 2.3.

[3]See in this sense J.C. Ginsburg (2014), 1381, stating that statutory licenses or privately negotiated accords within a statutory framework can ensure that "uses the legislator perceives to be in the public interest proceed free of the copyright owner's veto, but with compensation—in other words: permitted-but-paid". The author however restricts the use of statutory licenses for what she calls "distributive uses" (non-creative reuse of copyrighted works), as opposed to "productive uses". For this second category of uses, fair use "for free" should still be available.

[4]See detailed on this issue, with several examples of remuneration rights, C. Geiger (2015a).

[5]P.B. Hugenholtz (2016); P.B. Hugenholtz / M.R.F. Senftleben (2011), 8–9; M.R.F. Senftleben (2010), 521; C. Geiger (2008c), 178 et seq.

generated content",[6] as was recently done in Canada. This chapter is intended to fill that gap by exploring whether statutory licenses can offer a satisfying mechanism in the context of creative uses, in particular in the context of derivative works.

2 Statutory Licenses as a Tool to Secure Creativity and to Remunerate Creators

Statutory licenses are often considered technically as "limitations" to copyright law, as they limit the ability of the creator to decide if he wants to authorize a certain use or not, thus the exclusive character of copyright law. These limitations have always existed and are inherent to any copyright system.[7] If it is generally accepted that they have an important function in securing future creativity (Sect. 2.1), they are seldom considered as a mechanism to secure the financial interest of creators (Sect. 2.2). This might also be the result of an unclear and unstable terminology used in the context of "limitation-based" remuneration rights (Sect. 2.3).

2.1 Copyright Limitations as a Tool to Secure Creative Uses / Creativity

It is indisputable that copyright law must secure free spaces in order to enable the creative use of existing works. Herewith constitutional values such as the protection of freedom of expression, freedom of information and freedom of art can be secured, and the public interest in a comprehensive cultural life can be served.[8] In brief, limitations are about the promotion of creativity, or—to use an economic term—innovation. This is also one function that the exploitation rights have to fulfil.[9] According to a utilitarian approach, this is even the superior objective of the copyright system: "[t]o promote the Progress of Science and useful Arts", as it is written significantly in the American Constitution.[10] Thus, to a function-oriented

[6]See for example the European Commission's Green paper, COM (2008), 19–20.

[7]See also M.-C. Janssens (2009), 347, emphasizing that the balancing mechanism between exclusive rights and exceptions "is ingrained in the copyright system and is of paramount importance for its legitimacy and credibility" (emphasis added).

[8]C. Geiger (2004); C. Geiger (2015b), 115; D. Voorhoof, (2015), 331.

[9]See in this sense also A. Kur / M. Levin / J. Schovsbo (2011), 408: "[I]n spite of their canonisation as a special type of human rights, and irrespective of the strong flavour of personal rights permeating copyright law, IPR in the first place have been created to 'do a job' – namely to foster creativity and innovation".

[10]Article 1, Section 8, Clause 8 of the US Constitution of 1787. The Feist Court's observation is revealing in this sense: "The primary objective of copyright is not to reward the labor of authors, but '[t]o promote the Progress of Science and useful Arts'" (Feist Publications Inc. v. Rural Telephone Service Co., 499 U.S. 340 (1991), at 349).

view of the copyright system, it seems strange to differentiate between exploitation rights and copyright limitations, because both have the same goal. This means that copyright limitations cannot be separated from exploitation rights; both form a whole, which serves the promotion of creativity.[11] In this context, what should matter is only whether copyright regulation achieves the desired purpose.[12] If the objectives can be achieved by a greater curtailment of the exclusive right via copyright limitations, then there should be no objection to it. This is of course especially the case when the limitation creates a right to fair remuneration which secures creators' financial participation in the use of their work.

2.2 Copyright Limitations as Protection Mechanisms of the Interests of Creators

In fact, to foster creativity is not the only aim copyright law pursues. At least in Continental-European countries, the protection of the creator builds another essential basis for the justification of the system. Anyhow, to put the author in the center of the system does not conflict, as it is often claimed, with the above-mentioned utilitarian approach. On the contrary, both approaches complement one another very well: if one wants to reach an optimal promotion of creativity, it is absolutely consistent to allocate a special role to the person who brings about the social added value, i.e. the creator.[13]

If one considers the interest of the authors to participate adequately in the fruits of their work, it must not be forgotten that copyright limitations on no account mean that works can always be used free of charge. Legislators may provide a right to appropriate remuneration for all uses legitimated by copyright limitations. Recital 36 of the Directive of 2001 on the harmonization of copyright in the information society (InfoSo)[14] clarifies this unambiguously when it prescribes that the Member States "may provide for fair compensation for right holders also when applying the optional provisions on exceptions or limitations which do not require such compensation". In German law, for instance, remuneration is provided in most limitation provisions (this is what is often called—mostly in common law countries—perhaps misleadingly copyright "levy"[15]). These remunerations, which are split

[11]On this issue see C. Geiger / F. Schönherr (2012), 133.

[12]On the purpose of copyright protection, see C. Geiger (2013), 153.

[13]See C. Geiger (forthcoming 2016).

[14]Directive 2001/29/EC of the European Parliament and of the Council of 22 May 2001 on the harmonisation of certain aspects of copyright and related rights in the information society (InfoSoc), OJ No. L 167 of 22 June 2001, 10.

[15]We will get back to this problem of terminology. See *infra* Sect. 2.3.

between authors and exploiters most of the time in an author-friendly manner,[16] are in many cases much more interesting for the authors than the royalty payments they receive from contracting parties. Furthermore, these "limitation-based remuneration rights" are sometimes considered inalienable for creators,[17] in contrast to the exclusive right which is most of the time transferred to exploiters. Besides the protection provided through copyright contract law, copyright limitations can thus be considered additional and suitable instruments to achieve a reasonable balance of interests between authors and exploiters.[18] Given the fact that copyright contract law does not exist in many national legislations and that the results in those countries that have such rules are not yet fully satisfactory,[19] the limitation-based remuneration system seems to be an interesting and viable option.

Certain courts in Europe have already seen the potential of "limitation-based remunerations" for an effective protection of the creator. In a very interesting decision of 11 July 2002, the German Federal Supreme Court interpreted extensively the limitation for press review of Article 49 of the German Copyright Act in order to cover electronic press reviews made by companies for internal use, on the grounds that a considerable part of the received payment would flow to the authors themselves and that a narrow interpretation of the limitation would thus not improve the author's position.[20] This argumentation was taken up and brought further by the Swiss Supreme Court, which considered that the activity of a company commercially preparing and delivering electronic press reviews

[16]See even going further the recent decision of the Court of Justice of the European Union, Case C-572/13, Hewlett-Packard Belgium [2015], Judgment of the Court (Fourth Chamber) of 12 November 2015, according to which "Article 5(2)(a) and Article 5(2)(b) of Directive 2001/29 preclude national legislation, such as that at issue in the main proceedings, which authorises the Member State in question to allocate a part of the fair compensation payable to rightholders to the publishers of works created by authors, those publishers being under no obligation to ensure that the authors benefit, even indirectly, from some of the compensation of which they have been deprived" (at para. 49). On this case, see European Copyright Society (2016), 71.

[17]See e.g. section 63a of the German Copyright Act. The limitation-based remuneration claims can only be transferred in advance to a collective society. See also Article 5(2) of Directive 2006/115/EC of the European Parliament and of the Council of 12 December 2006 on rental right and lending right and on certain rights related to copyright in the field of intellectual property (codified version), OJ No. L 376 of 27 December 2006, 28: "The right to obtain an equitable remuneration for rental cannot be waived by authors or performers". In addition, in Luksan the CJEU opined that, "with regard to the right to the fair compensation payable to authors under the private copying exception, it does not follow from any provision of Directive 2001/29 [InfoSoc] that the European Union legislature envisaged the possibility of that right being waived by the person entitled to it" (CJEU, Case C-277/10, Martin Luksan v. Petrus van der Let [2012], Judgment of the Court (Third Chamber) of 9 February 2012, at para. 105, published in the electronic Reports of Cases). See also C. Geiger (2015a).

[18]R.M. Hilty (2005a), 325. In the context of the limitation for private copying, see also A. Dietz (2003), 347; C. Geiger (2008b), 121; S. Dusollier / C. Ker (2009), 352.

[19]For an evaluation see A. Dietz (2007), 465.

[20]Federal Supreme Court (Bundesgerichtshof) (2003), "Elektronische Pressespiegel", 11 July 2002, JZ 473.

(so-called "press clipping and documentation delivery services" or "value-added information services") is covered by limitation for personal use according to Article 19 of the Swiss Copyright Act, which allows the reproduction of a work also by third parties.[21]

2.3 *Not Only a Matter of Terminology: Copyright "Levies", Liability Rules, Statutory Licenses or "Limitation-Based" Remuneration Rights?*

In light of what has been argued previously, it can be considered misleading when the European legislator speaks of "compensation" in connection with copyright limitations and the right of creators to receive a fair remuneration for these permitted uses.[22] One reads, for example, in recital 35 of the InfoSoc Directive: "In certain cases of exceptions or limitations, rightholders should receive fair compensation to compensate them adequately for the use made of their protected works or other subject-matter" (emphasis added).[23]

This "compensation" or "indemnity" terminology seems to imply some kind of damage which has to be redressed. Given the above discussion, however, these terms appear to be inaccurate.[24] One would rather speak of "remuneration" instead of "compensation".[25] Hence, there would be a remuneration by way of a license and

---

[21]Swiss Supreme Court, 1st Civil Chamber, 26 June 2007, 39 IIC 990 (2008). On this decision, C. Geiger, (2008a), 943.

[22]See further on this issue C. Geiger / F. Schönherr (2014); C. Geiger / F. Schönherr (2012), 133.

[23]The French wording is very similar: "Dans le cas de certaines exceptions ou limitations, les titulaires de droits doivent recevoir une compensation équitable afin de les indemniser de manière adéquate pour l'utilisation faite de leurs œuvres ou autres objets protégés" (emphasis added).

[24]See also in this sense, "deploring the incoherence of the EU concept of fair compensation based on harm", M. Kretschmer (2011).

[25]See clearly in this sense the opinion of the Advocate General of the Court of Justice of the European Union V. Trstenjak delivered on 11 May 2010 in Case C-467/08, Padawan: "The right to 'fair compensation' within the meaning of Article 5(2)(b) of Directive 2001/29, as the German Government correctly points out, primarily has the character of a reward. This is apparent from the first sentence of recital 10, pursuant to which if authors or performers are to continue their creative and artistic work, they have to receive an 'appropriate reward' for the use of their work. Recital 35 makes clear that 'fair compensation' should also be classified in this category of rewards, where it is stated that in certain cases of exceptions or limitations, rightholders should receive fair compensation to compensate them adequately for the use made of their protected works or other subject-matter. On the other hand, legal categorisation of the legal concept of 'fair compensation' as a straightforward claim for damages, as the referring court apparently assumes, may not readily be confirmed" (para. 79 and 80 of the Opinion, emphasis added). Unfortunately, the Court of Justice did not follow the Advocate General's line of reasoning, and held that "fair compensation must be regarded as recompense for the harm suffered by the author", and that the level of compensation is linked to the harm caused (CJEU, Case C-467/08, Padawan (2010), Judgment of the Court (Third Chamber) of 21 October 2010, ECR I-10055, para. 40). On the issue of terminology, see further C. Geiger (2015a).

a remuneration through a copyright limitation. Terminologically, it would thus be preferable to use the term "limitation-based remuneration rights" than the more established and often misleading term "levies". The same can be said about the economically-oriented term "liability rule", often used to describe the kinds of legal situations where, instead of a possibility to forbid, the right owner only gets some monetary reward for the use of their works, as the notion of liability implies a prejudice that needs to be compensated.[26] The term "statutory license", which is often used for limitations coupled with a right to receive fair remuneration, seems more suitable to express the concept of remuneration for the use of a copyrighted work, although the term is itself not entirely satisfying, as it implies that there is an exclusive right and that the permission to use is given only by the law; it could as well be argued that the exclusive right is absent in those cases but that legislator considers that the use should be remunerated as a policy option to secure creators' interests. In fact, copyright limitations are to be understood as limits to the exclusive right of the authors, beyond which they may not have any control over their work anymore. Therefore it seems that it would be better to speak of limitations with remuneration (or "limitation-based remuneration claims") and limitations without remuneration.

Surprisingly, the wording in the German version of the same recital 35 is clearly more neutral: "In certain cases of exceptions or restrictions the right holders shall receive a fair equalization in order to receive an appropriate remuneration ["Vergütung"] for the use of their protected works or other subjects of protection".[27] Likewise, in the Lending and Rental Right Directive, the European legislator explicitly stated that authors and performers enjoy a non-waivable "right to obtain an equitable remuneration" for the rental of their work that cannot be waived.[28] The Court of Justice of the European Union (CJEU), interpreting this concept, ruled that the right to equitable remuneration had to be viewed "as enabling a proper balance to be achieved between the interests of performing artists and producers in obtaining remuneration for the broadcast of a particular phonogram, and the interests of third parties in being able to broadcast the phonogram on terms that are reasonable" (emphasis added).[29]

---

[26]See A. Kur / M. Levin / J. Schovsbo (2011), *supra* note 9, defining liability rules as a "legal structure permitting third parties to undertake certain actions without prior permission, provided that they compensate the injured person for the trespass" (emphases added). See also more generally on this issue the seminal article by G. Calabresi / A.D. Melamed (1972), 1089, reminding that the liability paradigm was primarily developed in the context of tort law.

[27]The German version of recital 35 is: "In bestimmten Fällen von Ausnahmen oder Beschränkungen sollen Rechtsinhaber einen gerechten Ausgleich erhalten, damit ihnen die Nutzung ihrer geschützten Werke oder sonstiger Schutzgegenstände angemessen vergütet wird" (emphasis added).

[28]See e.g. Article 5(2) of Directive 2006/115/EC, *supra* note 17.

[29]ECJ, Case C-245/00, SENA (2003), Judgment of the Court (Sixth Chamber) of 6 February 2003, ECR I-01251, para. 36.

3 Statutory Licenses, an Option in the Context of Creative Reuses and Derivative Works?

In order to avoid the exclusive right hindering creativity in the context of derivative works, the copyright systems foresee some specific limitations or open norms such as the fair use defence. As we will see, those limitations are currently not sufficient to address properly the issue of creative reuses, and courts had sometimes to rely on fundamental rights-based reasoning outside IP law in order to be able to overcome the hurdle of exclusivity. Thus, a specific statutory license or "limitation-based remuneration right" could be created. Such an approach could overcome the obstacles created by the international and constitutional protection of copyright, provided that a fair remuneration is paid to the creator of the original work.

3.1 Why Can the Exclusive Right Hinder Creativity in the Context of Derivative Works?

It has to be recalled that copyright does not solely protect the remuneration interest of the author who has already created a work, but also freedom of the author during the creation process. The free spaces granted by the law ensure the free creation of new works. However, concerning this matter the existing system still shows weaknesses.[30] If the creator intends to create a new work based on another[31] and when some of the expression of a previous work needs to be borrowed, this normally necessitates the authorization of the copyright owner of the original work.[32] If the original author refuses to grant the permission or asks for too high a price, the creative reuse will be hindered. This situation resembles private censorship, as private entities or individuals have the potential to decide what can be created or not and to block the dissemination of new works.[33] It is questionable how this situation can be reconciled with either the copyright's rationale of incentivizing creativity or the obligations imposed on the States by human rights such as freedom of expression and information. As we will see, some of these situations

[30]See B. Fitzgerald (2008), 46: "There is a growing need to sensibly articulate the right to engage in transformative reuse of copyright material in international and national laws".

[31]The technique of sampling in music or appropriation uses in visual arts are popular examples, among many others.

[32]This is usually deducted from Article 2(3) of the Berne Convention for the Protection of Literary and Artistic Works, according to which "translations, adaptations, arrangements of music and other alterations of a literary or artistic work shall be protected as original works without prejudice to the copyright in the original work".

[33]See in this sense A. Barron (2004), 80, underlying "the spectre of censorship, for to have a property right in a work is to have the ability to exclude others from using that work as a mean of expression".

have been already addressed by the courts and certain ad hoc solutions have been found.[34]

In a highly publicised case in which Victor Hugo's heirs tried to use the famous author's moral rights to prevent a sequel to the work "Les Misérables", the French Supreme Court gave priority to the freedom of creation.[35] Citing Article 10 (freedom of expression) of the European Convention on Human Rights (ECHR), it held that, subject to respect of the right to paternity and of integrity of the adapted work, freedom of creativity prevents the author of the work or his heirs from hindering the production of a sequel after the exploitation monopoly is expired.

The German Constitutional Court likewise recognised the admissibility of numerous restrictions of the exclusive right in the past when the interests of secondary authors and creativity were concerned. In "Germania 3", which concerned the refusal of the heirs of Bertolt Brecht to allow the use of passages from a play by their ancestor for insertion in a new play in order to permit a critical analysis in artistic form of some of his theories, the Court gave precedence to the freedom to create laid down in Article 5(3) (artistic freedom) of the German Basic Law over "a minor infringement of copyright that only involved a minimal financial loss for the right holders."[36]

More recently, in a decision which concerned the creative reuse of three copyright-protected photographs in a painting, the French Supreme Court, referring to Article 10 ECHR, reversed the lower court's finding of an infringement, on the ground of the Appeal Court's failure to show how exactly the fair balance between the freedom of artistic expression and the copyright-holder's interests had been achieved and for not having sufficiently justified its decision in the light of freedom of creativity protected by the ECHR.[37]

---

[34]Further on this issue see recently C. Geiger / E. Izyumenko (2014), 316; See also, in the context of copyright enforcement online, C. Geiger / E. Izyumenko (forthcoming 2016).

[35]French Supreme Court, 1st Civil Chamber, Hugo v. Plon SA, 30 January 2007, 38(6) IIC 736 (2007). For a comment, C. Geiger (2007b), 707.

[36]German Constitutional Court (Bundesverfassungsgericht) (2001), "Germania 3", 29 June 2000, para. 22, GRUR Int. 149. See also in this sense in the field of music, regarding the legality of a sample from a song by the German music band Kraftwerk, German Constitutional Court, First Senate, "Metall auf Metall", 31 May 2016, 1 BvR 1585/13: "If the creative development of an artist is measured against an interference with copyrights that only slightly limits the possibilities of exploitation, *the exploitation interests of the copyright holders may have to cede in favour of the freedom to enter into an artistic dialogue* [Art. 5(3) (*artistic freedom*) of the German Basic Law] (emphasis added)."

[37]French Supreme Court, 1st Civil Chamber, 15 May 2015, no. 13–27391, published in the Bulletin. For a comment, see C. Geiger (2015c), 1620. See also, with the same reasoning, the decision of the Supreme Court of the Netherlands of 3 April 2015, GS Media BV v. Sanoma Media Netherlands BV and Others, available at: docs.google.com/viewer?a = v&pid = sites&srcid = ZGVmYXVsdGRvbWFpbnxhZnJvaXBsZW98Z3g6ZGFlNjc3Mzhk-YjBjNWVm (accessed 1 December 2015). Many other examples could be given also in other fields of IP, where Courts have justified the creative use of a trademark or of a protected design with the right to freedom of expression protected by Article 10 ECHR (for trademark see the numerous cases quoted in: C. Geiger (2007a), 317; for designs, see e.g. the Court of Appeal of the Hague, 4 May 2011, 389526/ KG ZA 11–294; J. McCutcheon (2015), 192.

These solutions were found by using external mechanisms (fundamental rights) to secure the creative reuse of copyrighted works. However, this situation, relying on rules from outside the intellectual property system, might not be an ideal one and it would be preferable for these problems to be solved by the IP legislation itself.[38]

3.2 *What Are the Solutions Existing Within the System to Address These Situations?*

In Continental-European copyright systems, authors who wish to use existing works for artistic purposes can have recourse to the limitations and exceptions permitted by law, such as quotations, parody, free use ("freie Benutzung"),[39] and others. Such provisions can, however, in certain respect appear insufficient as a satisfactory guarantee of the freedom to create. On the question of the quotation exception, firstly, in certain countries it still seems to be restricted to the field of text. It is thus often impossible to quote an image. The French Supreme Court, for instance, still regularly recalls that "the integral representation of a work of whatever form or duration can never constitute a brief quotation."[40] Moreover, the quotation for artistic purposes frequently requires the breach of the strict limits imposed by the wording of the law.[41] Accordingly, it is not surprising that on numerous occasions judges have had no choice but to have recourse to fundamental rights such as the freedom of expression or the freedom of creativity in order to "push through" the quotation exception.[42]

---

[38]See, however, T.F. Cotter (2010), 746: "[I]f the right to prepare derivative works is sufficiently problematic from the standpoint of freedom of speech, perhaps a more direct approach would be to limit the right on First Amendment grounds rather than indirectly through the fair use doctrine."

[39]Article 24 of the German Copyright Act.

[40]French Supreme Court (2004), 1st Civil Chamber, "Utrillo", 13 November 2003, 35 IIC, 716.

[41]L. Bochurberg (1994), 128 et seq.

[42]See as examples the decisions of the French Supreme Court, 1st Civil Chamber, no. 13–27391, 15 May 2015, published in the Bulletin; Austrian Supreme Court (2002), "Medienprofessor", 12 June 2001, GRUR Int., 341; The Hague Court of Appeals (2003), Church of Scientology v. XS4ALL, 4 September 2003, 6 AMI, 222; Supreme Court of the canton of Zurich (2004), 9 September 2004, Medialex, 231; German Constitutional Court (2001), "Germania 3", 29 June 2000, GRUR Int., 149; Paris District Court (2000), 3rd chamber, "Utrillo", 23 February 1999, 184 RIDA, 374. However, there have admittedly been numerous decisions that have refused to apply the fundamental rights, holding that the balance between copyright and freedom of expression had already been implemented within copyright by means of the existing limits. See on this subject P.B. Hugenholtz (2001), 343; A. Strowel / F. Tulkens (2006); C. Geiger (2006), 371.

Parody, in turn, also has limited possibilities, since it often requires a humorous or satirical view[43] that is missing in many cases. Moreover, it is often interpreted very strictly in order to prevent abuses. In certain legal systems, there is the concept of the "free use of a work". This is the case under German law, where Article 24 of the Copyright Act permits the author to freely exploit a work created on the basis of another work, provided that "the personal characteristics of the first work are lost in the derived work".[44] However, here too, this possibility is interpreted very strictly by the literature and by judicial practice, and is rarely upheld.[45]

Unlike the Continental Europe's systems of strictly enumerated exempted uses, the common law countries often tend to frame copyright limitations as open-ended provisions, which allow reaction to new situations in a more flexible way. The US fair use constitutes perhaps the most prominent example thereof.[46] The landmark US Supreme Court's holding in Campbell v. Acuff-Rose Music constitutes a good illustration in the context of creative reuses.[47] In that case, the flexible nature of the clause allowed the Court ruling in favour of a 2 Live Crew's parody of Roy Orbison's "Oh, Pretty Woman", despite the commercial character of the derivative work.[48] It is, however, also true that the results of the application of the open-ended provisions are often said to be less predictable.[49]

Alternatively, an interesting solution could be found in introducing in copyright law a specific limitation for creative reuses, in the spirit of the "user-generated

---

[43]Consider, in this sense, the CJEU's recent holding that an expression of humour or mockery is an "essential characteristic" of a parody (CJEU, Case C-201/13, Deckmyn (2014), Judgment of the Court (Grand Chamber) of 3 September 2014, para. 20). For a comment see European Copyright Society (2015), 93.

[44]Analogously, see section 5(2) of the Austrian Copyright Act.

[45]See A. Dietz / C. Geiger / P. Wand / S. Merzbach (2006).

[46]The U.S. Copyright Act, S 107, provides that uses are fair and non-infringing depending on four factors: the purpose and character of the use; the nature of the copyrighted work; the amount appropriated from the copyrighted work; and the effect of the use upon the potential market for or value of the copyrighted work.

[47]Campbell v. Acuff-Rose Music, Inc., 510 U.S. 569 (1994).

[48]See also the United States Court of Appeals for the Second Circuit, 26 October 2005, Andrea Blanch v. Jeff Koons, The Solomon R. Guggenheim Foundation and Deutsche Bank, No. 05-6433-cv, in the case of an artist's appropriation of a copyrighted image in a collage painting. The Court explored all statutory factors of the fair use clause, weighed them together in the light of the purpose of copyright and came to the conclusion that copyright law's goal of "promoting the Progress of science and useful arts" would be better served by allowing the use than by preventing it. On the issue of appropriation art and copyright, see J. Bresler (2003), 15; W.M. Landes, (2000), 1.

[49]D. Nimmer (2003), 282: "It is largely a fairy tale to conclude that the four factors determine resolution of concrete fair use cases". In more recent times, many scholars have challenged this assumption, suggesting that the fair use rule as it is applied by US courts provides more legal security than it is sometimes assumed, see M. Sag (2012), 47; P. Samuelson (2009), 2537; B. Beebe (2008), 549; P.B. Hugenholtz / M.R.F. Senftleben (2011); M.R.F. Senftleben (2010).

content" exception as it was recently implemented in Canada.[50] It is however worth noting that the Canadian model is limited to non-commercial uses, and the wording of the provision as such is rather complex.[51] Interestingly, the possibility of an "exception for user-created content" was examined—back in 2008—by the European Commission in its Green Paper on Copyright in the Knowledge Economy.[52] In the public consultation launched in late 2013 on the review of the EU copyright rules, the Commission once again reflected on the potential introduction into the European copyright framework of an exception for transformative uses[53]; more recently, the European Parliament in its non-legislative resolution of 9 July 2015 also addressed the issue and called for a balanced solution in the case of transformative uses.[54]

---

[50]Section 29.21 (Non-commercial User-generated Content) of the Canadian Copyright Modernization Act (S.C. 2012, c. 20), that reads as follows: "(1) It is not an infringement of copyright for an individual to use an existing work or other subject-matter or copy of one, which has been published or otherwise made available to the public, in the creation of a new work or other subject-matter in which copyright subsists and for the individual – or, with the individual's authorization, a member of their household – to use the new work or other subject-matter or to authorize an intermediary to disseminate it, if (a) the use of, or the authorization to disseminate, the new work or other subject-matter is done solely for non-commercial purposes; (b) the source – and, if given in the source, the name of the author, performer, maker or broadcaster – of the existing work or other subject-matter or copy of it are mentioned, if it is reasonable in the circumstances to do so; (c) the individual had reasonable grounds to believe that the existing work or other subject-matter or copy of it, as the case may be, was not infringing copyright; and (d) the use of, or the authorization to disseminate, the new work or other subject-matter does not have a substantial adverse effect, financial or otherwise, on the exploitation or potential exploitation of the existing work or other subject-matter – or copy of it – or on an existing or potential market for it, including that the new work or other subject-matter is not a substitute for the existing one. (2) The following definitions apply in subsection (1): 'intermediary' means a person or entity who regularly provides space or means for works or other subject-matter to be enjoyed by the public. 'Use' means to do anything that by this Act the owner of the copyright has the sole right to do, other than the right to authorize anything."

[51]On the pros and cons of importing the Canadian user-generated content exception to other legal systems, see P.K. Yu (2014), 177. For a comment of Section 29.21 of the Canadian Copyright Modernization Act, see also C. Geiger (2016a).

[52]European Commission's Green Paper, COM (2008), 19–20. For a comment on this document, see C. Geiger / F. Macrez / A. Bouvel / S. Carre / T. Hassler / J. Schmidt-Szalewski (2009), 412. The authors envisaged the solution in a provision which would allow creative use of existing works only after the original author's death, thereby leaving derivative works intact (id., at 431). See also E. Lawson (2009), 61, examining "whether a copyright exception should be created for user-generated content on the basis that it is 'transformative'".

[53]European Commission (2013), 28–30. For an overview of responses to this consultation, see European Commission (2014), 67–71 covering the questions related to the user-generated content.

[54]European Parliament Resolution of 9 July 2015 on the implementation of Directive 2001/29/EC on the harmonisation of certain aspects of copyright and related rights in the information society, P8_TA-PROV (2015) 0273, para. 41, where the Parliament "notes with interest the development of new forms of use of works on digital networks, in particular transformative uses, and stresses the need to examine solutions reconciling efficient protection that provides for proper remuneration and fair compensation for creators with the public interest for access to cultural goods and knowledge" (emphasis added). C. Geiger / O. Bulayenko / T. Hassler / E. Izyumenko / F. Schönherr / X. Seuba (2015), 683.

The problem, however, remains that each of the above-discussed solutions presupposes that the use is free of charge, meaning that no remuneration will be paid to the creator.[55] This leads to a tendency of legislators and courts to define limitations narrowly and to exclude some important creative uses, generating additional uncertainties as to what is covered or not. As a consequence, creators refrain from using existing work, which in turn inhibits the creative process. Moreover, some uses made initially for non-commercial purposes can become commercially relevant afterwards because of their success. In this case, the initial creator should not have the possibility to block the exploitation of the new work, but should be entitled to participate in the fruits generated by the derivative creation.

Therefore, it would be better to create a specific statutory license for derivative works with a clear scope in order to facilitate creative uses.[56] The spirit of this limitation to the exclusive right can be found in the practice of the Court of Justice of the European Union, in particular in its famous Magill decision of 1995, where it was considered that refusing to grant a license just to block someone from commercializing a new product on the market was an abuse of dominant position.[57] In this sense, a "competition exception" was proposed in the context of a European

[55]See on this issue about US fair use: J.C. Ginsburg (2014), 1383 stating that "fair use is an on/off switch: either the challenged use is an infringement of copyright or it is a fair use, which section 107 declares 'is not an infringement of copyright.' As a result, either the copyright owner can stop the use, or the user not only is dispensed from obtaining permission, but also owes no compensation for the use". Thus, some US scholars have argued in favour of compulsory licensing to be applied to derivative works: Hon. J.A. Kozinski / C. Newman (1999), 512.

[56]See, in this sense, UN General Assembly, Report of the Special Rapporteur in the field of Cultural Rights, F. Shaheed (2014), para. 45 et seq. looking into statutory licenses as one of the possible mechanisms to remunerate the creators. Consider also, mutatis mutandis, R.M. Hilty (2015), 377, arguing that "in case enforcement of an IP right proves to be abusive, this right should be downgraded to a 'liability regime'", which would allow for "more balance [...] through monetary compensation to the right holder".

[57]ECJ, Joined cases C-241/91 P and C-242/91 P, RTE and ITP v. Commission (1995), Judgment of the Court of 6 April 1995, ECR I-00743. The finding however took years of litigation, which demonstrates the need for internal mechanisms inside copyright to avoid these kinds of situations from the start.

Copyright Code drawn up by a group of academics (the "Wittem Group") and could serve as an inspiration.[58]

In the same spirit, patent law provides a mechanism for creative reuse of protected inventions: to prevent the holder of a patent (who is in a dominant position in view of a patent of improvement) from using their right to impede the exploitation of this improvement, the creator can sue for the issue of a compulsory license based on reasons of dependency.[59] Such compulsory licenses are also foreseen in the TRIPs Agreement (Article 31), and the members of the WTO have wide discretion regarding the reasons that may give rise to the grant of such a license.[60]

The main disadvantage in all these cases is the fact that the license has to be ordered by a judge, a fact that favours those economic actors who have the resources to afford the associated legal costs of sometimes very long proceedings. In the meantime, innovation is blocked. Therefore, it seems that legal regulations for non-voluntary licenses based on a right to remuneration should be preferred,[61] which would be due at least in the case of a commercial use of the derivative work.

3.3 *What Are the Obstacles?*

Any domestic legislation implementing a "limitation-friendly" approach must of course comply with obligations resulting from international conventions, in particular with the so-called "three-step test"[62] included in many international treaties on

---

[58]The European Copyright Code, released on 26 April 2010, available at: www.copyrightcode.eu (accessed 1 December 2015). Version published in 33(2) EIPR 76 (2011). Article 5.4 (Uses for the purpose of enhancing competition), paragraph 2 of the Code reads as follows: "Uses of news articles, scientific works, industrial designs, computer programs and databases are permitted without authorisation, but only against payment of a negotiated remuneration, and to the extent justified by the purpose of the use, provided that: (i) the use is indispensable to compete on a derivative market; (ii) the owner of the copyright in the work has refused to license the use on reasonable terms, leading to the elimination of competition in the relevant market and (iii) the use does not unreasonably prejudice the legitimate interests of the owner of the copyright in the work."

[59]Article 24(2) of the German Patent Act; Article L. 613–15 of the French Intellectual Property Code.

[60]See also in this sense Article 12 of Directive 98/44/EC of the European Parliament and of the Council of 6 July 1998 on the legal protection of biotechnological inventions, OJ No. L 213 of 30 July 1998, p. 13, which also provides for compulsory licenses in cases of dependency.

[61]For such a proposal in the field of incremental creations such as software, R.M. Hilty / C. Geiger (2005), 641 et seq.

[62]Concerning the "three-step test" in general, see e.g. C. Geiger / D. Gervais / M.R.F. Senftleben (2015), 167.

copyright and intellectual property.[63] The three-step test requires the compliance of the contracting parties with a number of conditions when introducing limitations into their national copyright law. In order to fulfil the criteria, the limitation must (1) describe a certain special case; (2) not conflict with the normal exploitation of the work; and (3) not unreasonably prejudice the legitimate interests of the author and/or the right holder. At the third step, a fair balance of interests involved is required, whereas the second step shall ensure that the core of copyright is not eroded. In this spirit, the normal exploitation of the work is interpreted by some authors as including only the economic core of copyright.[64] Understood accordingly, the protected core arguably prohibits transforming the exclusive right totally into a right to receive a fair remuneration, but the possibility of a restriction should remain if important conflicting interests of the general public so require. Thus, for the purposes of a normative consideration of the three-step test, which is already advocated by some scholars,[65] it could be argued that the "normal" exploitation in some cases can also be achieved by limitation-based remuneration rights and that the exclusive right only covers the right to oppose the sole identical copy of the work (primary market) and not its creative use (derived markets).[66]

Apart from the international three-step test, the constitutional framework for copyright might pose yet another obstacle to a total transformation of the exclusive right into a limitation-based remuneration right. This is the situation in those countries where copyright is subsumed under the general right to property,[67]

[63]Article 13 of TRIPs; Article 9(2) of the revised Berne Convention, Article 10 of the WIPO Copyright Treaty, Article 16(2) of the WIPO Performances and Phonograms Treaty, as well as Article 5(5) of the InfoSoc Directive. C. Geiger (2007c), 486.

[64]M.R.F. Senftleben (2004), 182.

[65]In favour of a normative approach to the second step, M.R.F. Senftleben (2006), 407; C. Geiger (2008c), 194 et seq.; C. Geiger (2009), 627.

[66]See in this spirit the "Declaration on a Balanced Interpretation of the 'Three-Step Test' in Copyright Law" drawn up by a group of experts from various European countries, 39 IIC 707 (2008), especially para. 4: "Limitations and exceptions do not conflict with a normal exploitation of protected subject matter, if they are based on important competing considerations or have the effect of countering unreasonable restraints on competition, notably on secondary markets, particularly where adequate compensation is ensured, whether or not by contractual means". On this document, C. Geiger / J. Griffiths / R.M. Hilty (2008), 489.

[67]F. Yeoh (2015), 119: "The concept of copyright as 'property' and the 'economic' approach to copyright have ensured that the limitations to the 'monopolistic' rights of copyright owners are strictly interpreted".

which is the case in most European countries and seems to be the case in the US too,[68] even if it appears to have been less an issue in US courts so far.[69] At the European level, it is recognized that copyright enjoys protection according to Article 1 of the First Additional Protocol (property) to the ECHR.[70] Article 17 paragraph 2 of the Charter of Fundamental Rights of the European Union of 2000 (Charter) even contains the succinct clause "intellectual property shall be protected",[71] which can easily lend itself to abusive interpretations in the absence of any explanations of the scope of such protection.[72]

On the other hand, the potential negative consequences of the property approach should not be overestimated, as they could largely be remedied by the internal limits of the constitutional right to property. Even in a natural-law-based understanding, the constitutional notion of property has always been considered as a right inherently restricted by public interests. This principle of the "social bounds" of property ("Sozialbindung des Eigentums") for the benefit of society is reflected in both Article 1 of the First Protocol to the ECHR and Article 17 paragraph 1 of the

---

[68]See, for example, United States Court of Appeals of the Fifth Circuit, Chavez v. Arte Publico Press, 204 F.3d 601, at 605, note 6 (5th Cir., Feb. 18, 2000, revised 10 March 2000): "The Supreme Court held in Florida Prepaid that patents are considered property within the meaning of the due process clause. See Florida Prepaid, 119 S.Ct. at 2208. Since patent and copyright are of a similar nature, and patent is a form of property [. . .] copyright would seem to be so too" (emphasis added). See on this issue M.A. Carrier (2004), 1.

[69]For an alternative normative frame for copyright—such as the right to culture or the right to freedom of expression—Article 27 of the Universal Declaration of Human Rights of 1948 and Article 15 of the International Covenant on Economic, Social and Cultural Rights of 1966; or—on the national level—Article 34(1) of the Czech Charter of Fundamental Rights of 1993, Article 42 of the Lithuanian Constitution of 1992, Article 20 of the Spanish Constitution of 1978, and many others. For further examples of how the constitutional protection for copyright is framed under different domestic and supranational constitutional texts around the globe, see C. Geiger (2015d), 661. See also C. Geiger (ed.), "Intellectual Property and Access to Science and Culture: Convergence or Conflict?", CEIPI/ ICTSD publication series on "Global Perspectives and Challenges for the Intellectual Property System", Issue N° 3, forthcoming (2016c).

[70]ECtHR, Akdeniz v. Turkey (dec.), no. 20877/10, 11 March 2014; ECtHR, Neij and Sunde Kolmisoppi v. Sweden (dec.), no. 40397/12, 19 February 2013; ECtHR, Ashby Donald and Others v. France, no. 36769/08, 10 January 2013; ECtHR, Balan v. Moldova, no. 19247/03, 29 January 2008; ECtHR, Melnychuk v. Ukraine (dec.), no. 28743/03, 5 July 2005, ECHR 2005-IX; ECtHR, Dima v. Romania (dec.), no. 58472/00, 26 May 2005; ECommHR, Aral, Tekin and Aral v. Turkey (dec.), no. 24563/94, 14 January 1998; ECommHR, A.D. v. the Netherlands (dec.), no. 21962/93, 11 January 1994.

[71]Further on this, C. Geiger (2010b), 255.

[72]The Community legislator has already referred to Article 17(2) when opting for a "maximalist" conception of IP in the European Union, with an aim to implement a "rigorous", "more far-reaching" system of intellectual property protection (see e.g. recital 11 to the Directive 2001/29/EC (InfoSoc), OJ No. L 167 of 22 June 2001, p. 10.; recital 16 to the Directive 2006/115/EC, OJ No. L 376 of 27 December 2006, p. 28. See also the European Commission's Green paper, COM (2008), 4. The so-called "absolutist" logic has also influenced the case law of the Court of Justice of the European Union (see e.g. ECJ, Case C-5/08, Infopaq (2009), Judgment of the Court (Fourth Chamber) of 16 July 2009, ECR I-06569, where it was held that even certain parts of sentences may be considered a protected work).

EU Charter, which provide for the possibility of restrictions in the common interest.[73] This means that intellectual property can be limited in order to safeguard the public interest just like the right to physical property. This logic, clearly excluding an "absolutist" conception of IP, was envisaged by the drafters of both the ECHR and the Charter[74] and finds its further support in the judicial practice of the European Courts.[75]

3.4 How to Secure a "Fair Remuneration"?

The final important question that remains to be considered is how the "fair remuneration" could in practice be secured. In this sense, the share of the remuneration collected to which creators are entitled can be established by law or negotiated.[76] In the first situation, the solutions might be less nuanced, as some works are more successful than others, whereas in the second case the right owner, being not entitled to refuse authorization, could still negotiate the amount of remuneration

[73]For further discussion of a limited nature of the right to property in general and intellectual property in particular, C. Geiger (2013).

[74]Council of Europe, Preparatory Work on Article 1 of the First Protocol to the European Convention on Human Rights, CDH (76) 36, Strasbourg, 13 August 1976, entertaining an idea of a "relative" nature of a newly introduced property paradigm as opposed to an absolute right to own property in a sense it was understood by Roman law. Similarly, the preparatory documents of the EU Charter specify that "the guarantees laid down in paragraph 1 of Article 17 shall apply as appropriate to intellectual property" and that "the meaning and scope of Article 17 are the same as those of the right guaranteed under Article 1 of the First Protocol to the ECHR" (Note from the Praesidium, Draft Charter of Fundamental Rights of the European Union, Text of the Explanations Relating to the Complete Text of the Charter as set out in CHARTE 4487/00 CONVENT 50 (Brussels, 2000), 19–20).

[75]Particularly, as it concerns the CJEU, the latter has stated on numerous occasions that IP rights are not absolute and that a "fair balance" has to be struck between intellectual property protection and the other interests of fundamental importance: inter alia CJEU, Case C-580/13, Coty Germany (2015), Judgment of the Court (Fourth Chamber) of 16 July 2015, para. 34–35; CJEU, Case C-117/13, Ulmer (2014), Judgment of the Court (Fourth Chamber) of 11 September 2014, para. 31; CJEU, Case C-201/13, Deckmyn (2014), Judgment of the Court (Grand Chamber) of 3 September 2014, para. 26; CJEU, Case C-314/12, UPC Telekabel (2014), Judgment of the Court (Fourth Chamber) of 27 March 2014, para. 46 and 61; CJEU, Case C-360/10, SABAM v. Netlog (2012), Judgment of the Court (Third Chamber) of 16 February 2012, para. 41 and 51, published in the electronic Reports of Cases; CJEU, Case C-70/10, Scarlet Extended [2011], Judgment of the Court (Third Chamber) of 24 November 2011, para. 43 and 53, ECR I-11959.

[76]UN General Assembly, Report of the Special Rapporteur in the field of Cultural Rights, F. Shaheed (2014), para. 45.

to be paid. If no solution can be found, a regulatory authority could step in and mediate.[77] To this effect, the creation of an independent regulation authority such as an "Observatory on access to copyrighted work" could be envisaged,[78] on the model of some European competition authorities. More generally, statutory organized mediation is a regulatory option that has been underexploited so far and should gain much importance in the future in the debate on how to secure balanced solutions taking into account all interests.[79]

Yet another, less "intrusive" alternative would be subordinating creative uses to the mandatory collective administration of works, as this would not be a limitation but a way of exercise of the exclusive right, which would therefore be more likely to be compatible with the three-step test.[80] In order to avoid the same blockages as with the exclusive right, the tariffs asked by the collecting society could also be regulated or checked by the same independent authority to be created.

4 Conclusion

As we have seen, statutory licenses can be a workable option to secure creative reuses of copyrighted works, provided that a fair remuneration is secured to the creator. This could be guaranteed through the implementation of an independent public authority, which could check that access is granted at a fair price, taking into account the specificity of the work in question, such as the potential market for the derivative work, the fame of the original creator or work used, etc.

More fundamentally, there might be a need in the future to reconsider and reshape copyright as an "access right", meaning a right to grant access (and not to hinder it), as a right to say "yes" rather than a right to say "no", as an inclusive right rather than an exclusive right.[81] Such a rethinking of the legislative framework has nothing to do with an anti-copyright position, as it is sometimes portrayed by those reluctant to reform. In fact, in current discussions on the future of copyright

[77]J.C. Ginsburg (2014), 1446, recommending the implementation of "statutorily facilitated bargaining between agents representing copyright owners and users, backed up by last best-offer arbitration before the Copyright Royalty Board. Whichever method is employed to set the rates for permitted-but-paid uses, the copyright law should ensure that authors share in any statutory or privately ordered remuneration scheme".

[78]In this spirit, a specific provision on orphan works in the Canadian copyright law (Copyright Act, R.S.C., ch. C-42, Sec. 77 (1985), permits anyone who wants to make use of a work and cannot locate the copyright owner, to petition the Canadian Copyright Board for a license.

[79]C. Geiger / A. Wechs Hatanaka / X. Seuba (2013).

[80]S. von Lewinski (2004); C. Geiger (2007d); C. Geiger / F. Schönherr (2016); P.B. Hugenholtz / R. Okediji (2008), 19: "Although the practical effect of such a rule is similar to that of a statutory or compulsory license (providing for a right of remuneration), it is technically not a limitation, since the exclusive economic right remains intact and can still be enforced on behalf of right holders by designated collective societies".

[81]C. Geiger (2016b); S. Dusollier (2015), 101.

law, anyone questioning the functioning of the current system and bringing "access" arguments forward immediately risks being accused of being a greedy "pirate" who claims broad and free access on the Internet, stealing the bread out of the mouth of poor creators.[82] It has to be recalled: claiming access means not that the access should be for free, but that it should be possible under fair conditions and that copyright should not block future creativity.[83]

Acknowledgement The author is thankful to Elena Izyumenko, PhD Candidate at the CEIPI, for her research assistance and editorial support.

References

Barron, A. (2004), Commodification and Cultural Form: Film Copyright Revisited, New Formations, 58-81, Lawrence & Wishart

Beebe, B. (2008), An Empirical Study of U.S. Copyright Fair Use Opinions, 1978-2005, University of Pennsylvania Law Rev., 549-624

Bochurberg, L. (1994), Le droit de la citation, Masson

Bresler, J. (2003), Begged, Borrowed or Stolen: Whose Art is it Anyway? An Alternative Solution of Fine Art Licensing, J. of the Copyright Society of the USA, Vol. 50, 15

Calabresi, G. / Melamed, A.D. (1972), Property Rules, Liability Rules and Inalienability: One View of the Cathedral, Harvard Law Rev., 1089-1128

Carrier, M.A. (2004), Cabining Intellectual Property through a Property Paradigm, Duke Law J., 1-145

COM (2008), Green Paper: Copyright in the Knowledge Economy (466/3, 2008), Commission of the European Communities

Cotter, T.F. (2010), Transformative Use and Cognizable Harm, Vanderbilt J. of Entertainment and Technology Law, 701-749

Dietz, A. (2003), Continuation of the Levy System for Private Copying also in the Digital Era in Germany, Auteurs & Media, 347-350

Dietz, A. (2007), Les aspects contractuels du droit d'auteur en Allemagne, in: C. Geiger / M. Bouyssi-Ruch / R.M. Hilty (Eds.), Perspectives d'harmonisation du droit d'auteur en Europe, 465, Litec

Dietz, A. / Geiger, C. / Wand, P. / Merzbach, S. (2006), National Report, Germany, Proceedings of the ALAI Study Days, Copyright and Freedom of Expression

[82]Indeed, as rightly noted by R.M. Hilty, "an enhancement of copyright protection scarcely helps the creators of the works, but rather burdens the consumers", since "the borderline of conflicting interests runs not so much between creators and consumers as greatly emphasized by the traditional perception of copyright, [. . .] [but] arises from the fact that the exploiting copyright industry wants to optimise its profits by all the possible means they can deploy" (R.M. Hilty (2005b), 132–133).

[83]*See* in this sense also F. Gurry (2016), at 61, underlining that the role of copyright is "finding a balance between all the competing interests that surround the act of cultural creation. On the one hand, there are the interests of the creators, who derive their economic existence through the restriction on access that copyright entails. On the other hand, there are the interests of society and the general public. Access is the reason for which we are interested in cultural production" (emphasis added). More generally on the important issue of intellectual property and access to culture and science, see C. Geiger (2016c).

Dusollier, S. (2015), Inclusivity in intellectual property, in: G.B. Dinwoodie (Ed.), Intellectual Property and General Legal Principles: Is IP a Lex Specialis?, 101, Edward Elgar
Dusollier, S. / Ker, C. (2009), Private Copy Levies and Technical Protection of Copyright: The Uneasy Accommodation of Two Conflicting Logics, in: E. Derclaye (Ed.), Research Handbook on the Future of EU Copyright, 349-372, Edward Elgar
European Copyright Society (2015), Limitations and Exceptions as Key Elements of the Legal Framework for Copyright in the European Union – Opinion of the European Copyright Society on the Judgment of the CJEU in Case C-201/13 Deckmyn, IIC, 93-104
European Copyright Society (2016), ECS Position Paper on the Opinion of the Advocate General in the Case HP Belgium v. Reprobel pending before the Court of Justice of the EU, EIPR, 71-74
European Commission (2013), Public Consultation on the Review of the EU Copyright Rules
European Commission (2014), Directorate General Internal Market and Services, Report on the Responses to the Public Consultation on the Review of the EU Copyright Rules
Fitzgerald, B. (2008), Copyright 2010: The Future of Copyright, EIPR, 43
Geiger, C. (2004), Droit d'auteur et droit du public à l'information, approche de droit compare, Litec
Geiger, C. (2006), 'Constitutionalizing' Intellectual Property Law? The Influence of Fundamental Rights on Intellectual Property in Europe, IIC, 371-406
Geiger, C. (2007a), Trade Marks and Freedom of Expression – The Proportionality of Criticism, IIC, 317-327
Geiger, C. (2007b), Copyright and the Freedom to Create – A Fragile Balance, IIC, 707-722
Geiger, C. (2007c), From Berne to National Law, via the Copyright Directive: The Dangerous Mutations of the Three-Step Test, EIPR, 486-491
Geiger, C. (2007d), The Role of the Three-Step Test in the Adaptation of Copyright Law to the Information Society, e-Copyright Bulletin January March 2007, available at: portal.unesco.org/culture/en/ev.php-URL_ID=34481&URL_DO=DO_TOPIC&URL_SECTION=201.html
Geiger, C. (2008a), Rethinking Copyright Limitations in the Information Society: The Swiss Supreme Court Leads the Way, IIC, 943-950
Geiger, C. (2008b), The Answer to the Machine Should not be the Machine: Safeguarding the Private Copy Exception in the Digital Environment, EIPR, 121-129
Geiger, C. (2008c), Flexibilising Copyright – Remedies to the Privatisation of Information by Copyright Law, IIC, 178-197
Geiger, C. (2009), Implementing an International Instrument for Interpreting Copyright Limitations and Exceptions, IIC, 627-642
Geiger, C. (2010a), Promoting Creativity through Copyright Limitations, Reflections on the Concept of Exclusivity in Copyright Law, Vanderbilt J. of Entertainment & Technology Law, 515-548
Geiger, C. (2010b), Intellectual 'Property' after the Treaty of Lisbon: Towards a Different Approach in the New European Legal Order? EIPR, 255
Geiger, C. (2013), The Social Function of Intellectual Property Rights, Or how Ethics can Influence the Shape and Use of IP Law, in: G.B. Dinwoodie (Ed.), Intellectual Property Law: Methods and Perspectives, 153-176, Edward Elgar
Geiger, C. (2015a), Scope and Enforcement Tools to Assure Remuneration in the Case of Statutory Remuneration Rights, General report presented at the ALAI International Congress on the topic of "Remuneration for the Use of Works: Exclusivity vs. Other Approaches", Bonn (Germany), 18 June 2015 (proceedings forthcoming, together with O. Bulayenko, in: S. von Lewinski (ed.), "Remuneration for the use of works, Exclusivity vs. Other Approaches", De Gruyter, 2016)
Geiger, C. (2015b), Reconceptualizing the Constitutional Dimension of Intellectual Property, in: P. Torremans (Ed.), Intellectual Property and Human Rights, 3rd ed., 115-161, Kluwer Law International

Geiger, C. (2015c), Droit d'auteur et liberté d'expression artistique: art 'autorisé' et libre création ne font pas bon ménage, La Semaine Juridique 2015, 1620-1624

Geiger, C. (2015d), Implementing Intellectual Property Provisions in Human Rights Instruments: Towards a New Social Contract for the Protection of Intangibles, in: C. Geiger (Ed.), Research Handbook on Human Rights and Intellectual Property, 661-690, Edward Elgar

Geiger, C. (2016a), Propriétés intellectuelles, No. 58, 91-92, Thomson Reuters

Geiger, C. (2016b), Copyright as an Access Right, Securing Cultural Participation through the Protection of Creators' Interests, Max Planck Institute for Innovation and Competition Research Paper No. 15-07, in: R. Giblin / K.G. Weatherall (Eds.), What if We Could Reimagine Copyright?, ANU Press (Forthcoming)

Geiger, C. (ed.) (2016c), Intellectual Property and Access to Science and Culture: Convergence or Conflict?, CEIPI/ ICTSD publication series on "Global Perspectives and Challenges for the Intellectual Property System", Issue No. 3, 2016

Geiger, C. / Bulayenko, O. / Hassler, T. / Izyumenko, E. / Schönherr, F. / Seuba, X. (2015), The Resolution of the European Parliament of 9 July 2015: Paving the Way (Finally) for a Copyright Reform in the European Union?, EIPR, 683

Geiger, C. / Gervais, D. / Senftleben, M.R.F. (2015), Understanding the 'Three-Step Test', in: D. Gervais (Ed.), International Intellectual Property, A Handbook of Contemporary Research, 167-189, Edward Elgar

Geiger, C. / Griffiths J. / Hilty, R.M. (2008), Towards a Balanced Interpretation of the 'Three-Step Test' in Copyright Law, EIPR, 489-496

Geiger, C. / Izyumenko, E. (2014), Copyright on the Human Rights' Trial: Redefining the Boundaries of Exclusivity through Freedom of Expression, IIC, 316-342

Geiger, C. / Izyumenko, E. (2016), The Role of Human Rights in Copyright Enforcement Online: Elaborating a Legal Framework for Website Blocking, American University Int. Law Rev., (Forthcoming)

Geiger, C. / Macrez, F. / Bouvel, A. / Carre, S. / Hassler, T. / Schmidt-Szalewski, J. (2009), What Limitations to Copyright in the Information Society? A Comment on the European Commission's Green Paper 'Copyright in the Knowledge Economy', IIC, 412-433

Geiger, C. / Schönherr, F. (2012), Defining the Scope of Protection of Copyright in the EU: The Need to Reconsider the Acquis regarding Limitations and Exceptions, in: T.-E. Synodinou (Ed.), Codification of European Copyright Law, Challenges and Perspectives, 133-167, Kluwer Law International

Geiger, C. / Schönherr, F. (2014), Limitations to Copyright in the Digital Age, in: A. Savin / J. Trzaskowski (Eds.), Research Handbook on EU Internet Law, 110-142, Edward Elgar

Geiger, C. / Schönherr, F. (2016), Effective Harmonisation of Limitations to Copyright in the EU: An Opportunity for Collective Rights Management, in: R.M. Hilty / S. Nérisson (Eds.), Collective Management of Copyright in Europe, Springer (Forthcoming)

Geiger, C. / Wechs Hatanaka, A. / Seuba, X. (2013), Civil Enforcement of Intellectual Property Rights: CEIPI's Comments on the Public Consultation of the European Commission, with a Focus on Alternative Dispute Resolution Mechanisms, June 2013, available at: www.ceipi.edu

Ginsburg, J.C. (2014), Fair Use for Free, or Permitted-but-Paid?, Berkeley Technology Law J., 1383-1446

Gurry, F. (2016), Developments in the International Intellectual Property System, in: C. Geiger (ed.), The Intellectual Property System in a Time of Change: European and International Perspectives, Collection of the CEIPI, Volume 64, 57-65

Hilty, R.M. (2005a), Verbotsrecht vs. Vergütungsanspruch: Suche nach Konsequenzen der tripolaren Interessenlage im Urheberrecht, in: A. Ohly / T. Bodewig / T. Dreier / H.-P. Götting / M. Haedicke / M. Lehmann (Eds.), Perspektiven des Geistigen Eigentums und Wettbewerbsrechts, Festschrift für Gerhard Schricker zum 70. Geburtstag, 325-353, C.H. Beck

Hilty, R.M. (2005b), Five Lessons About Copyright in the Information Society: Reaction of the Scientific Community to Over-Protection and What Policy Makers Should Learn, J. of the Copyright Society of the U.S.A., 103-138

Hilty, R.M. (2014), La limitation de la propriété intellectuelle comme moyen d'encourager l'innovation, in: C. Geiger / C. Roda (Eds.), Le droit de la propriété intellectuelle dans un monde globalisé, Mélanges en l'honneur du Professeur Joanna Schmidt-Szalewski, 207-219, LexisNexis

Hilty, R.M. (2015), Legal Remedies Against Abuse, Misuse, and Other Forms of Inappropriate Conduct of IP Right Holders, in: R.M. Hilty / K.-C. Liu (Eds.), Compulsory Licensing. Practical Experiences and Ways Forward, 377-395, Springer

Hilty, R.M. / Geiger, C. (2005), Patenting Software? A Judicial and Socio-Economic Analysis, IIC, 615-646

Hugenholtz, P.B. (2001), Copyright and Freedom of Expression in Europe, in: R.C. Dreyfuss / D.L. Zimmerman / H. First (Eds.), Expanding the Boundaries of Intellectual Property: Innovation Policy for the Knowledge Society, 343, Oxford University Press

Hugenholtz, P.B. (2016), Flexible Copyright: Can EU Author's Right Accommodate Fair Use?, in: I.A. Stamatoudi (Ed.), The Future of Copyright, A European Union and International Perspective, 417-433, Kluwer Law International

Hugenholtz, P.B. / Okediji, R. (2008), Conceiving an International Instrument on Limitations and Exceptions to Copyright, Final Report March 2008, available at: www.ivir.nl/publicaties/download/937

Hugenholtz, P.B. / Senftleben, M.R.F. (2011), Fair Use in Europe: In Search of Flexibilities, Amsterdam: Institute for Information Law/VU Centre for Law and Governance 2011, available at: ssrn.com/abstract=1959554

Janssens, M.-C. (2009), The Issue of Exceptions: Reshaping the Keys to the Gates in the Territory of Literary, Musical and Artistic Creation, in: E. Derclaye (Ed.), Research Handbook on the Future of EU Copyright, 317-348, Edward Elgar

Kur, A. / Levin, M. / Schovsbo, J. (2011), Expropriation or Fair Game for All? The Gradual Dismantling of the IP Exclusivity Paradigm, in: A. Kur / M. Levin (Eds.), Intellectual Property in a Fair World Trade System – Proposals for Reforming TRIPS, 408-451, Edward Elgar

Landes, W.M. (2000), Copyright, Borrowed Images, and Appropriation Art: An Economic Approach, George Mason Law Rev., Vol. 9/1, 1-24

Lawson, E. (2009), Orphan Works and Transformative Works in the Knowledge Economy, Entertainment Law Rev., 61-63

Kozinski, Hon. J. A. / Newman, C. (1999), What's So Fair About Fair Use? The 1999 Donald C. Brace Memorial Lecture, J. of the Copyright Society of the U.S.A., 513-530

von Lewinski, S. (2004), Mandatory Collective Administration of Exclusive Rights – A Case Study on Its Compatibility with International and EC Copyright Law, e-Copyright Bulletin January March 2004, available at: portal.unesco.org/culture/en/files/19552/11515904771svl_e.pdf/svl_e.pdf

M. Kretschmer, Private Copying and Fair Compensation: An Empirical Study of Copyright Levies in Europe, an Independent Report Commissioned by the UK Intellectual Property Office, 2011

McCutcheon, J. (2015), Designs, Parody and Artistic Expression – A Comparative Perspective of Plesner v. Louis Vuitton, Monash University Law Rev., 192-217

Nimmer, D. (2003), 'Fairest of Them All' and Other Fairy Tales of Fair Use, Law and Contemporary Problems, 263-288, Duke University School of Law

Okediji, R. (Ed.) (2017), Copyright in an Age of Limitations and Exceptions, Cambridge University Press

Sag, M. (2012), Predicting Fair Use, Ohio State Law Journal, 47-91, The Ohio State University, Michael E. Moritz College of Law

Samuelson, P. (2009), Unbundling Fair Uses, Fordham Law Rev., 2537-2621

Senftleben, M.R.F. (2004), Die Bedeutung der Schranken des Urheberrechts in der Informationsgesellschaft und ihre Begrenzung durch den Dreistufentest, in: R.M. Hilty / A. Peukert (Eds.), Interessenausgleich im Urheberrecht, 159-186, Nomos

Senftleben, M.R.F. (2006), Towards a Horizontal Standard for Limiting Intellectual Property Rights? – WTO Panel Reports Shed Light on the Three-Step Test in Copyright Law and Related Tests in Patent and Trademark Law, IIC, 407-438

Senftleben, M.R.F. (2010), Bridging the Differences between Copyright's Legal Traditions – The Emerging EC Fair Use Doctrine, J. of the Copyright Society of the U.S.A., 521-552

Shaheed, F. (2014), Copyright Policy and the Right to Science and Culture, Human Rights Council, Twenty-eighth session, A/HRC/28/57 24 December 2014, available at: www.ohchr.org/EN/HRBodies/HRC/RegularSessions/Session28/Documents/A_HRC_28_57_ENG.doc

Strowel, A. / Tulkens F. (2006) (Eds.), Droit d'auteur et liberté d'expression, Larcier

Voorhoof, D. (2015), Freedom of Expression and the Right to Information: Implications for Copyright, in: C. Geiger (Ed.), Research Handbook on Human Rights and Intellectual Property, 331-353, Edward Elgar

Yeoh, F. (2015), Adaptations in Music Theatre: Confronting Copyright, Entertainment Law Rev., 119-129

Yu, P.K. (2014), Can the Canadian UGC Exception be Transplanted Abroad?, Intellectual Property J., 177-205

MIX
Papier aus verantwortungsvollen Quellen
Paper from responsible sources
FSC® C105338

If you have any concerns about our products,
you can contact us on
ProductSafety@springernature.com

In case Publisher is established outside the EU,
the EU authorized representative is:
Springer Nature Customer Service Center GmbH
Europaplatz 3, 69115 Heidelberg, Germany

Printed by Libri Plureos GmbH
in Hamburg, Germany